Manipulation

NEW TOPICS IN APPLIED PHILOSOPHY

Series editor: Kasper Lippert-Rasmussen

This series presents works of original research on practical issues that are not yet well covered by philosophy. The aim is not only to present work that meets high philosophical standards while being informed by a good understanding of relevant empirical matters, but also to open up new areas for philosophical exploration. The series will demonstrate the value and interest of practical issues for philosophy and vice versa.

ALSO PUBLISHED IN THE SERIES

Spying Through a Glass Darkly
The Ethics of Espionage and Counter-Intelligence
Cécile Fabre

Inheritance of Wealth
Justice, Equality, and the Right to Bequeath
Daniel Halliday

The Politics of Social Cohesion
Immigration, Community, and Justice
Nils Holtug

Not In Their Name
Are Citizens Culpable for their States' Actions?
Holly Lawford-Smith

Sharing Territories
Overlapping Self-Determination and Resource Rights
Cara Nine

Exploitation as Domination
What Makes Capitalism Unjust
Nicholas Vrousalis

Disability Through the Lens of Justice
Jessica Begon

What's Wrong with Lookism?
Personal Appearance, Discrimination, and Disadvantage
Andrew Mason

Manipulation

Its Nature, Mechanisms, and Moral Status

ROBERT NOGGLE

OXFORD
UNIVERSITY PRESS

Great Clarendon Street, Oxford, OX2 6DP,
United Kingdom

Oxford University Press is a department of the University of Oxford.
It furthers the University's objective of excellence in research, scholarship,
and education by publishing worldwide. Oxford is a registered trade mark of
Oxford University Press in the UK and in certain other countries

Published in the United States of America by Oxford University Press
198 Madison Avenue, New York, NY 10016, United States of America

British Library Cataloguing in Publication Data
Data available

Library of Congress Control Number: 2024949722

ISBN 9780198924890

DOI: 10.1093/9780198924920.001.0001

Printed and bound by
CPI Group (UK) Ltd, Croydon, CR0 4YY

The manufacturer's authorised representative in the EU for product safety is
Oxford University Press España S.A. of El Parque Empresarial San Fernando de Henares, Avenida
de Castilla, 2 – 28830 Madrid (www.oup.es/en or
product.safety@oup.com). OUP España S.A. also acts as importer into Spain
of products made by the manufacturer.

Contents

Acknowledgments

This book began in the late 1980s at the Ohio State University, in an undergraduate class on Shakespeare. That class was taught by one of the best professors I've ever met, Dr Phoebe Spinrad. She brought Shakespeare's characters to life, revealing *why* they say what they say and do what they do. For *Othello*, this required unravelling Iago's manipulation of the title character. *Othello* turned out to be, and remains, one of my favorite Shakespeare plays, and I wrote one of my papers for the class on Iago's manipulation of Othello. That humble undergraduate essay is the earliest seed from which this book springs. Thank you, Doctor, Professor, and Captain Spinrad!

A few years later, I was writing a doctoral dissertation on personal autonomy at the University of Illinois at Chicago. My advisor, Jerry Dworkin, suggested thinking about manipulation as a threat to autonomy. That suggestion led me back to Othello, whose story became a central example in a paper that was published in 1996 in *American Philosophical Quarterly*. Thank you, Jerry!

The topic of manipulation was not popular among philosophers when I first wrote about it in 1996, and it remained "under-theorized" for many years thereafter. The most notable exception, and, by my lights, the single best article ever written on the topic, was Marcia Baron's 2003 American Philosophical Association presidential address on "Manipulativeness." Among other things, that paper presented a vast array of examples of manipulation—including many that didn't fit into the theory I had developed in that 1996 paper. Baron's paper convinced me that my original theory was either wrong or at least incomplete, and that there was more work to do on the topic. Thanks, Marcia!

After 2010, philosophical interest in manipulation began to increase. Part of the reason for this was the popularity of Richard Thaler and Cass Sunstein's work on nudges (Thaler and Sunstein 2009), and part of it was the publication of a collection of philosophical essays on manipulation, edited by Christian Coons and Michael Weber (Coons and Weber 2014). A fortuitous conversation with Michael Cholbi at an APA meeting in 2016 alerted me to the growing philosophical interest in manipulation far sooner than I would have stumbled on it myself. That conversation nudged me to start doing the work that Baron's paper showed me needed to be done. Thanks, Michael!

My first forays back into the topic of manipulation were a paper on manipulation and nudges published in *Bioethics* in 2018, and an entry for the *Stanford Encyclopedia of Philosophy* on "The Ethics of Manipulation." I presented drafts of the former at the 2016 Western Michigan University Medical Humanities

Conference and the 2016 Northwest Philosophy Conference. I am grateful to audiences at both conferences, and anonymous readers for *Bioethics*, for their assistance in helping me refine my thinking about manipulation. And I am grateful to Ed Zalta at the *Stanford Encyclopedia of Philosophy* for allowing me to contribute to that fine enterprise, and for helpful feedback on the article. Some ideas, and small bits of text, from the SEP article ("The Ethics of Manipulation," https://plato.stanford.edu/archives/sum2022/entries/ethics-manipulation/) found their way into Chapters 1 and 3. To everyone who helped me think through and refine the contents of those two works, thank you!

A key task of this book is to find a way of thinking about manipulation that does justice to all the forms of manipulation discussed in Marcia Baron's 2003 paper. I worked out an early version of how to do this in a paper called "Trickery, Pressure, and a Unified Account of Manipulation." I presented a version of the paper at the 2017 Northwest Philosophy Conference. It was ultimately published in 2022 in *American Philosophical Quarterly* (Volume 57, number 4, 241–52). Chapter 4 reworks that material and includes a few bits of the original text. In many ways, that chapter is the core of this book. So, I am especially grateful to the audience at NPC and the reviewers at APQ for their comments and suggestions. Thank you!

Since several key early pieces of this work were presented at the Northwest Philosophy Conference, I want to thank the folks who keep that wonderful conference going. On several trips to present at that conference, I managed to squeeze in some hiking with my excellent CMU colleague, Matthew Katz. During those hikes, we would discuss the papers we were presenting, most of mine being early versions of work that developed into parts of this book. For those conversations, and for being such great company on our hikes, thanks, Matt!

In Autumn 2019, I was granted a sabbatical from Central Michigan University, during which I wrote early drafts of seven of the chapters of this book. Thank you, CMU!

A few weeks into that sabbatical, I had the extraordinary opportunity to present an early draft of some of the material for this book at a workshop on "The Ethics of Behaviour Prediction and Behavioural Influence." The workshop was organized by Thomas Douglas and Hazem Zohny at Oxford University and the Uehiro Centre for Practical Ethics, and held at Oxford in September 2019. The other workshop participants were Thomas Douglas, Kasper Lippert-Rasmussen, Elizabeth O'Neill, Kalle Grill, Jesper Ryberg, Elizabeth Shaw, Carissa Veliz, Moti Gorin, and Hazem Zohny. I learned a great deal from their helpful feedback at a crucial stage of this project, and from the work they presented. Since I was on sabbatical, I was able to combine the workshop with a quick trip (my first) to London. Of course, I visited the recreated Globe Theater to pay homage to William Shakespeare, whose study of manipulation in *Othello* has been both an inspiration for and a recurring theme in my work. To everyone who made both halves of that trip possible, thank you!

I was fortunate to be able to present chapter drafts of much of this book to various audiences. I presented a draft of parts of Chapter 5 at the 2019 Northwest Philosophy Conference and the 2020 Central Division American Philosophical Association conference. I learned much from the commentators—David Schwan and James Mahon, respectively—and from the audiences at both conferences. Thank you!

I presented a draft of Chapter 10 to a workshop on the "Ethics of Influence" organized by Peter Schaber, Holger Baumann, and Thomas Douglas and held at the University of Zurich in September 2022. The other workshop participants were Tom Douglas, Massimo Renzo, Luc Bovens, Gabriel DeMarco, Jennifer Blumenthal-Barby, Peter Ubel, Lisa Forsberg, Christine Clavien, and Peter Schaber. I learned a great deal from their presentations, from their feedback on my presentation, and from the many fascinating conversations throughout the conference. Thank you!

I presented material that found its way into Chapter 11 at a wonderful interdisciplinary conference on "Understanding & Combating Online Manipulation" organized by Daniel Susser, Lee McGuigan, Beate Roessler, and Helen Nissenbaum, and held at Cornell Tech in May 2023. I benefitted immensely from the outstanding and eye-opening interdisciplinary formal program, as well as the opportunity to converse informally with several people whose work I had long admired but whom I had never yet met in person, including Daniel Susser, Helen Nissenbaum, Thomas Nys, Sophie Gibert, Anne Barnhill, and—most of all—Marcia Baron. To those folks, and everyone connected with that conference, thank you!

I presented material that found its way into Chapter 9 at an innovative weeklong workshop on "Manipulation and Autonomy" in August 2023 at the University of Leiden's Lorentz Center. This event was organized by Michael Klenk, Magda Osman, Tom Dobber, Monika Betzler, and Matthias Uhl. I am grateful for the opportunity to participate in this innovative workshop. I learned something from everyone present, and I especially enjoyed and benefitted from presentations by and conversations with Guido Cassinadri, Jan Gogoll, Paul Nemitz, Christiane Turza, Christos Bechlivanidis, Micha Werner, Josefine Spürkel, Laurens Rook, Sunny Xun Liu, Jade Vrielink, Bram Vaassen, Shervin Mirzaei Ghazi, Giulio Mecacci, Antonia Kempkens, Matthias Uhl, and, most especially, Michael Klenk and Magda Osman. To everyone who made that event possible and so wonderful, thank you!

I presented additional material that found its way into Chapter 9 to an audience at Kings College London in October 2023, as one of the Yeoh Tiong Lay Lectures on Practical Agency, organized by Massimo Renzo. I am grateful to Massimo, the audience, and a great group of Massimo's students, for helpful questions, comments, and conversation. Thank you!

In 2020, there was a small matter of a global pandemic. Soon after things shut down, Tom Douglas invited me to participate in the monthly online meetings of a group of scholars working on behavioral influences and related topics. The group started out as a way for Tom and other Oxford folks to work around the pandemic shut downs to share and discuss work in progress on topics related to his project on arational influence. But it grew to include other scholars working on similar topics. I feel both grateful and honored to have been welcomed into that group. Over the course of a couple of years, the group kindly read and provided outstanding feedback on drafts of Chapters 5, 6, 9, and 11. Just as importantly, though, the group provided an opportunity to interact with an outstanding group of scholars, and to read and discuss their work. Having ongoing interactions with these scholars would be a blessing under any circumstances; it was doubly so during the pandemic. I learned something from everyone who participated in these meetings, and special thanks are due to Tom, of course, and to Holger Baumann, Emma Dore-Horgan, Felix Koch, Peter Schaber, Jonas Hertel, Juan Pablo Bermúdez, Lisa Forsberg, Maximilian Kiener, Robyn Waller, Rebecca Brown, Thomas Mitchell, Viktor Ivanković, Paul Martin, Muriel Leuenberger and, especially, Gabriel De Marco (who not only offered great real-time feedback, but who generously provided astute written comments on almost everything of mine that the group read). Thank you!

I am grateful to the folks at Oxford University Press for making this book a reality; thank you all! I am also grateful to Kasper Lippert-Rasmussen for his advice, encouragement, and help throughout the process, and to two anonymous readers for OUP for their careful evaluation and helpful suggestions about improving the book. Thank you!

Although they've already been mentioned, I want to offer special thanks to Thomas Douglas, Michael Klenk, and Massimo Renzo. They provided support, feedback, advice, and kind words at various and crucial points throughout this project. Their generous assistance, wise counsel, and kind words have helped me more than they probably know. Thank you!

I am both very certain and very sorry that I have forgotten—or never learned—the names of many people who have discussed, offered feedback on, or asked questions about the material in this book, or about manipulation more generally. Every one of these encounters has been valuable, and I regret that I can only offer you a collective acknowledgment. But each one of them has, in some way or another, helped move this project forward. So, to everyone who has ever asked a question, offered feedback, or just said a kind word, about this work at a presentation, at a conference or workshop, online, or in any other format, thank you!

Finally, none of this would have been possible without the love and support of my family. To my spouse, best friend, love of my life, and the smartest person I know, Sara, and to our three wonderful children, Spencer, Jessie, and Lucas, who fill our lives with laughter, joy, love, and hope, thank you!

1
Introduction

1.1. Introduction

We are social beings, interconnected and interdependent. Our lives, and the people and things we care about, can be affected by what other people do. Thus, it often *matters to us* what other people do. Not surprisingly, we often want to *influence* what other people do. In fact, many of the things *we* do, and many of the things we *say*, are attempts to influence what other people do.[1]

There are many ways to influence what another person does. Some involve giving reasons. This may involve pointing out *existing reasons* for doing one thing rather than another. Or it may involve creating new reasons by offering the other person something *in exchange* for doing one thing rather than another. These forms of influence treat other persons as beings who can appreciate and respond to reasons, and who can negotiate in good faith. Because these forms of influence treat other persons as rational beings, it is difficult to find any moral fault with them, provided that they are not used to get the other person to do something bad.

Other forms of influence are presumptively immoral—that is, morally wrong except in special circumstances. Coercion is a prime example. There is always a moral presumption against coercion, even though it may sometimes be justified, for example, if it is the only way to prevent someone from doing something very bad to someone else.

Rational persuasion, good-faith bargaining, and coercion have all been subjects of exhaustive philosophical scrutiny. However, philosophers have paid far less attention to other forms of influence. At least part of the territory between these better-understood forms of influence is occupied by manipulation.

Most of us, at some point or another, have experienced some form of influence that we would describe as manipulation. As we shall see in the next chapter, there is a bewildering variety of tactics and forms of influence that are commonly described as manipulation. For now, though, let's consider just a few examples of manipulation:

- In Shakespeare's *Othello*, Iago manipulates Othello by playing on his insecurities to make him jealous, and then working him into a rage that leads him to murder Desdemona.

[1] Some of the ideas presented in this chapter, and a few passages of the text, first appeared in Noggle (2022).

Manipulation. Robert Noggle, Oxford University Press. © Robert Noggle 2025.
DOI: 10.1093/9780198924920.003.0001

- One friend manipulates another into forgoing her plans to leave their small town to attend a big-city college by overemphasizing college costs, sensationalizing the city's crime rate, and downplaying the benefits of college.
- An abuser manipulates his partner by gaslighting her so that she doubts her own sound judgment that their relationship has become toxic.
- Another abuser manipulates his partner by playing on her fear of abandonment by threatening to break off their relationship unless the partner allows the abuser to control every aspect of her life.

While these are all clear cases of manipulation, there is no consensus about what *makes* them cases of manipulation. Moreover, for many kinds of influence, there is no clear consensus as to *whether* they count as manipulation. Here are a few examples:

- Dressing up for a job interview or first date.
- Infusing a house one is selling with the scent of fresh baked goods to entice buyers to purchase it.
- Encouraging healthier food choices by arranging a cafeteria so that more nutritious foods are easier to reach than less nutritious foods.
- Encouraging a patient to consent to a medical procedure by saying that it has a 90 percent success rate rather than a 10 percent failure rate.
- Advertising a product by associating it with images of youth, vigor, and fun.

1.2. Ordinary Manipulation

This book is about manipulation that influences *people*. We sometimes apply the term 'manipulation' to what might be described as gaming the system. The political theorist William Riker coined the term 'heresthetics' to apply to manipulation of this sort, what he called "structuring the world so you can win" (Riker 1986, ix). Other theorists call it "situational manipulation." Gerrymandering is a prime example: It changes the rules about how votes are grouped together, so that the outcome of an election changes even if no one's vote changes. Heresthetic or situational manipulation typically works by changing the rules governing some practice or process, or by exploiting loopholes in those rules. This form of manipulation may affect people indirectly, since people often react to changes in the rules or attempts to exploit loopholes, and to the outcomes that such tactics bring about. But because its primary target is something more like "the system," or the rules governing some process or practice, rather than persons, it is not the topic of this book.[2] This book is about manipulation that affects people *directly*.

[2] For discussion of situational manipulation and how it differs from manipulation that directly influences people, see section 4.10.

Moreover, this book is about manipulation as it occurs in ordinary life. Ordinary manipulation is quite different from what philosophers writing about free will sometimes call "manipulation." In the free will literature, the term 'manipulation' often refers to decidedly *extra*-ordinary interventions like brainwashing, direct neurological intervention, genetic engineering, or the intervention of supernatural beings. Often, these extra-ordinary interventions are imagined as completely programming or reprogramming a person's entire psychology. Furthermore, they are imagined as not just *influencing* behavior, but *determining* it. Extra-ordinary manipulation like this is often mentioned in arguments for the claim that causal determinism is incompatible with free will. These arguments rest on an analogy between people living in a causally determined world and the victims of extra-ordinary forms of manipulation: Since the victims of such manipulation seem to be unfree, people living in a causally determined world would also seem to be unfree. Or so the argument goes. Such examples may or may not tell us anything about free will. But they seem unlikely to tell us much about the ordinary manipulation that occurs in everyday life.

The ordinary forms of manipulation investigated in this book are not hypothetical. They are just as real, and just as much a part of our moral landscape, as other forms of influence like coercion, rational persuasion, and good-faith bargaining. The fact that manipulation is commonly distinguished from these other forms of influence raises an important question: Are *all* forms of influence that are not forms of coercion, rational persuasion, or good faith bargaining manipulation? Or is manipulation only a *subset* of the forms of influence that do not fit into those other categories? And if manipulation is only a subset of the influences that do not fit into those other categories, then how can we distinguish between those that count as manipulation and those that do not?

1.3. Manipulation as Immoral Influence

The question of what makes a form of influence manipulation is an interesting theoretical puzzle. But it is also a question with considerable practical importance. The term 'manipulation,' as it is commonly used in ordinary conversation, is not morally neutral. Calling someone manipulative is not like calling someone tall or talkative. It is to say something negative about that person's character. Saying that someone manipulated you is not like saying that someone greeted you. It is to make a moral complaint about how you were treated. This makes the term 'manipulation'—at least as it is used in ordinary conversation—quite different from the more neutral term 'influence.'

This is not to deny that the term 'manipulation' is *sometimes* used in a more neutral way, in effect as a synonym for 'influence.' Nor is it to deny that we could *decide* to use it this way, stipulating away its normal connotations of moral criticism.

But doing so seems artificial in a way that changes the subject. To investigate the concept of manipulation in a way that either ignores or artificially cleanses it of its negative moral connotations is to cease to investigate the concept as it is used in ordinary conversation. So, when we investigate what manipulation is, we should also investigate why it seems like a bad thing. Nevertheless, some readers might insist that our ordinary concept of manipulation does not have the negative moral connotations that I claim that it has. Readers taking that position are welcome to treat my use of the term 'manipulation' as a shorthand for those forms of manipulation that *do* seem morally disreputable.

1.4. Three Questions about Manipulation (or, What this Book is about)

This book is about the nature, mechanisms, and moral status of manipulation. To put it more simply, this book seeks to find out three things about manipulation: what it is, how it works, and why it's bad. Thus, it will address three main questions.

The first main question is: What is manipulation? Answering it will involve answering several more specific questions: What do all the various forms of manipulation have in common? What distinguishes manipulation from other forms of influence like rational persuasion, bargaining, and coercion? What state of mind must a person be in if that person can be correctly said to be engaged in manipulation? These questions concern the *nature* of manipulation.

The second main question is: How does manipulation work? Answering it will also involve answering several more specific questions: How can the manipulator influence what a person does without giving that person a reason to do one thing rather than another? How does Iago manage to turn Othello from a lovestruck newlywed to a murderous monster? Why do we fall for the manipulators in our own lives? These questions concern the *mechanisms* by which manipulation operates.

The third main question is: Why is manipulation bad? As with the other main questions, answering it will involve answering several more specific questions: Are we correct to regard manipulation as something immoral or at least morally disreputable? If so, why? Is manipulation always immoral, and if not, then what determines when it is immoral and when it is not? And when it *is* immoral, what makes it so? These questions concern the *moral status* of manipulation.

Although the three main questions are distinct, they are also interrelated. It will be difficult to discover how manipulation *works* without knowing what manipulation *is*. It will be difficult to discover why manipulation is *bad* without knowing what it is and, perhaps, how it works. But at the same time, an explanation of what manipulation is will seem incomplete if it does not help explain why manipulation seems like a bad thing. Moreover, certain claims about the nature of manipulation might clash with claims about its moral status. For example, suppose that we explain the nature of manipulation in such a way that it includes all forms of influence besides coercion, rational persuasion, and good-faith bargaining. Suppose that we also claim that manipulation is categorically immoral. The conjunction of those two claims would be that no form of influence other than good faith bargaining or rational persuasion is ever morally legitimate. This would be a quite radical conclusion.

All three of these questions about manipulation are interesting in their own right, as philosophical puzzles to be solved. But there are also practical reasons for wanting answers to them. As social beings, it is inevitable that we will attempt to influence each other. Thus, being able to identify when our influences are manipulative, and being able to tell when, if ever, manipulation is morally justified, will help us in our efforts to live morally good lives and to relate to one another in morally sound ways. Understanding how manipulation works will play a role in answering these practical questions. But it will also help with the practical task of combatting manipulation and, perhaps, recognizing it before we fall for it.

Understanding manipulation is also important for addressing several social and public policy questions. Take, for example, the debate about the "nudges" championed by Cass Sunstein and Richard Thaler (Thaler and Sunstein 2009; Sunstein 2014). A nudge is an easily resistible push in a direction that the nudger thinks is good for you. Some nudges seem like forms of rational persuasion in that they merely provide more or better information or make it easier to understand. But others fall into that uncertain territory between rational persuasion, coercion, and good-faith bargaining—the same territory that includes manipulation. These include encouraging healthier food choices by arranging a cafeteria so that more nutritious foods are easier to reach than less nutritious foods; encouraging patients to consent to a beneficial surgery by framing outcomes in terms of survival rates instead of fatality rates; and making saving for retirement a default that one must opt out of rather than into. There is a lively debate about whether nudges of this sort—or at least some of them—are manipulative.[3]

The worry that advertising might be manipulative goes back at least as far as the economist John Kenneth Galbraith's suggestion that advertising is "the competitive manipulation of consumer desire" that is analogous to demons afflicting consumers with desires for things they do not need (Galbraith 1958, 155, 153). Some critics see all forms of advertising as potentially manipulative. Others are

[3] For a sampling of this debate, see Hausman and Welch (2010), Blumenthal-Barby and Burroughs (2012), Nys and Engelen (2017), Wilkinson (2013), Grüne-yanoff (2012), and Moles (2015). Nudges will be discussed in detail in Chapter 11.

concerned mostly with advertising that does not impart factual information, since that form of advertising seems to influence behavior without providing a rational basis for purchasing decisions.[4] Some tactics that salespersons use to close the sale without providing reasons for buying also raise worries about manipulation.[5]

Concerns about manipulation in politics are probably as old as politics itself. Aristotle's discussion of how democracies descend into tyranny, and Herodotus's account of how Aristagoras got the Athenians to go to war against Persia, both mention tactics like appealing to emotions and the desire for gain that we would likely call manipulation.[6] Although it is easy to find clear cases of political manipulation either in history or current events, drawing the line between manipulation and legitimate political communication is more difficult. This concern is especially important in democracies, where political legitimacy derives from the will of the people. If the people have been manipulated into supporting a given policy or candidate, then we might wonder whether those choices succeed in conferring political legitimacy.[7] This concern is especially pressing because the rise of new technologies like the internet, data analytics, and artificial intelligence make manipulation more efficient and more effective than ever.

1.5. Methodology

Often, there is a clear and strong consensus about whether a particular influence is a form of manipulation. We noted a few such examples at the beginning of this chapter. But we also noted cases where we lack a clear consensus about whether to call an influence manipulation. In these latter cases, our judgments—what philosophers call "intuitions"—about whether manipulation occurs may be weak, or they may vary from person to person, or both. The fact that we sometimes disagree about whether a given influence is manipulation is part of what makes a philosophical investigation of manipulation important: We need a principled way to settle such disagreements.

However, those very disagreements make the quest for a theory of manipulation that *never* conflicts with *anyone's* intuitions a fool's errand. We must, of course, pay attention both to how the term 'manipulation' is commonly used in ordinary conversation, and to strong and widely shared intuitive reactions to specific cases.

[4] For a sampling of the debate about whether advertising—or some forms of it—is manipulative, see Crisp (1987), Beauchamp (1984), Santilli (1983), Arrington (1982), Phillips (1997), and Lippke (1999). Advertising will be discussed in detail in Chapter 11.

[5] See, for example, Holley (1986) and Alessandra, Wexler, and Barrera (1992). Sales tactics will be discussed in Chapter 11.

[6] See Aristotle, *Politics*, Book V, and Herodotus, *Histories*, Book V, ch 97.

[7] For a sample of discussions of political manipulation, see Goodin (1980), Claudia Mills (1995), Noggle (2021), and the papers collected in Le Cheminant and Parrish (2011).

But any attempt to build a philosophical theory that is consistent with *every* use of the term and *every* intuition is doomed to failure. We need something that is both more subtle and more messy.

The approach that seems best suited to our subject matter is a version of the method of "reflective equilibrium" that has become standard in moral philosophy.[8] To use this method, we abandon the impossible goal of a theory that fits *each and every* intuition about whether manipulation has occurred in each and every case. Instead, we adopt a goal of devising a theory that fits with our *strongest* and *most widely shared* intuitions. But this is not our only goal. We also adopt a goal of devising a theory that *explains* those intuitions. Such an explanation goes beyond mere consistency with our intuitions and seeks to identify some common feature shared by the forms of influence that our strongest and most widely shared intuitions identify as manipulation. Moreover, since the concept of manipulation has distinct negative moral connotations, a theory that explains our strongest and most widely shared intuitions about manipulation should also explain why we regard manipulation as a morally disreputable form of influence.

These goals also provide criteria for judging among *competing* theories: We should favor theories that *fit best* with our strongest and most widely shared intuitions about when manipulation is present and when it is absent. But we should also favor theories that offer the best and most compelling *explanations* for those intuitions. There is, of course, no guarantee that these two criteria will point in the same direction. But that is a bridge we needn't cross until we get to it.

In short, then, our goal is not to reverse-engineer *all* our intuitions about manipulation. Rather, it is to find some property that is present in most if not all the cases that our strongest and most widely shared intuitions identify as cases of manipulation, where this property also helps to explain our sense that manipulation is a morally disreputable form of influence. Once we have identified such a property, we will have good grounds to reconsider and, perhaps, abandon intuitions that manipulation occurs in cases when this property is absent, or intuitions that it does not occur when it is present. The willingness to reconsider intuitions that conflict with a theory that fits with and explains most of our strongest and most widely shared intuitions is a critical part of this method. In extreme cases, we should be willing to reconsider even *some* of our strong and widely shared intuitions if they conflict with a theory that offers an *especially* compelling explanation for *most* of our strongest and most widely shared intuitions.

In this way, we should expect to move back and forth between devising a theory to fit and explain our intuitions, and revising our intuitions in light of the

[8] See Rawls (1971, 20–21; 48–51); especially helpful discussions can also be found in Kagan (1991, 11–14) and Daniels (2020).

theory. The endpoint—the equilibrium that gives the method half of its name—occurs when we are satisfied that the theory is more reasonable than any of the intuitions that conflict with it, and that the theory both fits and explains all the intuitions that we are not prepared to give up. If we succeed in finding a theory that explains our strongest and most widely shared intuitions, then we should feel confident in using it to adjudicate cases about which we lack strong, widely shared intuitions.

It is a messy methodology, to be sure. And there is no guarantee that it will result in a single theory that achieves reflective equilibrium. But this is the best method that philosophers have devised for investigating concepts where there is consensus about some cases and disagreement about others. And we will not know whether the method succeeds or fails until we make a sustained effort to employ it. That is the goal of this book.[9]

1.6. Terminology, Names, and Other Preliminaries

Before we begin, a few preliminaries are in order. I will refer to the person whom the manipulator tries to influence as the "target." In definitions and other formal or semi-formal statements about manipulation or other influences, I will designate this person as "**T**," and I will designate the manipulator as "**M**." If I want it to remain an open question whether the influence counts as manipulation, I will speak of the "influencer" rather than the "manipulator," and designate that person as "**N**" (I use "**N**" rather than "**I**" to avoid confusion with the first person-pronoun). When I give names to participants in various examples, I will typically give the target a name beginning with "T" and the influencer or manipulator a name beginning with "I" or "M." I will typically use "**A**" to refer to something that the target may do. While this is typically an action (hence the "**A**"), I mean "doing" to be taken broadly enough to include such things as refraining from an action, or adopting or abandoning some mental or emotional state.

Often, I will give the manipulator/influencer a different gender from that of the target. I do this *only* to make it clear whether a pronoun refers to the influencer or to the target. I am certain that there are important and interesting things to say about the interaction between manipulation and gender. But exploring such matters is beyond the scope of this book.

[9] A very different methodology is suggested in a recent paper by Sophie Gibert (2023). Gibert is skeptical about the existence of a feature common to all forms of manipulation that explains their moral status (Gibert 2023, 370). Nevertheless, she claims that we can reach substantive conclusions about why manipulation is immoral (in cases where it is immoral) without completing the "definitional project" (Gibert 2023, 370). I am far less pessimistic about the "definitional project," and I am far less optimistic about the prospect of defending substantive claims about the moral status of manipulation without completing that project.

1.7. Plan of the Book

Chapter 2 explores the diversity of influences that seem like clear cases of manipulation. This will provide an initial data set of paradigm examples of manipulation, which we can use to build and test theories about the nature of manipulation. Since the topic of this book is ordinary manipulation as it occurs in real life, the examples come from real life or psychologically realistic fiction. They include (1) playing on the emotions; (2) misdirection and "misemphasis" (distorted emphasis); (3) gaslighting; (4) game switching (tricking someone into following the wrong norms for the situation); (5) social proof; (6) peer pressure; (7) emotional blackmail; (8) nagging; (9) charm offensives; (10) exploiting conflict aversion; (11) exploiting reciprocity; (12) negging; and (13) conditional flattery. The chapter also discusses the fact that some forms of influence can be used in ways that seem clearly manipulative, as well as in ways that seem clearly not manipulative.

Chapter 3 surveys several accounts of manipulation, to see how they stack up against the data set of paradigm examples of manipulation from Chapter 2. It argues that while most of them get something right about manipulation, they all face significant challenges. The chapter identifies two of the most promising accounts: one that sees manipulation as a form of trickery, akin to lying and deception, and one that sees it as a form of pressure that falls short of coercion. Each of these two accounts fails to identify manipulation in about half of the paradigm examples from Chapter 2. However, each one succeeds precisely where the other fails, so that these two accounts *together* properly identify manipulation in all the paradigm examples from Chapter 2.

Chapter 4 explores the significance of the finding from the previous chapter that some forms of manipulation seem to involve tricking the target into adopting a faulty mental state, while others seem to involve some kind of pressure. One obvious response to this finding would be to offer a disjunctive account, according to which manipulation consists of *either* trickery *or* pressure. But while such a theory would fit with our intuitions about all thirteen paradigm examples of manipulation, it fails on the other criterion of a good theory. For it would leave unanswered the deeper question of what those two forms of manipulation have in common. The chapter then embarks on a closer examination of manipulative pressure. It begins with the observation that *manipulative* pressure is usually described as being weaker than the pressure exerted by coercion. Thus, unlike coercive pressure, manipulative pressure does *not* make the action solicited by the manipulator the best or least bad option for the target of the manipulation. But if that is correct, then manipulative pressure only works when and because the target makes a mistake: The target chooses the action solicited by the manipulator even though it is not the target's best or least bad option. This conclusion allows us to identify a common feature in forms of manipulation that involve trickery and those that involve pressure: They both induce the target to make a mistake. This idea is the core of a new, unified account of manipulation—the Mistake Account. The Mistake Account characterizes manipulation as influence that operates by inducing the target to make a mistake.

Chapter 5 poses a question for the Mistake Account: For the purposes of defining manipulation, from what perspective should we judge whether something is a mistake? For example, Iago's influence on Othello is manipulative because the jealousy and anger that he gets Othello to feel toward Desdemona are mistaken. But is Iago's behavior manipulative because *Iago believes* that it is a mistake for Othello to be jealous and angry at Desdemona? Or is Iago's behavior manipulative because it *really is* a mistake for Othello to be jealous and angry at Desdemona? The Mistake Account regards manipulation as being similar to deception. These similarities suggest that: (a) *acting manipulatively* involves trying to get someone to make *what the manipulator thinks* is a mistake, but (b) someone has been successfully *manipulated* only when what the manipulator regards as a mistake *really is* a mistake. This way of defining "M acted manipulatively" and "T was manipulated" parallels how we define "D acted deceptively" and "T was deceived." These distinctions between attempted and successful influence reflect two distinct moral concerns: what happened to the target, and what the influencer was trying to do to the target. The second half of the chapter takes up the question of how best to characterize the intention that a person must have if we are to describe that person as acting manipulatively.

Chapter 6 draws on the findings of the previous two chapters to develop formal definitions of 'manipulation' and related terms. It also assembles the cumulative case in favor of the Mistake Account, and in so doing, shows how the Mistake Account properly identifies all the paradigm examples of manipulation from Chapter 2. It concludes by showing how the Mistake Account incorporates important insights from competing theories of manipulation.

Chapter 7 details the various sorts of mistakes the induction of which the Mistake Account regards as manipulation. It begins with the clearest case: mistaken beliefs. A belief is mistaken when it is false. Emotions can be mistaken either by failing to fit the facts (as when Othello is jealous of Desdemona despite having no reason for jealousy) or by being too strong or too weak for the circumstances (as when someone is excessively fearful of a small, well-behaved dog). Mistakes of attention and weighting occur when the amount of attention paid to some fact, or the amount of weight placed on it in decision-making, is disproportionate to its actual importance. Other sorts of mistakes involve the application of heuristics or packages of procedural knowledge in situations where they are not appropriate. The mistakes involved in manipulative pressure are also discussed. These are instances of what philosophers call "akrasia" or weakness of will.

Chapter 8 discusses psychological mechanisms that contribute to the mistakes that manipulators induce targets to make. It begins with a sketch of a simple model of decision and action. Next, it discusses how limits on time and information create challenges for decision-making. Because of these limits, most decision-making relies on a combination of fast, unconscious processes that identify promising courses of action, and slower, conscious processes that select among them. This is the basic insight of dual process theories of decision-making. Adding the findings and insights from these theories to the sketch of decision-making helps us see a variety of ways that manipulation operates. The chapter concludes with a discussion of several cognitive and decision-making biases that facilitate manipulation. These include the availability heuristic; framing effects; the status quo bias; the immediacy bias; and biases toward social conformity and against conflict.

Chapter 9 discusses the moral status of manipulation. It begins by observing that it seems implausible to claim that manipulation is *never* morally justified. It then argues that manipulation is both *prima facie* and *pro tanto* morally wrong. It is *prima facie* wrong because there are situations where it is not wrong at all. It is *pro tanto* wrong because there are situations where manipulation remains morally wrong, but its moral wrongness is outweighed by other considerations that favor engaging in manipulation as the lesser of two evils. For short, we can combine all of this into the claim that manipulation is "presumptively" wrong. The chapter then explores various possible explanations for manipulation's presumptive wrongness. These include the claim that manipulation harms the target, that it undermines the target's autonomy, and that it treats the target as a thing, or as a mere means to an end, rather than a person. However, each of these explanations faces serious problems. We will then turn to an explanation of manipulation's presumptive wrongness that derives directly from the Mistake Account: Being mistaken is a kind of failure and thus a kind of misfortune. Thus, manipulation is the deliberate infliction of a misfortune upon someone. While the fact that a mistake is a misfortune accounts for the presumptive wrongness of *all* instances of manipulation, it remains true that manipulation *often* harms the target or undermines the target's autonomy. Thus, while manipulation always inflicts the misfortune of making a mistake, it often inflicts far more serious misfortunes as well. In this, as in many other respects, manipulation resembles deception. Consequently, intuitions about when deception is morally justified can assist us in determining when manipulation is morally justified.

Chapters 10 and 11 apply the Mistake Account to influences other than the thirteen paradigm examples from Chapter 2. Chapter 10 discusses exotic forms of influence, and influences that pose special challenges for the Mistake Account. The first category includes influences like priming and conditioning. The second includes influences that produce systemic changes to the target's moods, levels of fatigue, etc. Chapter 11 focuses on more ordinary kinds of influence: nudges, advertising, sales tactics, and online influences. It serves as a kind of "field test" for the Mistake Account. It does not offer the final word on every practical question. Rather, it shows how the Mistake Account can provide plausible, practical advice about various forms of influence that raise pressing ethical and public policy questions. The chapter concludes with a few brief remarks about political manipulation.

2
Thirteen Forms of Ordinary Manipulation

2.1. Introduction

The term 'manipulation' is commonly applied to a large and diverse set of tactics and forms of influence. This chapter will document that diversity. Since our focus is ordinary, real-life manipulation, our examples will come either from real life or from psychologically realistic fiction. This chapter's main task is to identify and discuss various forms of influence that seem like clear cases of manipulation. The result will be a list of paradigm examples of manipulation, which will serve as a data set against which we will test various theories of manipulation in the next chapter.

2.2. Thirteen Manipulative Tactics

The tactics and forms of influence to be discussed here are ones that seem like clear cases of manipulation. I believe that most readers would describe most if not all of them as manipulation, or at least would not object to describing them so. Moreover, they are tactics and forms of influence that *have* been described as manipulation in contexts where there is no reason to think that such a description is idiosyncratic.

While I expect most readers to agree that the examples discussed here are indeed cases of manipulation, some readers may not see every single item on the list as a *clear* case of manipulation, or a case of manipulation *at all*. That possibility is one advantage of having a long list of examples: Even if you object to characterizing a few of them as manipulation, we will still have a long enough list to work with.[1] Moreover, in accordance with the methodology discussed in section 1.5, we should recognize that the most convincing theory of manipulation might provide compelling reasons to deny that one or more of these cases are genuine instances

[1] An alternative approach would be to employ social science methods to determine when people apply terms like 'manipulation' in scenarios where various forms of influence are present. Magda Osman and Christos Bechlivanidis have done some fascinating initial work of this sort (Osman and Bechlivanidis 2024a; 2024b). My hope is that the length of the list developed here makes that sort of investigation unnecessary for my purposes. We do not need a complete list, and the list developed here would be sufficiently long even if the social science approach uncovered some disagreements about whether a few of its members really are clear cases of manipulation.

Manipulation. Robert Noggle, Oxford University Press. © Robert Noggle 2025.
DOI: 10.1093/9780198924920.003.0002

of manipulation. Thus, we should see the list below as a *tentative* data set, such that a convincing account of manipulation should identify *most, if not all*, of them as cases of manipulation.

2.2.1. Playing on the Emotions

Playing on the emotions is a common manipulative tactic, and one that comes readily to mind when we think about manipulation. For compelling examples of this tactic, one can hardly improve on Shakespeare's *Othello*. Iago is the quintessential manipulator, and playing on the emotions is one of his favorite tactics. Consider this exchange from Act 4, Scene 1. Iago has gotten Othello to believe—mistakenly—that his beloved Desdemona is having an adulterous affair with his lieutenant. Othello's initial impulse is to murder them both. But his love for Desdemona begins to win out over his rage. This is a development that Iago seeks to reverse:

OTHELLO: Ay, let her rot and perish and be damned tonight, for she shall not live. No, my heart is turned to stone. I strike it and it hurts my hand. Oh, the world hath not a sweeter creature, she might lie by an emperor's side and command him tasks.
IAGO: Nay, that's not your way.
OTHELLO: Hang her! I do but say what she is. So delicate with her needle, an admirable musician. Oh, she will sing the savageness out of a bear! Of so high and plenteous wit and invention!
IAGO: She's the worse for all this.
OTHELLO: Oh, a thousand thousand times!—And then of so gentle a condition!
IAGO: Ay, too gentle.
OTHELLO: Nay, that's certain. But yet the pity of it, Iago! O Iago, the pity of it, Iago!
IAGO: If you are so fond over her iniquity, give her patent to offend, for if it touch not you it comes near nobody.
OTHELLO: I will chop her into messes! Cuckold me?
IAGO: Oh, 'tis foul in her.
OTHELLO: With mine officer!
IAGO: That's fouler.
OTHELLO: Get me some poison, Iago, this night. I'll not expostulate with her lest her body and beauty unprovide my mind again. This night, Iago!

When Othello's memory of Desdemona's "gentleness" begins to soften his anger, Iago jumps back in and suggests that if he loves Desdemona so much, he should just let her continue her adulterous affair. This rekindles Othello's rage and puts him back on the murderous path that Iago has planned for him.

Iago's manipulation of Othello both inflames and appeals to negative and violent emotions like anger, jealousy, and hatred. We often use terms like 'provoking' or 'inciting' or 'goading' when manipulation kindles emotions like these. But manipulators can employ many other emotions as well. Fear-mongering is a common form of emotional manipulation, especially in the political realm. Some of the most infamous political advertisements, such as the "Willie Horton ad" (about a criminal who committed violent crimes after being furloughed by Governor Mike Dukakis, who was George Bush, Sr.'s opponent in the 1988 US presidential election) and the "Daisy ad" (where a small child counts flowers just before a nuclear explosion) are often cited as paradigm examples of manipulative fear-mongering in politics.[2] In recent years, a great deal of fear-mongering has appeared over the topic of immigration. Fear often begets hatred, and hate is perhaps even more effective than fear for manipulating the public. Resentment over past injustices—real, exaggerated, or merely imagined—is also a potent lever for political manipulators. History abounds with examples of such tactics operating to galvanize support for wars, ethnic cleansing, and even genocide.

Yet manipulators sometimes play on more positive emotions. The manipulative appeal to sympathy is nicely illustrated in a scene from the 1949 Katherine Hepburn and Spencer Tracy film, *Adam's Rib* (Cukor 1949). Spouses and fellow attorneys Adam and Amanda Bonner have just represented opposing parties in a recent court case, and this has strained their marriage. During a meeting with a divorce attorney (Julie), Adam breaks down in tears, and the two decide to reconcile. Later, Adam announces that the Republicans have asked him to run for county judge. Amanda suggests that she is considering running for the same position as a Democrat:

AMANDA: Have they picked the Democratic candidate yet? I was just wondering.
ADAM: You were. But you wouldn't.
AMANDA: How do you know?
ADAM: Because I'd cry, and then you wouldn't.
AMANDA: What?
ADAM: I'd cry . . . the way I did in Julie's office today. Got me what I wanted. Got me you back.
AMANDA: Those were real, those tears.
ADAM: Of course they were. But I can turn 'em on anytime I want to. Us boys can do it, too. We just never think to.

Not only has Adam learned to produce "crocodile tears," but he has learned to deploy them to influence Amanda's behavior. This tactic works—when it does—by

[2] The former, of course, also appealed to racist attitudes. For a compelling analysis of the Willie Horton ad as an example of a racist dogwhistle, see Saul (2024).

engaging the target's sympathetic or empathetic feelings to get the target to do what the manipulator wants.

The use of crocodile tears is closely related to, and sometimes a part of, a tactic commonly known as the guilt trip. Here is an example from the psychologist George Simon's book about dealing with manipulative people. Janice's husband Bill is a drinker and philanderer. After leaving him, she is racked with guilt—an emotion to which she seems especially susceptible. Bill suggests that his bad behavior is the result of Janice's failure to support him during a difficult time at work, and that their separation will trigger a relapse in his drinking. While Janice is living elsewhere, Bill ratchets up the guilt:

> Bill told her not to worry that problems were mounting at work, that the kids seemed to be needing a lot of attention, or that he'd had episodes of heavy drinking again . . . On his last call, Bill's voice sounded shaky and his speech a little slurred as he told Janice not to worry about him, his temptations to drink, or the possibility that he might be losing his job soon. He insisted that he was handling the "deep pain" of their separation and the problems with their children as best as anyone could all by himself. (Simon 2010, 92)

Later, the hospital calls Janice to report that Bill has overdosed on pain medications. Simon indicates that this is little more than a ploy by Bill, but an effective one:

> [I]t didn't matter to her that the doctor said he hadn't really taken enough of his pain pills to do himself.any serious damage. She just looked at him, imagining the pain and anguish that must have "driven" him to do such a thing. Once again, she began to believe that she'd been too selfish (Simon 2010, 93)

We sometimes distinguish various forms of emotional manipulation according to which emotion is being targeted. Thus, we have: fear-mongering, guilt trips, crocodile tears, etc. The variety of emotions that a manipulator can leverage makes it difficult to settle on a single paradigm example of this form of manipulation. But since I am partial to *Othello*, I will use this one:

> ***Playing on the Emotions:*** Iago manipulates Othello by playing on his jealousy and anger to get him to murder Desdemona.

2.2.2. Misdirection, Misemphasis, and Other Distortion Tactics

Manipulators often influence someone's behavior by influencing how much attention that person pays to various facts. At the extreme, this may involve getting the target to overlook some fact entirely. This is the goal of misdirection. Misdirection typically involves drawing attention *away* from one thing by drawing it *toward* something else. Pickpockets use misdirection when they deliberately jostle their victims to draw attention away from the process of wallet extraction. Military planners use misdirection with decoys to divert attention away from the main attack. Stage magicians use misdirection to draw attention away from the mechanism by which a trick is done. Con artists use misdirection to focus their victims' attention on the prospect of a huge payoff and away from the fact that they are at the bottom level of a pyramid scheme. The goal of misdirection is to obscure some fact that might lead the target to do something other than what the manipulator wants—but *only if* the target pays attention to it.

The most successful instances of misdirection prevent the target from even noticing whatever fact the manipulator is trying to hide. Often, though, manipulators need not—or cannot—completely prevent the target from noticing something. In such cases, it is often sufficient for the manipulator to get the target to pay less attention to that fact than the target otherwise would. This can be done in much the same way as misdirection, by calling the target's attention to some other fact. The more attention one pays to one thing, the less is available for another.

Since we tend to pay attention to what we regard as important, and vice versa, changing how much attention someone pays to something usually affects how much weight that person places on it when deciding what to do. Thus, focusing someone's attention on some fact is a way of emphasizing that fact, and vice versa. Consequently, misdirection often functions as a way of *emphasizing* or *de-emphasizing* certain facts, to the manipulator's advantage. We might call this tactic "misemphasis." Although misdirection is one form of misemphasis, there are many others, including: repetition; the use of fine print; relative positioning of different items within a message; and differences in the volume, pitch, or speed of speech. Misemphasis can also include distortions like exaggeration and hyperbole, or downplaying and minimization. Often, merely changing the subject is enough to de-emphasize what was just being discussed.

Misemphasis can involve the manipulator de-emphasizing something that might make the target less likely to do what the manipulator wants. Or it can involve over-emphasizing something that might make the target more likely to do what the manipulator wants. Often, a manipulator will employ both tactics simultaneously. Thus, a manipulative car salesperson might overemphasize the already obvious sleekness of the sports car, while downplaying the fact that the price tag is above the customer's stated budget and that it lacks a back seat suitable for his children. Advertisements for dubious diet products emphasize a few success stories, while downplaying the fact that dramatic results are the exception rather than the rule.

All these tactics have a common feature: They involve changing the *salience* of some fact in a way that will make the target more likely to do what the manipulator wants. In cases of successful misdirection, the fact that the manipulator wants the target to ignore may have no salience at all, since it may go completely unnoticed. In less extreme cases, the manipulator changes the salience of facts of which the target is aware—increasing the salience of facts that support doing what the manipulator wants, and decreasing the salience of facts that support doing something else.

Since the pickpocket's use of misdirection is an especially clear case of this tactic, let us use it as our paradigm example of this form of manipulation:

> ***Misdirection/Misemphasis:*** The pickpocket manipulates his victim by jostling him so that he will not notice that his wallet is being extracted from his pocket.

2.2.3. Gaslighting

In recent years the term 'gaslighting' has become much more popular, while its meaning has become much less precise. It is commonly applied to a variety of interpersonal dynamics and influences, sometimes being used as little more than a synonym for 'manipulation' or 'deception.'[3] During the administration of the forty-fifth US president, the term became especially popular to describe that president's habit of denying plain and verifiable facts—denials accepted at face value by large swaths of the American public.

The term's original meaning—which I will use here—derives from the play *Gas Light* by Patrick Hamilton (Hamilton 1939) that was developed into a 1940 British film, *Gaslight*, and a 1944 American film of the same name, starring Ingrid Bergman (Cukor 1944). In the 1944 film, the nefarious Gregory enters the home of a rich opera singer and murders her for her priceless jewels, but is forced to flee the crime scene without them. Later, he marries the opera singer's niece, Paula, and convinces her that they should move into her aunt's old apartment, where Gregory hopes to find the jewels. To disguise both his identity and his search for the jewels, Gregory gradually convinces Paula that she cannot trust her own judgments and should simply accept whatever Gregory says. Over time, Gregory's efforts push Paula to the brink of insanity.

Gregory's tactics came to be known as "gaslighting." Some early uses of the term referred to deliberate efforts to drive someone insane. But that is not the use that I will adopt. Rather, I will use the term to apply to attempts to get someone to doubt their own judgment and rely on the manipulator's advice instead. An example of this use of the term appears in a 1975 scene from the American television show M*A*S*H (Philips 1975). Prior to the scene in question, Corporal "Radar" O'Reilly

[3] See Stark (2019) and Abramson (2024) for accounts of gaslighting similar to the one given here, and a discussion of other uses of the term. For a recent self-help book that seems to use the term 'gaslighting' as a synonym for manipulation more generally, see Sarkis (2018). For another recent self-help book that treats gaslighting as a dysfunctional relationship dynamic in which one person defines the reality of the other, see Stern (2018).

gets Colonel Blake to sign a pass allowing a medical orderly under his command to visit his family. He does this by surreptitiously slipping the pass into a stack of papers for Colonel Blake to sign. Before reaching his family, the orderly is detained by an officer who suspects that the pass was forged. Later, at a poker game, Blake is shown the pass, but does not remember signing it. The next day, the following exchange occurs:

COL. BLAKE: Radar, let me see the pass again . . . I just don't remember signing this.
CAPT. MCINTYRE: Well, who's to blame if you have amnesia?
COL. BLAKE: Aw, don't give me that amnesia bit. I remember seeing this last night at the poker game.
CAPT. MCINTYRE AND CAPT. "HAWKEYE" PIERCE, IN UNISON: What poker game?
COL. BLAKE: Radar, didn't we play poker last night?
CPL. O'REILLY: If you say so, sir.
COL. BLAKE: Oh, I get it. You're trying to gaslight me, right?

Here, McIntyre, Pierce, and O'Reilly try to get Col. Blake to doubt his own memory so that he will rely instead on what they tell him. As in the film *Gaslight*, we see a two-part process: undermining the target's confidence in his or her own judgment, and then getting the target to use this lack of confidence as a reason to rely on the manipulator's judgment instead.[4] It seems clear that this is an example of manipulation. Let us use the events from the 1944 film as our paradigm example of this form of manipulation:

> ***Gaslighting:*** Gregory manipulates Paula by undermining her confidence in her own judgment so that she will do as Gregory advises.

2.2.4. Game Switching

In a fascinating article, the philosopher Lisa Herzog (2017) discusses a phenomenon she calls "misleading about the game you are in." She gives this example:

> An engineer, Anne, is in negotiations with another engineer, Bert, from a different company. They discuss a deal about a new product that their companies

[4] In her excellent book on the topic, Kate Abramson (2024) treats gaslighting as a much more complex phenomenon that takes place over time and is focused less on getting the target to do some particular thing and more on undermining the target's standing as an agent who can challenge the authority of the gaslighter (Abramson 2024, 45–60). This phenomenon appears to be a more elaborate and complete version of what I am calling gaslighting here. Or, to put it another way, anyone who prefers Abramson's characterization of gaslighting should think of what I am discussing as a kind of "gaslighting lite."

> might develop together . . . Anne is keen to find out how large the other company's budget is: this would allow her to suggest a maximum price for her own company's contribution without putting the deal at risk. But during the first half of the negotiations, when they talk money, Bert is on guard not to reveal this information, because he is aware of its strategic importance. Later in the day, however, they walk over to the test stand where the prototypes are mounted. They get excited about the project, and start a heated discussion about how to solve the remaining technical problems. Both being engineers, and given that there are strong social norms about cooperation among fellow engineers, they are used to having collegial conversation in which they share their expertise. At one point, Anne notes, in a casual tone: "Well, that solution might work, depending on how much money you'd want to spend on it." In the heat of the moment, Bert readily reveals the information about his budget. (Herzog 2017, 250–51)

As Herzog observes, Anne gets Bert to operate according to the rules of the "collaboration between engineers" game rather than the "negotiating with a business rival" game. Of course, the term 'game' here is a metaphor. But it is a helpful one, for it evokes the idea of rules governing behavior—rules that often vary in important ways from one kind of situation to another. The rules appropriate for a brainstorming session between engineering team members are very different from those appropriate for a business negotiation between representatives of different companies.

Notice that Herzog's story is not one of deception.[5] Bert does not come to *believe* that Anne is a colleague working on the same team. Rather, Anne acts according to a set of behavioral norms and expectations, and this gets Bert to follow those same norms and expectations as well. As Herzog's metaphor suggests, these norms and expectations function like rules in a game. By following the rules of the "collaboration game," Anne tricks Bert into following those same rules instead of the rules governing the game that they are actually playing, i.e., the "business negotiation game." This process would seem to operate automatically rather than from a conscious decision. Thus, it does not require Bert to adopt any conscious belief that Anne is a colleague rather than a representative of a different company.

Herzog may be the first philosopher to discuss this form of influence. But once we see it, we can recognize it in many examples of influence that seem like clear cases of manipulation. For example, some forms of "social engineering" seem to involve triggering behavioral norms that are not appropriate to the situation. According to cybersecurity expert Ralph Moseley, "social engineering can be

[5] Herzog characterizes it as "misleading" rather than "deception."

defined as the act of manipulating an individual, or even a group, into giving away confidential information" (Moseley 2021, 95). Many forms of social engineering involve outright deception, as when a scam email purports to be from someone known to the recipient, or when a criminal dresses as a delivery person to gain access to a secure location. But others appear to operate without deceiving their targets into acquiring any false beliefs.

One such tactic is called "tailgating." This is a means of accessing secured areas simply by following closely behind someone authorized to enter the area. According to Moseley, "tailgating plays on the idea of common courtesy, that is, in the situation of having opened a secure door with a pass key or other device, the person will open the door for the person behind, even holding it open for them" (Moseley 2021, 99). Criminals sometimes combine this tactic with deception, for example by wearing a delivery person's uniform to deceive the target into believing that the criminal is authorized to enter. But the door-holding norm can be strong enough to drive behavior without the need for deception: Many people have so internalized this norm that it forms a habit that can be triggered automatically, with little or no conscious thought. Consequently, we can be tricked into thoughtlessly following this norm without ever considering—and thus forming a belief about—whether the person for whom we are holding the door belongs inside.

Herzog hesitates to label the phenomenon she describes as manipulation because she assumes that manipulation must be intentional, and she wants to leave open the possibility that the phenomenon she describes could occur unintentionally (Herzog 2017, 257 n. 4). But if we imagine Anne *intentionally* trying to get Bert to follow the rules of the "collaboration between colleagues" game instead of the "business negotiation" game, I think that most people would agree that Anne manipulates Bert. It is even more clear that tailgating is manipulative, since it is frequently offered as an example of social engineering, which is commonly described as a kind of manipulation. So let us take that as our paradigm example of this form of manipulation:

> ***Game Switching***: The "social engineer" manipulates the employee into allowing access to a restricted area by getting him to follow the behavioral norm of holding open the door for the person behind him.

2.2.5. Social Proof

We often assume that if others are doing something, then it is a sensible thing to do. This tendency is sometimes called "social proof." In his influential book, *Influence*, Robert Cialdini describes social proof like this: "We view a behavior as correct in a given situation to the degree that we see others performing it" (Cialdini 2008, 99). Often, the assumption that what others are doing is sensible is itself quite sensible. Sometimes there really is wisdom in a crowd, and following the lead of those around us can prevent or solve coordination problems. But it also leaves us susceptible to manipulation.

Of course, a decision to do what others are doing can reflect conscious, logical reasoning that weighs the probabilities that other people have better access to information relevant to the question of what to do. But conformity with the behavior of others can also result from cognitive habits or shortcuts—sometimes called *heuristics*—that predispose us to assume, more or less automatically, that what others are doing is sensible. Sometimes it may even result from a non-conscious tendency simply to imitate those around us. I will use the term 'social proof' to refer to the tendency—conscious or not—to assume that what other people are doing is sensible and thus worth imitating. Although we remain free to question and reject such assumptions, the fact that we do not always do so makes social proof a potent behavioral influence. This potency is enhanced in situations when we lack other sources of information that might counter the assumption that what others are doing is the sensible thing to do. Cialdini argues that this process helps to explain the tragedy of the People's Temple mass suicide in Jonestown, Guyana in 1977. Cialdini writes:

> [Reverend Jim] Jones sought to control the end of the Temple in his own way. He gathered the entire community around him and issued a call for each person's death to be done in a unified act of self-destruction. The first response was that of a young woman who calmly approached the now famous vat of strawberry-flavored poison, administered one dose to her baby, one to herself, and then sat down in a field, where she and her child died in convulsions within four minutes. Others followed steadily in turn. Although a handful of Jonestowners escaped and a few others are reported to have resisted, the survivors claim that the great majority of the 910 people who died did so in an orderly, willful fashion. (Cialdini 2008, 128)

Although Cialdini notes that several factors played a role in this tragedy, he argues that a key ingredient was the fact that the cult members were isolated from other sources of information about what to do—a situation that heightens the power of social proof to influence action:

> [T]he single act in the history of the People's Temple that most contributed to the members' mindless compliance that day occurred a year earlier with the relocation of the Temple to a jungled country of unfamiliar customs and people ... The environment—both physical and social—into which they were dropped must have seemed dreadfully uncertain ... [W]hen people are uncertain, they look to the actions of others to guide their own actions. In the alien, Guyanese environment, then, Temple members were very ready to follow the lead of others. (Cialdini 2008, 129)

Few examples of manipulation are more tragic and more paradigmatic than the tragedy of Jonestown, and it appears that social proof played a major role in it. Hence, we will use this as our paradigm example of manipulation involving social proof:

Social Proof: Jim Jones manipulated his followers by getting some of them to drink poisoned fruit punch and then relying on the tendency of the rest to do what others are doing to get them to drink the fruit punch as well.

2.2.6. Peer Pressure

Like social proof, peer pressure often increases social conformity. Indeed, the two forces often operate in tandem, so that it is sometimes difficult to tell them apart. Nevertheless, they are distinct forms of influence. Social proof involves an assumption—often tacit—that other people know what they are doing. By contrast, peer pressure involves caring about obtaining and retaining other people's approval. Often this concern for approval encourages the target to imitate the behavior of those whose approval the target seeks: If I don't do as my friends do, they will disapprove of me. But, unlike social proof, peer pressure can influence a person to do something different from what others are doing, so long as it is something on which the approval of those others depends.

Such is the case in a scene from the 1983 American film *A Christmas Story* (Clark 1983). A group of children are gathered at recess on a cold winter day. One child, Schwartz, wants another child, Flick, to put his tongue on a metal flagpole to see whether it will freeze. The following dialogue occurs:

SCHWARTZ: Well, I double-dare you.
NARRATOR: The exact exchange and nuance of phrase in this ritual is very important.
FLICK: Are you kidding? Stick my tongue to that stupid pole? That's dumb.
SCHWARTZ: That's 'cause you know it will stick!
FLICK: You're full of it.
SCHWARTZ: Well, I double dog-dare you!
NARRATOR: Now it was serious. A double dog-dare. What else was left but a "triple-dare you"? And finally, the *coup de grace* of all dares, the sinister triple dog-dare!
SCHWARTZ: I triple dog-dare you!
NARRATOR: Schwartz created a slight breach of etiquette by skipping the triple dare and going right for the throat.
FLICK: Alright, alright.

Flick is not being pressured to do what his peers are doing; he is being pressured to do something else, on which their approval will depend. He takes the dare to avoid their disapproval. That fact is what makes Flick's predicament a clear case of peer pressure.

Flick is threatened with the *disapproval* of his peers. More powerful forms of peer pressure can involve threats of complete ostracism from the social group. Peer pressure of this more extreme sort might be more aptly described as coercion than manipulation. While it can be difficult to draw a sharp line between coercive and manipulative peer pressure, it seems more accurate to describe peer pressure as manipulative when it appeals to the desire to "fit in" with one's current social group, to gain the approval of a more desirable group, or to simply achieve a generalized approval of one's peers. But even peer pressure that seems more aptly described as manipulation than coercion can be used in nefarious and aggressive ways, as when one group member mobilizes others to bully a classmate (Garandeau and Cillessen 2006), or to engage in other dangerous or anti-social behaviors.

Although adolescents are especially susceptible to peer pressure, adults are hardly immune. While most of us would refuse to stick our tongues onto frozen flag poles on a dare, peer pressure can still be a potent influence on our behavior, especially when combined with social proof. It is quite possible that both peer pressure and social proof contributed to the tragedy of Jonestown. Be that as it may, we will use Flick's misadventure as our paradigm example of this form of manipulation:

Peer Pressure: Schwartz manipulates Flick into sticking his tongue on the flagpole by "triple dog-daring him" and thus ensuring that his peers will disapprove of him if he fails to take the dare.

2.2.7. Emotional Blackmail

The term 'emotional blackmail' is sometimes used loosely to include forms of emotional manipulation like guilt trips, or to refer to any form of manipulation within a relationship. I will use the term more narrowly, to refer to a threat to engage in behaviors that cause the target to experience unpleasant emotions, typically in the context of a personal relationship. This more precise definition is closer to how psychologist Susan Forward describes it in her book, *Emotional Blackmail*:

> Emotional blackmail is a powerful form of manipulation in which people close to us threaten, either directly or indirectly, to punish us if we don't do what they want. At the heart of any kind of blackmail is one basic threat, which can be expressed in many different ways: *If you don't behave the way I want you to, you will suffer.* A criminal blackmailer might threaten to use knowledge about a person's past to ruin her reputation, or ask to be paid off in cash to hide a secret. Emotional blackmail hits closer to home. Emotional blackmailers know how much we value our relationship with them. . . . [T]hey use this intimate knowledge to shape the threats that give them the payoff they want: Our compliance. (Forward 2001, x)

Although she does not call it 'emotional blackmail,' Marcia Baron seems to have this tactic in mind when she writes about forms of manipulation that

> rely on a concern on the part of the person being manipulated either to retain a close relationship with the manipulator or simply to remain on good terms with him or her. Sometimes they require no more than a wish to avoid unpleasantness, or avoid creating a scene. (Baron 2003, 43)

In most cases, the emotional blackmailer threatens forms of suffering that require the existence of a relationship. Although this is often a romantic relationship, it need not be. Friendships and family relationships can also provide the context for emotional blackmail. Regardless of the nature of the relationship, emotional blackmail threatens the relationship itself, or forms of suffering that the target cannot escape without abandoning, damaging, or otherwise compromising the relationship. For this reason, a total stranger is seldom in a position to engage in emotional blackmail because nothing prevents a person from walking away from a stranger who makes the kinds of threats typical of this form of manipulation.

The most severe forms of emotional blackmail involve threats to the relationship itself. Less severe, but still powerful, forms involve the blackmailer becoming unpleasant to be around. This may involve sulking, imposing "the silent treatment" or becoming irritable or withdrawn. It may also involve unpleasant histrionics or "drama." Temper tantrums, especially when used deliberately in calculated attempts to get one's way, are often forms of emotional blackmail. Indeed, they are not significantly different from other tactics used by older children and some adults: Meeting requests to help around the house with foot-dragging, complaining, and specious arguments about the unfairness of having to contribute to the maintenance of the household. The common feature in all these tactics is the imposition of suffering, or at least unpleasantness, which is difficult to avoid because it takes place within a relationship, and which is calculated to change the other person's behavior.

Emotional blackmail is often accompanied by guilt trips. Although the two tactics are sometimes run together, I prefer to keep them separate. As I understand it, the motivational lynchpin of emotional blackmail is simply the unpleasantness of the consequences that the blackmailer imposes or threatens. Consequently, emotional blackmail can be used to induce compliance with a wide variety of demands. The motivational lynchpin of a guilt trip is, of course, guilt. Although guilt is an unpleasant emotion, its motivational force is more narrowly targeted toward actions that will atone for whatever bad thing the target has been made to feel guilty about. In ordinary contexts, it is seldom crucial to distinguish the two, but for our purposes, we will keep them separate.

Susan Forward offers this first-person account of Allen, who is being emotionally blackmailed by his new spouse, Jo:

> I know she loves me, but I don't like what's happening to us. If I suggest that we spend any time apart—my friends are always bugging me to go to the movies or hang out after work—she acts really hurt. She looks at me with those big sad eyes and says "What's the matter? You're bored with me? You don't want to be with me anymore? I thought you were wild about me." If I start to make plans, she pouts, pleads with me and lets me know how unhappy I'm making her in no uncertain terms. (Forward 2001, 15)

Assuming that Allen's account is accurate, and assuming that Jo's behavior is deliberately calculated to gain Allen's compliance, Jo's behavior seems aptly described as manipulation. So understood, let us take it as our paradigm example of this form of manipulation:

Emotional Blackmail: Jo manipulates Allen by deliberately being unpleasant to be around whenever he does not do what she wants him to do.

2.2.8. Nagging

Nagging is one of the least sophisticated forms of manipulation, but also one of the most effective. Sometimes the person doing the nagging offers a legitimate reason for doing something. But what gives nagging its manipulative character is not the content of what is said, but the fact that it is repeated to the point that it becomes annoying at best, and intolerable at worst. Nagging, in effect, is a kind of punishment that the manipulator inflicts on the target for not doing what the manipulator wants. This distinguishes nagging from mere repetition for emphasis, or to ensure that one's request is heard and remembered.

Nagging often goes hand in hand with emotional blackmail, especially in its more primitive forms like tantrums and drama. And in ordinary contexts, it is seldom necessary to distinguish them. However, one difference between them is that emotional blackmail is a threat to impose suffering in the future, if the target fails to do what the manipulator wants. Nagging, by contrast, first imposes the unpleasant consequence and then offers to remove it if the target complies. Although nagging is easy to resist in the short term, over time, it can wear down the target's resistance. In this, it is much like the urge to scratch an itch: the effort required to resist it becomes ever greater the longer it persists.

Nagging is such a crude tactic that it may not come readily to mind as an example of manipulation if we are accustomed to thinking about sophisticated manipulators like Iago. But this is no doubt why we can find it being used even by young children. The psychologist Harriett Braiker includes it among the manipulative tactics in her book on the topic (Braiker 2004, 134). Marcia Baron seems to have nagging in mind when she writes of:

> wearing another down until one gets one's way . . . by whining, complaining, or incessant arguing—though once again, if one is arguing with the aim of convincing, and not with the aim of wearing the other down, this should not count as manipulation, even if the effect is the same. (Baron 2003, 42)

So, despite its crudeness, nagging seems not only aptly described as a kind of manipulation, but indeed as a clear case of it. To sidestep the question of whether nagging by very young children is manipulative, let us take its use by an adolescent as our paradigm example of this form of manipulation:

> ***Nagging:*** The teen manipulates his parents by nagging them to let him take his gaming device to school, which the parents think is a bad idea.

2.2.9. Charm Offensive

In his book on psychopaths, Robert D. Hare (2011) relates this vignette about a law enforcement officer who has stopped a motorist for speeding:

> It is generally against protocol for a traffic violator to get out of the vehicle . . . And yet she emerged so confidently, smiled so winningly. She isn't really beautiful, but the direct eye contact she makes is powerfully attractive. He asks for her license and resists her attempts at conversation—for the moment. Finally, though, he gives in to her bantering style and writes out only a warning . . . The officer watches her climb back into the car and drive away, fighting to keep himself from waiving in her rearview mirror. (Hare 2011, 144)

The motorist has clearly manipulated the officer. She has charmed him, and thereby made him disinclined to write her a citation for speeding.

As Hare observes, "there are always people who use their appearance and charm—natural or contrived—to convince others to do their will" (Hare 2011, 144). Hare is describing what is often called a "charm offensive." A charm offensive is the mirror image of emotional blackmail. Whereas emotional blackmail involves threats to impose unpleasant consequences for noncompliance with what the manipulator wants, charm offensives offer pleasant consequences for compliance. Where emotional blackmail is the stick, the charm offensive is the carrot.

Charm offensives often involve sexual or romantic appeal, as in Hare's account. In such cases they trade on the appeal of being well-regarded by someone one finds romantically appealing. These charm offensives are often strengthened by the suggestion that a liaison might be possible if only the target will play his cards right and do what the manipulator wants. Such a prospect can motivate even people who would decline such a liaison if it were offered.

However, charm offensives need not have sexual or romantic undertones. Sometimes charm is based simply on making people feel good about themselves, whether through insincere flattery or simply a deliberate program of saying nice but true things about the target. Or it may be based on a sort of undefinable charisma, magnetism, or likeability that makes a person fun or exciting to be around. In such cases, the carrot may be the charmer's approval, or it may be the prospect of spending more time in the charmer's company. Often it is both.

Of course, charm and charisma are not vices in themselves, and there is nothing wrong with being someone whose company others enjoy. A manipulative charm offensive weaponizes these things to get the target to do the manipulator's bidding. This seems to involve two elements: First, the target must be gotten to care about the manipulator's approval, attention, or company. Second, the manipulator makes this approval, attention, or company dependent on the target doing what the manipulator wants. Since Hare's story implies that the motorist is deliberately doing both things to avoid a speeding citation, we will use it as our paradigm example of this form of manipulation:

> ***Charm Offensive:*** The motorist manipulates the police officer by getting him to have positive feelings toward her that make him care about gaining her approval, and making it clear that he can do this by letting her go without issuing a speeding citation.

2.2.10. Exploiting Conflict Aversion

In his fascinating study of con artists, R. Paul Wilson makes this observation about "short cons" (which take place over a matter of minutes): "Once caught in the middle of a short con, the mark can only escape by breaking social conventions and walking away or confronting the hustlers directly" (Wilson 2014, 198). Wilson observes that the aversion to breaking social convention exerts a powerful influence, even when the target begins to suspect that a con is afoot. Wilson continues:

> Most of the time, people don't like to rock the boat. Scammers abuse this tendency to comply by making it difficult or uncomfortable for the mark to raise an objection or change a course of action. This aversion to conflict is used in a con

game to make the mark feel like he is being unreasonable or even dishonorable by raising any concerns. (Wilson 2014, 120)

The natural human aversion to conflict can be exploited by manipulators in several ways. Manipulators often gain compliance by making a request in a situation where it would seem rude or socially awkward to refuse—what we often call putting someone "on the spot." As Marcia Baron observes, this manipulative tactic is often "employed by salespeople and telephone solicitors who are skilled at making it socially awkward not to buy anything or not to agree to the solicitor's proposal" (Baron 2003, 44).

Another version of this tactic involves not waiting for the target to respond to a request but instead expressing confidence—and perhaps gratitude—that the person will accept. A manipulator might also simply proceed as though the target has *already agreed* to the manipulator's request. To escape this trap, the target must interrupt the manipulator's action *and* deny both the manipulator's assumption that the request has been accepted, as well as the request itself. More extreme forms of this tactic may involve the manipulator simply doing something objectionable while counting on the fact that those around will simply not object because doing so creates conflict. The exploitation of conflict aversion may also play a role in the tactic of "tailgating" discussed earlier in this chapter (section 2.2.4): Shutting the door on someone about to walk through it, or asking someone to show identification, both involve a level of social conflict with which many people are uncomfortable.

Of course, there are good reasons for a certain level of aversion to conflict. At the social level, a reluctance to create conflict promotes social harmony and cohesion. At the individual level, conflict often invites unpleasant interactions or even violence. While it is reasonable to have some aversion to conflict, this aversion can be exploited by a manipulator, who may leverage it to get the target to acquiesce to being taken advantage of rather than creating conflict by objecting.

Of course, there is a great deal of individual variation in aversion to conflict. Some find conflict extremely aversive, while others seem to thrive on it. For those in the former category, merely declining a request can feel unacceptably rude. But even for people in the middle of this continuum, a clever manipulator can often make refusing the manipulator's request seem more like an unprovoked, hostile act than a simple exercise of the right to say no.

Let us use the con artist's version of this tactic as our paradigm example of this form of manipulation:

> ***Exploiting Conflict Aversion:*** The con artist manipulates his mark by relying on the mark's aversion to conflict so that he will not simply extract himself from the con when he starts to suspect that it is a con.

2.2.11. Exploiting Reciprocity

Our aversion to conflict is both part of the glue that holds society together, and a feature of human nature that manipulators can exploit. The same is true of our tendency to reciprocate. It is vital to the cooperation on which society depends. But the unscrupulous can use it to ensnare the unwary in a web of reciprocal obligation. Julius Caesar was said to have pardoned his enemies at least in part to put them in his debt, and the mafioso Don Corleone's largesse comes with strings: "Someday, and that day may never come, I will call upon you to do a service for me."[6]

In their textbook on persuasion, Robert Gass and John Seiter offer this example of how manipulators can exploit reciprocity, a tactic which they call "pre-giving":

> [I]n touristy areas of big cities . . . panhandlers have figured out a tricky way to get donations from unsuspecting tourists. The panhandlers wait a block or two from a well-known tourist attraction. When tourists walk by, clearly headed for the attraction, the panhandlers catch up with them, walk in stride, and proceed to "guide" the tourists to their destination. Once there, the panhandlers ask for a donation for the unrequested and unneeded service rendered. (Gass and Seiter 2013, 218)

This tactic exploits the fact that most people find it uncomfortable to refuse to reciprocate a favor that has been done for them—even if it is a worthless favor they did not request. This way of exploiting our tendency to reciprocate seems more clearly manipulative than ones where the target can escape the strings of reciprocity by declining the favor that had the strings attached. Thus, it seems an appropriate paradigm example of this form of manipulation:

> ***Exploiting Reciprocity:*** The panhandlers manipulate the tourists by doing small, unrequested favors for them and exploiting the tendency to reciprocate to get them to give the panhandlers money.

2.2.12. Negging

"Negging" is an especially sleazy form of manipulation practiced by especially sleazy characters who describe themselves as "pickup artists." Journalist Nicky Woolf offers this description of the tactic:

> A woman is drinking at a bar. She is alone; perhaps she is waiting for a friend. A man sidles up to her . . . "Your roots are showing," he says. She looks round,

[6] For Caesar, see Cicero (BCE 49); for the quote from Don Corleone, see Coppola (1972).

> confused. Perhaps she has misheard. "Your roots are showing," he says again, gesturing weakly at her hair . . . You may never have come across this bizarre phenomenon before, but in various forms it is being practised as a seduction technique around the world. Negging, as it is called, is in essence a trick. The idea is to undermine a woman's confidence by making backhanded or snide remarks—give a compliment with one hand, and take it away with the other. It is about control, putting the man in charge of the interaction by pushing the woman to earn his approval. (Woolf 2012)

Negging seems to involve a two-step process. First, the manipulator's negative remarks reduce the target's self-esteem. Second, the manipulator offers his own romantic attentions as a way to validate the target's self-image, restoring the self-esteem that he himself just diminished (Nicholson 2013; Green, Kukan, and Tully 2017).

Once we see the theory behind it, we can recognize similar tactics in other places besides night clubs. Some forms of advertising appear designed to make the target feel insecure about some aspect of his or her personal appearance, before pitching a product that will allegedly remedy the alleged defect about which the advertisement has cultivated the insecurity (Fennis and Stroebe 2021, 214). In other situations, this tactic may take the form of a challenge, where the manipulator expresses an unflattering assessment of the target, and then suggests that doing the thing that the manipulator wants will disprove that assessment. Schoolyard taunts sometimes take this form: A bully who tells another child that he is a coward if he doesn't perform some asinine stunt employs the same internal logic that the sleazy pickup artist uses: Here is an unflattering picture of yourself; here's what you can do to disprove it.

Negging seems clearly manipulative, and we can take the "pickup artist's" use of it as our paradigm example of this form of manipulation:

Negging: The so-called pickup artist manipulates a night club patron by first reducing her self-esteem, and then inducing her to regard dating him as a way to restore it.

2.2.13. Conditional Flattery

In negging, the manipulator says to the target: "Here's a *negative* portrayal of you; do X to *prove me wrong*." A tactic that we might call conditional flattery is the mirror image: "Here is a *positive* portrayal of you; do X to *prove me right*." Unlike more ordinary forms of flattery, this is flattery with strings attached: The manipulator paints an appealing portrait of the target, *but* it is one that applies *only if* the target does what the manipulator wants.

Marcia Baron offers this example of the tactic, which she takes to be "a clear case of manipulation":

> When Ayn Rand set out to have an affair with her protege, Nathaniel Branden, she wanted to feel morally in the clear about it. So . . . she sought the consent of her husband and . . . Branden's wife. Here (according to Barbara Branden) is the gist of what Rand said by way of asking them for their consent: "If the four of us were lesser people, it could never have happened and you could never accept it. But we're not lesser people." ' (Baron 2003, 37)

More mundane examples of this tactic are easy to find: "A strong man like you would have no trouble helping me move my new washing machine up the steps." "Someone with your organizational abilities would be a great committee chair." "Surely someone as brave as you would not mind getting up on that ladder to clean the gutters."

Narcy Recker, a nurse and astute observer of human behavior, calls this tactic the "conditional compliment." She writes that

> conditional compliments also give you a task to do, often with a deadline. Only if you accept the task, do you feel qualified to accept the compliment. If you do not do the task, then the possibility that you are not "as good" exists. This may leave you feeling unworthy and defeated. . . . A conditional compliment . . . may be a form of artful manipulation . . . particularly for individuals who are unsure and need the compliment as a positive reinforcement. (Recker 1993)

As with negging, the motivational lynchpin of conditional flattery seems to be the need for self-esteem. In negging, the *unpleasantness* of having one's self-esteem *deflated* makes people vulnerable to the manipulator's promise that it will be *restored* by doing what the manipulator wants. In conditional flattery, the *pleasantness* of having one's self-esteem *inflated* makes people vulnerable to the manipulator's promise that it will be *improved* by doing what the manipulator wants.

A possible example of conditional flattery can be found in Act 1, Scene 2 of Shakespeare's *Julius Caesar*, where Cassius tries to get Brutus to join the conspiracy to assassinate Caesar:

> O, you and I have heard our fathers say,
> There was a Brutus once that would have brook'd
> The eternal devil to keep his state in Rome
> As easily as a king.

Here Cassius offers Brutus an appealing portrait of himself as the worthy successor to his famous ancestor who, regarding monarchy as no better than rule by the devil, rid ancient Rome of its last king. But that self-image can only be claimed if Brutus helps rid present-day Rome of Caesar. Whether we should treat this as an example of manipulation depends on how we interpret the play. In a society like ancient Rome with a strong ethos of family honor, encouraging someone to live up to a famous ancestor *might* be less like manipulation than rational persuasion, at least in that social context. Thus, it is somewhat unclear whether we should regard Cassius as engaging in manipulation, or simply giving Brutus a reason for not flinching from his duty to rid Rome of a tyrant. Either way, though, the passage nicely illustrates the *structure* of conditional flattery, where a compliment is tied to doing what the manipulator wants.

Since the examples of Ayn Rand and Brutus pose problems of interpretation, let us use a generic case for our paradigm example of this form of manipulation:

> ***Conditional Flattery:*** The department chairperson manipulates an overworked faculty member into taking on an arduous task by praising her dedication and organizational abilities when making the request.

2.3. Some Caveats

We have now assembled a large and diverse list of tactics and forms of influence that seem aptly described as manipulation: (1) playing on the emotions; (2) misdirection/misemphasis; (3) gaslighting; (4) game switching; (5) social proof, (6) peer pressure; (7) emotional blackmail; (8) nagging; (9) charm offensive; (10) exploiting conflict-aversion; (11) exploiting reciprocity; (12) negging; and (13) conditional flattery, and we have identified a paradigm example of each of them.

I make no claims about the effectiveness of these tactics, though I suspect that all of them work at least some of the time. Nor do I claim that this is a perfect list. For one thing, it is almost certainly incomplete. For another, some classifications and distinctions may be somewhat artificial and arbitrary. There is some variation in how some terms relating to manipulation, such as 'gaslighting' and 'emotional blackmail,' are used in ordinary conversation. In such cases, I have simply chosen the usage that I prefer. These imperfections might be problematic if this were meant as a complete and precise taxonomy of manipulative tactics and the terms used to describe them. But it is not. Instead, it is simply meant to provide a list of examples that displays the diversity of ordinary forms of manipulation.

Some items on our list might not strike every reader as clear cases of manipulation; others may seem manipulative only in certain contexts or under certain conditions. Fortunately, the list would still be quite long and diverse even if not every reader agrees that everything on it is a clear case of manipulation. I am optimistic that most readers will agree that *most* of the items on this list *are* examples of manipulation, and that level of agreement will allow us to proceed.

We should remain open to the possibility that some forms of influence that initially seemed like manipulation might not share the features that, according to the best theory we can devise, are definitive of manipulation. After all, sometimes philosophical progress takes the form of discovering that some of our initial intuitions are not ultimately supportable. Even so, any attempt to construct an adequate theory of manipulation should aspire to accommodate as many of our strongest and most widely shared intuitions as possible. The number and diversity of tactics that seem like clear cases of manipulation will make this challenging.

2.4. What about Deception?

Some readers might wonder why this list of manipulative tactics omits lies, deception, innuendo, insinuation, and so on. These tactics, after all, often seem to go hand in hand with manipulation. If I say, "manipulation and . . .", the term 'deception' likely comes to mind. Moreover, the manipulative tactics discussed above are often accompanied by deception.

This is especially true of playing on the emotions. While Iago's stoking of Othello's anger in the scene quoted earlier does not involve deception, the ultimate cause of his anger is the fact that Iago has deceived Othello into believing that Desdemona has been unfaithful. But it also seems likely that Iago's earlier stoking of Othello's jealousy made him more susceptible to that deception, and less likely to see through it. Similarly, while the tactic of game switching need not involve deception, it might well be accompanied by it. Thus, Criminal Carl might seek entry into a secured area by using the tactic of "tailgating" which can operate without deceiving Employee Edna. But Carl might hedge his bets by dressing as a delivery person, so that if Edna stops herself from habitually holding the door to ask herself whether this person belongs there, she is more likely to form the false belief that he does.

The fact that manipulation and deception often complement one another raises the question of how the two phenomena are related. Different theories about manipulation say or imply different things about the relationship between manipulation and deception. The theory that I will develop and defend later in this book treats deception, insinuation, innuendo, and lies as forms of manipulation. Other theories, however, do not. Consequently, counting deception and related tactics as clear cases of manipulation that any credible theory of manipulation should identify *as* manipulation might seem like unfairly stacking the deck in favor of the theory that I will defend. Readers who regard deception, lies, insinuation, and the like as clear examples of manipulation are welcome to add those to the list here.

Readers who think that it is an open question whether such tactics are forms of manipulation may rest assured that I will, in due course, offer some reasons why they *should* count as forms of manipulation.

2.5. The Dual Use Phenomenon

Before concluding this chapter, we should note another important data point for which any adequate theory of manipulation should account: Many of the forms of influence we have discussed can be used in ways that seem clearly manipulative *and* in ways that do not.

This is especially true of emotional appeals. It is clearly manipulative for Iago to cultivate and appeal to Othello's jealousy and anger. But many forms of sincere moral persuasion involve appeals to empathy or sympathy. If Ingrid makes a sincere appeal to Tom's empathy to get him to care about the plight of children in a faraway land who are suffering from undeserved misery, her conduct does not seem aptly described as manipulation. Or consider gaslighting. It seems clearly manipulative for Gregory to undermine Paula's confidence in her own judgment to get her to listen to Gregory. But not every attempt to undermine someone's confidence in their own judgment seems manipulative. If your inebriated friend contends—implausibly—that she can drive home safely, then it does not seem manipulative to encourage her to place less confidence in her own judgment so that she trusts the judgment of her sober friends. Bill's making Janice feel guilty is a manipulative guilt trip. But it does not seem manipulative to get someone to feel guilt, or at least remorse, about having done something seriously wrong. Getting someone to agree to an onerous request to avoid the momentary social awkwardness of refusing is a manipulative exploitation of conflict aversion. But it does not seem manipulative to advise someone to give up their pocket money to a mugger to avoid a potentially violent conflict. The pickpocket's directing his victim's attention away from the fact that his wallet is being extracted is manipulative misdirection. But it does not seem manipulative to direct someone's attention to something important, such as a poisonous snake lurking nearby.

In short, many forms of influence that can be used manipulatively also appear to have non-manipulative uses as well. Let us call this the Dual Use Phenomenon:

> ***The Dual Use Phenomenon:*** Many forms of influence can be used in ways that seem like manipulation and in ways that do not seem like manipulation.

The Dual Use Phenomenon creates yet another challenge for an adequate theory of manipulation. As we shall see in the next chapter, many otherwise promising theories have difficulty meeting this challenge.

2.6. Conclusion

As we have seen, the tactics and forms of influence that are aptly described as manipulation are quite diverse. In the next chapter, we shall see that this diversity poses an important challenge to theorizing about manipulation. For it will prove difficult to find a theory of manipulation that identifies manipulation in all—or even most—of the examples where it clearly seems to be present.

3
Nine Accounts of Manipulation

3.1. Introduction

Chapter 2 explored the tremendous diversity of influences that seem like clear cases of manipulation. In this chapter, we will see that this diversity poses a significant challenge for any attempt to construct an account or theory of manipulation that distinguishes it from other influences. This chapter will examine nine different accounts of manipulation.[1] We will see that none of them adequately captures the diversity of influences that seem like clear cases of manipulation. Many fail to identify manipulation in cases where it seems clearly to be present. Others incorrectly identify manipulation in cases where it seems clearly to be absent. Some face additional problems as well. However, we shall also see that two of these accounts fail and succeed in complementary ways. One is strongest where the other is weakest, and vice versa. That fact will suggest that an adequate account of manipulation must somehow combine these two accounts—a task to be pursued in Chapter 4.

3.2. Expansive Accounts

To manipulate is to influence. Can we simply leave it at that? Social scientists sometimes use the term this way. For example, evolutionary psychologist David M. Buss characterizes manipulation as "the diverse tactics by which individuals influence and exploit the psychological mechanisms and behavioral machinery of others" (Buss 1992, 479). On Buss's definition, manipulating another organism resembles manipulating a non-living object.

We might call Buss's definition the "Maximally Expansive Account" of manipulation, since it would apply to *any* form of influence, *including* coercion and rational persuasion. It reflects his concern with seeking a scientific, value-neutral, understanding of how creatures get along in the world. Thus, this sense of the term 'manipulation' is best regarded as a technical term defined in a certain way for a specific scientific purpose. But this way of defining the term removes it from how it is used in ordinary conversation. In ordinary conversation, manipulation is understood to be distinct from other influences like coercion and rational persuasion.

[1] Many of the ideas presented in this chapter, and a few passages of the text, first appeared in Noggle 2022.

Manipulation. Robert Noggle, Oxford University Press. © Robert Noggle 2025.
DOI: 10.1093/9780198924920.003.0003

The maximally expansive definition of 'manipulation' may be suitable for certain scientific purposes, but it is not a plausible analysis of what we ordinarily mean when we use the term 'manipulation.'

Perhaps we simply need to make the account a bit less expansive. Perhaps we can define 'manipulation' as any influence *other than* coercion, rational persuasion, and good-faith bargaining. Let us call this the Moderately Expansive Account. Although this account is closer to how we use the term 'manipulation' in ordinary conversation, it faces two serious problems. First, it classifies as manipulation many tactics that most of us would hesitate to call manipulation. Consider, for example:

- A clergy member seeks to get her parishioners to feel empathy toward faraway people suffering from undeserved misfortune.
- A traffic safety agency uses graphic films of car crashes to instill in drivers a healthy fear of the dangers of drunk or distracted driving.
- One friend cheers up another by taking her to see a funny movie.
- A guide leads a large tour group by showing the people in front where to go, and relying on social proof to get the others to follow along.
- To help motivate student learning, a teacher feigns excitement about material that even he finds dull.

These are clearly not examples of rational persuasion, bargaining, or coercion. Yet most people would hesitate to call them manipulation. If someone *were* to describe them that way, we would suspect them of exaggeration, irony, or of stretching the term to make some sort of over-the-top complaint. Influences like this are not what we usually have in mind when we use the term 'manipulation.'

Exacerbating this problem is the fact that (as discussed in Chapter 1), in ordinary conversation, the term 'manipulation' suggests a moral complaint. But nothing about the examples above seems to warrant any sort of moral complaint. We would not ordinarily complain about others employing them, and we would likely regard anyone making such complaints as engaging in hyperbole. In short, some instances of influence that are neither rational persuasion, nor bargaining, nor coercion do not seem to be even presumptively immoral.

One response to this problem would be to claim that, contrary to first impressions, these forms of influence really *are* presumptively immoral. This would imply a very stringent ethics of influence. For it would claim that the only morally sound ways to influence others are by rational persuasion or good-faith bargaining.[2] This

[2] One might try to derive this view from Kant, by claiming that rational persuasion is the only form of influence that fully respects a person's status as a rational agent. But attaching Kant's name to this view does not make it any more plausible—even to people (like myself) who are sympathetic to Kantian moral philosophy. In section 9.8.2, we will see how a plausible account of manipulation can articulate a version of the idea that manipulation fails to respect the target's rational agency.

would be a very tough pill to swallow. The claim that it is morally wrong to cheer up a sad friend with a funny movie, to elicit empathy for the plight of those suffering undeserved misfortune, or to use social proof to help lead a large crowd on a tour, is implausible if not downright absurd.

A second response on behalf of the Moderately Expansive Account would be to abandon the connection between manipulation and moral disapproval. Thus, one might claim that manipulation in and of itself is not even presumptively immoral. Rather, one might claim, it is immoral only in certain contexts, such as when it is used to get someone to do something bad. Perhaps the term 'manipulation' only *seems* to have a negative moral connotation because it is *often* used in immoral ways.[3]

This response is unappealing for two reasons. First, it is doubtful that the term 'manipulation' only has a negative moral connotation because it is sometimes used in immoral ways. To see why, notice that the more neutral term 'influence' applies to something that can be used in immoral ways. Yet the term 'influence' does not have the same negative connotations that 'manipulation' has. Thus, if the term 'manipulation' has a negative moral connotation only because manipulation is sometimes used in immoral ways, then the same should be true of the term 'influence,' since it can also sometimes be used in immoral ways. But in ordinary conversation, the term 'manipulation' has significantly stronger negative moral connotations than the term 'influence.'

Second, adopting a definition of 'manipulation' stripped of its negative moral connotations would simply relocate important questions about manipulation. We want to know what forms of influence have the kind of presumptive immorality that we usually think of manipulation as having. If we characterize manipulation in a way that retains its negative moral connotations, then this question is simply the question of which influences count as manipulation. But if we strip the term of those negative moral connotations, the same question simply re-emerges in different words: Which forms of manipulation are presumptively immoral in the way that manipulation seemed presumptively immoral before we decided to use the term in a morally neutral way? The Moderately Expansive Account distorts the common meaning of the term 'manipulation' without making any progress toward solving the main questions about manipulation.

I am not interested in arguing with anyone who prefers to use the term 'manipulation' in a morally neutral way.[4] And I am happy to accommodate the linguistic

[3] I am grateful to one of the anonymous readers for pressing this objection.

[4] Allen Wood (2014) argues for defining 'manipulation' in a morally neutral way for methodological reasons. While I think that his point about not building presumptive immorality into the definition of the term is well taken, I think that it would be a mistake to ignore the term's moral connotations. A theory of manipulation can help illuminate why something seems immoral without building its apparent immorality into its definition. I will argue in Chapter 9 that the account of manipulation to be developed in this book does exactly that.

intuitions of anyone who thinks that the term 'manipulation' as used in ordinary conversation is morally neutral. Those who prefer a morally neutral analysis of the term 'manipulation' should interpret my use of the term as referring only to those forms of manipulation that *are* presumptively immoral.

3.3. Method-Specific Accounts

Psychologists who study manipulative behavior sometimes provide a loose definition of the term 'manipulation,' which they operationalize by constructing questionnaires or behavioral checklists that catalogue a variety of manipulative behaviors.[5] Could we simply dispense with the loose definition and instead define 'manipulation' by reference to a list of manipulative behaviors? According to what we might call the Method-Specific Account, we would define 'manipulation' by constructing a comprehensive list of the behaviors that count as manipulation, and using that list to distinguish manipulative from non-manipulative influences.

One challenge for this approach is the sheer diversity of forms of influence that seem like manipulation. Although the list of examples of manipulation developed in Chapter 2 is quite long, there is no reason to think that it is complete. This might not be a problem for certain purposes, like constructing psychological studies of the prevalence of manipulative behavior among various populations, its correlation with personality factors like emotional intelligence, and so on. But it will not help us determine whether some novel form of influence counts as manipulation. To address this worry, it might seem tempting to list as many clear cases of manipulation as we can think of, and then conclude the list by saying "and similar tactics." But this approach will face the problem of explaining what makes other tactics "similar" enough to the exemplars to count as manipulation. Answering that question would quickly push us back to our original task of determining what all forms of manipulation have in common.

Ultimately, we cannot discover *what manipulation is* simply by listing forms of manipulation. Discovering the nature of manipulation requires discovering what characteristic is *shared* by the various forms of manipulation that make them all instances of the same phenomenon. A list of manipulative influences is the starting point for such an investigation, not its end point. Of course, it is possible that there is no single characteristic shared by all and only those influences that we call manipulation.[6] This would be an interesting conclusion, but one that we should draw reluctantly, only after we have searched diligently for a characteristic common to all forms of manipulation. Until then, we should seek an account of manipulation

[5] For examples, see Austin and O'Donnell (2013); Austin et al. (2007); Hart et al. (2022); and Ioannidis (2021).

[6] Felicia Ackerman (1995) defends a view like this.

that goes beyond merely listing forms of manipulation to explain what makes them all examples of the same phenomenon.

3.4. Covert Aggression Accounts

Manipulation is often used as a tool of aggression in toxic and dysfunctional relationships. Thus, it is natural that its aggressive potential would be front and center in practical discussions about dealing with manipulative people. In an influential self-help book about dealing with manipulative people, psychologist George Simon claims that the "heart of most manipulation" is "covert aggression" (Simon 2010, 19). He sees manipulation as the tool of people who wish to act aggressively, but who do not want to be seen to be doing so: "When someone is being covertly aggressive, they're using calculating, underhanded means to get what they want or manipulate the response of others, while keeping their aggressive intentions under cover" (Simon 2010, 22). This aptly characterizes the kind of manipulation that Simon wants to help people avoid. But it does not seem promising as a *general* characterization of manipulation.[7] Some examples of manipulation do not seem to involve aggression. Consider this case:

> ***Bad Boyfriend***: Theresa has left a toxic relationship with Al, who is abusive, but also scrupulously monogamous. Theresa values Al's faithfulness so highly that she is considering going back to Al. Her friends know that if Theresa does this, Al's abuse will resume and escalate, which poses a grave threat to Theresa's mental and physical well-being. Unfortunately, their attempts to use rational persuasion to get Theresa to abandon her plan to reconcile with Al have failed. So, Theresa's friends employ Iago's manipulative tactics to drive Theresa into a jealous rage that quashes any thoughts of reconciling with Al.[8]

It seems obvious that Theresa's friends manipulated her. Since they employ the same tactics that Iago uses to manipulate Othello, it is difficult to see how we could deny that they, too, are engaged in manipulation. Yet it is *also* difficult to see anything aggressive in their behavior. Their only concern is with ensuring that their friend is safe from a dangerous situation. Hence, it seems incorrect to describe their action as aggression, covert or otherwise.

Perhaps, though, there is something subtly aggressive about resorting to manipulation, even out of concern for the well-being of the person one is manipulating. Something like this might be true. But if there is something subtly aggressive about

[7] In fairness to Simon, it is worth nothing that he only clams that the heart of *most* manipulation is covert aggression.

[8] Thomas Hill (1984) uses a similar story in his discussion of benevolent lies.

what Theresa's friends do, its very subtlety prevents us from using it to distinguish manipulative from non-manipulative behavior. If the aggression is something that we cannot recognize independently, but must only infer from the presence of manipulation, then defining manipulation as covert aggression will not help us identify manipulation in cases like ***Bad Boyfriend***, where the manipulators do not display any obvious form of aggression. If we wish to define manipulation as a form of aggression, then we need a way to recognize aggression in cases where we have not already decided that manipulation is present.

If there really is something subtly aggressive about what Theresa's friends do, it might become apparent when we have a better account of what manipulation is. Until then, defining manipulation as covert aggression *assumes* into existence something that a theory of manipulation should *discover*—a feature common to all instances of manipulation.

3.5. Bypassing Reason Accounts

It is often suggested that manipulation bypasses a person's reason.[9] It is less often said what, exactly, this means. Perhaps the most obvious interpretation is this: Whereas rational persuasion and good-faith bargaining provide reasons for doing something, manipulation does not. Such a claim might be a mere platitude that tells us what we already knew, namely that manipulation doesn't do what rational persuasion and good faith bargaining do. But if this claim is meant as a definition, then it would characterize manipulation as influence that is neither rational persuasion nor good faith bargaining. But this is just a version of the Moderately Expansive Account, which we have already rejected.

Thus, a credible definition of manipulation in terms of bypassing reason cannot simply explain "bypassing reason" by contrasting it with what happens in rational persuasion or good faith bargaining. Perhaps we might look to clearly manipulative influences that bypass the target's reason in some clear and obvious way as examples of what it means for manipulation to bypass reason. For example, suppose that subliminal advertising worked in the way that it is commonly—though probably inaccurately—portrayed. Suppose that a subliminal message urging you to "Drink Coke" could make you order a Coke without consciously deciding to do so. Or suppose that hypnosis could make a person act in some way suggested by the hypnotist, without that person making any conscious decision to do so. Or suppose that students could condition a professor to lecture from a doorway by being more attentive when she is closer to the door, without the professor even noticing what is happening (Brunvand 2001, 326–27). There is good reason for

[9] For example, Kumar (2016, 866) and Sunstein (2016, 82) seem to suggest such a view.

skepticism about whether subliminal advertising, hypnosis, or conditioning can control people in ways and to the degree that they are commonly portrayed. But if they *did* work the way that popular imagination supposes, then they would be clear examples of manipulation. According to popular imagination, these influences bypass reason in a very clear way: They drive behavior *directly* without engaging the target's processes of rational decision-making at all. Perhaps we can define manipulation in terms of bypassing reason, and characterize "bypassing reason" as what *these* influences do, at least in the popular imagination.

This approach faces a serious challenge, however. Defining manipulation as bypassing reason, understood as driving behavior directly, without engaging conscious decision-making at all, would set too high a bar for an influence to count as manipulation. This is because most *ordinary* forms of manipulation do not drive behavior directly, bypassing decision-making altogether. Instead, they typically *introduce* something into decision-making or otherwise alter its course. For example, gaslighting alters the course of the target's decision-making by getting the target to place more weight on the manipulator's advice. Conditional flattery and negging both alter the course of the target's decision-making by getting the target to choose the action that will improve or restore the target's self-esteem. Nagging and emotional blackmail alter the course of the target's decision-making by getting the target to choose actions that will prevent or eliminate negative consequences. While emotional appeals *sometimes* elicit unthinking, impulsive behaviors, they more commonly induce emotions that *influence decision-making* by making certain options seem more appealing or appropriate than others. In short, ordinary forms of manipulation are much more likely to *influence* decision-making than to *bypass* it.

Perhaps, though, we have been barking up the wrong tree by focusing on the "bypassing" part of "bypassing reason." Perhaps we should think of "bypassing reason" as bypassing *rational* decision-making. Thus, we might define manipulation as *non-rational influence*. However, this suggestion *sounds* more informative than it really *is*. To see why, consider appeals to emotion. Are they "non-rational influences"? If we say that they *are*, then we must conclude that sincere moral persuasion that appeals to empathy for those suffering undeserved misery is manipulative. That seems incorrect. But if we say that emotional appeals are *not* "non-rational influences," then we must conclude that Iago's playing on Othello's jealousy and anger is not manipulative. And that also seems incorrect.

Thus, the Dual Use Phenomenon (section 2.5) suggests that the "non-rational influence" version of the Bypassing Reason Account must say that *sometimes* emotions *are* non-rational influences and *sometimes* they *are not*. It is difficult to see how we could say this without a more general theory of the relationship between reason and emotion. But this issue is hotly contested. One traditional view—associated with Kant—sees emotions as inherently non-rational, so that, by definition, when they affect decision-making, they would be non-rational influences. By contrast, some contemporary philosophers and psychologists argue that emotions are essential to rational decision-making.[10] Naturally, there are a variety of positions between these extremes. Among those who deny that emotions are inherently non-rational, there is disagreement about when they help and when they hinder rational decision-making.[11] These differences imply different answers to the question of when emotions are *rational* influences versus when they are *non-rational* influences. Perhaps at some point a consensus on these matters will emerge. But until it does, we cannot know whether the "non-rational influence" version of the Bypassing Reason Account can properly distinguish manipulative from non-manipulative appeals to emotion.[12]

In a 2014 paper, Moti Gorin (2014a) proposes a more decisive objection to the Bypassing Reason Account. He offers examples of manipulation that do not bypass the target's reason, under various descriptions of what "bypassing reason" means. Perhaps the most compelling of these is a case he calls "***Lucrative Suicide***" (Gorin 2014a, 56), which goes like this: James will inherit a fortune if Jacques dies. James knows that Jacques believes that (a) God exists, and (b) if God did not exist, life would be so meaningless that there would be no reason to go on living. Hoping to inherit the fortune, James sets out to bring about Jacques's death. So, he provides Jacques with rational arguments against the existence of God. Jaques reflects on these arguments, evaluates them rationally, and concludes that God does not exist. That conclusion, together with his belief (b) that God's non-existence would make life meaningless, leads him to commit suicide—just as James had planned. Gorin claims that James manipulates Jacques, and this seems correct. This case poses a serious challenge to the idea that manipulation bypasses reason. James relies on Jacques's reasoning both to understand the arguments against God's existence, and to draw the conclusion that suicide is therefore reasonable. Assuming (as Gorin seems to) that there are rational arguments against God's existence (even if we do not regard them as decisive), James does not introduce any irrational influences into Jacques's thinking. It is thus difficult to discern any way that James's arguments bypass Jacques's reasoning. Yet James's behavior seems correctly described as manipulation.

[10] See e.g. Damasio (2005) and D. Evans (2002).

[11] Helpful overviews of the various positions can be found in Scarantino and de Sousa (2018), Scarantino (2006), and Greenspan (2004).

[12] Perhaps one could bite the bullet and claim that all appeals to emotion are manipulative, but deny that manipulation is always bad. A similar argument can be reconstructed from an interesting and provocative article by Sarah Buss (2005). Buss appears to adopt something like a Bypassing Reason Account of manipulation (Buss 2005, 208–10, esp. nn 19, 25). She then argues that manipulation, thus understood, is "integral to (most) early courtships" and thus essential for something intrinsically valuable (Buss 2005, 230). Thus, at the risk of oversimplification, the argument apparently assumes the correctness of (something like) the Bypassing Reason Account, observes that some reason-bypassing influences are (part of something) intrinsically good, and concludes that manipulation can be (part of something) intrinsically good. By contrast, I would argue that the intuition that manipulation is presumptively *immoral* is sufficiently strong to provide a good reason to reject the Bypassing Reason Account and look for something better, given that some reason-bypassing influences are indeed (part of) something intrinsically good.

Thus, it is extremely difficult to identify a sense of "bypassing reason" that convincingly distinguishes clearly manipulative from clearly non-manipulative influences. Nevertheless, it still seems not only possible but likely that manipulation has *some* sort of adverse relationship to reason. But the strategy of moving from that idea to a *definition* of manipulation does not seem promising. Perhaps, though, an acceptable account of manipulation will help illuminate its adverse relationship to reason. Indeed, we might find out more about the relationship between manipulation and reason if we avoid basing our theory of manipulation on what we assume that this relationship must be.

3.6. Covert Influence Accounts

If attempts to define manipulation in terms of "bypassing *reason*" are unsuccessful, perhaps we might define it in terms of bypassing *something else* instead. A promising suggestion is that manipulation bypasses the target's conscious awareness.

From this idea springs a family of theories that characterize manipulation as covert or hidden influence. Versions of this idea can be found in the work of Robert Goodin (1980, 8–9), Alan Ware (1981), and Alan Strudler (2005, 459). An especially influential version has been developed by Daniel Susser, Beate Roessler, and Helen Nissenbaum. They claim that manipulation consists of "imposing a hidden or covert influence on another person's decision-making" (Susser, Roessler, and Nissenbaum 2020, 26). On their view, "covertly influencing someone—imposing a hidden influence—means influencing them in a way they aren't consciously aware of, and in a way they couldn't easily become aware of were they to try and understand what was impacting their decision-making process" (Susser, Roessler, and Nissenbaum 2019, 4).

Other members of this family of theories claim that manipulation occurs when the manipulator's *intention*, rather than the influence itself, is covert. Radim Bělohrad, for example, claims that "the manipulator always projects intentions that differ from her real intentions" (Bělohrad 2019, 459). Gregory Whitfield makes a similar suggestion, writing that

> An act of manipulation is any intentional attempt by an agent (**A**) to cause another agent (**B**) to will/prefer/intend/act other than what **A** takes **B**'s will, preference or intention to be, where **A** does so utilizing methods that obscure and render deniable **A**'s intentions vis-à-vis **B**. (Whitfield 2022, 786)

An eclectic version of the Covert Influence Account might characterize manipulation as an influence in which *something* is hidden from the target. This version of the Covert Influence Account would properly identify manipulation in many of our paradigm examples. Iago's manipulation requires keeping the truth about

Desdemona's love and devotion hidden from Othello. Game switching seems unlikely to work on you if you realize that the influencer is getting you to play by the wrong rules. Gaslighting seems unlikely to work on you if you know that there is no good reason to doubt your own judgment. It might be psychologically if not conceptually impossible to misdirect someone who knows what one is trying to hide. When manipulation is facilitated by deception—as it so often is—then its effectiveness may depend at least partly on the truth remaining hidden.

But do *all* forms of manipulation require something to be hidden? Anne Barnhill argues that "manipulative guilt-trips, for example, can be plain as day" (Barnhill 2014, 60). Bělohrad replies by imagining a case where the guilt-tripper *announces* that she *intends to use guilt* to get the target to do something. Bělohrad claims that, in such a situation, if the target complies, it would not be because he was manipulated (Bělohrad 2019, 458–59).

Perhaps *guilt trips* either fail or cease to be manipulation if the target becomes aware of the manipulator's intention. But other forms of manipulation do not seem to require anything about the influence—including the intention behind it—to be hidden. Consider a teen nagging her parents for a new phone. It is difficult to see how anything about this situation is covert. The teen's intention is quite transparent—to get the parents to buy a new phone—as is the means being used to achieve this. A group of teens might employ peer pressure to get a fellow to smoke without hiding their intention or how they hope to achieve it. Tantrums, the "silent treatment", and other forms of emotional blackmail can succeed—and would still seem to be manipulative—even if the intention behind them is obvious. Realizing that someone is trying to get you to accept a request by making it awkward to refuse does not make the behavior any less manipulative. In short, many forms of manipulation seem likely to work—while still counting as manipulation—even when everything about the attempt to influence is out in the open.[13]

Whitfield attempts to address proposed counterexamples like this by claiming that manipulation only requires "plausible deniability" about one's intentions (Whitfield 2022, 795). It is not entirely clear what exactly "plausible deniability" means in this context. But whatever it means, the attempt to achieve it does not seem necessary for an influence to count as manipulation. Suppose that the nagging teen announces: "I'm going to keep nagging you until you give in." Whatever "plausible deniability" might mean, the teen in our example has surely abandoned it. And she has been "truly explicit about her intentions" in a way that Bělohrad (2019, 458) suggests is incompatible with manipulation. Yet there is no reason to think that such an announcement must prevent the nagging from succeeding. Nor is there any ground for thinking that, if it does succeed, it no longer counts as manipulation.

[13] In his extensive critique of Covert Influence Accounts, Michael Klenk (2022b, 91–96) offers additional counter-examples to the claim that manipulation must be covert.

Of course, manipulators often do hide their plans. But this is simply because people do not like being manipulated and will often resist attempts to manipulate them. If a manipulator announces his plans, the target will likely try to thwart them. But this is not unique to manipulation. A villain is more likely to succeed at stealing your car, trampling your flowerbed, or kicking you in the shin, if he doesn't announce his plan ahead of time so that you can take steps to thwart it. The fact that manipulators often hide their intentions does not distinguish manipulation from other things that people do not like having done to them.

So, while manipulation *often* involves something hidden, it is possible—though perhaps uncommon—for manipulation to occur in which nothing is hidden. This fact poses an enormous—perhaps insurmountable—problem for Covert Influence Accounts.

3.7. Endorsement Accounts

We have just observed that people generally do not like being manipulated. Perhaps that idea can be harnessed to characterize what manipulation is. James Fishkin writes that:

> A person has been manipulated . . . when she has been exposed to a message intended to change her views in a way she would not accept if she were to think about it on the basis of good conditions—and in fact she does change her views in the manner that was intended. (Fishkin 2011, 32–33)

These remarks suggest what we might call the Subjective Endorsement Account of manipulation: T has been manipulated if T was influenced in a way that T would not accept or endorse. Or, to put it the other way around, an influence is manipulative if the target would object to being subjected to it. On this view, it is not just that we object to influences that are manipulative; but our objecting to them is what *makes* them manipulative.

Suppose that Tim watches a video showing the graphic effects of a car crash caused by distracted driving, which causes him to quit checking his phone while driving. We might imagine Tim endorsing this form of influence. By contrast, it seems safe to regard Othello's attempt to kill Iago at the end of the play as evidence of Othello's objection to Iago's influences on him. The Endorsement Account would correctly say that Iago's influence on Othello is manipulation, and the video's influence on Tom is not. So far, so good. But consider this case:

White Supremacist Will denies that he has any reason to care about people who are not white, or to feel any empathy for any suffering they might endure. Isabel tries to get Will to feel empathy toward the non-white victims of a vicious hate-crime. She relays to Will vivid but truthful accounts of the crime's psychological and physical effects on the victims. This causes Will to feel empathy toward the hate-crime victims. But his racist views do not change. He continues to maintain that empathy toward white people is appropriate but empathy toward people who are not white is not. Consequently, he finds Isabel's influence objectionable because it gets him to feel empathy toward people whom he regards as undeserving of it.

According to the Subjective Endorsement Account, Will's objection would render Isabel's appeal manipulative. This seems incorrect. Appeals to empathy are potent tools for combatting racism precisely because they help people recognize that they share a common humanity with those against whom they have been discriminating—even if they do not *want* to recognize this. It is difficult to believe that this is manipulation.

Clearly, the problem is the subjectivity of the Subjective Endorsement Account. Perhaps we need something less subjective. A promising suggestion appears in Thomas Hill's paper on benevolent lies:

> Manipulation, broadly conceived, can perhaps be understood as intentionally causing or encouraging people to make the decisions one wants them to make by actively promoting their making the decisions in ways that rational persons would not want to make their decisions. (Hill 1984, 258)

Hill provides various examples of influences that cause someone to decide in a way that a rational person would not want. They include subliminal advertising, hypnosis, intoxicants, playing on psychological weaknesses, and deliberately withholding or selectively presenting information.

It is unclear whether Hill is simply offering an observation about how rational people regard manipulation, or whether he is offering a definition of manipulation. Be that as it may, defining manipulation as influence to which a *rational* person would object might seem like a promising way to address the problems with the Subjective Endorsement Account. After all, there is something clearly irrational about Will's objection to Isabel's appeal to empathy. He appeals to a morally irrelevant distinction to determine who deserves his empathy and who does not. Consequently, it seems like Will's objection would not be one that a rational person could make. So, on what we might call the *Rational* Endorsement Account, Will's objection would *not* make Isabel's influence manipulative.[14]

[14] Alan Wood (2014, 35) offers an account of manipulation that contains elements of an endorsement approach, though it is not clear whether it is best seen as an example of the subjective endorsement approach or the rational endorsement approach.

But matters are not so simple. Clearly *Will*'s objection to Isabel's appeal to empathy is not rational. But that is not enough to show that there is *no* rational objection to Isabel's appeal. Might a rational person object to Isabel's influence simply because it is an appeal to emotion? If we hold an extreme Kantian view that regards emotions as non- or irrational forces, then we might think that any appeal to emotion is something to which a rational person would object. If, on the other hand, we reject the idea that reason and emotion must always be opposed to one another, we might claim that a rational person would not object to Isabel's emotional appeal. But presumably we would still want to claim that it is rational for Othello to object to Iago's emotional appeals. Thus, we face a problem that should be familiar from our discussion of Bypassing Reason Accounts: Whether a rational person would object to an emotional appeal depends on the answer to questions about the relationship between emotion and reason. And those questions seem unlikely to be settled any time soon. Given the important role that emotional influences play in everyday life, this is a huge drawback for the Rational Endorsement Account (just as it is for the Bypassing Reason Account).

3.8. Manipulator-Based Accounts

Perhaps the common thread that unites all forms of manipulation is not to be found in the tactics or forms of influence, but rather in the person wielding them. Perhaps the key to understanding manipulation is to first understand something about the manipulator.

We might turn, for example, to Marcia Baron's important 2003 paper, "Manipulativeness" (Baron 2003), which investigates the character of the manipulator. Baron's analysis focuses not on manipulation *per se*, but on the trait of "manipulativeness," which she treats as an Aristotelian vice. That is, manipulativeness is an excess regarding

> how much to steer others—and which others, and how, and when, and toward what ends; and more generally, to what extent—and how and when and to whom and for what sorts of ends—to seek to influence others' conduct. (Baron 2003, 48)

Thus, we might see manipulativeness as an excessive propensity to influence, which causes the manipulative person to go wrong in terms of when, how, and how much to influence others.[15] In keeping with an Aristotelian approach to virtues and vices, Baron claims that there is a vice that involves deficiency in those qualities that are excessive in manipulativeness. This vice is a sort of "isolationism"

[15] As Baron notes, this way of looking at a vice is an oversimplification (Baron 2003, 38). Nevertheless, it is close enough for present purposes.

that involves "refraining from offering potentially helpful counsel; or refraining from trying to stop someone from doing something very dangerous, for example" (Baron 2003, 48).

Baron's discussion of *manipulativeness* does not offer an explicit definition of *manipulation*. Instead, she offers an impressive and diverse list of examples of manipulation, and refrains from trying to isolate a single essential feature that unites them. Might we nevertheless extrapolate an analysis of manipulation from her analysis of the manipulative person? Unfortunately, this seems unlikely, at least if we understand the vice of manipulativeness according to the standard Aristotelian account. On this account, the vice of manipulativeness would be a propensity to influence others for the wrong reasons, in the wrong amounts, and in the wrong ways. But this formula tells us nothing about what those wrong reasons, wrong amounts, and wrong ways *are*. What *are* the wrong ways to influence others? When, for example, is an appeal to emotion the right way to influence, and when is it the wrong way? What are the right reasons for employing a given form of influence? These are the questions that we would need answered to define manipulation. But they are questions that an Aristotelian account of manipulativeness does not answer.

A somewhat different way to characterize *manipulation* in terms of the *manipulator* has been proposed by Michael Klenk. On Klenk's view, the nature of manipulation is not to be found in the manipulator's tactics, but in the manipulator's state of mind. The defining feature of this state of mind is a kind of carelessness or negligence. According to Klenk,

> A manipulator is negligent in the sense that they ultimately choose their means of influence because it is effective in getting the manipulatee to believe, feel, or desire in a certain way and not because it reveals reasons to the manipulatee. (Klenk 2022a, 112)

Klenk extracts an account of the nature of *manipulation* from this account of the *manipulator*'s state of mind: "We have a case of manipulation if and only if the manipulator does not care whether his or her means of influence reveals eventually existing reasons to the manipulatee" (Klenk 2022b, 97). Thus, manipulation occurs when an influencer chooses an influence because it is likely to get the target to do what the manipulator wants, regardless of whether it does that by revealing to the target reasons for doing that thing.

This account faces two challenges. First, Klenk has not yet offered a full account of when an influence reveals reasons and when it does not. What sort of reasons are relevant? Objective? Subjective? Prudential? Moral? And what counts as revealing a reason? For example, do appeals to emotion reveal reasons? Without a more complete account of what a reason is and what it means to reveal it, the proposal is difficult to evaluate. Second, this account seems to yield odd judgments about when manipulation takes place. According to the definition quoted above, manipulation occurs when the influencer chooses a form of influence for its effectiveness, without regard to whether it reveals reasons. This definition will yield odd results in cases where the most effective influence *is* one that reveals reasons. Consider this case:

> ***Car Seller***: Ike wants to sell Titus a certain car. Although Ike is happy to employ sales tactics like misdirection, charm offensives, and gaslighting, to sell cars, he suspects that Titus is likely to be impervious to them. However, the car that Ike wants Titus to buy is extremely suitable for Titus's needs. So Ike engages in rational persuasion that shows Titus the good reasons he has to buy this car. However, Ike chooses this approach purely because he thinks that it is the best way to get Titus to buy the car. If Ike had judged that gaslighting, a charm offensive, or misdirection would have been more effective, he would have used it instead.

The definition quoted above counts Ike's behavior as manipulation, since he chose it for its effectiveness in getting Titus to do what Ike wants, rather than because it would reveal Titus's reasons to him. But it seems odd to say that rational persuasion, even in this case, counts as manipulation. Ike's willingness to influence by any means necessary clearly makes Ike a manipulative person. But it seems odd to say that rational persuasion that reveals Titus's reasons to him counts as manipulation, even when it is chosen simply for its effectiveness.

Baron and Klenk both offer important insights about what it is to be a manipulative person. But neither of their theories, at least in their current forms, seems to offer a convincing account of manipulation that properly distinguishes manipulative from non-manipulative influences.

3.9. Trickery Accounts

The word 'manipulation' is often uttered in the same breath as the word 'deception', and the two concepts are often assumed to be closely related. For example, discussions of whether advertising is manipulative sometimes involve claims that it creates misleading associations or false impressions about products (Beauchamp 1984, 10–16). In a discussion of promises, T. M. Scanlon labels as "manipulation" the deliberate creation of false expectations (Scanlon 1998, 298).

However, manipulation does not always involve deception. Consider playing on the emotions, for example. While it often involves deception—as we see in the case of Iago and Othello—it need not. A manipulative appeal to anger might require only that the target fixate on some actual injury done to him by the person at whom the manipulator wants the target to be angry. Manipulative fear mongering might, likewise, require nothing more than getting the target to fixate on some actual danger. To recognize non-deceptive emotional manipulation, we might treat manipulation not as a form of deception, but as a broader category of which deception is a special case. Thus, we might claim that whereas deception tricks someone into adopting a faulty belief, manipulation tricks someone into adopting *any* faulty mental state—belief, desire, emotion, etc.

In a 1996 paper, I argued that manipulation involves getting someone's beliefs, desires, or emotions to fall short of the ideals that apply to them (Noggle 1996, 44). For example, the ideal of a belief is to be true, so lies and deception are manipulative because they get the target's beliefs to fall short of that ideal. The ideal for emotion is appropriateness to the situation, so manipulative playing on the emotions occurs when the manipulator gets the target to feel an emotion that is inappropriate for the situation. Thus, Iago manipulates Othello because the jealousy he gets Othello to feel is inappropriate to Othello's situation (since Desdemona loves and has been faithful to Othello all along).

Thus, what we might call the Trickery Account generalizes from the form of trickery inherent in deception. Whereas deception tricks someone into adopting a faulty *belief*, manipulation tricks someone into adopting a faulty mental state of any kind: belief, desire, emotion, or other mental state.[16]

Several philosophers have defended versions of this account. For example, Anne Barnhill writes that "manipulation is directly influencing someone's beliefs, desires, or emotions such that she falls short of ideals for belief, desire, or emotion in ways typically not in her self-interest *or likely not in her self-interest in the present context*" (Barnhill 2014, 77, emphasis original). Jason Hanna characterizes manipulation as influences that "affect the target's deliberation for the worse" so that "the target acts on the basis of bad reasons, or fails adequately to reflect on reasons, or attends to irrelevant considerations, or places more (or less) weight on certain considerations than those considerations properly merit" (Hanna 2015, 630–31). Each of the items on Hanna's list can be construed as a kind of faulty mental state that the manipulator induces the target to adopt.

Claudia Mills offers a somewhat different account of manipulation that can be seen as a version of the Trickery Account. She writes that:

> manipulation in some way purports to be offering good reasons, when in fact it does not. A manipulator tries to change another's beliefs and desires by offering her bad reasons, disguised as good, or faulty arguments, disguised as sound—where the manipulator himself knows these to be bad reasons and faulty arguments. (Mills 1995, 100)

[16] A 1980 paper by Vance Kasten may anticipate this view. Kasten writes that "being manipulated involves being misled" (Kasten 1980, 54). While most of his examples involve deception, he also includes "playing on . . . inappropriate guilt feelings" as a form of manipulation (Kasten 1980, 54). Thus, his use of 'mislead' seems to apply to inappropriate emotions as well as false beliefs.

It seems reasonable to assume that it is ideal for beliefs and desires to be based on good reasons. If so, then it would seem correct to say that those based on bad reasons are therefore faulty or non-ideal. In this way, we can interpret Mills's view as a version of, or at least a close cousin to, the Trickery Account.

A similar picture of manipulation emerges from the work of the political theorist Keith Dowding (2016, 2018). Dowding does not define manipulation directly. Instead, he proposes ideal conditions for political discourse meant to exclude influences like manipulation. These conditions suggest that manipulation is persuasion in which the persuader appeals to reasons that the persuader does not accept or emotions that the persuader does not feel. Here again, the idea that manipulation gets the target to accept reasons that the manipulator does not accept as good, or emotions that the manipulator does not regard as appropriate, seems like a version of, or a close cousin to, the idea that manipulation induces the target to adopt mental states that are faulty.

Dowding's theory has built into it an answer to a question facing all versions of the Trickery Account: Does manipulation occur when the target adopts a mental state that *really is* faulty? Or does manipulation occur when the target adopts a mental state that the *manipulator believes* is faulty? Is Iago's behavior manipulative because *Iago believes* that Othello has no reason to be jealous, or because there *really is* no reason for Othello to be jealous? By defining manipulation in terms of a reason that the influencer does not accept or an emotion the influencer does not feel, Dowding's theory characterizes manipulation in terms of *what the influencer regards as* a faulty mental state. This is the answer I gave in my earlier work, and it seems implicit in Mills's account as well. By contrast, Hanna (2015, 633) explicitly defends defining manipulation in terms of an objective standard. Barnhill suggests that our use of the term 'manipulation' is simply inconsistent on this question (Barnhill 2014, 66–67).

Despite these differences, the accounts just discussed share the core idea that manipulation involves *tricking* the target into accepting or adopting something *faulty*: non-ideal mental states, bad reasons, or a faulty appreciation of the reasons for deciding one way or another. Because the idea of a faulty mental state plays a key role in it, some scholars characterize this as a "norm-based" approach (Klenk 2022a, 112).

The fact that it defines manipulation as inducing the target to adopt a *faulty* mental state allows the Trickery Account to accommodate the Dual Use Phenomenon discussed in section 2.5. For example, the Trickery Account classifies a guilt trip as manipulative insofar as it induces the target to feel guilt that is *inappropriate* given the actual facts. But it would not say that it is manipulative to get someone to feel an *appropriate* level of remorse for having done something genuinely wrong. Similarly, the Trickery Account would say that inducing someone to feel excessive or inappropriate fear is manipulative. But it would not say that it is manipulative to induce someone to have an appropriate level of fear for something that is genuinely dangerous.

Another important advantage of the Trickery Account is that it suggests an explanation of manipulation's moral status. Since it regards manipulation as similar to deception, it suggests that the reasons why manipulation seems immoral are similar to the reasons why deception is immoral. In both cases, the influencer attempts to introduce faulty elements into the target's decision-making. This degrades the target's ability to make rational, autonomous decisions that reflect a proper appreciation of what is true, good, and important.

The Trickery Account is sufficiently promising that it makes sense to spell out exactly which of the forms of manipulation from Chapter 2 it properly identifies, and how it does so. Thus:

Playing on the Emotions: According to the Trickery Account, it is manipulation to get someone to do something by tricking that person into having a faulty emotion—one that is inappropriate given the circumstances. Thus, Iago's getting Othello to be jealous of and angry at Desdemona is manipulation because these emotions are inappropriate since Desdemona has not been unfaithful. But the Trickery Account would *not* say that it is manipulation to get someone to have an *appropriate* emotion, as when one person gets another to feel appropriate empathy for those suffering undeserved misery, for example.

Misdirection/Misemphasis: According to the Trickery Account, it is manipulation to get someone to do something by tricking that person into a faulty pattern of attention—that is, paying insufficient attention (or no attention at all) to something important, or too much attention to something unimportant. Thus, the pickpocket's jostling of his victim so that he will not notice that his wallet is being extracted is manipulation because it induces the victim to fail to notice something important. But the Trickery Account would *not* say that it is manipulation to direct someone's attention toward something that *is* important, as when one person directs another's attention to a hidden danger, for example.

Gaslighting: According to the Trickery Account, it is manipulation to get someone to do something by tricking that person into an inappropriate pessimism about that person's own judgment. Thus, Gregory's undermining of Paula's confidence in her own judgment is manipulation because her judgment is perfectly sound. But the Trickery Account would *not* say that it is manipulation to get someone to doubt that person's own judgment when it really is compromised, as when the person is angry or intoxicated, for example.

Game switching: According to the Trickery Account, it is manipulation to get someone to do something by tricking that person into following faulty rules or norms—that is, rules or norms that are not appropriate for the actual situation. Thus, the social engineer's getting the employee to hold open the door to a secured area is manipulation because the door-holding norm is inappropriate in that situation. But the Trickery Account would *not* say that it is manipulation to get someone to follow a norm that is *appropriate* to the situation, as when security staff reminds employees to follow the "secured area" protocols when entering the building, for example.

Social Proof: According to the Trickery Account, it is manipulation to get someone to do something by tricking that person into a faulty use of the social proof heuristic—that is, using it in situations where the fact that others are doing something is not a good reason to do the same thing. Thus, Jim Jones's relying on his followers' tendency to do what others are doing was manipulation because the situation was one where other people's behavior was a poor guide. But the Trickery Account would *not* say that it is manipulation to use social proof to solve a coordination problem, as when the tour guide shows the people in front where to go and relies on social proof to induce the others to follow along, for example.

Thus, the Trickery Account properly classifies many of our paradigm examples of manipulation. And it does this without falling afoul of the Dual Use Phenomenon.

Despite these advantages, the Trickery Account faces a huge problem: There are many clear cases of manipulation that the Trickery Account fails to identify as such. When Jo manipulates Allen by making it clear that their relationship will be strained if he does not do what she wants, she does not seem to get Allen to adopt any faulty mental states. Jo *might* be bluffing, of course, and if she is, then her manipulation *would* include an element of trickery. But if Jo is not bluffing, then it does not seem correct to describe her behavior as tricking Allen into adopting a mental state that is faulty in any way analogous to the faultiness of a false belief. When Schwartz uses peer pressure to manipulate Flick into sticking his tongue to the flagpole, it does not seem correct to say that Schwartz tricked Flick into adopting a mental state that is faulty in the way that a false belief is faulty. When the con artist relies on his mark's aversion to conflict to manipulate him into continuing to play a game that he suspects is rigged, it does not seem correct to describe the con artist as tricking the mark into adopting a mental state that is faulty in the way that a false belief is faulty.[17] (Certainly, con artists often do employ trickery, but *this* particular tactic does not seem best described as trickery.) The target of nagging does not seem to be tricked into adopting a faulty mental state so much as worn down. Indeed, nagging is such an unsubtle tactic that it would be odd to describe it as a form of trickery.

[17] A die-hard defender of the Trickery Account might claim that these are not cases of manipulation, or that, if they are, then they are cases of situational rather than psychological manipulation. But as we saw in Chapter 2, tactics like these are commonly labelled as manipulation. In section 4.10 we shall see that these tactics are different from situational manipulation.

It appears, then, that the Trickery Account fails to identify a variety of influences that seem like clear cases of manipulation. Many forms of manipulation, such as emotional blackmail, peer pressure, nagging, and exploiting conflict aversion, do not seem to rely on anything aptly described as trickery. Hence, the Trickery Account appears to be seriously under-inclusive.

3.10. Pressure Accounts

Manipulation is normally understood to differ from both rational persuasion and coercion. Bypassing Reason Accounts focus on the distinction between manipulation and rational persuasion, but as we saw, those accounts face serious challenges. Perhaps we can do better by focusing on the distinction between manipulation and coercion. Coercion uses threats, which exert what we might think of as a kind of psychological pressure on the target. This pressure varies according to the magnitude of the threat. A mobster's threat to break both of your legs if you squeal exerts more pressure than his threat to break one of your fingers. Both are, perhaps, coercive, but different threats can exert different amounts of pressure and still be coercive.

However, we can imagine forms of pressure that do not rise to the level of coercion. And since manipulation is generally understood as distinct from coercion, perhaps we can understand manipulation as pressure that is too weak to constitute coercion. Several philosophers have suggested that we can understand at least some forms of manipulation in this way.

For example, Ruth Faden, Tom Beauchamp, and Nancy King (Faden, Beauchamp, and King 1986), contrast three ways that a physician might get a patient to take a prescribed drug. At one extreme, the physician might coerce the patient to take the drug. At the other, the physician might rely only on rational persuasion. Manipulation, they say, falls in between these two extremes:

> [S]uppose the physician has made clear that he or she will be upset with the patient if the patient does not take the drug, and the patient is intimidated . . . [T] he patient agrees to take the drug because it appears that acceptance will foster a better relationship with the doctor . . . [T]he patient does not find it overwhelmingly difficult to resist the physician's proposal, but . . . it is nonetheless awkward and difficult to resist. (Faden, Beauchamp, and King 1986, 258)

Marcia Baron offers a similar account of manipulative pressure:

> Manipulation may involve a threat that does not rise to the level of being coercive but differs mainly just in the degree of resistibility. Whereas the coercive threat does not leave one a reasonable alternative to doing the coercer's bidding, the

> manipulative threat does. To say "I'll kill your children unless you help me rob a bank" is coercive, at least if the threat is credible; to say "I won't be your friend anymore/marry you/play in your band unless you help me rob a bank" is not coercive, but is . . . generally manipulative. (Baron 2003, 40–41)

Joel Feinberg may have had a similar picture in mind when he wrote that tactics for getting someone to do something

> can be placed on a spectrum of force running from compulsion proper, at one extreme, through compulsive pressure, coercion proper, and coercive pressure, to manipulation, persuasion, enticement, and simple requests at the other extreme. The line between forcing to act and merely getting to act is drawn somewhere in the manipulation or persuasion part of the scale. (Feinberg 1989, 189)

The idea that manipulation is a form of pressure—what we might call the Pressure Account—has considerable appeal. It offers a plausible and straightforward analysis of tactics like nagging, emotional blackmail, and peer pressure—which are tactics that other prominent theories fail to correctly identify as manipulation. Moreover, the Pressure Account offers a persuasive analysis of the difference between manipulation and coercion: While they both involve pressure, coercive pressure differs from manipulative pressure because it leaves the target with no reasonable alternative to doing what the influencer demands.

However, the appeal of the Pressure Account is sharply limited because the account fails to identify as manipulative several of our paradigm examples of manipulation from Chapter 2. For example, it is not clear that tactics like misdirection, misemphasis, gaslighting, and game switching involve anything aptly described as pressure.

For this reason, most philosophers who discuss manipulative pressure explicitly claim that it constitutes only *one* form of manipulation. Baron, for example, discusses a wide variety of forms of manipulation, and claims only that manipulation *sometimes* involves non-coercive threats (Baron 2003, 41). Faden, Beauchamp, and King define manipulation disjunctively, so that it includes both manipulative pressure that involves "non-coercively altering the actual choices available" and non-pressure forms of manipulation that involve "nonpersuasively altering the other's perception of those choices" (Faden, Beauchamp, and King 1986, 354). Joel Rudinow's early account of manipulation (Rudinow 1978) recognizes forms that involve pressure as well as forms that involve deception.

Thus, even those who propose the Pressure Account recognize that it only applies to some forms of manipulation. In this, then, the Pressure Account is like the other accounts we have examined here, in that it cannot accurately identify manipulation in all of the clear examples from Chapter 2. But there is something particularly striking about the pattern of *which* cases the Pressure Account gets *right* and *which* it gets *wrong*. The forms of manipulation that it *fails* to recognize are ones that the Trickery Account easily recognizes.[18] And the forms of manipulation that the Pressure Account accurately recognizes are forms that the Trickery Account fails to recognize. This latter fact is worth documenting in a bit more detail. Here are the examples from Chapter 2 that the Pressure Account correctly identifies as manipulation:

Peer Pressure: By threatening that Flick will lose respect from his peers if he refuses to take the dare, Schwartz exerts psychological pressure on Flick. Insofar as this pressure does not rise to the level of coercion, it is manipulative.

Emotional Blackmail: By threatening that Allen will suffer the unpleasant consequences of a strained relationship with Jo if he does not do what Jo wants, she exerts psychological pressure on Allen. Insofar as this pressure does not rise to the level of coercion, it is manipulative.

Nagging: By continually inflicting the unpleasant experience of being nagged about bringing the gaming device to school, the teen exerts psychological pressure on the parent. Insofar as this pressure does not rise to the level of coercion, it is manipulative.

Exploiting Conflict Aversion: By arranging matters so that the mark must experience unpleasant, socially awkward conflict if he leaves the rigged game before its conclusion, the con artist exerts psychological pressure on the mark. Insofar as this pressure does not rise to the level of coercion, it is manipulative.

Exploiting Reciprocity: By arranging matters so that the tourists will experience the unpleasant social awkwardness of refusing to reciprocate a favor if they refuse to give them money, the panhandlers exert psychological pressure on the tourists. Insofar as this pressure does not rise to the level of coercion, it is manipulative.

3.11. Conclusion

Most of the accounts we have examined get something right about manipulation. Manipulation is often—though not always—a tool of aggression, benefitting the manipulator at the expense of the target, and in such cases it is most effective and most insidious when the aggressive intent is hidden. More generally, manipulation often—though again not always—works best if some aspect of the manipulator's plan remains hidden; this is probably why we regard manipulation as being sneaky and underhanded. Manipulation seems to stand in an antagonistic relationship to

[18] The same might be true of the relationship between the Pressure Account and the Covert Influence Account. But for reasons that will become clear in the next chapter, I am more interested in the relationship between the Pressure Account and the Trickery Account.

reason, even if it is not obvious what that relationship is. It seems correct to characterize *manipulative people* as ones who are both too eager to influence others and careless about how they influence others, though it is difficult to extract an account of *manipulation* from these important insights. The Trickery Account and the Pressure Account both seem promising, but each one fails to properly identify a large swath of manipulative tactics. Interestingly, though, each of these latter accounts seems strongest precisely where the other is weakest. That striking fact is the starting point for the next chapter.

4

A Unified Account of Manipulation

4.1. Introduction

Chapter 3 concluded with a curious observation. Two otherwise promising accounts of manipulation—the Trickery Account and the Pressure Account—each seem weakest precisely where the other is strongest. The Trickery Account fails to properly identify paradigm examples of manipulation that the Pressure Account easily identifies, and vice versa. This observation suggests that a fruitful strategy would unify these two accounts in some way. Developing such a unified account of manipulation is the goal of this chapter.[1]

4.2. Pressure versus Trickery

Let us begin by taking a closer look at the strengths and weaknesses of the Trickery Account and the Pressure Account. Consider this example:

> ***University I***: Tara and Mandy are casual friends who graduated from their small-town high school last year. Tara has considerable academic promise, deep intellectual curiosity, and parents who value higher education. Nevertheless, she initially decided not to attend university after graduation, and remained in their hometown, working at a low-paying retail job. Now, however, she has reconsidered and is planning to attend university in a nearby city in the autumn. Mandy has no desire to attend university or to leave their small town. But most of Mandy's close friends have already moved away, leaving Tara as one of her only friends still living in their small town. So, while they are not extremely close friends, Mandy does not want Tara to attend university. Mandy knows that a university education would be a good opportunity for Tara, and that scholarships and her parents' help will make it affordable. She also knows that their friendship is not deep enough to provide a good reason for Tara to forgo her education and remain in their hometown. Consequently, Mandy doubts that using rational persuasion will get Tara to change her mind about attending university.

[1] This chapter is a revised and expanded version of Noggle (2020). Most of the ideas, and small bits of the text, were previously published in that article.

Manipulation. Robert Noggle, Oxford University Press. © Robert Noggle 2025.
DOI: 10.1093/9780198924920.003.0004

Now let us imagine that Mandy resorts to various manipulative tactics to try to get Tara to change her mind:

Playing on the Emotions: Mandy knows that Tara will easily make new friends at university. But she plays on Tara's fears of loneliness by emphasizing that she will be alone in a new city. Although she knows that Tara is not responsible for Mandy's happiness, she tries to make Tara feel guilty about leaving her behind. Although she knows that Tara's parents have been wonderful, Mandy tries to make Tara feel resentful toward them so that she will forgo a university education out of spite.

Misdirection/Misemphasis: Mandy repeatedly overemphasizes the charms of small-town life, while downplaying its lack of opportunities for career and intellectual growth. In addition, Mandy repeatedly draws Tara's attention to the city's higher crime rate and directs her attention away from the excitement of city life.

Gaslighting: Mandy attempts to undermine Tara's faith in her own judgment by exaggerating her past mistakes and portraying them as evidence that her judgment is not trustworthy. She does this to make it more likely that Tara will follow Mandy's advice to stay home instead of attending university.

Nagging: Mandy continually pesters Tara about her decision to attend university, hoping that she will eventually give in and reconsider. Her nagging does not provide Tara with any new information; it is simply meant to annoy her so much that she gives in.

Emotional Blackmail: Mandy makes it clear that she will immediately stop being friends with Tara unless she withdraws her application to university.

Exploiting Reciprocity: Before asking Tara to withdraw her university application, Mandy does several small favors for Tara, hopeful that she will feel obligated to do this much larger favor in return.

Thus, we are imagining that Mandy employs many of the tactics discussed in Chapter 2. In Chapter 3, we saw that the Trickery Account—which characterizes manipulation as inducing faulty mental states—correctly identifies some of these tactics as manipulation:

Playing on the Emotions: Playing on Tara's fears and inducing her to feel guilt and resentment is manipulation because these emotions are unfounded or inappropriately strong given Tara's actual circumstances.

Misdirection/Misemphasis: Overemphasizing the advantages of staying home and the disadvantages of attending university is manipulation because it encourages Tara to adopt a faulty weighing of the pros and cons of her options.

Gaslighting: Making Tara doubt her own judgment is manipulation because it encourages Tara to adopt a faulty assessment of her own judgment.

But, as we also observed in Chapter 3, the Trickery Account fails to identify manipulation in Mandy's other tactics. Nagging, emotional blackmail, and exploiting reciprocity all seem like intuitively clear cases of manipulation. But they do not seem to involve getting the target to adopt any faulty mental states. The target of emotional blackmail may have a completely accurate assessment of the threat being made against her (and the likelihood of it being carried out). The target of nagging may have a perfectly accurate assessment of the pros and cons of giving in. The target of exploiting reciprocity may fully understand that what has been given to her is much less than what is being asked in return. Although such tactics are *often* accompanied by trickery, they can nevertheless operate without any trickery, and when they do, they still seem like clear cases of manipulation.

Before turning to the Pressure Account, which *does* properly identify such tactics as manipulation, let us consider what may seem like an obvious way to rescue the Trickery Account. Could we claim that Mandy's nagging, emotional blackmail, and exploiting reciprocity really do trick Tara into adopting a faulty mental state, namely a *faulty decision* not to attend university? If we count a bad decision as a faulty mental state, then the Trickery Account would seem to identify all of Mandy's tactics as manipulation.

But counting it as manipulation to induce someone to make a bad decision is less appealing than it may seem at first glance. To see why, consider this case:

> ***University II:*** Ursula is the only other of Mandy's friends still residing in their small town. Like Tara, Ursula, is also considering attending university this autumn. Unlike Tara, Ursula is currently underprepared—emotionally, financially, and academically—for university education and life in the city. Were she to attend university this autumn, she would likely wash out with crippling debt and crushed self-esteem. Ursula would be wise to take a gap year during which she can become more independent, earn money, and take community college courses to prepare for university. However, Ursula underestimates the challenges of university, and overestimates her current capacities to meet those challenges. Consequently, she has decided to attend university this autumn. But, as with Tara, Mandy would like her to change her mind.

Suppose that Mandy employs the same pressure-based manipulative tactics on Ursula that she employs on Tara: She nags Ursula just as much as she nags Tara. She threatens to withdraw her friendship unless Ursula withdraws her application to university. She does trivial favors for Ursula before asking her to withdraw her application to university. Assume that these tactics succeed, so that Ursula decides not to attend university this autumn. Given Ursula's circumstances, this is a *better* decision than she would have made without Mandy's influence.

Mandy's actions are the same in both cases. And they are clearly manipulative in ***University I.*** Consequently, it is reasonable to think that they are manipulative in ***University II***. Revising the Trickery Account to treat a *bad decision* as a faulty mental state will enable it to identify Mandy's use of nagging, emotional blackmail, and exploiting reciprocity on *Tara* in ***University I*** as manipulation. But it will *not* enable it to identify her use of the very same tactics on *Ursula* in ***University II*** as manipulation. The decision that Mandy gets Tara to make is faulty. But the decision that Mandy gets Ursula to make is not faulty. Indeed, it is better than the decision that Ursula would have made without Mandy's influence. Modifying the Trickery Account to treat a bad decision as a faulty mental state would commit it to saying that Mandy manipulates Tara but not Ursula, even though Mandy's behavior is identical in both cases. That cannot be correct. Thus, this strategy to rescue the Trickery Account seems like a dead end.

So, the Trickery Account remains unable to recognize manipulation in several tactics that are clear examples of manipulation. But the Pressure Account correctly identifies manipulation in several clear cases of manipulation where the Trickery Account does not:

Nagging: Continually asking, pleading with, or otherwise pestering Tara imposes a cost—in the form of annoyance—on Tara for failing to comply with Mandy's wishes. This puts pressure on Tara to comply, and the Pressure Account identifies this as manipulation.

Exploiting Reciprocity: Doing favors to make Tara feel obligated to comply with Mandy's wishes imposes a cost on Tara for failing to comply, in the form of discomfort that people commonly feel when violating the social norm of reciprocity. This puts pressure on Tara to comply, and the Pressure Account identifies this as manipulation.

Emotional Blackmail: Threats by Mandy to withdraw her friendship threaten to impose costs on Tara for failing to comply with Mandy's wishes. This puts pressure on Tara to comply, and the Pressure Account identifies this as manipulation.

Notice that these tactics work exactly the same way when directed at Ursula as they do when directed at Tara. Hence, the Pressure Account correctly recognizes that Mandy's use of these tactics is equally manipulative in both cases.

Thus, the Pressure Account successfully identifies many tactics that seem like clear cases of manipulation. However, as we have seen, the Pressure Account fails to properly identify *other* clear cases of manipulation. Tactics like gaslighting and misdirection/misemphasis, for example, do not involve pressure, yet they are clear cases of manipulation.

Playing on the emotions is a bit more complicated. Experiencing certain emotions—like guilt—is unpleasant. Thus, inducing someone to feel an unpleasant emotion imposes a psychological cost on that person. Perhaps, then, the Pressure Account could treat inducing someone to feel an unpleasant emotion as a form of pressure. Thus, we might count Mandy's use of the guilt trip as a form of pressure because it gets Tara to feel an unpleasant emotion.

However, this attempt to rescue the Pressure Account faces a problem. If we count Mandy's guilt trip as manipulative because guilt is an unpleasant emotion, we would *also* have to classify as manipulative any attempt to get someone to feel an *appropriate* level of guilt, e.g., for some genuine and so-far unrepented wrongdoing. Yet this seems incorrect. Getting someone to feel an appropriate level of guilt—or at least remorse—for a genuine instance of wrongdoing does not seem manipulative, even if that emotion is unpleasant. Similarly, it does not seem manipulative to get someone to feel an appropriate level of fear toward something that is genuinely dangerous, even though fear is unpleasant. Thus, this way of trying to make the Pressure Account handle manipulative playing on the emotions seems like a dead end.

The discussion so far points to the following observation: Manipulation sometimes seems like trickery, and sometimes seems like pressure. Yet trickery and pressure seem very different from one another. What should we make of this?

Since manipulation involves *psychological* processes, perhaps psychologists can provide insight into its true nature. Unfortunately, however, scholarly psychological literature is rather unhelpful in this regard. As we noted in section 3.3, psychologists who study manipulation often characterize it by reference to a list of manipulative behaviors. For example, Elizabeth Austin and colleagues have developed two such lists. They form the basis for their Emotional Manipulation Scale (EMS) and their Management of the Emotions of Others Scale (MEOS) (Austin et al. 2007; Austin and O'Donnell 2013). These scales include tactics like guilt trips and feigned anger, which seem best described as trickery. But they also include tactics like charm offensives and using unkind words to control people's behavior, which seem best described as pressure. Pavlos Ioannidis has developed a scale for measuring manipulative behavior in romantic relationships (Ioannidis 2021). It contains behaviors best describe as trickery, like feigned emotions, guilt trips, and induction of unwarranted jealousy, as well as behaviors best described as pressure, like emotional blackmail and charm offensives. In their studies of manipulation among children, Shelley Hart and colleagues (Hart et al. 2022) have developed a "Trashy Tricks Rating Scale" to measure, and help children identify, manipulative behavior. It contains tactics best described as trickery, like feigned emotions ("faking") and guilt trips ("pouting") as well as tactics best described as pressure, like tantrums and "drama," charm offensives and being "whiny."

When the terms 'manipulation' and 'manipulative' appear in psychological descriptions of personality types and disorders, they commonly refer to both trickery and pressure tactics. For example, the Machiavellian personality is characterized in part by a tendency to engage in manipulation. The standard scale for identifying this personality type is the MACH-IV (Christie and Geis 1970). It includes among manipulative behaviors several that seem to involve trickery, such as lying and withholding one's true purposes when interacting with others. But it also includes flattery, which can be seen as a form of positive pressure related to the charm offensive. Psychopaths are consistently described as manipulative; tactics used to illustrate this quality include trickery tactics like conning, and deception, but also pressure-based tactics like charm offensives and emotional blackmail (Hare 2011; see also Potter 2006). A study by Len Bowers indicates that psychiatric nurses use the term 'manipulation' to refer both to pressure-based tactics (like bullying and threats) and to trickery-based tactics (Bowers 2003).

A similar picture emerges from various self-help books for dealing with manipulative people. Some use the term 'manipulation' mainly to refer to various forms of trickery (Stern 2018). Others use it mainly to refer to pressure (Braiker 2004; Forward 2001). Still others use it to refer to both (G. K. Simon 2010).

In short, psychologists who study manipulation, and who help people deal with the manipulators in their own lives, use the term 'manipulation' to apply *both* to tactics that involve trickery *and* to tactics that involve pressure.

4.3. A Disjunctive Account?

One might conclude from the discussion so far that the term 'manipulation' refers to two irreducibly different forms of influence—trickery and pressure. Perhaps, then, we should simply join the Pressure Account and the Trickery Account together and claim that manipulative influences are those that involve *either* pressure *or* trickery. Indeed, as we noted in section 3.10, scholars who have discussed forms of manipulation involving pressure do *not* typically claim that *all* forms of manipulation involve pressure. Thus, analyses of manipulation as pressure are often *already* parts of broader theories of manipulation that can best be seen as disjunctive.

A disjunctive account which characterizes manipulation as influence that employs *either* trickery *or* pressure would correctly identify all our paradigm examples of manipulation—something that existing accounts cannot do. However, this wider coverage comes at a price. Simply saying that manipulation is *either* trickery or pressure tells us nothing about what both forms of manipulation have in common that makes them manifestations of the same phenomenon. On the face of it, trickery and pressure do not seem very much alike. Yet our use of the term 'manipulation' to refer *both* to influences that involve trickery *and* to influences that involve pressure suggests that we think that they have something in common.

This commonality—if it exists—might also help explain why both forms of manipulation seem to have a similar moral status. This is especially significant because, as we noted in section 3.9, the Trickery Account provides a compelling explanation for why manipulation seems morally wrong. On this account, manipulation resembles deception, and is immoral for similar reasons. But since pressure seems different from deception, it is difficult to see why manipulative pressure would be wrong for reasons similar to those that make deception wrong. Thus, a disjunctive account of manipulation seems likely to imply a disjunctive account of its moral status.[2] This puts the disjunctive account even further away from our ordinary way of thinking about manipulation, which seems to assume that its various forms are all forms *of the same thing*, and all wrong for similar reasons. Of course, our ordinary way of thinking about manipulation might be wrong. But we should only accept this conclusion reluctantly, if we cannot provide a unified account that explains what manipulation that involves trickery has in common with manipulation that involves pressure. Fortunately, I think that we *can* provide such an account.

4.4. Non-Coercive Pressure

The key to developing a unified account of manipulation lies in the Pressure Account's claim that manipulative pressure is *non-coercive*. What does that mean?

Although coercion has received significant philosophical attention, no consensus has emerged on several key questions about it: Does coercion always involve threats, or can offers also be coercive? If coercion always involves threats, then how can threats be distinguished from offers? Is 'coercion' a "success term," so that we should only say that coercion occurs when the target gives in to the coercer's demands? Are moral norms of some sort built into the definition of 'coercion'? Should we regard coerced actions as fully voluntary? To what extent should we excuse actions done under coercion?

Fortunately, we need not settle any of those questions here. For our purposes, a very weak claim about coercion will suffice. Let's call it ***Condition C***:

***Condition C: N** coerces **T** to **A** only if **N** credibly threatens to do something that will make the consequences for **T** of failing to **A** worse than the consequences of **A**-ing.*

Put a bit more simply, **N** coerces T to do **A** only if **N** credibly threatens that if T refuses to do **A**, then **N** will make things worse for T than they would have been if T had done **A**. Notice that Condition C is only a *necessary* condition for coercion, not a sufficient one. Moreover, it is a claim that any plausible theory of coercion should accept. It would seem odd to say that someone was coerced into **A**-ing by a threat that was too small to make refusing to **A** worse than **A**-ing. (For example, "Your money or your life" is coercion. "Your money or I will call you a banana-head"

[2] Christian Coons and Michael Weber make a similar point (Coons and Weber 2014, 7).

is not.) Something like Condition C is included—either explicitly or implicitly—in the most influential philosophical accounts of coercion. For example, in his groundbreaking work on the topic, Robert Nozick suggests that, for **P** to coerce **Q** into *refraining from A-ing*, it must be true that "**Q** believes that . . . **P**'s threatened consequence would leave **Q** worse off, having done **A**, than if **Q** didn't do **A** and **P** didn't bring about the consequence" (Nozick 1969, 443).[3] Similarly Joseph Raz claims that a necessary condition for **P** to coerce **Q** into refraining from **A**-ing is that "**Q** believes that it is likely that **P** will bring about **C** if **Q** does **A** and that **C** would leave him worse off, having done **A**, than if he did not do **A** and **P** did not bring about **C**" (Raz 1988, 149). Joel Feinberg claims that "coercion proper" occurs only when "the costs of the threatened consequences exceed the costs of complying with the demand" (Feinberg 1989, 203). Alan Wertheimer argues that "having 'no *acceptable* alternative' but to succumb to a coercive proposal" is necessary for coercion (Wertheimer 1990, 267, emphasis original); this only seems possible when the costs of complying are less than the costs of refusing.

While Condition C is overwhelmingly plausible as a *necessary* condition for coercion, it does not seem to be *sufficient*. For example, an employer threatening to fire a non-performing employee unless the employee does the job for which the employee was hired fulfils Condition C, but it does not seem like coercion (Kiener 2020). Scholars disagree about what additional conditions must be met for genuine coercion to occur. Some argue that it must also be morally wrong for **N** to impose the relevant costs on T for not **A**-ing. A similar suggestion is that **N**'s threat, if carried out, must make T worse off than T ought to be (Wertheimer 1990). Some argue that **N** must make the cost of non-compliance significantly larger than that of compliance. Some claim that this cost must be high enough to make compliance the only "reasonable option," or to render **N**'s compliance less than fully voluntary.[4]

Let us return to the concept of *coercive pressure*. Of course, it is not literal pressure, in the form of a physical force. Rather, it is a metaphor for the influence created by a threat to impose some disincentive for failing to comply with the coercer's demand. It seems natural to think of *coercive pressure* as pressure which meets the minimum threshold for coercion, as expressed in Condition C. This would mean that coercive pressure involves disincentives that make refusing to perform the action demanded by the coercer worse for the target than performing it. Since Condition C is necessary but not sufficient for "genuine coercion" or "coercion proper," exerting coercive pressure is necessary but not sufficient for genuine coercion or coercion proper. Nevertheless, such pressure is still "coer*cive*" in the sense that it meets the threshold level required for coercion. Let us call the action that the

[3] In his comprehensive discussion of coercion, Scott Anderson interprets Nozick as claiming that P coerces Q into not-Aing only if P credibly threatens that "if Q performs A, then P will bring about some consequence that would make Q's A-ing less desirable to Q than Q's not A-ing" (Anderson 2011, 14).

[4] For helpful overviews of these matters, see S. Anderson (2011) and Kiener (2020).

coercer—or any influencer—tries to get the target to perform the *solicited action.* Coercive pressure involves a threat to make the consequences of *failing* to perform the solicited action *worse* for the target than the consequences of performing it. Thus, coercive pressure involves threats that make the solicited action the target's least bad alternative.

As we have seen, cases of manipulation that seem best described as involving pressure are distinct from coercion. That is, even when manipulation resembles coercion in that it involves pressure, there still seems to be a clear difference between the two. In particular, the pressure exerted in forms of manipulation that involve pressure is less intense than the pressure exerted in coercion. In short, manipulative pressure is weaker than coercive pressure. Consequently, it makes sense to think that manipulative pressure involves disincentives that are *smaller* than those involved in coercive pressure, i.e., the minimum level of pressure required for coercion. As we have just seen, coercive pressure involves disincentives that are large enough to make the solicited option less bad for the target than the alternatives. Putting these ideas together yields the following conclusion: Pressure is *manipulative* (rather than coercive) when it involves disincentives that worsen the consequences of failing to perform the solicited action, but *not enough to make the solicited action the target's least bad option.*

We have been speaking of manipulative pressure in terms of *dis*incentives. Could *incentives* constitute a form of manipulative pressure as well? It seems reasonable to think so. Charm offensives involve incentives, that is, offers of positive consequences for performing some action: If you do as I wish, you will earn my approval. Let us call the pressure exerted by disincentives (i.e., threats of negative consequences) *negative pressure.* We may then call the pressure exerted by incentives (i.e., offers of positive consequences) *positive pressure.*[5]

As we have seen, *negative* manipulative pressure is too weak to make the solicited action the target's *least bad* option. Thus, it would make sense to say that *positive* manipulative pressure is too weak to make the solicited action the target's *best* option. Of course, "least bad" and "best" are just different ways to describe an *optimal* choice, i.e., a choice for which no better alternative is available. Thus, we can say that *both* negative and positive manipulative pressure are too weak to make the solicited action the target's optimal choice. Let us call an incentive or disincentive—or the pressure it exerts—*optimalizing* when it is large enough to make choosing

[5] I am using the term 'coercive pressure' in a way that is slightly different from how Feinberg uses the term. Feinberg uses the term to refer to pressure created by the threat to impose a cost of *any magnitude* for refusing to do what the influencer demands (Feinberg 1989, 193). What Feinberg calls 'coercive pressure,' I am calling 'negative pressure,' since it imposes a *cost* for *refusing* to do what the influencer demands. As I shall use the term, 'coercive pressure,' is negative pressure that is strong enough to make *refusing* to do what the influencer demands *worse* for T than doing what the influencer demands (that is, pressure that is strong enough to make complying with the coercer's demand the target's least bad option).

the solicited action optimal for the target (i.e., better or less bad than any available alternative). So, an optimalizing *disincentive* threatens *bad* consequences for failure to comply that are large enough to make compliance optimal for the target. This happens in coercion.[6] An optimalizing *incentive* offers *good* consequences for compliance that are large enough to make compliance optimal for the target. This happens in good-faith bargaining. By contrast, *non-optimalizing* incentives or disincentives are too small to make the solicited action the target's optimal choice. Since manipulative pressure must involve non-optimalizing incentives or disincentives if manipulation is to remain distinct from both good faith bargaining and coercion, we can say that:

> *M exerts* ***manipulative pressure*** *on T to do A only if M creates a non-optimalizing incentive for doing A, or a non-optimalizing disincentive for failing to do A.*

4.5. A Puzzle about Manipulative Pressure

The claim that manipulative pressure is non-optimalizing neatly distinguishes it from coercion and from good-faith bargaining. However, it also creates a puzzle. If manipulative pressure does not make the solicited action the target's best (or least bad) option, then how does it get the target to perform that action?

Consider Tara again. Mandy's use of manipulative pressure creates an incentive to withdraw her application to university. Depending on the tactic, that incentive might involve obtaining relief from annoying nagging, avoiding a strain on their friendship, or avoiding the awkwardness of refusing to reciprocate a favor. It would be farfetched to regard any of these incentives as being strong enough to make withdrawing her application to university Tara's *optimal* choice. And yet it is not at all farfetched to imagine those tactics working to get Tara to withdraw her application *anyway*. It is not farfetched because we have all seen people give in to pressure that is non-optimalizing in the same way that the pressure Mandy imposes on Tara is non-optimalizing. In fact, most of us have done this ourselves. But how can that possibly be? Why would anyone give in to pressure that is too weak to make complying one's optimal choice?

The simple answer is this: Manipulative pressure works, when it does, because *the target makes a mistake*. Once we see that manipulative pressure cannot make the solicited action the target's optimal choice if manipulation is to remain distinct from coercion and bargaining, this becomes the only answer possible.

[6] Sometimes it may be rational to refuse to choose the action that coercive pressure has made optimal. The target may judge that it is better to pay the price of the coercer following through on his threats to demonstrate that he will not give in to coercion. To allow for such possibilities, we should take "optimal" to mean least bad in terms of its immediate effects, ignoring any strategic or long-term reasons that the target might have for refusing to acquiesce.

Of course, we *could* imagine that Tara makes this mistake because she acquires the false belief that attending university is far less desirable than it had seemed. But to imagine this is to imagine the wrong thing. We are not imagining how Mandy might *trick* Tara into falsely believing that a university education is less desirable than retaining Mandy's friendship or ending her nagging. Instead, we are imagining that Tara gives in to Mandy's pressure even though she knows that doing so is suboptimal. Why would she do this?

The short answer is that it is simply human nature that we sometimes knowingly choose the lesser good. We avoid exercise, we eat too many sugary foods, we put off medical check-ups, we spend too much time on social media. We do these things even when we know that, in so doing, we are choosing the lesser good over the greater good. There is a rich philosophical tradition investigating this phenomenon, which philosophers call "akrasia" or "weakness of will." Roughly, a person displays akrasia, or makes an akratic choice, when that person chooses what the person knows is the lesser good. Thus, to choose akratically is to knowingly make a sub-optimal choice.

Once we see this, we can see that akrasia is central to the effectiveness of manipulative pressure. If non-optimalizing positive pressure gets you to perform the solicited action, despite judging the incentive to be insufficient to make it your best option, you have acted akratically. Similarly, if non-optimalizing negative pressure gets you to perform the solicited action, despite judging the threat to be insufficient to make it your least bad option, you have acted akratically. The role of akrasia distinguishes manipulative pressure from coercion on the one hand, and honest bargaining on the other. It is not akratic to choose an option that has been made best by an incentive, or made least bad by a disincentive. But it *is* akratic to give in to an incentive or disincentive which you know does neither. Thus, successful manipulative pressure requires the target to choose akratically.

A *complete* answer to how manipulative pressure works would require solving the philosophical puzzle of akrasia. A solution to *that* puzzle is beyond the scope of this book. But what we already do know about akrasia will go a long way toward helping us understand how manipulative pressure works. We are especially likely to choose the lesser good when it is more appealing in the short term than the greater one. Thus, it is the short-term unpleasantness of exercise that leads us to forgo it despite its greater long-term benefits. Our propensity to consume sugary foods is the mirror image. Short-term pleasure leads us to choose them despite their health consequences, which will only catch up to us later. Not only do we tend to choose smaller goods available sooner over larger goods available later, but this tendency increases drastically as "soon" gets closer and closer to "now" (Ainslie 2001).[7]

[7] This will be discussed in more detail in sections 7.9 and 8.6.6.

These facts help to explain why manipulative pressure often succeeds. Even if Mandy's approval is insufficient to make staying home Tara's best option overall, its immediacy might induce Tara to stay home anyway. Similarly, if Mandy threatens to dissolve their friendship if Tara does not withdraw her application to university, she might give in so she can avoid that immediate unpleasantness. And she might do this despite knowing that the long-term consequences of forgoing university are worse overall. Indeed, such an *immediate* threat would probably be more effective than a prediction that if Tara goes off to college the two of them will *eventually* drift apart. More generally, when the manipulator offers *immediate rewards* for performing the solicited action, or threatens *immediate punishment* for failing to do so, the tendency to choose smaller, immediately available goods over larger goods available later may induce the target to make what the target knows is a suboptimal choice.

In addition, some incentives and disincentives are especially likely to induce akratic choices. Some things are just more tempting than others. And some people are more susceptible than others to certain incentives. People who are insecure—or who are made insecure by the manipulator—are susceptible to akratically giving in to threats to withdraw approval, or offers of greater approval, even when they know that the manipulator's approval is not worth what must be done to obtain it. People who are impulsive, who lack self-control, or who have akratically strong appetites or addictions, are also easy targets for manipulative pressure. The "honey trap" of spy stories manipulates those who akratically give in to lust. People whose greed can lead them to act against their better judgment are lucrative marks for con artists. Quick-tempered people are easily manipulated to akratically choose retribution for affronts, whether they are real, imagined, or engineered by the manipulator.

Thus, the wielder of manipulative pressure exploits the target's susceptibility to akrasia. Depending on the situation and the target, this might simply be the general human tendency to choose a smaller but immediately available good over a larger good for which one must wait. Or it may be the tendency to react akratically to certain kinds of incentives or disincentives. Or it may be a special vulnerability of that particular person to react akratically to some particular incentive or disincentive.

4.6. The Mistake Account of Manipulation

So, manipulative pressure succeeds when and because the target chooses akratically. Whatever else an akratic choice might be, making one is clearly a mistake. This way of thinking about manipulative pressure reveals an underlying similarity between manipulation that involves pressure and manipulation that involves trickery: Both induce the target to make a mistake. Manipulative trickery involves inducing the target to adopt a mistaken belief, desire, emotion, judgment, or other mental state. Manipulative pressure involves inducing the target to respond akratically to a non-optimalizing incentive or disincentive.

Thus, we have identified a common feature shared by forms of manipulation that involve trickery and those that involve pressure: Both work by getting the target to make a mistake. What initially seemed like two distinct *forms of manipulation*—pressure and trickery—simply represent two different *kinds of mistakes* that the manipulator might get the target to make. Manipulative trickery induces faulty mental states that will make the target more likely to do what the manipulator wants. Manipulative pressure induces an akratic—and thus mistaken—reaction to a non-optimalizing incentive or disincentive designed to get the target to do what the manipulator wants. Thus, we can formulate what I will call the Mistake Account of manipulation:

> *Manipulation is an influence that operates by inducing the target to make a mistake.*[8]

4.7. Accommodating Two Accounts of Akrasia

Because it can accommodate cases of manipulative pressure, the Mistake Account is an improvement over the Trickery Account. But the Mistake Account also remedies another serious, but less easily noticed, shortcoming in the Trickery Account. To see this problem, consider two ways that we might imagine Mandy's emotional blackmail working:

> ***Mandy's Emotional Blackmail, Version 1:*** Mandy threatens to end their friendship immediately unless Tara withdraws her application to university. Upon hearing this threat, Tara temporarily changes her mind about her friendship with Mandy: Contrary to the evidence and her earlier judgments, Tara temporarily comes to believe that their friendship is more important than a university education. This change in Tara's judgment only lasts while Mandy is engaged in her emotional blackmail, but that is long enough for Tara to withdraw her application to university.
>
> ***Mandy's Emotional Blackmail, Version 2:*** Mandy threatens to end their friendship immediately unless Tara withdraws her application to university. Despite judging a university education to be more important than her friendship with Mandy, Tara responds akratically to the prospect of immediately losing the friendship and withdraws her application.

[8] In Chapter 6, this idea will be refined into a more formal definition.

Assume that in both versions, Mandy's behavior is identical, and Tara recognizes that she has made a mistake soon after she withdraws her university application. It seems correct to say that, in both versions, Mandy manipulated Tara.

The Trickery Account successfully identifies Mandy's behavior as manipulation in the first version: Mandy gets Tara to adopt a false belief about the importance of her friendship with Tara. But the Trickery Account falters with the second version. Here, Tara's decision reflects her akratic response to the possibility of losing Mandy's friendship. Notice that this response does not arise from any false belief about the value of Mandy's friendship, nor does it seem to involve any other faulty mental state. Hence, the Trickery Account cannot correctly identify Mandy's behavior as manipulation in this version, since Mandy does not induce any faulty mental state. And as we saw in ***University II,*** we cannot rescue the Trickery Account by treating Tara's *decision* to forgo college as a mistaken mental state.

Thus, the Trickery Account implies that manipulation occurs in Version 1 but not Version 2. But Mandy's behavior seems equally manipulative in both versions. Moreover, it is difficult to believe that whether Mandy manipulates Tara should depend on something so subtle as the difference between: (a) Tara briefly and irrationally adopting a new judgment that losing Mandy's friendship would be worse than forgoing university, and (b) Tara akratically acting against her judgment that forgoing university would be worse than losing Mandy's friendship.

Version 2 is an example of what we might call the "classical" conception of akrasia. This involves deliberately choosing something that, *at the time of the choice*, the chooser recognizes as the lesser good. Many philosophers claim that this phenomenon is fairly common in real life. But this view has been challenged recently, most notably by Richard Holton (2009). On Holton's view, cases like Version 2 seldom occur in real life, and most cases of weakness of will are more like Version 1: Someone abandons a prior decision because she temporarily and irrationally adopts a judgment that favors an option that she previously, and more rationally, regarded as sub-optimal.[9]

The difference between choosing against one's judgment about what is best and temporarily *changing* one's judgment about what is best is very subtle. As Alison McIntyre notes, it can be difficult to tell—even for oneself—whether one chose the lesser good because one temporarily rationalized that the lesser good is better after all, or whether one chose the lesser good while simultaneously recognizing it to be lesser (McIntyre 2006, 286–87).[10] In part, this is because people often engage in *ex post facto* rationalization for why they chose as they did. For example, we can easily imagine that in Version 2, Tara might rationalize her decision by claiming

[9] Some philosophers use the terms 'akrasia' and 'weakness of will' to mark the distinction between what happens in the two versions of this case. Others use both terms to apply to both versions. I will follow the second convention.

[10] Mario Rizzo (2016) makes a similar observation in the context of behavioral economics.

to have believed—at the time, at least—that her friendship with Mandy was very important. In addition to the empirical difficulties in determining whether a given instance of akrasia was more like Version 1 or Version 2, there are complex conceptual arguments about how we should understand this phenomenon.[11]

Consequently, it seems wise to avoid claiming—as the Trickery Account does—that whether manipulation occurs depends on whether something more like Version 1 or Version 2 occurs. Although correctly identifying manipulation may sometimes require attention to subtle psychological details, it is difficult to believe that it would depend on psychological differences as subtle as those that separate Version 1 from Version 2, or upon conceptual matters as arcane as the correct philosophical analysis of akrasia.

Here the Mistake Account's handling of manipulative pressure is superior to that of the Trickery Account. The Mistake Account identifies Mandy's emotional blackmail as manipulation equally well in Version 1 *and* Version 2. Its ability to count inducing akrasia as manipulation is not held hostage to philosophical debates about the nature of akrasia, or to the subtle differences between mistakenly choosing against one's judgment about what is best and mistakenly *changing* one's judgment about what is best.

We can remain neutral about such matters by stating that someone "reacts akratically toward" an incentive or disincentive if that person either (1) mistakenly abandons a prior judgment that the incentive or disincentive is not optimalizing, or (2) mistakenly reacts to it *as though* the person believed it to be optimalizing despite judging otherwise. On the Mistake Account, a non-optimalizing incentive or disincentive is manipulative if it induces the target to react akratically towards it.

4.8. Paternalistic Manipulative Pressure

Earlier, we rejected an attempt to modify the Trickery Account to enable it to recognize manipulative pressure by treating the target's *decision* as a mistaken mental state. The problem was that this way of modifying the Trickery Account does not work in cases like ***University II***, where the manipulator uses pressure to get the target to make a *better* decision than the one the target would have made without the pressure. A similar thing happens in cases of paternalistic manipulative pressure: These are cases where a well-meaning person uses manipulative pressure paternalistically, that is, to deliberately get the target to make a decision that is better for the target than the one that the target was going to make. It is worth pausing to

[11] For a critique of Holton's view, see Mele (2010). For an overview of the debate about akrasia and weakness of will, see Stroud and Svirsky (2019). Due to the complexity of these issues, I will strive to make my remarks here compatible with a wide range of views about akrasia.

show how the Mistake Account *can* properly identify paternalistic manipulative pressure.

Typically, people do what they think it is best for them to do. However, people are sometimes mistaken about what that is. Paternalistic manipulation occurs when the manipulator wants the target to do what is best for the target, and thinks that the target is mistaken about what that is. Of course, such a situation would be better addressed through rational persuasion to help the target see what really is best to do. But our concern here is with paternalistic *manipulation*, and, more specifically, *paternalistic manipulative pressure*. This would take the form of an incentive or disincentive to which the target responds akratically—that is, responding as though it was stronger than it really is. This akratic reaction would lead the target either to temporarily reverse the target's prior judgment about what is best overall, or to act akratically against the target's judgment about what is best overall. Either way, the manipulator's goal is to get the target to act contrary to what the target *mistakenly* thinks there is most reason to do. In this way, the manipulator seeks to induce in the target a peculiar sort of akrasia, one where the akratic choice is better than the non-akratic choice. Nomy Arpaly and Timothy Schroeder have labelled such cases as "inverse akrasia" (Arpaly and Schroeder 1999, 162).

The possibility of inverse akrasia creates the possibility of paternalistic manipulative pressure. Recall that manipulative pressure induces the target to mistakenly treat an incentive or disincentive as being bigger than it really is, either because of some special vulnerability like an addiction, or because of the general human tendency to treat immediate rewards as more valuable than they really are. Nothing prevents a manipulator from harnessing the tendency to irrationally overreact to an incentive or disincentive to get the target to make a better choice than the one the target was originally inclined to make.

Recall that in ***University II***, Ursula plans to attend university this autumn even though she is not currently prepared, academically, mentally, or financially, to do so. Because she does *not* fully appreciate the reasons for waiting to attend university, she mistakenly judges it best to attend university this autumn. Moreover, Ursula judges attending university this autumn to be more important than maintaining her friendship with Mandy. Now imagine that Mandy's motives are paternalistic rather than selfish: She is not concerned about keeping her friend home with her; she just wants what is best for Ursula. And she realizes that, contrary to what Ursula thinks, what is best for her is to take a gap year. Now imagine that Mandy employs the same emotional blackmail on Ursula that she did in the original version of the case. It is still no more farfetched to imagine Ursula reacting akratically to Mandy's threats to end their friendship than it is to imagine Tara doing so. The difference is that in Ursula's case, the decision to withdraw her application to university is a case of *inverse* akrasia. Tara and Ursula both respond akratically to Mandy's pressure: Mandy's non-optimalizing pressure leads both of them to act contrary to what they take themselves to have most reason to do. It's just that Ursula is wrong about what she has most reason to do, so that her akratic reaction to the non-optimalizing pressure is *inverse* akrasia. In this way, the Mistake Account recognizes the existence of paternalistic manipulative pressure.

4.9. Is Non-Optimalizing Pressure Always Manipulative?

It is worth emphasizing that the Mistake Account characterizes manipulative pressure in terms of non-optimalizing incentives or disincentives *only when they are akrasia-inducing.*[12]

Consequently, offering a non-optimalizing incentive or disincentive is not always manipulative.[13] Often, the person offering the incentive or disincentive will not even know whether it is optimalizing for the other party. For example, I might offer someone $20 to mow my yard without knowing whether that incentive is sufficient to make mowing my yard that person's optimal choice. So long as there is nothing akrasia-inducing about my offer, there is no reason to think that this constitutes manipulative pressure.

In fact, even *knowingly* offering a non-optimalizing incentive or disincentive is not always manipulative. If I am engaged in good-faith, honest bargaining, I will typically look for the least costly (for me) incentive that makes taking the deal optimal for you. Consequently, I might begin by offering incentives that I think are non-optimalizing and gradually increasing them until I find one large enough to make the deal optimal for you. If this is part of the normal process of trying to find the least costly (for me) incentive that will make the deal optimal for you, and if the progressively larger incentives being offered are not akrasia-inducing, then there is no reason to think that this constitutes manipulative pressure. No doubt some negotiation tactics *are* calculated to get the other party to react akratically to an incentive. However, in the context of honest, good-faith bargaining, offering a non-optimalizing incentive is not *automatically* manipulative. By contrast, consider this case:

> ***Lawn Mower:*** Trisha is a teenager who has set aside her afternoon to earn money by mowing someone's lawn. Her neighbors, Harriet and Mack, have identically sized lawns, live the same distance from Trisha, and would each like their lawn mowed. Harriet offers Trisha $30.00 to mow her lawn. Mack knows about Harriet's offer, but he also knows that Trisha has a pathological weakness

[12] One might wonder whether "akrasia-inducing" should be understood as "intended to induce akrasia," or as "actually inducing akrasia." This question will be discussed in Chapter 5.

[13] This is why the statement at the end of section 4.4 contains an "only if" rather than an "if and only if."

for ice cream. So, instead of matching or beating Harriet's offer, Mack offers to pay Trisha $15.00, plus two scoops of her favorite ice cream in a waffle cone—a treat that both Trisha and Mack know to be priced at $4.00. Mack vividly describes the treat's gustatory qualities, and he offers to give it to Trisha before she begins mowing.

Clearly, Mack's offer is manipulative. But its manipulativeness is not simply a matter of it being non-optimalizing. Rather, it is manipulative because it is calculated to get Trisha to choose akratically the lesser good over the greater. It exploits both Trisha's weakness for ice cream and the normal human tendency to overvalue smaller goods available immediately.

Finally, it is not necessarily manipulative to offer non-optimalizing incentives for doing what the target has already decided to do. Thus, a gym might offer modest, non-optimalizing rewards for maintaining one's exercise program. So long as the rewards are not ones to which people are apt to respond akratically, there is no reason to think that they are manipulative. Quite the opposite, in fact: Incentives to do what one has already decided to do can help protect against akrasia rather than inducing it.

4.10. Manipulative Pressure and Situational Manipulation

The Mistake Account's analysis of manipulative pressure sheds light on the distinction between what is sometimes called "psychological manipulation" and what is sometimes called "situational manipulation." An example from Joel Rudinow's classic paper on manipulation (Rudinow 1978) illustrates this distinction: A malingerer named Smith asks a hospital admitting physician to admit him to the psychiatric ward, on the grounds that he "had another terrible battle with his wife and . . . if he is not admitted he will . . . wind up drunk, brawling, and finally either in the emergency ward or in jail" (Rudinow 1978, 340). The admitting physician refuses to admit him on these grounds. Smith responds: "All right then . . . I will climb to the top of the water tower and create such a scene that you'll have to admit me" (Rudinow 1978, 340). Later, a police officer brings Smith to the psychiatric ward, reports that he is suicidal, and requests that he be admitted. Although the admitting physician is not fooled, her hospital's rules force her to admit the malingerer at the police officer's request.

It seems correct to say that Smith has manipulated both the police officer and the admitting physician. But what he does to them is quite different. Smith clearly gets the police officer to adopt a mistaken belief that Smith is suicidal. But this is very different from what he does to the admitting physician. That more closely resembles the sorts of tactics that the political theorist William Riker called "heresthetic" manipulation, which he described as "structuring the world so you can win" (Riker 1986, ix). A paradigm example of heresthetic manipulation is the "poison pill" amendment, when legislators who oppose a bill attach an amendment to it that makes it unappealing to its supporters. This resembles what Smith does to the admitting physician: He changes the situation so that it is no longer viable to do other than what the manipulator wants.

At first glance, the difference between what happens to the police officer and what happens to the admitting physician in Rudinow's example seems clear enough. It seems equally clear that one involves manipulation of the police officer's *psychology* and the other involves manipulation of the physician's *situation*. But explaining this distinction precisely is more difficult than we might expect.

It is tempting to say simply that situational manipulation changes the target's external situation rather than the target's psychology. But that cannot be right, for two reasons. First, even clear cases of situational manipulation change the psychology of people involved. Consider a poison pill amendment. This is a clear case of situational manipulation, but it changes people's decision about whether to vote for the bill to which the amendment has been attached. Second, even clear cases of psychological manipulation sometimes involve changes to the external situation. When Iago famously plants Desdemona's handkerchief to make Othello believe that Desdemona gave it to Cassio, he changes the external situation: He moves the handkerchief from one place to another. But this nevertheless seems like a clear case of psychological manipulation.

A more promising suggestion is offered by Anne Barnhill, who suggests that we distinguish between (a) manipulation that "changes the options available to the person or changes the situation she's in, and thereby changes her attitudes," from (b) manipulation that "changes a person's attitudes directly without changing the options available to her or the surrounding situation" (Barnhill 2014, 53). Boiled down, the suggestion is that situational manipulation changes the person's options, while psychological manipulation changes how the person thinks about those options.

This proposal properly distinguishes what happens to the police officer from what happens to the admitting physician: Smith changes the admitting physician's options and not just her perception of them. But this proposal faces problems when we try to categorize cases of manipulative pressure. Mandy's emotional blackmail changes the "external or objective features" of Tara's choice situation, which "changes the options available to" Tara. Mandy makes Tara's option of attending university more costly than it had been, and she entirely eliminates Tara's option of *attending university while remaining friends with Mandy*. So this proposal would classify Mandy's emotional blackmail as *situational* manipulation. But this does not seem correct. Emotional blackmail seems like a clear case of *psychological* manipulation.

But Barnhill offers another, more refined, suggestion. It emerges from this example:

> ***Camping Trip I***: Your partner wants to go on a family camping trip, but you don't. While you're discussing it, your partner calls out to your children, "Hey, kids! Who wants to go on a camping trip?" The children cheer. You correctly judge that it's better to go on the camping trip (despite its drawbacks) than to disappoint your children. You agree to go on the camping trip (Barnhill 2014, 54).

According to Barnhill, in this case, "the way that your partner manipulated you . . . is that he changed the situation (i.e., he got the kids excited about camping), such that the ideal response for you to have is his desired response" (Barnhill 2014, 54). Barnhill's analysis of this example leads her to make a more refined proposal about how to distinguish psychological from situational manipulation. The key, according to Barnhill, is the difference between:

(A) Manipulation that involves "making someone have a non-ideal response, either by influencing her directly . . . or by changing the situation in a way that will cause her to have a non-ideal response to the new situation" (Barnhill 2014, 54–55) and
(B) Manipulation that involves "changing the situation so that the target's ideal response to the new situation is the manipulator's desired response" (Barnhill 2014, 55).

Barnhill's analysis locates the key difference between psychological and situational manipulation. The analysis of manipulative pressure developed here can help us see this even more clearly. To see how, let us embellish Barnhill's case to help amplify its crucial feature. Imagine that you have had a busy week, and simply want a quiet, relaxing weekend. Had they not been alerted to the possibility of camping, the kids would have found other things to do, and would have been reasonably content. All in all, everyone's weekend would have been just fine. That being the case, staying home would have been your optimal course of action—until your partner opened his big mouth. Once that happens, and the kids are alerted to the possibility of a camping trip, the situation changes. Suppose that, once the kids see camping as a possibility, they will be surly and ill-tempered if you do not go camping, and this will make everyone's weekend miserable. Thus, your partner's announcement not only changed the situation, but it did so in a way that *changed what is optimal for you*: Before, staying home was optimal. Now, going camping is optimal.

These elaborations make it more plain why Barnhill's case is not only *not* a case of *psychological* manipulation, but also *not* a case of *manipulative pressure* either.

It is now a case of *situational* manipulation. But this is not simply because your partner changed your options. It is because he changed those options in such a way that the option he wants you to choose *is now your optimal choice.* To see this more clearly, imagine this contrasting version of Barnhill's case:

> ***Camping Trip II*:** You hate camping, yet the family has been camping for the past three weekends in a row—and you've been miserable each time. Bad weather is forecast for the coming weekend, plus it's black fly season and the kids' allergies are all peaking. Your weekend preference is to take the kids to a cultural event that the kids will probably enjoy, though they won't know that until they experience it. When your partner suggests camping, you explain your reasons for rejecting the suggestion. Your partner then brings in the kids and says, "how about camping this weekend?" knowing that they'll want to go camping again. You know that they will be disappointed temporarily if you refuse. But you also know that camping again this weekend will be miserable for everyone, and that everyone would have more fun attending the cultural event instead. Yet you find it difficult to disappoint your children. So you give in, realizing that this will doom the entire family to a miserable weekend.

In ***Camping Trip II***, camping is *not* your optimal choice. (This is true regardless of whether you are choosing for selfish reasons or for the benefit of the entire family.) More importantly, it *remains sub-optimal* even *after* your partner announces the possibility to the children. But you make that sub-optimal choice anyway. Now the case is a clear example of manipulative pressure *and* a clear example of *psychological* manipulation.

Notice that the key difference between the cases is whether the influence makes the solicited action optimal for you, or whether it induces you to choose it *akratically* despite it *not* being optimal. In ***Camping Trip I*** (Barnhill's original version), involving the children changes the balance of reasons so that agreeing to the camping *trip becomes your optimal choice.* In ***Camping Trip II***, involving the children does *not* make the camping trip optimal. Instead, it induces you to make a *mistake* by *reacting akratically* to the children's excitement and the prospect of their immediate disappointment.

Thus, we can distinguish situational manipulation from manipulative pressure by noting that the former makes the solicited action optimal for the target, while the latter induces the target to *mistakenly* react to it *as though* it were optimal. This way of making the distinction captures the idea that psychological manipulation involves manipulating the person and that situational manipulation involves manipulating the situation. In situational manipulation, there is no need to manipulate the person into mistakenly treating the sub-optimal action as optimal. Instead, one simply arranges things so that the solicited action *really is optimal.* Thus, situational manipulation has less in common with psychological manipulation than it does with coercion. In both cases the influencer arranges matters so that the solicited action really is the target's best or least bad option.

But this does not mean that situational manipulation is indistinguishable from coercion. As we noted earlier, the application of coercive pressure is necessary but not sufficient for coercion. This fact suggests a tripartite distinction among forms of negative pressure. Non-optimalizing negative pressure is manipulative. Optimalizing negative pressure is situational manipulation when the additional conditions for coercion proper are not met. Optimalizing negative pressure is coercion proper when the other conditions for coercion *are* met. Defining those other conditions for coercion proper is beyond the scope of this book. But their existence suggests a way to distinguish among manipulative pressure, situational manipulation, and coercion.

4.11. Conclusion

As we have seen, the Mistake Account has considerable advantages over other accounts of manipulation. In the next chapter, we will address questions about the mental state of the manipulator, including one that the Mistake Account inherits from one of its two "parents," the Trickery Account.

5

Perspective, Intent, and Manipulation

5.1. Introduction

This chapter addresses two important questions about the state of mind of the manipulator. The first is one that the Mistake Account inherits from the Trickery Account: If manipulation involves getting someone to make a mistake, whose perspective determines what counts as "getting someone to make a mistake"? Call this the *Perspective Question*. The second concerns the extent to which manipulation requires some sort of intention on the part of the influencer, and if so, what the content of that intention must be. Call this the *Intention Question.*

5.2. The Perspective Question

Should we say that someone is manipulated only if that person makes what *really is* a mistake? Or should we say that someone is manipulated only if that person makes what the *manipulator believes* is a mistake? Is Iago's behavior manipulation because *Iago believes* that Othello has no reason to be jealous, or because there *really is* no reason for Othello to be jealous?[1]

Since the Perspective Question also arises for the Trickery Account, it has been discussed by some of that account's proponents. However, no consensus has emerged. As we noted in section 3.9, some defend an influencer-subjective standard, according to which manipulation occurs when the influencer attempts to get the target to adopt what the *influencer regards* as a faulty mental state. Others defend an objective standard according to which manipulation occurs when the influencer attempts to get the target to adopt a mental state that *really is* (objectively) faulty.

Had there been a consensus about how the Trickery Account should answer the Perspective Question, we might have been able to import it directly into the Mistake Account. Instead, we shall have to start from scratch. It will be less cumbersome to focus first on manipulative trickery, which involves mistaken

[1] Defining manipulation in terms of what the *target* takes to be a mistake is a non-starter. Since a person who believes that **P** will typically also believe that not-**P** is a mistake, any attempt to convince such a person that not-**P** will at least initially be regarded by that person as an attempt to induce a mistake. Hence, defining manipulation as inducing what the target regards as a mistake would imply that most instances of rational persuasion are manipulative. This would be absurd.

Manipulation. Robert Noggle, Oxford University Press. © Robert Noggle 2025.
DOI: 10.1093/9780198924920.003.0005

mental states like beliefs, emotions, and patterns of attention, and then apply whatever answer emerges to manipulative pressure, which involves akratic mistakes. Suppose, then, that influencer **N** gets **T** to adopt mental state **S**. Matters are simple when **S** is *both* objectively mistaken *and* believed by **N** to be mistaken: The Mistake Account correctly identifies these as clear cases of manipulation. Matters are also simple when **S** is *neither* objectively mistaken *nor* believed by **N** to be mistaken. The Mistake Account correctly finds no manipulation in such cases.

But what happens when **N** regards **S** as mistaken when, objectively, it is not? Or when **S** is objectively mistaken, but **N** does not know that? Cases like these pose a problem for the Mistake Account—a problem that can only be solved by answering the Perspective Question. Consider this example of the first kind of problem case:

***Irene's New Coworkers*:** Irene has just taken a new job. Two of her new coworkers, Billy and Todd, have known each other since childhood—a childhood in which Billy bullied Todd mercilessly. Billy remains contemptuous of Todd even now, but he hides this from Todd and pretends to be Todd's friend, while ridiculing and undermining him behind his back. Through a combination of naïveté and self-deception, Todd regards Billy as a true friend, and dismisses his childhood bullying as "kids being kids." Todd tells Irene that Billy is his good friend, and Irene believes him. However, Irene sees their friendship as an obstacle to her own career advancement, and she resolves to drive a wedge between them. Irene repeatedly draws Todd's attention to what both she and Todd initially regard as Billy's good-natured kidding. But Irene insinuates that Billy's behavior displays a thinly veiled contempt for Todd. "Wow," Irene sometimes says, "you two must be really good friends for you to let him talk to you that way." At other times, Irene simply asks questions like, "Did you notice how Billy just took credit for your work?" or "Did you hear what Billy said about you?" Irene thinks she is cherry-picking from the banter that she regards as part of their rough-and-tumble friendship. When Todd finally becomes irritated at Billy's behavior, Irene plays on this irritation so that it grows into resentment and anger toward Billy. Consequently, Todd comes to resent Billy's behavior toward him and to dislike Billy himself. Although Irene thought she was getting Todd to adopt a *mistaken* attitude toward Billy, it turns out that Todd's new attitude is far more appropriate than the one it replaced.

We must be careful to *avoid* imagining that Irene induces Todd to adopt any *objectively* mistaken mental states, like a belief that Billy did something that he did not do. For that would make Irene's case one of straightforward manipulation, since she would have gotten Todd to adopt mental states that are both objectively faulty and believed faulty by Irene. Imagine instead that Irene's tactics involve focusing Todd's attention on *actual* instances of contemptuous behavior by Billy and insinuating that they are signs of contempt—which they *are*—and getting Todd to feel emotions that are *appropriate* for someone who has been treated contemptuously. Thus, we must imagine Irene *only* inducing Todd to adopt mental states and attitudes that Irene regards as mistaken but which, objectively speaking, are not mistaken at all.

Now consider an example of the second kind of problem case, where **S** is objectively mistaken, but **N** regards it as non-mistaken:

> ***Aunt Vicky and Vaccines:*** Aunt Vicky is fearful of vaccines. She is not a full-fledged vaccine skeptic, but she fixates on the rare adverse events associated with vaccines so that they loom far larger in her thinking than is rational given their rarity. Because she lacks experience with diseases like polio, measles, and diphtheria, she fails to appreciate the dangers of refusing the vaccines against them. Consequently, she has developed an irrational—but sincere—*fear* of the vaccines against these serious illnesses. Vicky tries to get others—including Cousin Carl—to share these fears. Vicky's efforts result in Carl acquiring an irrational fear of vaccines. This fear is objectively mistaken, but Vicky believes that it is appropriate.

Did Irene manipulate Todd? Did Aunt Vicky manipulate Carl? I would not expect people to have clear, strong, and uniform intuitions about these cases. Thus, determining what to say about them is not simply a matter of reverse-engineering our initial, intuitive reactions to them. Instead, my plan is to work out the most sensible thing for the Mistake Account to say about them, given its own internal logic and, especially, the analogies that it draws between manipulation on the one hand, and lying and deception on the other. We have already seen how the Mistake Account properly identifies manipulation in all the paradigm examples of manipulation from Chapter 2, and how it does so without running afoul of the Dual Use Phenomenon. We have also seen that no other account of manipulation does these things. Consequently, it seems reasonable to let the Mistake Account guide our judgments about cases where our initial intuitions are less clear and less uniform than the intuitions that guided our development of that account. In other words, we can rely on the Mistake Account's claim that manipulation resembles lying or deception to give a principled answer to the Perspective Question.

5.3. Lying, Deception, and Manipulation

The Mistake Account draws a parallel between manipulation on one hand and lying and deception on the other. All three of these forms of influence involve getting the target to make a mistake.

However, one important *difference* between deception and lying is that 'deceive' implies *success* in changing the target's belief, while 'lie' does not. Consider this case:

> ***Candy in the Cupboard, Part I:*** Tim, Larry, and Dora all correctly believe that there is candy in the cupboard. Larry and Dora also believe that if Tim *continues* to believe that there is candy in the cupboard, he will devour it all before they get any. Consequently, Larry and Dora both want to make Tim believe (falsely) that there is *no* candy in the cupboard. Larry flat-out lies, saying, "There is no candy in the cupboard." Dora, however, does not want to lie outright, so she resorts to "mere" deception. In Tim's presence, she walks to the cupboard, makes an ostentatious show of searching about, and then makes the following true but deceptive statements: "I really wish we had some candy. Maybe I will buy some next time I go to the store." Larry and Dora both intend to cause Tim to acquire a false belief that there is no candy in the cupboard. But their efforts fail, and Tim retains his belief that there is candy in the cupboard.

It would be correct, if a bit stilted, to say:

(1) **Larry lied to Tim about the cupboard's contents, but Tim nevertheless continued to believe that it contains candy.**

A more natural and less stilted way to say the same thing would be to say:

(2) **Larry lied to Tim, but Tim didn't fall for it.**

But it would be odd to say:

*(3) **Dora deceived Tim, but Tim didn't fall for it.**

Instead, we would say:

(4) **Dora *tried to deceive* Tim, but Tim didn't fall for it.**

In short, I cannot be said to have *deceived* you unless I *succeeded* in getting you to believe something false. If I believe that P is false and try to get you to believe P, but you nevertheless do not come to believe P, then I have merely *tried* to deceive you. But if I lie to you, telling you that P is true when I believe it to be false, then even if you do not come to believe P, I have still *lied* to you.

What about manipulation? Consider this case:

> ***Snow Flurries I*****:** Tim is trying to decide whether to attend a party this evening that Maddie does not want him to attend. Maddie sees that the weather forecast predicts light snow flurries, but no accumulation. Maddie relays this information to Tim, but she deliberately makes the forecast seem worse than it is. For example, she reports the prediction as "snow" rather than "snow flurries," and leaves out the part about no accumulation being expected. She then ominously recounts graphic tales of accidents on slippery roads. She does this to make Tim excessively afraid of driving tonight, so that he will not attend the party.

Suppose, however, that Maddie fails to make Tim too afraid to drive to the party. We would not say:

*(5) **Maddie manipulated Tim, but Tim didn't fall for it.**

Instead, we would say:

(6) **Maddie *tried to* manipulate Tim, but Tim didn't fall for it.**

So, the term 'manipulate' seems to operate like the term 'deceive' in that both imply success in changing the target's state of mind in the way that the influencer intended. This finding is hardly earth-shattering on its own. But it does suggest that, linguistically and conceptually, the term 'manipulate' is closer to the term 'deceive' than to the term 'lie.' This suggests that if we want to develop the Mistake Account's parallel between one of those two other concepts, we should pursue the parallel with 'deceive' rather than the parallel with 'lie.'

5.4. Deception, Manipulation, and Another Kind of Failure

An attempt at deception fails if the would-be deceiver fails to get the target to believe what the would-be deceiver thinks is false. If Dora believes that the cupboard contains candy, and she tries to get Tim to believe that the cupboard is devoid of candy, then her attempt at deception fails if Tim does not come to believe that the cupboard is devoid of candy.

But there is another, more complicated way that an attempt at deception can fail. Consider this next chapter in our candy saga:

> ***Candy in the Cupboard, Part II:*** Larry suspects that Tim did not fall for his lie or Dora's attempted deception. Since he remains concerned that Tim will devour

all the candy, Larry removes it from the cupboard. Dora does not know that Larry removed the candy, so she still believes (falsely, now) that there is candy in the cupboard. However, like Larry, Dora suspects that Tim did not fall for the lie or attempted deception. Since she still wants to prevent Tim from devouring the candy that she mistakenly believes to be in the cupboard, Dora tries once more to get Tim to believe that there is no candy in the cupboard. "Dammit!" she exclaims, after making another show of searching the cupboard, "I really wish we had some candy." This time, however, Dora's ruse causes Tim to believe that the cupboard is devoid of candy. But this belief turns out—unbeknownst to Dora—to be true.

This time, Dora succeeded in getting Tim to believe something which Dora *thought* was false, but which, in reality, was *true*. That being the case, it would seem odd to say:

*(7) **Dora deceived Tim into believing that the cupboard is devoid of candy.**

The reason this sounds odd, of course, is that Dora got Tim to believe something that was objectively *true*. It seems odd to say that one person deceived another into believing that P when P turns out to be true. Thus, it seems to be a necessary condition for *being deceived about P* that one acquired a belief about P that really is false, and not merely believed to be false by the would-be deceiver. Hence, there appears to be an *objective* standard for *being deceived about P*: One can only be deceived about P if one acquires an objectively false belief about P.

Before moving on, we should address a slight complication. Although Dora did not deceive Tim about the contents of the cupboard, she probably did deceive him about something else—the content of her own mind. But this is a different matter. For even if Dora succeeded in making Tim acquire a false belief *about Dora's beliefs* (i.e., that Dora believed that the cupboard was devoid of candy), Dora did not succeed in making Tim acquire a false belief *about the contents of the cupboard*. Hence, she did not deceive Tim *about the contents of the cupboard*. To avoid making the text needlessly cumbersome, I will stipulate that, unless otherwise specified, when I talk about the belief that the deceiver wants the target to acquire, I mean a belief about the state of the world and not a belief about what the would-be deceiver believes.

5.5. Deceiving versus Acting Deceptively

So, we would *not* say that Dora *deceived* Tim about the contents of the cupboard when the proposition that Dora got Tim to believe turned out—unbeknownst to

Dora—to be *true*. But our reluctance to say that Dora deceived Tim in this case is not a moral free pass for Dora. She *tried* to deceive Tim, even though she did not succeed. The actual contents of the cupboard do not change the fact that she *intended* to get Tim to have a false belief. Accordingly, we might say that Dora *acted (or behaved) deceptively* toward Tim. This accusation is based on Dora's *belief* that the proposition she wanted Tim to believe was false, and not on whether it was actually false. Thus, we employ an *influencer-subjective* standard for whether someone *acted* or *behaved deceptively*. That is, whether **N** acted deceptively depends on **N**'s beliefs about what is true and what is false.

Thus, there is an asymmetry: To determine whether an influencer *acted deceptively*, we ask whether *the influencer believed* that the relevant proposition was false. But to determine whether someone has been *deceived*, we ask whether the relevant proposition *really was false*. Tim was deceived (about the contents of the cupboard) only if what he came to believe really was false. But Dora acted deceptively only if she tried to get Tim to believe something that she, Dora, believed to be false.

The existence of such an asymmetry may seem puzzling. Why do we employ an objective standard for whether a person was deceived, but a subjective standard for whether someone acted deceptively? The answer is that the asymmetry reflects two related but distinct concerns about deception.[2] One concern is the badness of acquiring a false belief. Since belief aims at truth, believing falsely is a kind of failure. Sometimes this failure is the fault of the believer. Sometimes it is no one's fault at all. But when a false belief is the deliberate work of another person, it takes on a special character that goes beyond a simple failure. To deceive someone is to inflict a false belief upon that person. It turns the other person into a victim, someone who is not merely foolish, but someone who has been made a fool of. Thus, someone who is deceived suffers a complex misfortune that combines the failure of believing falsely with the victimization of having that failure deliberately inflicted.

Now this more *complex* misfortune—being *tricked* into adopting a false belief—happens *only* when the person has been gotten to believe something that *really is false*. It makes sense to have a label for that misfortune. And so we do: We call it 'being deceived.' It is a bad thing that only happens to someone who *really is tricked* into believing something that *really is false*. Although this label only applies when the misfortune is the result of another person's deliberate behavior, its emphasis is nevertheless on what happens to the victim of deception.

[2] The distinction here is similar to one that Bernard Williams (2004) draws between the values of accuracy and sincerity. Williams claims that these values reflect distinct concerns about the truth. Roughly, accuracy is our concern with having true beliefs, and sincerity is our concern that people avoid asserting what they believe to be false.

A second concern about deception is the behavior of the deceiver. If being deceived is a misfortune, then it is presumptively immoral to attempt to inflict that misfortune upon someone.[3] This is true whether or not the attempt succeeds. When we criticize someone for attempting to deceive, that is, for *acting deceptively*, we focus on what the influencer did rather than on what happened to the target. In particular, we focus on the presumptive immorality of intending to get someone to adopt a false belief. But whether this presumptively immoral intention exists depends *not* on whether the relevant proposition *really was* false, but on whether the influencer *believed* it to be false. Consequently, *acting deceptively* is a presumptively immoral behavior that occurs when the influencer tries to trick the target into believing a proposition that the *influencer believes* is false. The influencer-subjective standard for 'acting deceptively' or 'trying to deceive' reflects this concern with the intentions of the deceptive person.

Thus, the asymmetry between the objective standard for 'deceived,' and the influencer-subjective standard for 'acted deceptively,' reflects the fact that sometimes we want to emphasize the objective misfortune that has befallen the deceived person, and sometimes we want to emphasize the subjective bad intention of the person who has acted deceptively.

5.6. Manipulating versus Acting Manipulatively

It seems reasonable to have a similar pair of related but distinct concerns about manipulation: We care about the misfortune of being tricked into making a mistake in how we feel, what we pay attention to, our confidence in our own judgments, our reactions to incentives and disincentives, etc. This concern is with what happens to the target of manipulation, and it applies only when the target is induced to make what *really is* a mistake. We are also concerned with the *intention* to get someone to make a mistake. That intention remains presumptively immoral even if the person trying to induce the mistake is wrong about it being a mistake.[4]

This parallel between deception and manipulation suggests an *objective* standard for *being manipulated* and an *influencer-subjective* standard for *acting manipulatively*. Accordingly, we should *not* say that Todd was manipulated. Despite Irene's efforts, Todd made no mistake. In fact, his overall state of mind became less mistaken because of Irene's influence. Thus, Todd did not suffer the misfortune of having been induced to make a mistake. He did not suffer this misfortune because,

[3] To say that something is "presumptively" immoral is just to say that it is immoral unless justified in some way. For example, an action like shoving someone is presumptively immoral, even though there are situations in which it is morally justified, such as when shoving someone is the only way to save that person from being hit by a truck. The various ways that something can be presumptively immoral are discussed in more detail in Chapter 9.

[4] These ideas will be developed in more detail in section 9.8.

objectively, Todd's attitude toward Billy became *less* mistaken. Since the Mistake Account identifies manipulation with being induced to make a mistake, it should deny that Todd has suffered the misfortune of having been manipulated.

But Irene deserves blame even though Todd escaped the misfortune that Irene tried to inflict on him. He escaped this misfortune because of Irene's own mistake. The fact that Irene's mistake allowed Todd to avoid the misfortune of having been induced to make a mistake does not get Irene off the hook, morally speaking. Her attempt to inflict this misfortune upon Todd is subject to moral criticism even though—unbeknownst to her—it resulted in Todd having an objectively *more appropriate* attitude toward Billy. The fact that Irene was wrong about the appropriateness of the feelings she induced in Todd does not make Irene any less blameworthy for acting with bad intent, that is, for *trying* to inflict a misfortune upon Todd. Irene acted manipulatively because her *intent* was to induce Todd to make a mistake. It seems proper to conclude that while Todd was definitely *influenced* by Irene, and while Irene *acted manipulatively* toward Todd, Todd was, nevertheless, *not manipulated*. Irene's attempt at manipulation failed—though not for the usual reason that such attempts fail.

What about Vicky? Certainly, her conduct is far from ideal. Her critical thinking is deficient—perhaps culpably so—and the irrational fear she spreads may induce people to make harmful decisions. We can rightly accuse her of recklessly spreading irrational fears. But the fact that Vicky's behavior is deficient in *some* respects does not make it deficient in *every* respect. In particular, Vicky's intention was *not* to inflict a *mistaken* fear on Carl, for she is sincere in her fear and does not regard it as mistaken.

To determine what to say about Vicky and Carl, it will be helpful to return to the analogy between manipulation and deception. Consider this case:

Highway Mix-up: Sincere Sally falsely believes that Interstate Highway 75 North goes to Chicago. Driver Dan asks her how to get to Chicago. Sally tells him, sincerely but mistakenly, that taking I-75 North will get him to Chicago. Driver Dan believes her, and thus acquires a false belief.

Sally might have committed some sort of epistemic sin, but she did not *act deceptively*, for she did not *try* to get Dan to make a mistake. Her sincerity is a defense against the charge of having acted deceptively. Similarly, regardless of the epistemic sins of which Vicky may be guilty, she did not *try* to get Carl to make a mistake. If we follow the parallel between manipulation and deception, we should regard Vicky's sincerity as a defense against the charge that she acted manipulatively.

So, Irene acted manipulatively, but Todd was not manipulated. Vicky did not act manipulatively. What about Carl? Was Carl manipulated?

Carl's situation is trickier. Vicky's influence caused him to adopt a mistaken fear. But it was not Vicky's intention to get Carl to make a *mistake*, for she regards the fear as reasonable. Carl's situation parallels Dan's situation. If we think of deception as something that is done intentionally, then, strictly speaking, we should not say that Dan was deceived. If *being deceived* names the misfortune of being *deliberately* induced to make a mistake (i.e., believing something false), then the parallel between deception and manipulation suggests that *being manipulated* should also name the misfortune of being *deliberately* induced to make a mistake. Just as we should not say that Dan was deceived, we should *not* say that Carl was manipulated. The fear that Carl acquired was mistaken, but Vicky did *not* intend for Carl to acquire a *mistaken* fear. Vicky attempted to get him to adopt *what she sincerely regarded* as an appropriate fear. She was *not acting manipulatively* because she was *not trying to get Carl to make a mistake*. Consequently, it would be best to say that Carl was mistaken but not manipulated.

Here, though, I suspect that some people's intuitions will differ, both about whether we should say that Dan was deceived, and about whether we should say that Carl was manipulated. So far, my strategy has been to suggest filling in the under-developed parts of the Mistake Account's notion of manipulation in ways that parallel our concept of deception. This strategy relies on the fact that our intuitions about deception are relatively well-behaved, i.e., strong, clear, and widely shared. But here we reach a point, I think, where our intuitions *about deception* are less well-behaved.

I think that the most common thing to say about the ***Highway Mix-up*** case is that Dan was not deceived because Sally did not act deceptively. That is why I contend that we should not say that Carl was manipulated because Vicky did not act manipulatively. But some readers may have different intuitions about what we should say about Dan. While I would prefer not to say that Sally deceived Dan, saying that Dan *was* deceived is not *grossly* incorrect, given that Sally did, in fact, cause him to have a false belief. Although the view that one is deceived only if one is *deliberately* gotten to believe something false seems to be dominant among philosophers, it is certainly not universal.[5]

Moreover, in ordinary conversation, we sometimes speak of a person being deceived by an inanimate object, when no intention to deceive was present. For example, it is neither incomprehensible nor obviously wrong to say that a driver was deceived by black ice. But perhaps we can treat such statements as metaphorical: It is *as though* the black ice was trying to deceive the driver. We tend to use such metaphors when either or both of these conditions are met: (1) the object was deliberately designed to induce a false belief, as when a trap has been deliberately camouflaged, or (2) the object is especially likely to induce a false belief, as with black ice. In the first kind of case, we can call the object deceptive in a *derivative* sense because it is an expression or effect of someone's intent to induce a false

[5] See Mahon (2016, 40–41) for discussion and references.

belief. The second kind of case is more properly seen as *metaphorical* (personification, to be precise). Notice that it would seem odd to describe something as deceptive if neither condition were met, even if, for some reason, the object caused someone to have a false belief. For example, it would seem odd to say that a clearly visible stop sign is deceptive simply because I failed to notice it.

If we treat the claim that an inanimate object like black ice is deceptive by treating it as a metaphorical claim that it is *as if* the object was trying to deceive, then perhaps we should say something similar when a *person* accidentally or unintentionally causes another to have a false belief: Insofar as Sally caused Dan to acquire a false belief, in certain respects it is *as though* Sally was trying to deceive him. Just as a driver might lament his false belief by claiming that he was "deceived by the black ice," so Dan might lament his false belief by saying that he was "deceived by Sally."

Thus, we can make sense of why some people might want to say that Dan was deceived, and why the rest of us can readily understand such a claim. We can treat this as a sort of metaphorical use of the term 'deceived.' However, while such usage is comprehensible, it is potentially misleading since it does not wear its metaphorical nature on its sleeve. Thus, we should recommend that anyone who describes someone in Dan's situation as having been deceived should make it clear that he was *accidentally* or *unintentionally* deceived.[6]

Similarly, we might treat the claim that Carl was manipulated as metaphorical: Insofar as Vicky's influence caused him to acquire a mistaken fear, in certain respects it was *as though* Vicky was trying to manipulate him. Here again, while such usage is comprehensible, and perhaps even tempting, it is potentially misleading because it creates the false impression that Vicky *intended* to trick Carl into acquiring a mistaken fear. Carl may have suffered the misfortune of acquiring a mistaken fear, but he did not suffer the indignity of someone deliberately tricking him. Still, we can understand why some people might want to say that Carl was manipulated, and why the rest of us can make sense of such a claim. But we can also recommend that anyone who describes someone in Carl's situation as having been manipulated should make it clear that he was *accidentally* or *unintentionally* manipulated.

This analysis addresses certain puzzling cases that have arisen in discussions of the Perspective Question. Consider, for example Anne Barnhill's case, ***Guilt Trip***, in which Mike induces in Janice a level of guilt which Mike thinks appropriate, but which many people would regard as inappropriate. Barnhill notes that such people might be "inclined to call Mike's behavior manipulation, since Mike makes Janice feel what they judge to be an inappropriate amount of guilt" (Barnhill 2014, 67). Jason Hanna offers a structurally similar case called ***Racist Candidate***, in which a

[6] Seana Shiffrin (2019) argues, persuasively, that unintended deception can sometimes be negligent, and develops an interesting account of when and why that is the case.

candidate plays on the racist fears of the voters—fears that readers will presumably regard as objectively inappropriate. However, the candidate believes that these fears are appropriate. Hanna writes that "perhaps the candidate has not *attempted* to manipulate the voters, but there is a strong case that the voters have nonetheless been manipulated" (Hanna 2015, 633, emphasis original).

Both cases are structurally similar to ***Aunt Vicky and Vaccines***, which is, in turn, similar to ***Highway Mix-up***. The Mistake Account claims that Mike and the racist candidate are not acting manipulatively. They are not trying to induce any mistakes, since they do not regard what they are trying to induce as mistakes. This corresponds to what we say about Sally: She does not act deceptively because she does not regard the belief she is trying to impart to Dan as mistaken.

If we speak strictly, so that being manipulated only occurs when an *attempt* to manipulate succeeds, then we should say that neither the voters nor Janice are manipulated. While this may seem odd, it is no odder than saying that, speaking very strictly, Dan is not deceived by Sally, since Sally was not *trying* to get him to believe something false.

Of course, we need not, and often do not, speak quite so strictly. We sometimes say, speaking loosely and metaphorically, that Sally deceived Dan, to mean that Sally *unintentionally* got Dan to believe something false. Likewise, we can say, speaking loosely and metaphorically, that Vicky manipulated Carl, the racist candidate manipulated the voters, and Mike manipulated Janice. When we say these things, we mean that Vicky, the candidate, and Mike *unintentionally* got Carl, the voters, and Janice to make mistakes. This metaphorical sense of the terms 'deceived' and 'manipulated' draws attention to the fact that *what happened to the targets* resembles what happens to targets of full-blooded, intentional deception and manipulation.

5.7. Contested Mistakes

The Mistake Account's parallel between manipulation and deception also helps us decide what to say in cases where there is no consensus about whether something is a mistake. Often, discussions about manipulation take place against a background where it is possible to settle the question of what is and what is not a mistake. But sometimes this is not possible. In cases of moral and political influence, for example, the question of what is and is not a mistake may be contested, and there may be no clear way to settle it.

For example, suppose that an anti-abortion activist tries to get others to adopt the same level of empathy toward human embryos as they feel toward human newborns. Suppose, further, that the activist believes that embryos *are* persons, and thus that it is *appropriate* to feel the same level of empathy toward embryos and newborns. Since the activist does not regard it as a mistake to feel the same empathy toward embryos and newborns, the Mistake Account will say that the activist has not acted manipulatively, since she is not trying to induce a mistake. Consequently, if we speak very strictly, anyone whom the activist successfully influences is not manipulated. But what if we wish to speak a bit less strictly, in the way that we did when discussing cases like ***Aunt Vicky and Vaccines***? This question is more challenging than the corresponding question about Aunt Vicky. This is because the question of whether it is a mistake to empathize with embryos is less amenable to being settled even by those who accept the same set of empirical facts than, say, the question of whether it is a mistake to fear the measles vaccine. Consequently, reasonable people might disagree about whether those whom the activists successfully induce to feel empathy toward embryos really have made a genuine mistake. Thus, they will disagree about whether those successfully influenced have been manipulated in the looser, metaphorical sense of the word.

At first glance, this may seem odd. But it is no odder than what we say in similar cases of deception. If our activist simply *asserts* that embryos are persons, and if the listener accepts the assertion as true, was the listener deceived? In the strictest sense, the answer is no, because the activist did not *try* to induce a *false* belief. But what about the looser, metaphorical sense of 'deceived'? Answering this question presumes an answer to the contested question of whether embryos are persons. And here we see, yet again, the parallel between manipulation and deception: Whether the metaphorical sense of both 'manipulated' and 'deceived' applies depends, in both cases, on the truth of propositions whose truth is contested. The possibility of such cases does not make our concept of deception unacceptable. Consequently, there is no reason to think that similar cases make the Mistake Account's understanding of the concept of manipulation unacceptable.

5.8. Manipulation, Intention, and Mens Rea

Answering the Perspective Question tells us something about the state of mind that one must have to be properly described as acting manipulatively: One must regard what one is trying to induce in the other person as a mistake. But what else, if anything, must be in a person's mind if that person is to be properly described as acting manipulatively? What sort of intention must be present? Must a person who is acting manipulatively recognize the manipulative character of the behavior? Must manipulators think of what they are doing *as manipulation*?

Fortunately, we do not need to start from scratch in answering these questions. In a 2014 paper, Marcia Baron discusses these matters and offers a persuasive account of the state of mind required for a person to be engaged in manipulation. I will use her discussion as a starting point. Baron begins by reiterating two claims from her 2003 paper, namely, that "manipulation requires intent," but that it "does not require that one knows one is manipulating or being manipulative" (Baron

2014, 100–101).[7] Consequently, "one can manipulate another without realizing at the time that one is doing so" (Baron 2014, 102, n. 9). To support this claim, Baron offers this example:

> Suppose you agree to do something because you are nervous around the person who requested it, eager not to displease her, and fearful that you will displease her if you decline her request. You may feel you have no real choice. This seems to me not yet to be a case of manipulation. What is missing is her intent to get you to do what she wants and . . . to do so by taking advantage of your eagerness not to disappoint her (perhaps also cultivating it, or speaking in a way that feeds your fear of her disapproval or rejection). She may not need to know that it is her intent to get you to do what she wants, but it has to be the case that it is. Otherwise, she is not manipulating you. (Baron 2014, 101)

This seems correct. While the recipient of the request may feel unable to decline, this is not the deliberate work of the requestor. Nor has the requestor done anything to make the request more difficult to decline. Someone who is eager not to disappoint may well choose akratically to agree to a request even though doing so is worse than disappointing the requestor. But if the requestor does nothing to try to induce such a mistake, it seems incorrect to say that the requestor has acted manipulatively. The fact that I might react mistakenly to what you do seems insufficient, by itself, to ground an accusation that you acted manipulatively.

5.9. The Content of the Intention

So it seems correct to say that acting manipulatively requires some sort of intent. But this does not tell us *what*, exactly, the person acting manipulatively must intend.

The most obvious suggestion would be to say that acting manipulatively requires the intent to manipulate. That is, we might say that Marvin acts manipulatively toward Tony only if Marvin intends *to manipulate Tony*. Baron rejects this suggestion: "Should we say that one must intend to manipulate the other? No, at least not under that description. That would unduly limit what can count as manipulation" (Baron 2014, 103). Baron gives no examples of how this suggestion would "unduly limit" what counts as manipulation, but it is easy enough to see what she might have in mind.

If we require a manipulator to intend *to manipulate*, that is, to think of what they are doing *as manipulation*, then it would be impossible for someone who lacks the

[7] She initially expresses less certainty about the second claim, but eventually re-endorses it.

concept of manipulation to act manipulatively. But it seems obvious that a person can act manipulatively without having the concept of manipulation. Perhaps very young children cannot be said to act manipulatively. But it seems reasonable to think that a child can act manipulatively before acquiring the *concept* of manipulation. Moreover, on this suggestion, merely refusing to recognize one's behavior as manipulative would render one immune from accusations of acting manipulatively. This problem is especially serious because the term 'manipulation' carries a sense of moral criticism. Since most people want to avoid moral criticism, those who act manipulatively have good reason to avoid thinking of their attempts to influence *as manipulation*. If we say that one manipulates only if one thinks of what one is doing *as manipulation*, then one could render one's manipulation morally innocent simply by refusing to think of it as manipulation. This cannot be correct. An influence does not cease to be manipulative, or cease to be morally blameworthy, simply because the influencer refuses to think of it that way.

So it seems that we should say that manipulation must be done intentionally, but that we should not require the manipulator to think of the intended behavior *as manipulation*. What, then, should we say about the content of the intention necessary for a person to be acting manipulatively? Here is Baron's suggestion:

> So maybe this: to lead the other to do x, and to lead the other to do so by ____ [and here we would sketch methods the agent might employ, which would in fact be manipulative]? (Baron 2014, 103)

On this proposal, the intent required for manipulation would be the intent to get someone to do what one wants, by some means. That is, the manipulator must have some sense of how to get the target to do what the manipulator wants. After all, "getting someone to do **A**" is not like raising one's arm, i.e., something that one simply *does*. Instead, it is more like getting a kite out of a tree, i.e., something that one cannot do without some plan for *how* one will do it, e.g., climbing the tree, using a pole to knock the kite down, etc. In other words, getting someone to do A is not a basic action. Rather, it is something that one does *by* doing something else—like making the other person angry, or offering an incentive, or getting the other person to believe a certain thing, etc.

But Baron's suggestion also requires that the means by which the manipulator intends to get the target to do a certain thing must be, in fact, manipulative, even if the manipulator does not think of it that way. Applied to the Mistake Account, this proposal would be that the manipulator must intend to get the target to do what the manipulator wants by inducing the target to make (what the manipulator regards as) a mistake. On Baron's proposal, the manipulator need not think of the action as manipulation. I think that we should go a step further and say that the manipulator need not even consciously think of the action as attempting to get the target to make a mistake.

5.10. The Minimum Conditions for Acting Manipulatively

If we hold that the manipulator need not think consciously: "I shall manipulate that fellow" or even "I shall get that fellow to make a mistake," then what must be true of the manipulator's state of mind? And how can we square this looseness in what we require of the manipulator's mental state with our earlier claim that acting manipulatively is defined in terms of what the manipulator thinks is a mistake?

Let's begin with the first question: What are the minimum conditions on the influencer's state of mind necessary for that person to count as acting manipulatively? To answer this question, it may help to imagine manipulation by someone with just enough cognitive sophistication to be acting manipulatively. Accordingly, let us consider the elementary-aged children from the American animated holiday special, *A Charlie Brown Thanksgiving* (Melendez and Roman 1973).[8] Charlie Brown is a timid, indecisive, and insecure child often described as "wishy-washy." His grandmother will be hosting his family's Thanksgiving dinner at her home. A day or so before Thanksgiving, his friend Peppermint Patty calls, and the following dialogue occurs:

PEPPERMINT PATTY: Listen, I really have a treat for you. My dad's been called out of town. He said I can go to your house and share Thanksgiving with you, Chuck.
CHARLIE BROWN: Well, I, uh . . .
PEPPERMINT PATTY: I don't mind inviting myself over because I know you kind of like me, Chuck.
CHARLIE BROWN: Well, I, uh . . .
PEPPERMINT PATTY: Okay, that's a date. See you soon, you sly devil.

Since Charlie Brown is not planning to host Thanksgiving dinner, he surely knows that he should tell Peppermint Patty that she is not invited to dinner. Why doesn't he? Peppermint Patty puts him on the spot. To prevent her from showing up at a non-existent dinner, he must do more than simply not inviting her. He must endure the immediate social awkwardness of interrupting and then contradicting her to rescind an invitation whose existence she has just asserted. Moreover, Charlie Brown is "wishy washy"—insecure and unassertive—and this makes it harder for him to endure that social awkwardness. These factors explain why Charlie Brown makes the akratic choice not to dis-invite Peppermint Patty, despite knowing that it will be worse overall if she shows up to a non-existent Thanksgiving dinner.

But should we say that Peppermint Patty acts manipulatively? That depends on her state of mind. We can certainly attribute to her the intention to get herself invited to Thanksgiving dinner, as well as the intention to do this by inviting

[8] The main characters appear to be around eight years old, though they are portrayed as being somewhat more cognitively sophisticated than typical children of that age.

herself to dinner. But that is not quite enough for it to be true that she acts manipulatively. Something more is needed, though it is something that she might not have consciously in mind when she acts. Consider this bit of dialog, near the end of the story, between Peppermint Patty and her friend Marcy (who often calls Peppermint Patty "sir"):

MARCY: Now, wait a minute, sir. Did he invite you here to dinner or did you invite yourself and us too?

PEPPERMINT PATTY: Gee, I never thought of it like that. Do you think I hurt old Chuck's feelings? I bet I hurt his feelings, huh? Golly, why can't I act right outside of a baseball game?

Marcy gets Peppermint Patty to see something about inviting herself that she did not see before. We can interpret the story in two different ways here. On the interpretation that is probably closer to the writers' intentions, Peppermint Patty realizes that Charlie Brown was not planning to host Thanksgiving dinner, and that he only agreed to do so because she invited herself. Marcy's question helps her see that it was precisely her inviting herself that made it difficult for Charlie Brown to undo the invitation. On this interpretation, Peppermint Patty realizes *after the fact* that she got Charlie Brown to make a mistake—failing to rescind her self-invitation. That is, she only realizes after the fact that inviting herself made it difficult for him to un-invite her. Perhaps, at the time, she really did assume that she would be invited, given her belief that Charlie Brown likes her. She may even have thought of herself as saving the notoriously shy Charlie Brown the trouble of asking her to attend by simply confirming an invitation that she assumed Charlie Brown wanted to offer. In this interpretation of the story, it does not seem quite right to say that Peppermint Patty *acts manipulatively*. Rather, she does something closer to what Vicky does: she induces a mistake without intending to.[9] To her credit, Peppermint Patty regrets having done this once it is pointed out to her.

To see what else must be true for Peppermint Patty to have acted manipulatively, we must retell the story in a way that the writers probably did not intend. Suppose that Peppermint Patty thinks that Charlie Brown will not invite her to Thanksgiving dinner because his parents do not want extra guests, and he places great value on not upsetting his parents. Suppose that she also knows that, despite all this, Charlie Brown is so "wishy washy" that if she invites herself to dinner, he will not object. These beliefs do not need to be conscious in her mind when she invites herself to dinner. Indeed, some of them may be things that she only believes in some "deep down" sense. But her possession of these beliefs would mean that, from

[9] Consequently, we could say that, even in this interpretation of the story, Peppermint Patty manipulates Charlie Brown in the loose, metaphorical sense that does not require her to have tried to induce a mistake. But that is not the sense of 'manipulate' that we are investigating here.

her perspective, she would be trying to get Charlie Brown to make a mistake, to do something he knows he should not do.

I doubt that this version of the story is the one that the writers had in mind. But it helps us see the bare minimum of what a person must believe and intend in order to act manipulatively. When she invites herself to dinner, Peppermint Patty may only be thinking of this as a way to get invited to dinner. But if she knows—at least in some "deep down" sense—that inviting herself to dinner is something that will likely get Charlie Brown to make a mistake, then she fulfills the minimum conditions for acting manipulatively.

Peppermint Patty's case is complicated partly because she is a child, and partly because akratic mistakes are more subtle than mistakes like inappropriate emotions. So let us consider briefly how what we have said would apply to a case of manipulation that involves trickery rather than pressure. Consider again Iago and Othello. At various points in the play, Iago tries to make Othello suspicious of Desdemona. He does this deliberately, and so we would expect him to have a conscious intention to make Othello suspicious of Desdemona. Now, it does not seem too farfetched to imagine Iago becoming so engrossed in his machinations that he is not always thinking consciously to himself that the suspicions he is trying to arouse are misplaced. It seems correct to say that, *even when this happens*, Iago is still acting manipulatively. Indeed, it seems *incorrect* to say that he *ceases* to act manipulatively whenever the thought that Othello has no reason to be suspicious fades from his conscious awareness. Thus, we should *not* say that Iago *only* acts manipulatively when his suspicion-mongering is accompanied by the *conscious* thought that the suspicion is unwarranted. What must be true instead, is that from his perspective, the suspicion *is* unwarranted. And this can be true even if some of the beliefs that make up his perspective are not within the field of his conscious attention while he is acting.

Although this example is in some ways simpler than that of Peppermint Patty, it raises a subtle worry that the Peppermint Patty example does not. What we have just said about Iago may seem to break the parallel between manipulation and deception—a parallel that has guided us throughout this chapter. We normally define 'acting deceptively' in terms of what the deceiver *believes* to be false and not "what is false *from the deceiver's perspective*." Aren't we imposing a looser condition on *acting manipulatively* than we do on *acting deceptively*? What justifies this difference given the stress we have placed on keeping the concepts of deception and manipulation harnessed together so tightly?

Fortunately, this difference is less substantial than it might initially seem. With deception, one seeks to get someone to believe some proposition. But when we call a proposition to mind, it is common for us to also call to mind whatever judgment we have made as to its truth or falsity. If D tries to get T to believe that P, it is natural for D to have in mind not only the intention to get T to believe that P, but also D's judgment about whether P is true or false. Consequently, it is difficult to imagine a case where D tries to get T to believe that **P** without **D** having some conscious thought of whether **P** is true or false. Difficult, but not impossible. Consider this case:

> ***Deep Cover***: FBI Agent Donnie has infiltrated a criminal organization in Chicago. He has memorized his fictitious biography, and thoroughly practiced acting and conversing in ways appropriate to it. His college training in method acting helps him suppress his awareness that he is acting while he is in character. Although Donnie was born and raised in Chicago, his cover story is that he lived in Boston until moving to Chicago last year. During a casual conversation, a mobster remarks on Donnie's ability to navigate Chicago's surface streets, and asks him, "Are you sure you're not from here?" He answers, in his well-practiced Boston accent, "Do I *sound* like I'm from Chicago?" He gives this answer in character, without any conscious thought that, in reality, he *is* from Chicago.

Cases like this are probably rare for people who are not actors or undercover agents. But there is no reason to think that they are impossible. Moreover, if we ask whether Donnie acts deceptively, the answer is clearly "Yes." Consequently, it seems that the necessary mental condition for acting deceptively is not an explicit, conscious awareness of one's belief in the falsity of what one is trying to get the other person to believe. Donnie acts deceptively not because he is consciously aware that what he wants the mobster to believe is false. He acts deceptively because he *would* become consciously aware of this if he were to reflect on it. It's just that he has taught himself *not* to reflect on such things. To maintain the parallel with deception, we should say that someone engages in manipulation if that person has a mental state similar to the one that makes it the case that Donnie engages in deception.

It is tempting to characterize this mental state by way of a conditional. Thus, we might say that **M** must intend to get T to make what **M** *would regard* as a mistake *if **M** were* to reflect on it. Unfortunately, however, such conditionals have a way of getting out of hand and running amok.[10] Suppose that I believe that Jones is innocent of some crime that others attribute to him, so I stand up for Jones and encourage you to trust him. However, when I consider the matter more carefully, I put together several things I know and conclude that Jones probably *did* commit the crime of which he is accused. That is, my reflection on what I know about Jones causes me to draw the *new* conclusion—and form the *new belief*—that Jones probably committed the crime. Thus, I tried to get you to believe something that, *on reflection*, I *now* believe to be false. But it seems incorrect to say that I acted deceptively *or* manipulatively.

What we need is a way to specify **N**'s perspective on what is a mistake without requiring that **N** *consciously* believes that it is a mistake *at the time of acting*, and *without* counting **N** as regarding something as a mistake just because **N** *would* come to see it that way *if* **N** worked out all the implications of what **N** already believes. We

[10] I am grateful to Thomas Douglas and Gabriel DeMarco for pointing out this problem.

need to distinguish what **N** *already* believes—even if **N** is not consciously aware of it—from new beliefs that **N** might *acquire* if **N** were to draw new conclusions from all the things that **N** already believes. The distinction we need is roughly the one that philosophers sometimes make between occurrent belief and dispositional belief, or between explicit belief and implicit or tacit belief.[11] Unfortunately, although philosophers often make this distinction, there is no well-developed consensus about how it should be made.

To avoid having to fill in this philosophical gap, I propose a workaround. Let us say that a person's "perspective" includes everything that the person *currently* believes, including beliefs not currently within that person's conscious awareness, such as their tacit, implicit, or dispositional beliefs. Thus, a person's perspective includes those beliefs of which the person could become immediately aware simply by considering whether the person believes a certain thing. But it does not include new beliefs that the person could form by engaging in conscious inferences from existing beliefs. We can now say that the manipulator seeks to induce the target to make what is, *from the manipulator's perspective*, a mistake. So, the manipulator need not be consciously aware of regarding it as a mistake; it simply must be true that, from the manipulator's perspective, it *is* a mistake.

This is not an unnatural way to use the term 'perspective.' It seems natural to say that, from *Donnie's* perspective—as opposed to his fictitious character's perspective—it is a mistake to think that he grew up in Boston. It's just that, in playing his role, he acts as though his perspective were other than it is. But this does not change what his actual perspective implies about whether he grew up in Chicago. We can say, then, that a person who acts manipulatively must intend to influence someone by doing something to induce in the target something that is, from the influencer's perspective, a mistake, whether or not the influencer is conscious of this. Since it is cumbersome to speak of "what is, from the influencer's perspective, a mistake, whether or not the influencer is conscious of this," I shall often say "what the influencer *regards as a mistake*," or "what is a mistake from the influencer's perspective." But I shall always mean these shorter statements as abbreviations for the longer one.

5.11. Conclusion

Having worked out what mental state a person must have if that person can be properly said to be acting manipulatively, we can now spell out the Mistake Account in more detail and with more precision. That will be the main task of the next chapter.

[11] See Schwitzgebel (2021) for an overview of the distinction(s), and see Lycan (1986) and Audi (1994) for two classic papers on the topic.

6
The Mistake Account
Definitions and Defense

6.1. Introduction

Chapter 4 introduced the Mistake Account, which characterizes manipulation as an influence that involves getting the target to make a mistake. Chapter 5 examined what mental state a person must have if it is proper to say that the person acts manipulatively. We are now in a position to work out a more formal definition of 'manipulation' and related terms. That is the first task of this chapter. Once this has been done, we will take stock of the cumulative case in favor of the Mistake Account. The chapter will conclude with a brief discussion of how the Mistake Account incorporates the best elements from rival accounts of manipulation.

6.2. Defining 'Acting Manipulatively'

In Chapter 5, I argued that 'acting manipulatively' is best treated as *attempting* to manipulate. It might seem sensible first to define 'manipulate,' and then to define 'acting manipulatively' as an attempt to manipulate. But I shall proceed in the opposite order, since some of the conditions on the mental state of the manipulator will be easier to formulate if we begin by thinking about when to say that a person acts manipulatively.

According to the Mistake Account, manipulation is a mistake-inducing influence. Thus, someone who tries to manipulate another person tries to influence that person by getting that person to make a mistake. Thus, as a first approximation, we might suggest:

(1) M acts manipulatively toward T if and only if M tries to influence T by getting T to make a mistake.

But this would be over-inclusive. Suppose that Marvin wants Tyler to sweat, so he reverses the numbers on the thermostat. This leads Tyler to mistakenly turn the heat up rather than down. According to (1) Marvin manipulated Tyler into sweating. This seems like an odd thing to say.

It would not be so odd, though, to say that Marvin manipulated Tyler into turning up the heat. So perhaps we should say that

Manipulation. Robert Noggle, Oxford University Press. © Robert Noggle 2025.
DOI: 10.1093/9780198924920.003.0006

(2) **M acts manipulatively toward T if and only if M tries to influence *T's actions* by getting T to make a mistake.**

This is narrower than (1), but it is a bit *too* narrow. Influences that seem aptly described as manipulation sometimes affect things besides actions. For example, the manipulative tactic of "tailgating" (see section 2.2.4) involves getting the target to hold open a door to a secure location *out of habit*. On some philosophical theories of action, this sort of habitual behavior might not count as an action, *per se*. It seems best to avoid definitions of manipulation that require taking a stand on contentious issues in action theory. It seems better, then, to say:

(3) **M acts manipulatively toward T if and only if M tries to influence *T's behavior* by getting T to make a mistake.**

In case it is not already clear, the word 'behavior' here is meant to include actions, as well as other forms of behavior that might not quite fit a certain definition of action. Nevertheless, (3) still seems a bit too restrictive. Manipulation often involves getting someone to *feel* a certain way or to *believe* a certain thing. Of course, this is often a means to getting the target to *behave* a certain way, as when Iago gets Othello to feel jealousy in order to get him to behave murderously. But sometimes the manipulator's main concern is with the mental state of the target, and not with any overt behavior.[1] Sometimes a manipulator may simply want the target to feel a certain way or believe a certain thing, without that being part of a larger plan to get the target to behave a certain way. Perhaps the manipulator's only or main goal is to get the target to love or respect the manipulator, or to be dependent on or subservient to the manipulator. Sometimes, a manipulator seeks to control the target's beliefs and feelings for no other reason than to have that control, so that changing the target's mental state is not a mere means to changing the target's behavior. Or the manipulator might intend to get the target to feel a certain way as a prelude to changing the target's behavior in some direction on which the manipulator has not yet decided. It seems best, then, to amend the previous proposal:

(4) **M acts manipulatively toward T if and only if M tries to influence T's behavior *or mental state* by getting T to make a mistake.**

This is better. But perhaps it would be better to be more precise about what it means to get T to make a mistake. The mistakes involved in manipulation occur in the target's head, so to speak. That is, they are mistakes that occur within the target's psychology. If you are swinging a hammer to strike a nail, and I bump your

[1] Kate Abramson observes that this is often the case in the more elaborate forms of gaslighting that she discusses (Abramson 2024, 51–60).

arm so that you miss, it is not too farfetched to say that I induced you to make a kind of mistake. Doing so might well change your mental state—it might make you angry, for example. But this is not the kind of mistake that seems to be required for manipulation. If I make you angry by bumping your arm so that you miss the nail you are trying to hit with the hammer, it would sound odd to say that I manipulated you. So we should specify that the mistake occurs within the psychological states or processes of the target. Hence:

> **(5) M acts manipulatively toward T if and only if M tries to influence T's behavior or mental state by causing *a mistake in T's psychological states or processes.***

However, (5) seems to suggest that there must always be two separate things: A mistake and a resulting behavior or mental state. Certainly, they often *are* separate things: The mistaken jealousy that Iago induces is distinct from the murderous actions that Iago hopes that the jealousy will get him to perform. But sometimes the mental state the manipulator seeks to elicit and the mistake that the manipulator seeks to induce are one and the same. This will often be the case in manipulation intended merely to get the target to believe a certain thing or feel a certain way, rather than to do a certain thing. Accordingly, we might modify (5) like so:

> **(6) M acts manipulatively toward T if and only if M tries to influence T's behavior or mental state by causing a mistake in T's psychological states or processes *(where the influence itself might constitute the mistake in T's psychological states or processes).***

This parenthetical makes it clear that the mistake and the influence do not have to be separate things. In the interests of brevity, however, I will suppress the parenthetical from now on, and treat its content as implicit in the formulations to follow.

I should also note that I regard it as implicit in statements like "**A** tries to make **X** happen by **Y**-ing" that **A** intends for **A**'s doing **Y** to play a role in making **X** happen. Thus, I mean for (6) and similar formulas to imply that **M** intends for the mistake to play a role in bringing about the influence on **T** that **M** is trying to achieve. Most often, the role will be causal, so that **M** means for the mistake to cause the changes to T's behavior or mental state that **M** wants to bring about. When the mistake and the influence are the same thing, then the mistake will play a conceptual role—that of identity—in bringing about the change that **M** wants.

One final issue about the mistakes mentioned in these formulae should be addressed. We are treating "**M** acts manipulatively toward **T**" as "**M** tries to manipulate **T**." As I argued in section 5.6, whether a person tries to manipulate depends on the influencer's perspective. But, as we noted in section 5.10, we should not require the manipulator to be consciously aware of this fact at the time of acting. Modifying (6) accordingly yeilds:

M acts manipulatively toward T if and only if M tries to influence T's behavior or mental state by causing *what is, from M's perspective,* a mistake in T's psychological states or processes.

I believe that with this statement, we have arrived at an adequate definition of 'acting manipulatively.' For brevity, I shall sometimes characterize **M**'s acting manipulatively toward **T** as **M** trying to induce **T** to make a mistake. This and similar statements should be understood as abbreviations for this more precise formula.

6.3. Indirect Manipulation and Pre-existing Mistakes

It is worth digressing briefly to note that a manipulator need not always induce a mistake directly. A manipulator might introduce into the target's mental states or processes something that is *not* a mistake, in order to cause something that *is* a mistake in those states or processes. Manipulators often use this indirect strategy when they wish to take advantage of a mistake that already exists in the target's mental states or processes.

To see how this might work, consider this version of a case we encountered in section 5.3:

Snow Flurries II: Tim is trying to decide whether to attend a party this evening that Maddie does not want him to attend. Maddie sees that the weather forecast predicts light snow flurries, but no accumulation. Maddie knows that Tim is irrationally fearful that snow flurries almost always turn into blizzards. While Tim is deciding whether to attend the party, Maddie reads the forecast verbatim. She does this to trigger Tim's irrational fear about snow flurries turning into blizzards, so that he becomes fearful of driving to the party.

Surely Maddie's behavior in ***Snow Flurries II*** is just as manipulative as it is in ***Snow Flurries I.*** But in ***Snow Flurries II***, Maddie exploits the fact that Tim *already* has a mistaken mental state—namely the irrational fear that snow flurries usually turn into blizzards. So, unlike in the original version, she does not exaggerate the weather forecast. Instead, she simply uses it to trigger Tim's *existing* mistake, namely his irrational fear that snow flurries usually turn into blizzards, to induce in Tim a *new* mistake, namely, an excessive fear that driving *tonight* will mean driving through a blizzard.

Such cases are likely to occur when a manipulator wishes to get the target to apply some pre-existing *general* mistake to a particular situation and thus to make a *new, more specific* mistake. Consider this case:

> ***Anger Mismanagement:*** Mark knows that Tony has a pathologically short temper. He wants to arrange an altercation between Tony and his neighbor Ned. Mark remembers that, when Tony first moved in, Ned complained to Mark about the loud music that Tony played while unloading his belongings. So Mark tells Tony this, being very careful not to exaggerate, embellish, or otherwise lead Tony to make any mistake *about the nature of Ned's remark*. But Tony's quick temper leads him to become extremely—and inappropriately—angry with Ned over this remark.

It seems clear that Mark manipulated Tony. But he did not induce a mistake directly. Rather, he got Tony to believe something which was not a mistake, but which would interact with Tony's mistakenly short temper to produce a new mistake—inappropriate anger at Ned.

Similar examples involve mistaken general beliefs. Consider this case:

> ***Inherited Guilt:*** Mark wants Trina to leave her boyfriend Lance. Mark knows that Trina has an irrational belief in inherited guilt, according to which each person is morally blameworthy for evils done by their ancestors. Mark also knows that one of Lance's great-great-great grandparents worked as an accountant for a firm connected with the Atlantic slave trade. Mark tells Trina this, and this causes Trina to loathe—and then leave—Lance.

Here again, Mark does not *directly* cause Trina to make a mistake. He merely informs Trina of something true. But he does this to get Trina to combine that truth with her *existing* mistaken belief in inherited guilt to induce in her a misplaced loathing for Lance.

A more complicated example of this phenomenon appears in Moti Gorin's ***Lucrative Suicide*** case (Gorin 2014a, 56) that we discussed in section 3.5: Jacques believes that God exists, but that if God did not exist, there would be no reason to go on living. Wanting to bring about Jacques's death, James provides Jacques with rational arguments against God's existence. These arguments cause Jacques to conclude that God does not exist. That conclusion, together with his belief that if God does not exist, there is no reason to go on living, leads him to commit suicide—just as James had planned.

It seems correct to say that James manipulates Jacques. As we saw in section 3.5, Gorin uses this case to argue that manipulation need not bypass reason, since James provides only good reasons for thinking that God does not exist. But the case also illustrates the indirect form of manipulation we are discussing here. For if we assume that James only offers objective, non-mistaken, non-distorted arguments against the existence of God, then he does not seem to induce Jacques to make a mistake *directly*. But those arguments, together with Jacques's mistaken belief that if God does not exist there is no reason to go on living, cause him to conclude that he lacks any reason to go on living. That *this* is a mistake is, I hope, self-evident.

6.4. Defining 'Manipulated'

Since 'acting manipulatively' is best seen as attempting to manipulate, we can define '**M** manipulated T' as a successful manipulative act. However, what counts as a successful manipulative act is more complicated than it may first appear because there are multiple ways for the would-be manipulator to fail, and a definition of 'manipulated' must rule out each one.

There are two obvious ways that an attempt at manipulation can fail. First, the would-be manipulator might fail to get the target to make what, from the manipulator's perspective, is a mistake. For example, in the case of ***Snow Flurries I*** (section 5.3), Maddie might try to get Tim to be excessively afraid of driving through snow flurries, but Tim may remain unafraid. Second, the target's making this mistake might fail to cause the behavior or mental state that the would-be manipulator wants to elicit from the target. For example, Tim might become fearful, but drive to the party anyway, or find other transportation.

A third way that the would-be manipulator could fail is less obvious: It could turn out that what is a mistake from the manipulator's perspective is not really a mistake at all. Recall the case of ***Irene's New Co-workers*** from section 5.2: Irene tries to get Todd to feel resentment and suspicion toward Billy. Irene thinks that these feelings are mistaken, because she believes that Billy is a good friend to Todd. But, unbeknownst to Irene, Billy is a bully merely pretending to be Todd's friend. Irene succeeds in getting Todd to feel suspicion and resentment toward Billy. But while Irene *thinks* that these attitudes are mistaken, *in reality*, they are quite appropriate. Thus, Irene's attempt at manipulation causes Todd's feelings to become more appropriate rather than mistaken. We saw in section 5.6 that we should say that Irene failed to manipulate Todd. That argument was based on an analogy with deception: If I get you to believe something that I believe to be false, I nevertheless fail to deceive you if it turns out that what I believed was false is actually true. Irene acted manipulatively, and while she succeeded at *influencing* Todd, she did *not manipulate* him because she did not induce him to make an *actual* mistake.

Accordingly, a definition of "M manipulates T" must include three distinct success conditions. Thus:

M manipulates T if and only if:
(1) M acts manipulatively toward T, and
(2) Each of these conditions is met:
a. What, from M's perspective, is a mistake really is a mistake;
b. T makes (approximately) this mistake; and
c. T's making this mistake has the (approximate) effect on T's behavior or mental state that M intended.

There are a couple of important things to note about this definition. First, conditions (2b) and (2c) require only approximate success. This makes explicit a looseness that commonly attends our notion of a successful action. If Karen tries to kill Victor by shooting him, we would say that she succeeded even if she was aiming at his head but the bullet struck his heart instead. If Joltin' Joe tries to hit the baseball out of the park, we would say that he succeeded even if the ball went over the left field wall when he was aiming for the center field wall. Of course, if Joe specifically intended to hit the ball over the center field wall—pointing to that spot before the pitch—then matters would be different. But manipulators need not, and typically do not, have similarly specific intentions about the fine-grained psychological details of their plans. Consider, for example, this case:

The Onerous Favor: Mike wants his casual acquaintance, Tess, to give up a week of her vacation to help remodel Mike's kitchen. Mike attempts to use a charm offensive to get Tess to care more than is reasonable about disappointing Mike so that she will agree to this onerous request. So, Mike lavishes attention on Tess, laughs at her jokes, lights up when Tess enters the room, flatters Tess, and so on. However, the effect of all this is that Tess arrives at the mistaken belief that she and Mike are much closer friends than they really are. On this basis, she agrees to Mike's request. However, she does this not because Mike has gotten her to feel excessively averse to disappointing him, but because she has acquired the mistaken belief that Mike is a good friend, and on that basis she does not regard the request as onerous.

Mike intended to get Tess to make a certain mistake, but the actual mistake she made was not quite the one Mike had in mind. It still seems correct, though, to say both that the mistake that Mike actually got Tess to make was approximately the mistake he intended, and that Mike successfully manipulated Tess.

Similarly, if we imagine that Iago intended to get Othello to murder Desdemona by poisoning her, the fact that he smothers her instead does not seem to undermine our judgment that Iago successfully manipulated him. Of course, if there is too much difference between the mistake that the influencer intended to induce and the mistake the target actually made, or between the intended and actual effects of that mistake, then it may be more apt to say that the attempted manipulation was not successful after all. Imagine that Iago's attempts to manipulate Othello backfire and drive him closer to Desdemona, but, after becoming intoxicated at a banquet celebrating their renewed devotion, Othello accidentally kills Desdemona when his drunkenness causes him to mistake her for an intruder. We would not say that Iago's attempt at manipulation was successful, even if, in this roundabout way, it played a causal role in the accident, or the mistake that led to it.

It is notoriously difficult to specify how deviant a causal chain must be between an intention and an action, or between an action and its consequences, before we say that the action was not successful. These are general problems for action theory, however, and not unique to attempts to define the particular kind of action we are considering here. If asked how close "approximate" means in the success conditions above, I shall simply answer: as close as we would normally require when judging *any* action attempt to be successful.

Second, the definition above applies only to the strict sense of the term 'manipulate.' As we noted in section 5.6, the term 'manipulate' is sometimes used in a looser, metaphorical sense that does not require an *intention* to manipulate. Thus, we might say that:

M manipulates T in the loose, metaphorical sense if and only if M causes a mistake in T's psychological states or processes, and this changes T's behavior or mental state.

6.5. Other Definitions

With these definitions in hand, we can define some other terms, such as the adjective 'manipulative.' When this term is applied to persons, we can say that:

A person is manipulative if and only if that person has a propensity to act manipulatively.

Having such a propensity does not, of course, imply that the person always acts on it, or even that the person always acts on it when it is possible to do so. Manipulative people are often content to use non-manipulative methods to get what they want—when those are likely to succeed. Some manipulative people have the attitude described by Claudia Mills and Michael Klenk: They see reasons as levers and choose good ones or bad (and thus manipulative) ones depending on what seems most likely to work (Mills 1995, 100–101; Klenk 2022b). Others might only use manipulation as a last resort, hoping to minimize the potential costs of being regarded by others as a manipulative person.

Drawing on discussions in Chapter 5 and above, we can define various senses in which an *inanimate object* can be manipulative. Sometimes we call an object manipulative because it was deliberately designed to influence behavior in a mistake-inducing way. We might call this the *derivative* sense of 'manipulative':

Something, S, is manipulative in the derivative sense if S has been designed to influence the behavior or mental state of those interacting with it by inducing what, from S's designer's perspective, are mistakes in their psychological states or processes.

The derivative sense of 'manipulative' would apply to inanimate objects—such as specific tactics, messages or contrivances—designed by manipulators to further their manipulative endeavors. Such things are, so to speak, extensions of the manipulator. Their design expresses, as it were, the manipulative intent of the designer.

But we sometimes describe something as 'manipulative' in a looser, more metaphorical sense as well:

Something, S, is manipulative in the metaphorical sense if S tends to influence the behavior or mental states of those interacting with S by inducing mistakes in their psychological states or processes.

This sense resembles the metaphorical sense (discussed in section 5.6) in which we might say that a person manipulates unintentionally. It is parallel to the metaphorical sense in which one might say that black ice is deceptive. This metaphorical sense focuses only on what happens to the person who is influenced. It captures the fact that, for certain purposes, we are more interested in what happens to that person than in what the influencer does.[2] In particular, the metaphorical sense of 'manipulative' captures the fact that *part* of what is bad about being induced to make a mistake does not depend on whether someone deliberately induced the person to make it.[3]

In an incisive discussion of what it might mean for a machine to manipulate, Jessica Pepp and her colleagues seem to have this metaphorical sense of 'manipulative' in mind when they speak of the "loose talk" approach to manipulation by inanimate objects (Pepp et al. 2022, 99).[4] As they point out, this way of

[2] This point is implicit in Michael Klenk's analysis of manipulative technology: rather than focusing on the manipulator and what it takes to act manipulatively, he opts instead to "focus on the patient perspective and ask what it takes to be manipulated" (Klenk 2022a, 108).

[3] As I noted earlier (sections 5.5–5.6) and as I will discuss in greater detail later (section 9.8), some of what is bad about being manipulated deliberately by another person *does* depend on the mistake being deliberately induced. So, being manipulated in the metaphorical sense is not bad in exactly the same way that it is bad to be deliberately manipulated by another person.

[4] Similarly, Sven Nyholm suggests that, even if they lack the agency required for manipulation in the strict sense, it might still be true that "technologies can relate to people in a manipulation-like way" (Nyholm 2022, 238).

speaking offers a way to reconcile the idea that manipulation proper requires a level of intent currently unavailable to machines, and the desire to obtain "a better understanding of the potential harms that machines can generate and to allow us to think through who bears responsibility for those harms, how we ought to mitigate them, and similar practical questions" (Pepp et al. 2022, 100–101). As they also note, this metaphorical or "loose talk" use of the term 'manipulative' will be most useful if we limit its application to inanimate objects that have a *significant tendency* to influence people in the way that manipulation does (Pepp et al. 2022, 102).

Finally, we can define a very broad sense in which something can be manipulative. This sense is a disjunction of the metaphorical sense and the derivative sense:

Something, S, is manipulative in the broad, disjunctive sense if S *either* tends *or* is intended to influence the behavior or mental states of those interacting with S by inducing mistakes in their psychological states or processes.

Finally, we can define 'manipulation' itself:

Manipulation: a process by which one or more persons or things manipulate, or act manipulatively toward, one or more other persons.

6.6. Manipulation as a Process

As this last definition indicates, manipulation is a *process*. Sometimes, it might be a very uncomplicated process: The influencer induces a mistake, and that mistake influences the target's behavior or mental state. Such instances of manipulation are discrete, isolated, well-defined events that occur over short periods of time. The relatively uncomplicated nature of such instances of manipulation makes them relatively easy to understand and analyze. It would be a good deal more difficult to identify what makes an influence manipulative, and what separates manipulative from non-manipulative influences, without focusing on individual, well-defined tactics, taken in isolation from one another. Consequently, this book has emphasized, and will continue to emphasize, individual, isolated instances of manipulation.

But the fact that we treat individual instances of manipulation in isolation for purposes of analytical clarity does not mean that this is how manipulation typically happens in real life. Of course, sometimes manipulation *does* consist of a single form of influence deployed in isolation over a short timeframe. But manipulation often—perhaps more often than not—takes place over a longer period of time, during which multiple tactics are employed, sometimes serially, and sometimes in tandem.

For example, Iago engages in insinuation, playing on the emotions, and outright deception, in a multiplex and iterated process that gradually transforms Othello from a loving husband to a murderer. Charm offensives can lay the groundwork for emotional blackmail by making the target overvalue the relationship so that threatening it will be more potent. Gaslighting can lay the groundwork for exploiting social proof by making the target more doubtful of being able to make sound judgments, and thus more likely to take cues from others. A manipulator might carry out game switching by following the inappropriate norms and relying on social proof to help get the target to act on them as well. Negging can clear the way for gaslighting by reducing the target's self-esteem so that it becomes easier for the manipulator to reduce the target's confidence about being able to make sound judgments.

Manipulative relationships often involve complex, long-term manipulative processes by which one form of manipulation leaves the target susceptible to another and another, and where many manipulative tactics are intertwined and layered atop one another. In such cases, it may be both difficult and relatively unimportant to individuate specific instances of manipulation in the ongoing manipulative process. Indeed, there may be no clear fact of the matter how many instances of manipulation occur in a complex, multi-element process of manipulation that occurs over time.

Moreover, some elements in a complex web of manipulation might not even be manipulative had they not been embedded in a larger manipulative process. A manipulator might employ isolation, or intoxication, or fatigue, or confusion in ways that will facilitate manipulation. Similarly, a manipulator might cultivate a trusting relationship with the target to make the target easier to manipulate. Such things, taken in isolation, might not be manipulative. But when used to make the target more likely to make a mistake, they become part of a larger manipulative process.[5]

[5] This fact provides a response to an otherwise puzzling case posed by Moti Gorin called "***Trust Me***" (Gorin 2014a, 58). Here, the influencer undertakes a process of providing the target with good reasons to trust him, so that he will believe the "egregious" lie that he plans to tell the target two months from now. However, before he finishes his plan, the influencer permanently leaves the country and never tells the lie. Although the influencer never gets the target to believe the egregious lie, Gorin claims that this is a case of manipulation. However, the analysis here suggests that it is more aptly described as an *incomplete manipulative process*. The element of the process that would have been manipulative in and of itself—i.e., the egregious lie—does not occur. And the elements that do occur are not manipulative when separated from the element that would have been manipulative in and of itself. For a somewhat different analysis of Gorin's example, according to which it is a mistake for the target to trust the influencer, see Bělohrad (2019, 453–54).

6.7. The Case for the Mistake Account: Coverage

Over the past few chapters, many considerations in favor of the Mistake Account have emerged. It seems useful to gather them all in one place and thus to display the cumulative case in favor of this theory about what manipulation is.

The strongest evidence favoring the Mistake Account is its ability to identify manipulation in a wide variety of cases where we have strong, clear, and widely shared intuitions that it is present. On this criterion, the Mistake Account is far superior to any of its rivals. It successfully identifies manipulation in each of the thirteen paradigm examples of manipulation from Chapter 2. As we saw in Chapter 3, none of the Mistake Account's rivals does this. This point is important enough to spell out in detail:

1. ***Playing on the emotions:*** Iago manipulates Othello by playing on his jealousy and anger to get him to murder Desdemona. The Mistake Account recognizes Iago's behavior as manipulation because Othello's jealousy and anger are mistaken, since Desdemona has done nothing to warrant them.
2. ***Misdirection/misemphasis:*** The pickpocket manipulates his victim by jostling him so that he does not notice that his wallet is being extracted from his pocket. The Mistake Account recognizes the pickpocket's behavior as manipulation because it induces the victim to mistakenly pay attention to the less important fact that he is being jostled, instead of the more important fact that his wallet is being removed.
3. ***Gaslighting:*** Gregory manipulates Paula by undermining her confidence in her own judgment so that she will do as Gregory advises. The Mistake Account recognizes Gregory's behavior as manipulation because nothing is wrong with Paula's judgment, and thus it is a mistake for her to doubt it.[6]
4. ***Game Switching***: The "social engineer" manipulates the employee into allowing access to a restricted area by getting him to follow the behavioral norm of holding open the door for the person behind him. The Mistake Account recognizes the social engineer's behavior as manipulation because it is a mistake to follow a rule or norm that is appropriate for entering public areas when one is, in fact, entering a restricted area.
5. ***Social Proof:*** Jim Jones manipulated his followers by getting some of them to drink poisoned fruit punch and then relying on the tendency of the rest to do what others are doing to get them to drink the fruit punch as well. The Mistake Account recognizes Jones's behavior as manipulation because it is

[6] The Mistake Account would also identify the more elaborate form of gaslighting that Abramson (2024) discusses as manipulation. Indeed, the more radical kind of undermining of agential authority that Abramson sees as the goal of the forms of gaslighting that she discusses is an even bigger mistake than what is induced in the "gaslighting lite" discussed here.

a mistake for his followers to treat the fact that others are drinking the fruit punch as a good reason to believe that it is a sensible thing to do.

6. ***Peer Pressure:*** Schwartz manipulates Flick into sticking his tongue on the flagpole by "triple dog-daring him" and thus ensuring that his peers will disapprove of him if he fails to take the dare. The Mistake Account recognizes Schwartz's behavior as manipulation because he gets Flick to akratically choose to risk freezing his tongue to the flagpole rather than enduring the loss of his peers' esteem. (However, if we imagine—somewhat implausibly—that Flick would suffer more from his peers' disapproval than from freezing his tongue to the flagpole, then this would no longer be a case of psychological manipulation, since Schwartz would be threatening something worse than what he is trying to get Flick to do, and it would not be a mistake for Flick to comply.)
7. ***Emotional Blackmail:*** Jo manipulates Allen by deliberately being unpleasant to be around whenever he does not do what she wants him to do. The Mistake Account recognizes Jo's behavior as manipulation either because Jo is bluffing, and thus inducing a mistaken belief, or because she is counting on Allen to react akratically to her demands—that is, by treating Jo's threat of a foul mood as creating a stronger reason than it really does. (However, if we imagine that Allen would suffer more from Jo's foul mood than from never getting to do what he wants, then this would no longer be a case of psychological manipulation, since Jo would be threatening something worse than what she is trying to get Allen to do, and it would not be a mistake for Allen to comply.)
8. ***Nagging:*** The teen manipulates his parents by nagging them to let him take his gaming device to school, which the parents think is a bad idea. The Mistake Account recognizes this behavior as manipulation because it seeks to induce the parents to act akratically by making what they regard as a worse choice overall in order to escape the annoyance of the nagging. (However, if we imagine that the nagging is especially severe and the reasons against letting the teen take the device to school are especially weak, then the suffering imposed by the nagging might be worse overall than complying. Such a case would no longer involve psychological manipulation, since the influencer would be threatening something worse than what he is trying to get the target to do, and it would not be a mistake for the target to comply.)
9. ***Charm Offensive:*** The motorist manipulates the police officer by getting him to have positive feelings toward her that make him care about gaining her approval, and making it clear that he can do this by letting her go without issuing a speeding citation. The Mistake Account recognizes the motorist's behavior as manipulation either because she leads the officer to believe—falsely—that a romantic liaison might be possible if he refrains

from issuing the citation, or because it induces him to akratically prioritize gaining her approval over doing his duty. (However, if we imagine a different kind of case, where the reasons against doing what the charmer wants are weak, then the advantages of retaining the charmer's approval might be enough to outweigh the disadvantages of doing what the charmer wants. Such a case would no longer involve psychological manipulation, since the influencer would be offering something good enough to make it worthwhile to do what the influencer wants, so it would not be a mistake for the target to comply.)

10. ***Exploiting Conflict Aversion:*** The con artist manipulates his mark by relying on the mark's aversion to conflict so that he will not simply extract himself from the con when he starts to suspect that it is a con. The Mistake Account recognizes the con artist's behavior as manipulation because he gets the mark to mistakenly choose the greater evil of losing his money over the lesser evil of enduring the momentary awkwardness of extracting himself from the situation.
11. ***Exploiting Reciprocity:*** The panhandlers manipulate the tourists by doing small, unrequested favors for them and exploiting the tendency to reciprocate to get them to give the panhandlers money. The Mistake Account recognizes the panhandlers' behavior as manipulation because they seek to induce the tourists to choose akratically to give up money to reciprocate a small, unrequested favor to avoid the minor awkwardness of violating the norm of reciprocity.
12. ***Negging:*** The so-called pickup artist manipulates a night club patron by first reducing her self-esteem, and then inducing her to regard dating him as a way to restore it. The Mistake Account recognizes the pickup artist's behavior as manipulation because he first induces the patron to mistakenly underestimate her own self-worth, and then to mistakenly see dating him as a way to regain it. It may also induce her to react akratically to the prospect of regaining her self-esteem, which is likely to be less important to her than exercising discretion about whom she dates.
13. ***Conditional Flattery:*** The department chairperson manipulates an overworked faculty member into taking on an arduous task by praising her dedication and organizational abilities when making the request. The Mistake Account recognizes the chairperson's behavior as manipulation insofar as it induces the faculty member to react akratically to the minor benefit of being called dedicated and organized, so that she chooses it at the much greater expense of taking on an arduous assignment.

Chapter 7 will discuss in more detail the mistakes made in these cases. But it should be clear enough that something aptly described as a mistake is being induced in each of these examples of manipulation. This is enough to show that the Mistake Account promises to handle the great diversity of manipulative influences.

6.8. The Mistake Account and the Dual Use Phenomenon

In section 2.5, we saw that many types of influence seem to have both manipulative and non-manipulative uses. Appeals to emotion are a case in point: Iago's appeals to emotion are manipulative, but it does not seem manipulative to appeal to empathy in sincere moral persuasion. Guilt trips are manipulative, but it does not seem manipulative to try to induce remorse in a so-far remorseless wrongdoer. Undermining someone's confidence in being able to make good decisions is manipulative gaslighting if the person's judgment is sound. But it is not manipulative to convince an intoxicated person to be less confident about being able to make a good decision about whether it is safe to drive home. Getting someone to agree to an onerous request to avoid the momentary social awkwardness of refusing is a manipulative exploitation of conflict aversion. But advising someone to give up their pocket money to a thug to avoid a potentially violent conflict is not manipulative.

As we saw in Chapter 3, this phenomenon poses an enormous challenge for efforts to define manipulation. But the Mistake Account handles it easily. Iago's appeals to emotion are manipulative because the emotions he seeks to induce are not appropriate given the facts of the situation. By contrast, empathy is an *appropriate* response to the undeserved suffering of others, so trying to get someone to feel empathy toward those experiencing such suffering is not an attempt to induce a mistake. Guilt trips are manipulative when and because the guilt being induced is mistaken—either not appropriate at all, or out of proportion to the circumstances. But it is appropriate to feel remorse about an actual wrong-doing, and so trying to induce someone to feel appropriate remorse at having done something genuinely wrong is not an attempt to induce a mistake. It is a mistake to distrust one's own *sound* judgment, so getting someone to do so is manipulative gaslighting. But it is appropriate to doubt one's judgment when it is impaired, so trying to get an inebriated friend to be less confident about the decision to drive home is not manipulative. Getting someone to incur the large cost of an onerous task to avoid the much smaller cost of social awkwardness is manipulative because it induces an akratic—and thus mistaken—overreaction to the immediate cost of social awkwardness. But suggesting compliance with a street thug that costs a few dollars in order to avoid violent conflict is not manipulative, precisely because choosing the lesser of the two evils is not a mistake.

The ability to recognize that many forms of influence have both manipulative and non-manipulative uses, and to distinguish which is which in an intuitively correct way, is a major strength of the Mistake Account.

6.9. The Mistake Account and the Parallel with Deception

Chapter 5 discussed the parallel that the Mistake Account draws between manipulation and deception. This parallel is an important advantage of the Mistake Account, for several reasons.

First, in ordinary conversation, manipulation and deception often go together, and are often mentioned in the same breath. Moreover, it would sound odd for one person to complain about having been manipulated and for another person to object that it was not manipulation because it was deception instead. Although these facts are not definitive proof of a parallel between deception and manipulation, they do suggest a connection. The parallel that the Mistake Account draws between deception and manipulation eliminates the chance that the theory will force us to say something that, as far as I can tell, we never say, namely that something was not manipulation because it was deception instead.

Second, the parallel that the Mistake Account draws between deception and manipulation ensures that whether an influence is manipulation will never depend on whether we describe it in terms of a mistaken belief or some other mistaken mental state. Recall the ***Snow Flurries I*** case from section 5.3, in which Maddie tries to get Tim to be excessively fearful of driving through snow flurries. Imagine that Maddie succeeds in getting Tim to be excessively afraid to drive. How should we describe what Maddie did? We could describe Maddie as inducing in Tim a mistaken *fear* of driving through the flurries. Or we could describe Maddie as inducing in Tim a mistaken *belief* that snow flurries constitute a significant hazard, and then claim that this mistaken belief causes the fear that keeps Tim from driving.

Notice that, on the second description, we could say that Maddie deceives Tim, and that his subsequent behavior is caused by that deception. Now, if we define manipulation in a way that separates it from deception, it could turn out that whether Maddie manipulated Tim might depend on whether we should describe what happened as an instance of deception. But that seems implausible. The question of whether Maddie manipulated Tim should not depend on whether we think of Maddie as getting Tim to acquire a false belief that gives rise to his excessive fear, or as getting Tim simply to have an excessive fear that is not caused by a false belief. This point does not apply just to emotional manipulation. As we saw in section 4.7, it also applies to manipulative pressure, since cases of akrasia can typically be described either as involving or as not involving a mistaken judgment about what is best. The same is true of confidence in one's judgment, patterns of attention, and so on. In short, most, if not all, of the mistakes involved in manipulation can be described either as involving or as not involving a false belief. Often, there will be no clear fact of the matter which description is more accurate.

But because the Mistake Account treats manipulation as a broader category which includes deception, it will never make the presence of manipulation depend on how we choose to describe a case that can be described equally well as involving a false belief or not. It will never turn out, for example, that whether Maddie manipulated Tim depends on whether we choose to describe her as getting Tim to believe that it is dangerous to drive through snow flurries or as simply getting him to fear doing so.

Third, the parallel that the Mistake Account draws between manipulation and deception provides principled ways to extend and develop the concept of manipulation, and to decide what to say about cases about which we have weak or conflicting intuitions (as we did in Chapter 5). Thus, the Mistake Account allows us to use a fairly well-understood concept—deception—as a template for extending the concept of manipulation. As we shall see in section 9.10, this parallel can also help guide our moral judgments about manipulation.

6.10. The Mistake Account and its Rivals

In addition to these advantages, the Mistake Account incorporates many of the best features of rival accounts of manipulation.

As we noted in Chapter 3, the Covert Influence Account fails to recognize forms of manipulation—like nagging—that can be both effective and manipulative even if they are out in the open. Nevertheless, manipulation *often* involves influences that are hidden. Manipulators often try to hide both what they are doing and why they are doing it. The Mistake Account explains why this is the case. For if manipulation involves getting someone to make a mistake, it is easy to see why manipulators try to keep things hidden. If you know that I am trying to get you to make a mistake, you are far more likely to avoid making it. Consequently, a manipulator who keeps things hidden is often much more likely to succeed. Iago cannot very well let Othello know that he believes that the jealousy he wants Othello to feel is baseless. Thus, the Mistake Account explains why manipulators *often* hide *something* important, namely, that it is crucial to their plans for the target to make a mistake. But the Mistake Account explains why manipulation is often covert without building covertness into the definition of manipulation.

The Covert Aggression Account fails to recognize the existence of paternalistic manipulation. Nevertheless, manipulation *often* induces the target to do something that makes the target worse off. In this sense, then, manipulation is often aggressive. In such cases, manipulators will often try to hide that fact. The Mistake Account explains this imperfect connection between manipulation and covert aggression. Getting someone to act contrary to their own interests often requires getting them to make some sort of mistake. Consequently, manipulators have good reason to hide the fact that this is what they are trying to get the target to do.

The Mistake Account also captures the most important insight of the Bypassing Reason Account. In fact, the Mistake Account supplies an explanation of the specific sense in which manipulation is opposed to reason or rational decision-making.

While the Mistake Account denies that manipulation must always bypass rational decision-making, it does entail that, in every instance of manipulation, something has gone wrong with the target's decision-making. What has gone wrong, according to the Mistake Account, is that a mistake has been introduced into the decision-making process. In this specific sense, the Mistake Account agrees that manipulation always involves what we might best describe as a "misfiring" of rational decision-making.

6.11. Conclusion

This chapter has refined the Mistake Account by developing formal definitions of key terms related to manipulation. It has also assembled the strong cumulative case for the Mistake Account. The next chapter examines the various kinds of mistakes that manipulators induce their targets to make.

7
Mistakes and Manipulation

7.1. Introduction

As its name suggests, the central idea of the Mistake Account is that of a mistake. Any attempt to define manipulation in terms of inducing a mistake must explain what sorts of things count as mistakes. Although we have mentioned various mistakes in earlier chapters, we have not yet examined them in detail. This chapter will do that.

7.2. Why "Mistakes"?

Before we begin, we should address a more basic question: Why think of manipulation as influence that gets the target to *make a mistake*? Why not think of it as influence that gets the target to adopt non-ideal mental states (Noggle 1996), or as influence that fails to track reasons (Gorin 2014b, 97; 2018)? The short answer is that we *can* think of manipulation in these ways, at least if we think of them as just different ways of expressing the same idea as inducing a mistake. Presumably it is a mistake to adopt mental states that are farther away from some ideal than one's previous mental states. Presumably it is a mistake to deliberate in a way that fails to track reasons. Readers who prefer those ways of describing what happens in manipulation may regard the concept of a mistake as a shorter way to say much the same thing.

Thus, my preference for the term 'mistake' is *largely* just that—a preference. But I think that it is a sensible one. The concept of a mistake is more clear and more familiar than the alternatives. Consider the "falling short of ideals" definition. To determine whether it applies, we must determine what mental states are ideal, which presumably means something like "maximally rational." This is a tall order. What, exactly, is the *ideal* amount of fear to experience toward, say, driving in a snowstorm or hiking through bear country? Defining manipulation in terms of a failure to track reasons presents different problems. There are many competing views about the nature of reasons and rationality. Defining manipulation in terms of influences that fail to track reasons would require determining which kind of reasons—subjective, objective, procedural, strategic, ecological—we mean when defining manipulation as influence that fails to track them.

The simplicity of the concept of a mistake is even more of a virtue when we ask about the influencer's state of mind. Most real-world manipulators lack

Manipulation. Robert Noggle, Oxford University Press. © Robert Noggle 2025.
DOI: 10.1093/9780198924920.003.0007

such sophisticated concepts as "tracking reasons" and "non-ideal mental states." Determining whether someone intends to induce a non-ideal mental state, or a failure to track reasons, will often require determining whether the person is trying to do a thing of which that person has no concept. By contrast, we all know what it means to make a mistake. *That* concept is quite basic: Even for relatively unsophisticated agents, there will usually be a relatively clear answer to the question of whether that agent is trying to get someone to make a mistake. Indeed, if we ask whether Iago tried to get Othello to adopt a non-ideal mental state, or to deliberate in a non-reason-tracking way, we are likely to begin with the simpler question: Did Iago try to get Othello to make a mistake? So why not just use the simpler, more basic concept of a mistake to begin with?

Whether we call them non-ideal mental states, failures to track reasons, or—as I prefer—mistakes, a theory that characterizes manipulation in terms of the attempt to induce them will not be complete without discussing them in some detail. Let us turn now to that task.

7.3. Mistaken Beliefs

It is difficult to imagine a more straightforward example of a mistake than believing something false. This is the mistake that the deceiver seeks to induce, and the Mistake Account treats deception as a special case of manipulation. So it makes sense to start with this mistake:

It is a mistake to believe something that is false.

Although this statement is correct, it is too narrow for our purposes. Sometimes the manipulator does not need to—and may not even try to—get the target to *believe* something false. It may often suffice to create something less than a false *belief*, such as a false appearance or false impression. In fact, in some forms of manipulation, trying to get the target to adopt a full-blown false *belief* might be counter-productive. Take the tactic of tailgating discussed in section 2.2.4. This tactic seems to work by making it *seem* like the manipulator belongs in the restricted area, and by discouraging the target from thinking enough to form any *belief* about the matter. Someone who considers a question like "does this person belong here?" enough to form a *belief* may realize that what merely *seems* to be true might well be *false*. Thus, we might imagine a manipulator trying to induce a false impression or a false "seeming" rather than a false belief. Here is how William Tolhurst describes "seemings":

> Like beliefs, seemings have a mind-to-world direction of fit unlike other states, e.g., desires and intentions, that have a world-to-mind direction of fit . . . Beliefs and seemings are supposed to fit the way the world is. Those that do not are

> defective, false or nonveridical . . . Though seemings are intimately related to beliefs, they constitute a distinct mental state type because it may seem to **S** that **p** even though **S** does not believe that **p.** (Tolhurst 1998, 293)

Philosophers have posited a number of other belief-like states, including "aleifs" (Gendler 2008), "bimaginings" (Egan 2008), "in-between believing" (Schwitzgebel 2001), and "quasi-beliefs" (Noggle 2016b), to name a few. Such states are *belief-like* in having what is sometimes called a "mind-to-world direction of fit." That is, such states *fail* or are *defective* if they do not conform to the facts about the world. Less metaphorically, such states *purport* or *function* to represent the way the world actually is. They are *mistaken* when the world is not the way that they represent it to be. There is a great deal of debate about the existence and nature of belief-like states, and their role in epistemology and philosophical psychology.[1] Fortunately, we need not settle these debates here. We need only to widen our original statement to cover whatever belief-like states might exist:

> ***Belief Mistake I:*** *It is a mistake to believe, or to have a belief-like state toward, a proposition that is false.*

But this is not the only kind of belief-related mistake that a manipulator might induce. In gaslighting, for example, the manipulator gets the target to *doubt* that the target's judgment is reliable.[2] The early stages of Iago's manipulation of Othello might be more aptly described as an attempt to get Othello to *doubt* that Desdemona is faithful than to get him to *believe* that she is not. Or consider the "doubt is our product" campaign by the US tobacco industry, which sowed doubt about the link between cigarettes and cancer (Hanson and Kysar 1998). Unfortunately, recent history has seen the proliferation of various tactics aimed at sowing doubt about everything from vaccines to climate change to the reliability of voting machines. We could, of course, treat statements of the form "**S** doubts that **P**" as statements of the form "**S** believes that it is doubtful that **P**." But this seems needlessly complicated, especially since we should also count the flipside—suspecting what is false—as a mistake. So let us simply define a second sort of belief mistake:

> ***Belief Mistake II:*** *It is a mistake to doubt something that is true, or to suspect something that is false.*[3]

[1] On seemings, see McAllister (2018) and P. J. Werner (2014); on other belief-like states, see, e.g., Schwitzgebel (2001) and Bortolotti (2010).

[2] Readers who prefer not to count doubting one's sound judgment as mistakenly doubting *that one's judgment is sound* are free to treat it as a separate kind of mistake, e.g., doubting the reliability of an epistemic practice that is, in fact, reliable.

[3] Readers who prefer to speak of "degrees of belief" are free to recast both forms of belief mistake in terms of credences that disobey Bayesian principles.

7.4. Game/Script Mistakes

Belief mistakes involve *declarative* knowledge, or what is sometimes called "knowing that." Another important class of mistakes involves *procedural* knowledge, or what is sometimes called "knowing how." Two common forms of procedural knowledge mistakes will not concern us much here: One is where procedural knowledge is absent or incomplete, as when someone does not know how to drive a car with a manual transmission. The other is when someone's procedural knowledge contains a mistake, as when someone keeps ruining the cake by following a flawed procedure calling for light rather than thorough stirring of the ingredients. Although the Mistake Account would classify influencing behavior by inducing either of these mistakes as manipulation, they do not figure prominently in real-world cases of manipulation.

The kind of procedural knowledge mistake most commonly induced by manipulators occurs when someone misapplies procedural knowledge to a situation where it is not appropriate. Usually this involves packages of procedural knowledge about how to navigate some type of social interaction. These packages of procedural knowledge include instructions about how to play one's part and achieve one's goals in that particular type of interaction, as well as behavioral norms and expectations that apply to the people involved in it. Thus, they provide knowledge about how to act, and tools for understanding and predicting the behavior of others. Consider, for example, the procedural knowledge involved in eating at a restaurant. It delineates various roles which participants play—customer, waiter, etc.—as well as procedural information about what the occupant of each role must do for the interaction to occur successfully. It will also often include behavioral norms and expectations about how the participants should conduct themselves. This might include various rules of etiquette, expectations about tipping, etc.

Adapting some terminology from psychology and artificial intelligence (e.g., Schank and Abelson 1977), we might call these packages of behavioral norms and procedural knowledge "scripts." Scripts define how various kinds of interactions are supposed to work, and how the participants are supposed to behave. Thus, the script we follow—and expect others to follow—differs according to the situation we are in. We act and expect others to act very differently at a formal dinner versus a pickup basketball game or a contract negotiation.

A manipulator can influence someone's behavior by getting that person to follow the wrong script for the situation. This seems to be what happens in Lisa Herzog's example (section 2.2.4), where Anne tricks Bert into following the rules appropriate for collaboration between fellow members of an engineering team, when in fact they work for different companies, whose interests are not completely aligned. Herzog uses the example to explore issues in social epistemology, such as how the epistemic value of an utterance depends on its social context (Herzog 2017, 253).

But her example is relevant to discussions of manipulation because the sort of "games" that Herzog discusses include, or at least imply, rules governing how to behave. In addition to whatever epistemic mischief Anne does about whom to trust and so forth, it is striking that she gets Bert to do something that he should not do—i.e., revealing proprietary information that he should not reveal to someone outside his own company.

Thus, what Herzog calls a "game" is a situation for which one set of rules is appropriate, and another set of rules is inappropriate. These sets of rules are, of course, what we have just been calling scripts. Both terms—'rules' and 'scripts'—are evocative names for packages of procedural knowledge, including behavioral norms and expectations, and I will treat them as synonyms here.

Although Herzog does not explicitly say so, it seems unlikely that Bert forms a conscious *belief* that he is operating in a collaborative situation. Indeed, if such a thought were to occur to him consciously, it seems likely that he would reject it and subsequently become more careful about what he divulges to Anne. Instead, Anne's own behavior appears to activate Bert's "collaborating engineers" script, which he then follows without consciously questioning its appropriateness.

This is not to say that Anne turns Bert into an unthinking zombie. But it seems likely that scripts can be activated automatically, without any conscious decision, and that once activated, they can influence behavior without the person noticing this influence. One reason for thinking so is that scripts are probably involved in automating complex behavior so that it requires little if any conscious attention, as when one's internalized procedural knowledge of how to drive a car allows one to perform many components of that task (like signaling before a lane change or making small adjustments to speed and lane position) without conscious thought. If that is correct, then it seems likely that scripts can be triggered and influence action automatically, without conscious intention. We will explore ways in which manipulation can exploit processes that facilitate automatized action in more detail in the next chapter. For now, though, it is enough to say that it is a mistake to follow a script that does not match the situation. Thus, we can define the following type of mistake:

> ***Game/Script Mistake:*** *It is a mistake to act according to a script, i.e., a package of procedural knowledge and behavioral norms and expectations similar to the rules of a game, that is not appropriate to one's actual situation.*

Although manipulation that induces this sort of mistake seems to have been largely unnoticed by philosophers writing about manipulation, it is probably very common. Con artists, salespersons, and others who want you to lower your guard might trigger your "friendly encounter" script—even when it is so obvious that this person is not your friend that it would be counter-productive to try to get you to believe it. The induction of game/script mistakes probably also plays a role in forms of manipulation that rely on pretense. The effectiveness of pretending to be a physician, maintenance worker, police officer, etc., may often have as much to do with triggering implicit procedural knowledge as with causing the target to form an explicit belief that the manipulator is who he pretends to be.[4]

7.5. Heuristic Mistakes

Closely related to game/script mistakes are mistakes involving decision-making rules commonly employed to make fast decisions. As we will discuss in more detail in Chapter 8, human decision-making often takes place under time constraints that require taking shortcuts that *usually* yield good decisions much faster than more elaborate forms of deliberation. These shortcuts are often called heuristics. One example, discussed by Gerd Gigerenzer, concerns imitation. Simply stated, this rule is "do what the majority of your peers do" (Gigerenzer 2007, 217). Gigerenzer observes that the reliability of a given heuristic depends on the situation and environment. The imitation heuristic works well when the environment is relatively stable, feedback on decisions is absent, and mistakes are dangerous (Gigerenzer 2007, 218). For example, this heuristic works well when one is deciding what foods are safe to eat, at least when it is safe to assume—as it *usually* is—that others will reject unsafe foods. As Gigerenzer notes, "Relying only on individual experience to learn which berries found in the forest are poisonous is obviously a bad strategy" (Gigerenzer 2007, 219). However, in other situations, the imitation heuristic can yield bad, even disastrous decisions. The tragic People's Temple mass suicide (section 2.2.5) may have been driven in large part by people employing this heuristic in a situation for which it was tragically inappropriate. Although fruit punch is normally safe to drink, the possibility of it being poisoned with cyanide by a fanatic, and the fact that it was not safe to assume that others would reject poisoned substances, made the situation unstable in a way that made the imitation heuristic unreliable. Thus, Jones's followers made what we might call the

> ***Heuristic Mistake:*** *It is a mistake to use a decision-making rule in a situation for which it is not reliable.*

As we have seen, it is not always a mistake to employ the imitation heuristic. Consequently, the influence tactic that Cialdini calls "social proof" is not always manipulative. Social proof is manipulative when the influencer induces the target

[4] The fact that the manipulator might not know or care which mechanism operates is another reason for requiring only that the target make "approximately" the mistake that the manipulator is trying to induce (see section 6.4).

to make the heuristic *mistake* of relying on the imitation heuristic in a situation where it is not reliable.

7.6. Mistakes of Attention and Weighting

Attention is a limited resource, best spent on selecting and executing the best action for the circumstances. Attention wasted on what is not important reduces the attention available for what is. Wasting one's attention on what is not important is a mistake. But it makes mischief mainly by contributing to the worse mistake of failing to pay attention—or enough attention—to what *is* important. Mistakes of attention are a main source of human error in accidents and other failures, both prudential and moral. The most straightforward kind of attention mistake is what we might call

> ***Attention Mistake I:*** *It is a mistake to pay too little attention to something important to the decision at hand, and/or to pay too much attention to something unimportant to that decision.*

This is the mistake induced by the manipulative tactic of misdirection: The pickpocket gets you to devote so much attention to the fact that you've just been jostled that you don't notice that he is relieving you of your wallet. The fraudster focuses his mark's attention on the potential of a large payoff so that he won't notice that he's entering the bottom level of a pyramid scheme. The Mistake Account regards such tactics as forms of manipulation because they induce someone to make Attention Mistake I.[5]

Sometimes distraction interferes not with decision-making, but with the task itself. Certain kinds of tasks require extremely focused attention, so that any distraction may degrade performance. But it often matters what one pays attention *to*. Typically, someone learning a new skill must pay attention to the details of its execution. But once the skill has been mastered, paying too much attention to those same details can degrade performance by interfering with the neural circuits that have already learned to perform the task without conscious attention (what athletes sometimes call "muscle memory"). Gigerenzer suggests a devious way to use this in a tennis match: "ask your tennis opponent what he is doing to make his forehand so brilliant today. You have a good chance of making him think about his swing and weakening his forehand" (Gigerenzer 2007, 36). It would be natural for

[5] This seems to be the mistake being induced in Moti Gorin's "***Global Warming***" case (Gorin 2014a, 58), where a politician obscures his support of unpopular green energy policies by adopting popular policies about other matters simply to make his green energy position less noticeable. For a similar analysis of this example, see Bělohrad (2019, 454).

the victim of such a tactic to complain later that it was a mistake to be so focused on the details of his forehand that it interfered with the very thing he was trying to attend to. Thus, we have...

> ***Attention Mistake II:*** *It is a mistake to pay too much attention to aspects of a task when doing so will degrade task performance.*

Attention mistakes—especially of the first type—are closely related to what we might call Weighting Mistakes. When making a decision, it is a mistake to place too little weight on something important, or too much weight on something unimportant. More precisely:

> ***Weighting Mistake:*** *It is a mistake to place weight on some fact during decision-making that is disproportionate to that fact's importance for that decision.*[6]

As we noted in section 2.2.2, paying attention to something is often closely related to placing weight on it during decision-making: The more important something seems, the more attention we usually pay to it, and the more attention we pay to something, the more important it seems. Thus, influences that change how much attention a person pays to something will often influence how much weight the person places on it during decision-making. Thus, mistakes of attention and weighting are often intertwined and mutually reinforcing. Often, both mistakes can be induced by changing the *salience* of some fact: The more salient it is, the more attention we are likely to pay to it, and the more weight we are likely to give it during decision-making. Complicating matters still further is the fact that manipulation that involves attention, salience, and emphasis often interacts with emotional manipulation. Engaging the emotions is an effective way to make something more salient, and thus influencing how much attention we pay to it and how much weight we give it during decision-making.

Although inducing an Attention Mistake is one way to induce a Weighting Mistake, it is not the only way. Weighting Mistakes can also be induced by changing *how* rather than *how much* a person thinks about some fact. A luxury car salesperson might associate concerns about fuel efficiency with penny-pinching and poverty to get an upscale customer to place less weight on the fact that the car under consideration is a gas guzzler. Exaggeration, hyperbole, and other

[6] Proponents of "one-reason decision-making," such as Gigerenzer, suggest that decision-making often does, and often should, proceed not by weighing competing considerations as though putting them on a scale, but by identifying a hierarchy of criteria to be considered in lexical order, so that decisions are made according to the top ranked criterion, with lower ranked criteria only serving to break ties (Gigerenzer 2007; Gigerenzer and Todd 1999). In this form of decision-making, the weight placed on a factor is reflected in its place in the lexical hierarchy. Thus, the weighing mistake in one-reason decision-making would involve placing a less important reason higher than it should be in the decision tree of lexically ordered reasons.

distortions can also change the relative weights a person assigns to various facts during decision-making. Tone and facial expressions in speech, and visual effects in writing or media, can also be used to make one thing seem more important—and thus deserving of extra weight during decision-making—than another.

Inducing weighting mistakes is the goal of the tactic that I called misemphasis in section 2.2.2. It occurs in the ***University I*** case from section 4.2, where Mandy emphasizes the charms of small-town life, while downplaying its lack of opportunities for career and intellectual growth, and when she emphasizes the downsides of college life, including debt, having to attend classes, and the city's higher crime rate. Mandy's goal is to get Tara to place more weight on the cons of going off to college, and less weight on the pros—even though she realizes that the pros actually outweigh the cons. In this way, Mandy behaves somewhat like politicians who use "spin" to emphasize their accomplishments and downplay their failings, or what purveyors of sketchy weight loss and exercise programs do when they highlight success stories and downplay the fact that those stories are not typical.

Weighting mistakes help to illustrate why I (now) prefer to think of manipulation in terms of inducing mistakes rather than inducing non-ideal mental states. For complex decisions, there may be no uniquely rational amount of weight to give to competing considerations. For example, if someone must choose between a job that promises a fulfilling career and a job in a more desirable location, then placing negligible weight on one fact or the other is probably a mistake. But it is not clear that there is a uniquely rational way to rank them, and thus no *ideal* amount of weight to give them relative to one another. Consequently, defining manipulation in terms of deviations from some ideal level of weight may be tantamount to defining it in terms of something that does not exist. By contrast, denying that there is, or always is, a uniquely correct answer to the question of how much weight a given factor merits in some particular decision is perfectly consistent with there being weightings that are clearly mistaken.

7.7. Mistaken Emotions

The philosophical literature on emotions is vast.[7] Much of it is concerned with the proper definition of emotions and theories about their essential nature. Fortunately, we need not settle those questions here, since there is wide agreement on the feature of emotions that is most central to our purposes. In their survey of the literature on emotion, Andrea Scarantino and Ronald de Sousa write that "Despite the great diversity of views on the nature and function of emotions we have documented, a broad consensus has emerged on a number of topics" (Scarantino and

[7] Good overviews—on which I have drawn—can be found in chapter 2 of Tappolet (2016) and Scarantino and de Sousa (2018).

de Sousa 2018, 56). One of them is that "emotions have intentionality or the ability to represent" (Scarantino and de Sousa 2018, 56); another is that "emotions can be appropriate or inappropriate with respect to their intentional objects" (Scarantino and de Sousa 2018, 58). Thus, the Mistake Account's assumption that there is such a thing as an emotion being inappropriate is consistent with the philosophical consensus.

But what *makes* an emotion inappropriate or, in our terms, mistaken? There are three plausible standards by which we might judge the appropriateness of an emotion. According to what we might call the Prudential Standard, an emotion is mistaken if being in that emotional state is contrary to the person's interests. According to what we might call the Moral Standard, an emotion is mistaken if it is morally blameworthy to be in that emotional state, or if it would be morally better not to be in it. According to what we might call the Fittingness Standard, an emotion is mistaken if it fails to be "fitting," where fittingness is a standard internal to the emotion itself. In selecting the proper standard, we should remember that our task is not to identify the standard of appropriateness for emotions that is correct in and of itself. Rather, it is to identify the standard by which the Mistake Account should treat an emotion as mistaken.

Let us begin with the Prudential Standard. Would it make sense to say that an emotion is mistaken in the sense relevant to manipulation if it is imprudent to experience that emotion in the situation at hand? The suggestion has some initial appeal, since manipulators often influence their targets in ways contrary to the targets' interests. But we have seen that manipulation can sometimes be benevolent or paternalistic. Recall Theresa, from the ***Bad Boyfriend*** case from section 3.4, who is tempted to return to her abusive ex-partner, Al. Her friends try to prevent this by making Theresa angry about something that Al did not, in fact, do. Theresa's anger is prudent, at least in the sense that it prevents her from doing something detrimental to her interests—returning to an abusive relationship. Nevertheless, it seems clear that inducing her to be angry about something that Al did not do is manipulative. If the Mistake Account is to get this case right, it cannot locate the mistake her friends induced her to make in terms of having an *imprudent* emotion. More generally, adopting the Prudential Standard would leave the Mistake Account unable to properly identify cases of paternalistic emotional manipulation, since the emotions induced in such cases would be beneficial to the target, and thus appropriate according to the Prudential Standard.

Consider next the Moral Standard. According to this standard, an emotion is mistaken if it would be better, morally speaking, not to be in that emotional state under the circumstances. This might seem like a plausible suggestion in some cases: For example, Othello's jealousy does seem immoral. But given that Desdemona has not been unfaithful, it is difficult to know whether Othello's jealousy seems mistaken because it is immoral, or whether it seems immoral because it is mistaken. We might try to sidestep this question by saying that jealousy is always immoral. But that won't work for all cases of emotional manipulation: If a con artist bilks naïve philanthropists of their savings by falsely promising to donate the money to fictitious victims of some fictitious disaster, he is manipulating them at least in part by playing on their empathy. But empathy seems an unlikely target for moral condemnation. Rather, what makes this empathy a mistake is that the people at whom it is directed do not exist. Finally, consider the ***Snow Flurries I*** case from section 5.3: Maddie gets Tim to be so afraid of driving through snow flurries that he skips a party that Maddie wants him to skip. Certainly, fear can sometimes be a moral failing. But that does not seem to be true of Tim's fear, and thus it seems an implausible account of why Tim's fear is mistaken. Our sense that Maddie manipulates Tim does not depend on whether we can think of some respect in which Tim's fear is immoral. So, it seems like the Moral Standard is not a promising way for the Mistake Account to characterize mistaken emotion.

Thus, we are left with the Fittingness Standard, according to which an emotion is mistaken if it is not "fitting." As Justin D'Arms and Daniel Jacobson note, "the fittingness of an emotion is like the truth of a belief" (D'Arms and Jacobson 2000, 72). As Christine Tappolet explains, "emotions are assessable in terms of how they fit the world. My fear can be appropriate or not, depending on whether what I am afraid of is fearsome, that is depending on whether it calls for fear" (Tappolet 2016, 10–11). Scarantino and de Sousa write that "We may for instance say that fear is *rational in terms of fittingness* just in case it is directed towards things that are truly dangerous, because this is what fear represents. Being afraid of a shark swimming alongside you is fitting, because the shark is dangerous" (Scarantino and de Sousa 2018, 48). By contrast, fearing a guppy swimming alongside you would not be fitting. Importantly, the question of whether an emotion is fitting is distinct from the question of whether it is prudent or moral. As D'Arms and Jacobson write, "an emotion can be fitting despite being wrong (or inexpedient) to feel. In fact, the wrongness of feeling an emotion never, in itself, constitutes a reason that the emotion fails to be fitting" (D'Arms and Jacobson 2000, 69).[8]

As we have seen, fear is fitting if the object of the fear is truly dangerous. Adopting the fittingness standard for the Mistake Account's notion of mistaken emotion would imply that the reason why Maddie's behavior is manipulative is that it is not fitting to fear driving through snow flurries, because this is not a dangerous thing to do. This seems correct. By contrast, it would not be manipulative to get a Florida tourist who is heedless of the danger posed by alligators to fear swimming in waters where they lurk. This also seems correct.

Let us consider some other emotions. Guilt is fitting when one is responsible for having done something wrong. It is not fitting to feel guilty about something

[8] They mean 'wrong' and 'wrongness' in the sense of morally wrong and moral wrongness.

that one had no hand in, such as surviving through sheer luck an accident that killed others (so-called "survivor's guilt"). Nor is it fitting to feel guilty about something bad that was not also wrong, such as the unavoidable pain of a necessary and consented to medical procedure. Adopting the fittingness standard for mistaken emotions would allow the Mistake Account to say that, when Mandy induces Tara to feel guilty about the prospect of leaving her behind to attend college in the city, her behavior is manipulative because it induces Tara to feel an unfitting guilt over something that it would not be wrong for her to do. This seems correct. But getting someone who *has* done something wrong to feel guilt—or at least remorse—would not be manipulative. Again, this seems correct.[9]

Similarly, it is fitting to feel empathy toward someone who is suffering a genuine misfortune. Thus, adopting the fittingness standard for mistaken emotions allows the Mistake Account to say—correctly—that it is not manipulative to get someone to feel empathy for people who are genuinely suffering. But adopting this standard would allow the Mistake Account to identify manipulation in scams that evoke empathy for someone who is not suffering, or who is merely feigning suffering (or who isn't even real).

It is fitting to feel anger toward someone who has mistreated you or someone you care about. But it is not fitting to feel anger toward someone who had no role in the mistreatment. Nor is it fitting to be angry when someone does something that you do not like, but about which you have no legitimate complaint. Thus, for example, it would not be fitting to be angry at someone who beat you fair and square in a race and won the prize. It is common for disappointment to turn to anger, and this anger might fit the situation if it is directed, say, at one's own contribution to the disappointment: "I'm not angry at him for winning; I'm angry at myself for not training more diligently." Such anger might be neither helpful nor healthy, but if it is directed at some malfeasance by your "past self" that deprived you of a victory you otherwise would have achieved, then it might be fitting. But if the race was fair, it is not fitting to be angry *at* the winner. Nor is it fitting to be angry at yourself if you did everything possible within the rules to win. In such a situation disappointment or sadness is fitting, but not anger. Employing the fittingness standard for mistaken emotions in the Mistake Account would imply that trying to get someone to feel angry at having been beaten in a fair competition would be manipulative. This seems correct.

Adopting the fittingness standard for mistaken emotions can illuminate the pathways by which emotional manipulation can operate. The similarity between the fittingness conditions between two emotions often makes it possible for a

[9] Interestingly, we sometimes use different terms for what seem like the same emotion depending on whether the emotion seems fitting. Thus, we often say "remorse" rather than "guilt" or "a healthy respect" rather than "fear" when we want to emphasize that the emotion is appropriate. I will sometimes follow this practice.

manipulator to convert one to another. Suppose Larry and Wendy are co-workers vying for the same opportunity for a promotion, and that Wendy won the promotion while Larry lost. It would be fitting for Larry to be disappointed. While it might be *natural* for Larry to be angry as well, anger would only be *fitting* if the decision to promote Wendy rather than Larry had been unfair in some way. But a manipulator wanting to get Larry to be angry and not merely disappointed could easily do this by making it *seem* to Larry that the decision was unfair. And once Larry had been gotten to be angry, one could easily imagine anger being directed wherever the manipulator wants—at the co-worker, at the person who made the promotion decision, or at the organization. This pathway seems an easy one to get someone to traverse precisely because the fittingness conditions for anger and disappointment are similar.

We can see the same phenomenon with the movement from fear to anger or hate: If something is dangerous, fear is fitting. But if someone can be gotten to regard the danger as the deliberate work of some other person, then it will be easy enough to convert that fear into anger or even hatred. Or consider envy. According to D'Arms and Jacobson, "envy portrays a rival as having a desirable possession that one lacks, and it casts this circumstance in a specific negative light" (D'Arms and Jacobson 2000, 66). Thus, envy is only fitting if the other person really does have the thing that you want, *and* if there is something unfair about this situation. Because the fittingness conditions for envy resemble those for disappointment and those for anger, we can see how easy it might be for a manipulator to move someone from disappointment to envy, and from envy to anger or even hatred. It is a fairly small step from disappointment at not having **X** to the thought that it is unfair that the other person has **X** and you do not, and from there to the thought that the other person has wronged you by having **X** when you do not. It is, of course, a mistake to infer one from the other, but it can be an easy mistake to make. And it can be an easy mistake for a manipulator to *get a disappointed person to make.*

It should be clear from all of this that the fittingness standard is the most appropriate standard for the Mistake Account to use in characterizing mistaken emotions.[10] Consequently, we can define one kind of emotional mistake as follows:

> ***Mistaken Emotions I:*** *It is a mistake to have an emotion that is not fitting given the facts of the situation.*

[10] Much of the work developing the concept of fittingness has been done by proponents of neo-sentimentalist meta-ethics, which seeks to tie moral judgments to emotions. Some theorists in this tradition are drawn to the concept of emotional fittingness as a way to reconcile claims about the emotional nature of moral judgments with the idea that moral judgments can be wrong or mistaken. However, the fact that the Mistake Account adopts much of what scholars of neo-sentimentalist meta-ethics say about fittingness does not tie the Mistake Account to that meta-ethical view.

7.8. Emotional Excess and Defect

An emotion can also be mistaken in regard to its strength or intensity. Indeed, it may be more common for an emotion to go wrong in this way than for it to be the wrong emotion for the situation. The classic source for the idea that the strength or intensity of an emotion can go wrong is, of course, Aristotle. On Aristotle's view, an emotion goes wrong if it is not the right emotion for the situation, or if it is felt with the wrong intensity for the situation.

For reasons similar to those discussed in the previous section, the Mistake Account should also employ the fittingness standard for determining whether the strength or intensity of an emotion is mistaken. Thus, we should think of fittingness as encompassing both whether the emotion itself fits the facts of the situation, and whether its strength or intensity fits those facts. D'Arms and Jacobson put the point this way:

> [C]onsiderations of fittingness can be divided into two kinds, corresponding to two dimensions of fit: one can criticize an emotion with regard to its size and its shape. An emotional episode presents its object as having certain evaluative features; it is unfitting on grounds of shape when its object lacks those features . . . An emotion can also be criticized for its size. While such criticism typically implies that it has the right shape, one can nevertheless urge that an emotional response is unfitting because it is an overreaction. Thus your envy might be too large for the circumstances, if what you have is almost as good as your rival's. Then you would not be warranted in being much pained over such a trifling difference. (D'Arms and Jacobson 2000, 73–74)

By the same token, the amount of anger that would be a fitting response to having one's house burned down by an arsonist would not be a fitting response to having one's flower bed accidentally stepped on. Similarly, the amount of fear that would be fitting when encountering a grizzly bear would be unfitting when encountering a bumble bee (unless, of course, one has a life-threatening allergy to their stings). More generally, we can say:

Mistaken Emotions II: *It is a mistake for one's emotion to be too strong or too weak given the facts of the situation.*

Thus, it would be manipulation for a Florida hotel manager to make his guests so afraid of alligators that they stay on the alligator-free hotel grounds and take all their meals from the hotel restaurant. But it would not be manipulation to induce those tourists to be sufficiently fearful of alligators that they do not let their children swim where alligators lurk. When Maddie gets Tim to be so fearful of the light snow that he skips the party that he wants to attend, this seems to be manipulation. It's not that snow flurries warrant no concern at all (after all, they might portend worsening conditions later), but that Maddie gets Tim to be excessively fearful of something that warrants no more than mild apprehension that conditions might worsen. By contrast, the efforts of therapists to reduce excessive fears, anxiety, etc., are not only not manipulation, but they can make patients less susceptible to emotional manipulation by others.

It is often easier for a manipulator to get someone who already feels an emotion to feel it to an excessive degree than to get someone to feel the emotion in the first place. Getting someone to feel an emotion that is not fitting at any strength will often require getting that person to believe (or at least suspect) something false, as we see in *Othello*, where Iago must get Othello to falsely believe (or at least suspect) that Desdemona has been unfaithful in order to get him to feel jealousy and anger. Similarly, since it seems easier to ramp up an emotion than to tamp it down, it seems likely that manipulation that induces mistaken emotional intensity will more often involve inducing excessive rather than deficient emotional intensity.

One might worry that this kind of mistaken emotion will be difficult to specify because emotional intensity is a matter of degree, and because it will be difficult, if not impossible, to specify exactly what level of intensity of some emotion is appropriate to the circumstances. How intensely should someone fear the prospect of that alligator attack in Florida, for example? And if we cannot answer that question, how can we know whether someone has induced, or tried to induce, a mistaken level of fear?

This concern certainly complicates the application of the Mistake Account, but it is less of a problem than it may initially seem, for several reasons. First, even though it is difficult and maybe even impossible to specify a precise level of rational fear (or "healthy respect") of alligators, there *are* levels of fear that are clearly excessive and clearly deficient. Even if—as seems likely—there is a range of non-mistaken levels of alligator fear, this will seldom matter when it comes to identifying manipulation. If a manipulator chooses to influence someone's level of alligator fear, this will usually be part of an attempt to influence that person's overall behavior. And doing *that* will typically require making a *significant* change in the person's level of fear, one that would likely push it into one of the clearly mistaken extremes. If my goal is to get you to spend your entire Florida vacation in my alligator-free resort, then I will try to get you to feel a clearly excessive fear. If my goal is to lure you into an alligator-infested swamp to secure your demise, I will try to get you to feel a clearly deficient fear. Questions about whether it is manipulative to get you to feel just a little less or just a little more fear will seldom raise questions about manipulation, since such changes are unlikely to be useful to the manipulator.

Second, we must remember that whether an influencer *acts manipulatively* depends on whether the influencer tried to induce in someone else what the *influencer* regards as a mistake. So the fact that *different* reasonable people might disagree about, for example, how much one should fear alligators in Florida, is not especially relevant to the question of whether a *particular* person *acted manipulatively*. The answer to *that* question depends on what level of fear the *influencer* regards as excessive or deficient. And that question often will have a fairly determinate answer. Of course, this will not help us determine whether the objective standard for being manipulated (in the strict sense) has been met. But when our focus is on whether someone acted manipulatively—as it often is—the problem of differing views about what level of emotional intensity is mistaken will not arise.

Third, we must remember that the criterion for manipulation is inducing a *mistake*. The Mistake Account does not claim that it is manipulation to induce someone to feel an emotion at anything other than the exact perfect intensity. If there is a range of acceptable levels of intensity for some emotion, then inducing someone to feel an emotion with an intensity within that range will not be manipulation. This is an advantage of moving from defining manipulation in terms of departures from "ideal settings" (Noggle 1996) to defining it in terms of mistakes. The fact that there may be no unique, maximally rational level of intensity for a given emotion does not threaten a standard that defines manipulation in terms of a *mistaken* level of emotional intensity.

Finally, the challenge is not significantly different from the challenge of identifying deception with regard to vague propositions. Suppose that Alice says to Beth, "There are many varieties of apples for sale at the farmer's market," and Beth believes her. But when Beth goes to the market, she is disappointed to find that there are precisely five different varieties available. Has she been deceived? To answer this question, it would seem natural to ask, not whether Beth regards five as "many," or whether in some objective sense five is "many," but whether Alice regards five as "many." If Alice does not regard five as "many," then she acted deceptively. The fact that there may be no uniquely, objectively correct answer to the question of whether five *really is* "many" may make it impossible to answer the question of whether Beth was deceived. But we hardly take such cases as counterexamples to the idea that a person is deceived when **N**'s successful attempt to get her to believe what **N** regards as false causes her to believe what really is false. Sometimes we must rest content with a well-defined answer to the question of whether someone *acted deceptively*, but no well-defined answer to the question of whether the other person *was deceived*. By the same token, sometimes we must rest content with a well-defined answer to the question of whether someone *acted manipulatively*, but no well-defined answer to the question of whether the other person was *manipulated*.

7.9. Akratic Mistakes

Chapter 4 argued that manipulative pressure is best understood as the pressure exerted by non-optimalizing incentives or disincentives, which change behavior when and because the target responds akratically to them. As we also noted, there are several different theories about how akrasia occurs, and thus several different ways that manipulative pressure might operate. Indeed, it seems likely that akrasia occurs in more than one way, so that manipulative pressure can work in more than one way. Consequently, the task of specifying the mistake that constitutes the akrasia induced by manipulative pressure might seem hopelessly complicated. Fortunately, we can bypass many of these complications by making the following observation, which should apply to all forms of pressure-induced akrasia: A person who gives in to a non-optimalizing incentive or disincentive reacts to it *as though* it were optimalizing. And this requires reacting to that incentive or disincentive *as though* its magnitude were larger than it really is. This observation suggests the following characterization of the mistake induced by successful applications of manipulative pressure:

> *It is a mistake to respond to an incentive or disincentive as though its magnitude were greater than its true magnitude.*

However, complications arise when we consider what "true magnitude" means when applied to an incentive or disincentive. The true magnitude of an incentive or disincentive is not a fixed quantity. Instead, it depends on the preference structure or utility function of the person being subjected to it. And this depends, in turn, on the person's values, goals, preferences, plans, priorities, and so on.

Consider an incentive of $20.00. Its "true magnitude" depends on various facts about the person to whom it is offered. If it is offered to a poor high school student as compensation for an hour of work at a fast-food restaurant, it might have a fairly high magnitude. If it is offered to a successful attorney for the same hour of fast-food employment, its magnitude will be laughably small. This is a well-known fact about financial incentives, but it applies to other incentives as well. An incentive of an ice cream cone will have different magnitudes depending on, among other things, whether the recipient is lactose-intolerant. The disincentive created by a threat to withdraw one's friendship depends on how much the target values that friendship.

So how should we think of the "true magnitude" of some incentive or disincentive for the purposes of determining whether someone's reaction to it is mistaken? Recall that the Mistake Account defines "**N** acts manipulatively toward T" in terms of **N** trying to get T to make a mistake. Notice that trying to get *the target* to make a mistake is not the same as trying to get the target to do something that it would be a mistake for *the influencer* to do. This detail is important because what is a mistake for one person might not be a mistake for another. Suppose that Fred plans to go fishing on his vacation, but Nick does not. It would be a mistake for Fred to fail to pack his fishing gear, but it would not be a mistake for Nick to fail to pack his. Consequently, what the influencer regards as a mistake *for the target* may be different from what the influencer would regard as a mistake *for the influencer*. Thus, whether the influencer is trying to get the *target to make a mistake* depends on what the influencer thinks would be a mistake *for the target to make*, since this may be different from what the influencer thinks would be a mistake for the influencer to make. To continue our earlier example, assuming that Nick knows about Fred's fishing plans, if Nick tries to get Fred to fail to pack his fishing gear, then Nick tries to get Ted to make a "packing-mistake"—even though it would *not* be a "packing-mistake" for Nick to fail to pack his own fishing gear.

Thus, if acting manipulatively involves **N** trying to get T to make a mistake, then it involves **N** trying to get **T** to make what (**N** thinks) would be a mistake for T, and not what (**N** thinks) would be a mistake for **N**. Applying this reasoning to actual cases yields plausible results. Suppose that Nora knows that Ted is an alcoholic, and that Tammy is a non-disordered connoisseur of Scotch whisky. It would be manipulative for Nora to exploit Ted's alcoholism by offering him a $20.00 bottle of Cutty Sark for his $500 bicycle that he uses to commute to work. For it would be an addiction-induced mistake for Ted to make such a trade. (He would be akratically reacting to the incentive of the cheap Scotch as though it were a bigger incentive than it really is.) But it would not be manipulative for Nora to offer Tammy a $500 bottle of 18-year-old Macallan double-cask single-malt for her $500 bicycle that she never uses. For it would not be a mistake for Tammy to treat that incentive as being sufficient to justify such a trade. Notice that these judgments do not rest on what Nora herself would regard as a mistake *for Nora*. For example, if Nora is no Scotch connoisseur, and if the Macallan is missing the label and documentation that would allow it to be re-sold for its market value, then it would clearly be a mistake for *her* to accept *either* bottle of Scotch for her $500 bicycle. What matters is whether Nora tries to get the target to make what, *for the target*, would be a mistaken overreaction to the incentive she offers.

One might worry that this extra level of perspective-dependence makes manipulative pressure significantly different from other forms of manipulation like deception—which was, after all, the Mistake Account's model for manipulation. It is true that we do not normally need this extra layer of perspective-taking when thinking about deception. But that is not because of some deep difference between deception and manipulation. Rather, it is because we usually specify the content of a belief in such a way that a false belief is what we might call a "person invariant" mistake. If there are no cookies in the cupboard, then it is a mistake to believe the proposition "there are cookies in the cupboard," no matter who you are (so long, of course, as we are all talking about the same cupboard). Consequently, there is no difference between what it would be mistaken for Tim to believe versus what it would be mistaken for Dora to believe.

But there *can* be such a difference in non-deceptive manipulation, and not just manipulative pressure. Iago's manipulation of Othello involves getting Othello to be angry with Desdemona when *Othello* has no good reason to be angry with her. Suppose that we re-told the story so that *Iago* has some reason to be angry with Desdemona—one that would not be a reason for Othello to be angry with her. In that version of the story, Iago's making Othello angry with Desdemona would still be manipulation because what matters is whether it is a mistake *for Othello* to be angry with her. Similarly, it would be manipulation for Mike to get Thaddeus to be terrified of a honeybee whose sting would do him only minor harm, even if *Mike* has a severe bee-sting allergy that makes it fitting *for Mike* to have a strong fear of honeybees.

The fact that other forms of manipulation display the same target-dependence that manipulative pressure displays might not seem comforting if our worry is that this feature destroys the parallel between manipulation and deception. But it turns out that we can duplicate this phenomenon *even in some cases of deception* because the content of some beliefs can be specified so that believing them can be a person-*variant* mistake. Suppose that Dave knows that he can run a five-minute mile and that Tracy cannot. If Dave tries to get Tracy to believe that she can run a five-minute mile, he would be inducing her to believe, falsely, the proposition that "Tracy can run a five-minute mile." Stated this way, the mistake is person-invariant. But if we state the content of the belief as "I can run a five-minute mile," then the parallel with manipulative pressure emerges. Dave deceives Tracy if he gets her to believe "I can run a five-minute mile" even though it would not be a mistake *for Dave to believe* "I can run a five-minute mile." Whether Dave deceives Tracy depends on whether he gets Tracy to believe something that would be a mistake *for Tracy* to believe.

Of course, we do not generally specify belief contents in this first-person way. But the fact that, when we do, deception involves inducing someone to believe something that would be a mistake *for the target to believe* demonstrates that the apparent dissimilarity between deception and other forms of manipulation is an artefact of how we normally specify the contents of beliefs, and not a deep difference between deception and other forms of manipulation. Thus, we need not be troubled by the need to specify akratic mistakes in terms of what would be a mistake *for the target to make.*

Taking all these considerations into account, we can say:

Akratic Response Mistake: *It is a mistake to respond to an incentive or disincentive as though its magnitude is greater than it is, given one's preferences, values, plans, priorities, etc.*[11]

7.10. Conclusion

We have now discussed the main kinds of mistakes induced in all the forms of manipulation that we discussed in Chapter 2.

The various forms of manipulative pressure all induce akratic response mistakes. Playing on the emotions induces one of the two emotional mistakes. Misdirection and misemphasis induce attention and weighting mistakes. Gaslighting induces the target to mistakenly doubt that her own judgment is sound. Game switching induces a game/script mistake. Social proof, when it is manipulative, induces a heuristic mistake. Negging and conditional flattery can involve either pressure or deception, or some combination of the two, and so they induce either mistaken beliefs, akratic response mistakes, or both.

It appears, then, that all the forms of manipulation that we have examined can be seen to involve the influencer's attempt to induce the target to make one of these mistakes. I have not claimed that the list of manipulative tactics in Chapter 2 is complete. Nor would I claim that this chapter provides a complete list of mistakes the deliberate induction of which is manipulative. For example, we might imagine complicated cases of manipulation that involve getting the target to place more (or less) credence in a proposition than the evidence for it warrants. But we need not cover every single mistake that a manipulator might seek to induce in order to illustrate and defend the Mistake Account's analysis of manipulation. I take it that we have done enough here for that purpose.

[11] Strictly speaking, it is better not to call a decision that results from an Akratic Response Mistake a "mistaken decision." This is because the existence of inverse akrasia entails that a decision can be akratic but not mistaken, at least in the sense that it can promote the decision-maker's interests better than the non-akratic decision would have. What is mistaken in an akratic decision is not the content of the decision, but the *process* by which it arose. (This is one reason why the definitions of manipulation developed in section 6.2 include the phrase "or processes.") If we do choose to call an akratic decision mistaken, we should keep in mind that we are speaking loosely, and that the mistake is *not* in the *content* of the decision but in the akratic *process* by which it arose.

8
The Psychology of Manipulation

8.1. Introduction

The previous chapter discussed the kinds of mistakes the induction of which constitutes manipulation. This chapter will sketch some of the psychological processes that manipulators use to get people to make those mistakes.

8.2. Decisions and Actions

Let us begin with a rough sketch of the processes by which behavior is produced.[1] When someone does something, it is often because the person *decided* to do (or to try to do[2]) that thing. As I shall use the terms, to *decide* is to settle the question of what to do, and a *decision* is what settles it. Someone who decides to do something becomes strongly inclined to do that thing. The person will then normally at least try to do that thing, unless something prevents it, or the person revokes the decision. (Some philosophers use the term 'intention' for what I am calling a 'decision.') I shall use the terms 'decision-making' and 'deciding' interchangeably to refer to the process of settling the question of what to do.

When a person does **A** because that person *decided* to do **A**, I will call the action *deliberate*. (Many philosophers would call this an intentional action.) The process of making a decision plays a key role in initiating a deliberate action. But some of our behavior is not initiated in this way. What I shall call non-deliberate behavior occurs without a decision to initiate it.[3] Habits, reflexes, and stimulus-response patterns are among the processes that can initiate non-deliberate behavior.

The fact that non-deliberate behavior is not initiated by a decision does not put it beyond conscious control, however. We can interrupt, override, or resist the processes that initiate non-deliberate behavior, and we can interrupt such behavior if it has already begun. Thus, I might habitually pet the cat when it sits next to me.

[1] When possible, I will side-step debates in action theory about the nature of intention and intentional action, the distinction between full-fledged actions and "mere" behavior, and so on. When this is impossible, I shall fill in the sketch in ways that I find most plausible, or that reflect the most prevalent scholarly opinions.

[2] In the interests of brevity, I will generally omit this qualification unless it is relevant.

[3] Some philosophers claim that a behavior that does not result from a decision is not an action; in speaking of non-deliberate *behavior*, I am neither endorsing nor rejecting this view.

Manipulation. Robert Noggle, Oxford University Press. © Robert Noggle 2025.
DOI: 10.1093/9780198924920.003.0008

Although I might normally do this without deciding to, I can decide to override the habit-created impulse to do so, if I notice it before my hand reaches the cat. If I have already begun petting the cat, I can decide to stop. Thus, deliberate action happens only if a decision initiates it, while non-deliberate behavior may commence and continue unless the person decides to override or interrupt it. If I fail to notice that I am engaged in, or about to initiate, some non-deliberate behavior, then I may fail to override or interrupt it, even if it is contrary to my current goals. For example, I might find myself absent-mindedly petting the cat out of habit, before I realize that this activity is getting cat hair all over the blazer I put on to attend an important meeting.

Deliberate action arises from a decision-making process which raises and settles the question of what to do. Some deliberate actions are complexes that include non- or less deliberate components. Driving to my office is a deliberate action—a thing that I decide to do. But it includes many components that are so habitual that I do not need to decide to initiate them. These include slowing down to avoid colliding with the car in front of me, keeping my car centered in my lane, and shifting the gears of a manual transmission.

Deciding what to do may involve more or less elaborate processes of conscious practical reasoning, problem-solving, weighing of pros and cons, etc. I shall generally reserve the term 'deliberation' to refer to processes like this, that is, processes of consciously thinking about what to do. Thus, deliberation often plays a role in the decision-making process. But it need not. Often, decision-making involves simply recognizing that there is an obvious thing to do and deciding to do it. If I try to open the door to my car and find it locked, it is obvious that I should unlock it, and decision-making may consist of nothing more than recognizing the obviousness of that course of action and deciding to do it. Often, we decide to do something—like petting the nearby cat—simply because we want to, and without thinking about it. Any deliberation that takes place in such a case is likely to be very minimal, consisting of little more than briefly considering whether there is any reason not to do the thing we feel like doing. But even that minimal form of deliberation may well be absent. For example, someone who acts impulsively, or on a strong emotion, may simply decide to do something without bothering to consider whether there are reasons not to.

Often, then, a default action comes to mind as the obvious or appealing thing to do, and deliberation, if it occurs at all, involves quickly scanning for reasons not to ratify that default. More elaborate deliberation might occur when there is no default action, either because I don't know what I feel like doing, or because no course of action seems like the obvious thing to do. It may also occur when there is some problem with the default action. If I feel like petting the cat but realize that this will get fur on my blazer, I may weigh the pros and cons of petting the cat versus a blazer free of cat hair. If I try to unlock the car and discover that my keys are missing, I may engage in more elaborate deliberation about what to do next. This may include weighing the pros and cons of calling a tow truck, searching my house for the keys, or brainstorming ways to unlock the car without keys.

Although philosophers tend to focus on decisions that result from elaborate forms of deliberation, the vast majority of our decisions involve little or no deliberation. Nevertheless, they still settle the question of what to do; they just employ little if any conscious thought in doing so. Such decisions are sometimes disparaged as "snap decisions." It is certainly true that a snap decision can be unwise; indeed, many of our most unwise decisions are of this variety. But sometimes they are just what we need. If a piano is falling on me, a snap decision to move to the right rather than the left is probably wiser than wasting time deliberating about which direction to move.

8.3. The Limits of Deliberation

One need not be in the path of a falling piano to face the problem of insufficient time for deliberation. Full deliberation can take more time than you have even when you do have some time. Deliberation is especially slow when there are multiple options, when the outcomes of one's options are uncertain, or when all the obvious options are bad. As Chris Mills aptly puts it, "our decisions are subject to cognitive scarcity" (Mills 2018, 403). But a more fundamental reason for deliberation to take more time than we have involves the nature of deliberation itself.

Consider what *maximally complete* deliberation would look like. Before I start deliberating, I would first decide *whether* to deliberate at all, as opposed to simply doing what I feel like, or what seems like the thing to do. Many considerations might be relevant to that decision. How likely is it that what seems like the thing to do is, in fact, a good thing to do? What are the potential costs and benefits of taking the time to deliberate? How likely is it that I failed to notice some compelling reason not to do what I feel like doing or what seems like the obvious thing to do? Once I decide to deliberate, I must determine what my options are, what I need or want to achieve, and the likely consequences of my various options. Identifying options is itself an open-ended process. At any given time, there is an indefinitely large number of things that I could do. My first task is to narrow down my options to those that might have a positive effect on my interests and goals. If my narrowed-down list of options includes ones that could further *competing* interests and goals, then I will need to prioritize them. This process itself might be open-ended, as it might involve critical reflection about my interests and goals and the importance I place on them. In any case, I will need to determine the likely effects of each option that might further my interests and goals. For each of these deliberative tasks, I will need to determine what information is relevant. If I am missing relevant information, I may then need to deliberate about whether to try to obtain it or whether to ignore it. For each bit of information that I bring to bear on one of these deliberative tasks, I might inquire about how certain I am that the information is accurate and complete.

In short, deliberation requires inputs, which implies some prior determination of which factors are relevant to the situation about which deliberation is to take place. And here a regress threatens: Before deliberation begins, we must select the inputs into it. But selecting the inputs for deliberation is a mental process that requires its own inputs. So, we must first select the inputs into the process of selecting inputs into deliberation. But that process also requires its own inputs, and so on. In theory, this regress could be infinite. But it need not be infinite in practice to be paralyzing. Clearly, we must have some way of avoiding or terminating it. And the processes that terminate it cannot be instances of deliberation or rely on the outputs of deliberation, since that would simply start a new regress.[4]

Of course, it always remains possible to cut off this regress, or to avoid it entirely, by simply *deciding*—deciding to stop deliberating, or deciding not to deliberate at all. But to cut off the original regress without triggering a new one, such a decision cannot itself result from full and complete deliberation. But now we must worry that any decision capable of cutting of the regress will be arbitrary, and an arbitrary decision seems little better than the regress it quashes.

Fortunately, an arbitrary decision is not the only solution to the regress problem. Our evolutionary history has provided us with various mechanisms that allow us to terminate or avoid the regress without making our decisions arbitrary. Many of these mechanisms enabled our pre-human ancestors—and continue to enable non-human animals—to behave in advantageous ways without complex deliberative faculties.

Some of these evolutionarily old mechanisms make salient stimuli that are crucial for survival and then prime action appropriate to them. For example, there appears to be an ancient, hard-wired "snake detection module" built into the human brain (Öhman, Flykt, and Esteves 2001). If a snake slithers across your room, it will command your attention, and it will likely trigger emotional responses that prepare you for action. Even catching a snake-shaped object out of the corner of your eye will likely direct your attention to finding out whether it really is a snake, and taking appropriate action if it is. Similar mechanisms are likely to operate for such things as abrupt drop-offs, and the eyes of potential predators. Such modules drive attention toward important environmental cues. They save us the trouble of having to decide whether the cliff edge, or a snake in our path, or eyes staring at us through the grass, are worth paying attention to.

[4] For similar observations, see Arpaly and Schroeder (2012).

8.4. Bounded Rationality, Heuristics, and Dual Process Theories

It is easy to see how evolutionarily old danger-detection modules helped our ancestors, and continue to help non-human animals, make good decisions in a timely way. But since contemporary environments tend to be devoid of predators, precipices, and serpents, they are of limited use in solving our versions of the problem of time pressures on decision-making.

A more comprehensive solution involves the kinds of short-cuts discussed within the "bounded rationality" approach to decision-making favored by researchers like Herbert Simon and Gerd Gigerenzer. This approach begins with the observation that "decision-making agents in the real world must arrive at their inferences using realistic amounts of time, information, and computational resources" (Gigerenzer and Todd 1999, 24). A key feature of bounded rationality is the focus on satisficing rather than optimizing, that is, choosing an option that is good enough rather than continuing to seek the very best option even after a good-enough option has been identified (Simon 1956).[5]

Another is the use of cognitive and decision-making shortcuts called heuristics (Gigerenzer and Todd 1999). Heuristics can contribute to the speed of decision-making in several ways. Consider the "do as others do" heuristic discussed in section 7.5. This heuristic is action-guiding in a very direct way because its output can be used to settle the question of what to do. Other heuristics are what we might call "procedural" heuristics because they tell us *how* to do something rather than *what* to do. This category includes one of Gigerenzer's main examples: the heuristic that tells us to catch a fly ball by moving toward it in such a way as to keep it at a constant angle in one's visual field (Gigerenzer 2007, 8–13). These heuristics help settle questions about *how* to do what we've decided to do. Other heuristics speed decision-making by helping us draw conclusions about facts relevant to deliberation. For example, Gigerenzer suggests that, in making purchasing decisions, we often use brand name recognition as a proxy for quality (Gigerenzer 2007, 126–29).[6]

Heuristics can be used consciously. Indeed, Gigerenzer advocates using heuristics consciously and deliberately to speed up and improve certain forms of medical decision-making (Gigerenzer 2007, 158–78). However, Gigerenzer also maintains that heuristics form the basis of unconscious processes that can produce a "gut feeling" or "intuition." This, according to Gigerenzer, is a "judgement (1) that appears quickly in consciousness, (2) whose underlying reasons we are not fully

[5] On the psychological benefits of satisficing, see Schwartz (2005). While it is widely held that satisficing is often rational, there is some debate among philosophers over whether it is rational *in itself*, or simply in the strategic sense of being an optimal decision rule. For a sampling of this debate, see the papers in Byron (2004). Nothing here turns on the outcome of that debate.

[6] This heuristic will be discussed in more detail in section 11.6.

aware of, and (3) is strong enough to act upon" (Gigerenzer 2007, 16). On this view, heuristics are involved in at least some of the unconscious processes whose outputs—such as default or recommended actions—can then be used in conscious decision-making.

Similar ideas emerge from Gary Klein's work on what he calls *recognition-primed decision-making* (Klein 2017). Based on extensive studies of the decision-making of experts like experienced lead firefighters, Klein argues that experts often simply recognize the situation and know what to do. One of Klein's most striking findings is that experts deliberating under time pressure seldom compare multiple options. Instead, their experience allows them to grasp the situation quickly and effortlessly, and to identify a candidate action that is likely to be satisfactory. Deliberation then takes the form of determining whether this candidate action really is likely to succeed. Additional deliberation might occur if the situation does not behave as expected, or if the initial candidate action is rejected as unsatisfactory or fails after being attempted. Klein's research indicates that recognition-primed decision-making occurs when the decision-maker has extensive experience with the kind of situation at hand. By contrast, decision-makers who lack such experience tend to engage in deliberation that compares the pros and cons of multiple options (Klein 2017, 21–24; 96–102).

Importantly, much of the work that goes on in recognition-primed decision-making does not involve conscious deliberation. On Klein's view, recognition is not a deliberate, conscious mental process, but rather an automatic reaction to the situation:

> we size the situation up and immediately know how to proceed: which goals to pursue, what to expect, how to respond. We are drawn to certain cues and not others because of our situation awareness. (This must happen all the time. Try to imagine going through a day without making *these automatic responses.*) (Klein 2017, 35, emphasis added)

Thus, the processes that harness the expert's experience and tacit knowledge to identify what is important in the situation, what goals might be achieved, and what course of action might achieve those goals, are unconscious and automatic. Indeed, Klein notes that experts often describe the candidate option as simply obvious or report knowing what to do without knowing *how* they know (Klein 2017, 33–44).

In short, then, both Klein and Gigerenzer distinguish between conscious deliberation about what to do, and non-conscious automatic processes that yield judgments about what to do. This resembles a distinction that is the cornerstone of *dual process theories* of cognition and decision-making. Such theories have become influential in psychology, behavioral economics, and other areas. They posit two distinct types of mental processes or mental systems. Type 1 or "System 1" processes are automatic, fast, and unconscious. Type 2 or "System 2" processes are slow, conscious, and deliberate.[7]

Because they involve conscious attention, Type 2 processes are more familiar. In his popular book, *Thinking, Fast and Slow*, Daniel Kahneman describes Type 2 processes ("System 2") as allocating "attention to the effortful mental activities that demand it, including complex computations" (Kahneman 2013, 21). He also notes that Type 2 or System 2 processes "are often associated with the subjective experience of agency, choice, and concentration" (Kahneman 2013, 21). Moreover, he observes that "when we think of ourselves, we identify with System 2, the conscious reasoning self that has beliefs, makes choices, and decides what to think about and what to do" (Kahneman 2013, 21). By contrast, he describes Type 1 or System 1 processes as operating "automatically and quickly, with little or no effort and no sense of voluntary control" (Kahneman 2013, 20). Type 1 or System 1 processes assist conscious decision-making by "effortlessly originating impressions and feelings that are the main sources of the explicit beliefs and deliberate choices of System 2" (Kahneman 2013, 21).

In one of the most sophisticated statements and defenses of dual process theory, Jonathan Evans and Keith Stanovich (Evans and Stanovich 2013) isolate the most essential elements that define the two types of processes. They conclude that:

> the defining characteristic of Type 1 processes is their autonomy. They do not require "controlled attention," which is another way of saying that they make minimal demands on working memory resources . . . [T]he execution of Type 1 processes is mandatory when their triggering stimuli are encountered and they are not dependent on input from high-level control systems . . . Into the category of autonomous processes would go some processes of emotional regulation; the encapsulated modules for solving specific adaptive problems that have been posited by evolutionary psychologists; processes of implicit learning; and the automatic firing of overlearned associations. (Evans and Stanovich 2013, 236)

Thus, Type 1 processes are automatic and do not require working memory, which is associated with conscious attention. By contrast, Type 2 processes require working memory, and thus conscious attention, and are associated with abstract and hypothetical reasoning of the sort needed for conscious deliberation.

For our purposes, the most important idea from dual process theories is that automatic, nonconscious Type 1 processes produce inputs for Type 2 processes of conscious deliberation. That is, the outputs of Type 1 processes—which some

[7] Construing this distinction in terms of two separate "systems" rather than two kinds of processes is somewhat misleading because there is likely no meaningful sense in which all the Type 1 processes constitute a single system. But speaking of two systems has become common in popular discussions of dual processing theories.

theorists call "intuitions"—are inputs into more reflective, Type 2 processes of deliberation. This idea is one that dual process theories share with the work of Klein and Gigerenzer. In a fascinating paper co-written with Kahneman, Klein writes that in his model, "the performance of experts involves both an automatic process that brings promising solutions to mind and a deliberate activity in which the execution of the candidate solution is mentally simulated . . ." and that the "intuitive judgments and preferences have the characteristics of System 1 activity: They are automatic, arise effortlessly, and often come to mind without immediate justification" (Kahneman and Klein 2009, 519).

Gigerenzer has been critical of certain aspects of dual process theories (Kruglanski and Gigerenzer 2011). Yet, as we saw, he acknowledges that unconscious processes can produce "intuitions" or "gut feelings" that can serve as inputs into conscious decision-making. Moreover, he writes that

> Music and sports are examples about how skills are learned in a deliberate fashion but at some point become intuitive; that is, attention is no longer directed to the movements and people cannot explain how they do what they do . . . In general, many, but not all, skills are learned deliberately and then become intuitive or turn into gut feelings. . . . The transition from deliberate to intuitive rules is a valuable process given that attention is a scarce resource. (Kruglanski and Gigerenzer 2011, 102)

Despite his disagreements with some of the details of dual process theory, then, Gigerenzer endorses what, for our purposes, is its central idea: Fast, automatic mental processes that require no conscious attention or effort provide at least some of the inputs for conscious deliberation and decision-making.

Such processes help to solve the regress that would otherwise leave us paralyzed by the need to select inputs into the processes that select inputs into the processes . . . that select inputs into the process of deliberation. As Evans notes, it has been "long recognized in psychology" that "the locus of conscious attention must be determined by mostly *pre*conscious processes" (Evans 2010, 202, emphasis original). Often, these preconscious processes focus our attention on a particularly promising course of action. Sometimes this is all we need, and conscious decision-making simply ratifies the course of action suggested by the fast preconscious automatic processes. In other cases, more elaborate conscious deliberation may occur. As Evans writes:

> Our intuitions often suggest an immediate answer or decision that we may be tempted to accept without any serious reflection. After all, intuition is effortless and reflection is hard work. This suggested inference or action we call the *default* or intuitive response. Often this default is accepted and acted upon. However, the reflective mind can also intervene by overriding this default response and

> replacing it with one which is more considered, based on slower, reflective thinking. (Evans 2010, 204)

Stanovich makes a similar point:

> One of the most critical functions of Type 2 processing is to override Type 1 processing. This is sometimes necessary because autonomous processing has heuristic qualities. It is designed to get the response into the right ballpark when solving a problem or making a decision, but it is not designed for the type of fine-grained analysis called for in situations of unusual importance . . . (Stanovich 2011, 20)

But even when more elaborate, conscious deliberation occurs, it draws upon the outputs of the fast preconscious automatic processes. For those processes focus our attention on the most relevant features of the situation, such as threats that might be present, opportunities to further our goals, etc. Thus, these fast preconscious automatic processes cut off the deliberative regress. But whether they do so in a way that is *superior* to an arbitrary decision to stop deliberating, or to forgo it entirely, depends on the *quality* of what they provide to decision-making.

The fact that Type 1 processes are automatic and require no conscious attention makes them fast and effortless. But these characteristics also make them vulnerable to errors. This vulnerability is sometimes overstated in the literature on dual process theories, especially that portion taking the "heuristics and biases" approach associated with Kahneman and Amos Tversky. System 1 is sometimes characterized as an impulsive simpleton whose foolishness contrasts with the cognitive sophistication and rationality of System 2. It is easy to think of System 2 as "Reason with a capital R." If we accept this characterization, we might be tempted to think of Type 1 processes as bypassing reason. This might tempt us to equate influences that employ them with manipulation.

However, we should resist the temptation to regard Type 1 processes as stupid, and the related temptation to equate influences that employ them with manipulation. As Evans and Stanovich write:

> Perhaps the most persistent fallacy in the perception of dual-process theories is the idea that Type 1 processes (intuitive, heuristic) are responsible for all bad thinking and that Type 2 processes (reflective, analytic) necessarily lead to correct responses. (Evans and Stanovich 2013, 229)

If anything, these remarks do not go far enough. Anyone who has taught—or even learned—formal logic will remember just how easy it is for our conscious logical reasoning processes to make mistakes. Similarly, complex mathematical calculations are paradigm examples of Type 2 processing, and they are hardly free of errors. Moreover, when Type 2 processes do yield correct answers, they are often very slow—a fact whose consequences range from merely inconvenient to potentially lethal.

By contrast, Type 1 processes often provide reliable outputs with astonishing speed. They perform a vast array of vital cognitive functions, from visual processing to reading to facial recognition to language parsing. They enable us to do things that we could never manage if we relied only on Type 2 processes: catching a ball, riding a bicycle, driving a car, playing a musical instrument, reading these words, etc. For the most part, these tasks are performed very accurately. Moreover, fast automatic preconscious processes allow experts to quickly, accurately, and effortlessly solve problems that non-experts can solve only through arduous and time-consuming conscious reasoning. Some of Klein's most interesting work, for example, concerns how these processes allow experienced firefighters to make good decisions almost effortlessly in complicated, life-and-death situations (Klein 2017).

One advantage of Type 1 processes is that they draw upon a vast store of implicit knowledge, rather than the limited amount of information that can be held in mind consciously. As Henning Plessner and Sabine Czenna observe,

> implicit knowledge is assumed to reflect one's entire prior experiences with a judgmental object or a decision option. As such, it can contain the integration of much more information than one would be able to handle explicitly and thus provides a valuable resource for judgment and decision making . . . Taken together, on the basis of our two systems framework, we expect people to benefit from their intuition when they possess implicit knowledge that goes beyond their explicit knowledge in a given judgment or decision task. (Plessner and Czenna 2008, 257–58)

Ultimately, identifying manipulative influences with Type 1 processes and non-manipulative influences with Type 2 processes would give too much credit to the latter and too little to the former. Moreover, it would lead to decidedly counter-intuitive implications. If you are engrossed in a good book and haven't noticed the errant baseball on a collision course with your head, and I yell out "Hey!" to get you to look up, then I have employed a Type 1 process. But it hardly seems correct to say that I manipulated you. Or consider Iago's manipulation of Othello. Much of this involves Iago getting Othello to draw false conclusions about Cassio and Desdemona. But Othello seems to draw these conclusions *consciously and deliberately*—he works through them in those wonderful soliloquies, after all—and so they seem to involve Type 2 processes. But it would be very odd to say that Iago does not manipulate Othello on these occasions because he triggers only his Type 2 processes.

While it is important not to overstate the vulnerability of Type 1 processes to error, it is also important not to understate it. Researchers working within the "heuristics and biases" approach have documented many specific error types to which Type 1 processes are susceptible. And even those who tout the powers of Type 1 processes acknowledge their limitations. Klein, for example, carefully documents breakdowns in recognition-primed decision-making that occur when the decision-maker first misreads the situation and then fails to notice discrepancies between the actual situation and this initial read. In their co-written paper, Kahneman and Klein identify conditions under which the processes that underlie recognition-primed decision-making are most trustworthy. Their main finding is that these processes can yield astonishingly good answers when they reflect a high degree of learning and experience gained under conditions similar to those in which they are subsequently deployed (Kahneman and Klein 2009, 524–25).

Evans and Stanovich provide a similarly balanced assessment of the reliability of Type 1 processing:

> Although the correlation between nonoptimal responses and Type 1 processing is no doubt modest in benign environments, it can be quite high in hostile environments . . . [F]or an environment to be classified as benign, it must not contain other individuals who will adjust their behavior to exploit those relying only on Type 1 processing . . . [A]n environment can turn hostile . . . if other agents discern the simple cues that are triggering Type 1 processing—and the other agents start to arrange the cues for their own advantage. (Evans and Stanovich 2013, 229)

As this quote suggests, the vulnerabilities of Type 1 processes can be exploited by other agents. The Mistake Account claims that when other agents do this to change someone's behavior in ways that induce mistakes, those agents are engaged in manipulation. But this is not because they are using Type 1 processes. Rather, it is because Type 1 processes—like Type 2 processes—are vulnerable to certain kinds of mistakes, and inducing mistakes is central to manipulation. In the next sections, we shall examine some of these vulnerabilities, and the role they can play in manipulation.

8.5. The Springs of Action: Processes and Vulnerabilities

The forgoing discussion of dual process theories helps flesh out our earlier sketch of "the springs of action." It also helps us see our vulnerabilities to various kinds of errors, some of which can be exploited by manipulators.

Let us start from the beginning. Perceptual cues from the environment are registered by both conscious awareness and non-conscious Type 1 processes. The latter draw on the agent's implicit knowledge, experience, and expertise to provide an initial interpretation of the situation, a sense of what aspects of it are most important, and, often, a recommendation about what to do. Thus, they set the stage for decision-making, that is, for settling the question of what to do. If the Type 1 processes have already identified a promising course of action, the agent may simply ratify this recommendation. If not, or if the Type 1 processes issue no recommendation, then the agent may do nothing at all, act according to the current dominant inclination, continue a complex action—like driving to work—already underway, or begin deliberating about what to do.

An agent who *does* engage in conscious deliberation will not start from scratch. The Type 1 processes will have already begun setting the stage. They will have already identified certain aspects of the situation as important by making them salient and drawing attention to them. They will have already brought to the agent's conscious attention pre-existing beliefs, desires, and goals relevant to the situation. And they may have already generated new beliefs about, or relevant to, the situation. Thus, the Type 1 processes provide an initial set of inputs from which deliberation can begin.

The agent might take these inputs at face value and deliberate accordingly. Alternatively, the agent might engage Type 2 reasoning processes to evaluate any of these inputs. This might lead the agent to accept, reject, modify, or supplement any or all of them. The agent might redirect attention to some aspect of the situation not already made salient by the Type 1 processes. The agent might question and perhaps reject some of the "intuitions" generated by the Type 1 processes about matters of fact. The agent might call to mind intermediate or long-range goals, or factual or means-end beliefs that seem relevant to the decision at hand. The agent might engage in conscious reasoning or problem-solving to generate new factual or means-ends beliefs or intermediate goals. The agent might weigh the considerations for and against one or more options. The agent might even engage in meta-deliberation about whether to maximize or satisfice, whether to seek additional information relevant to the decision, etc. But even when these more elaborate forms of conscious deliberation occur, they do not start from nothing. Automatic Type 1 processes set the stage. This is true even when the agent's conscious, Type 2 processes reject some or all the initial inputs delivered by the Type 1 processes.

This description surely oversimplifies the processes leading to action, and it may be incorrect in certain details. But its main outlines will suffice to identify vulnerabilities to mistakes, and thus, to manipulation. Errors can occur at virtually every point in these processes. Hence, there are many different opportunities for a manipulator to introduce mistakes into them.

Let us begin with one of the most common pathways to action: the one where Type 1 processes identify a candidate action, and the agent ratifies it with little if any deliberation. The manipulative tactic of game switching probably works by inducing an error into this process. The scripts that underlie this form of manipulation are prime candidates for the kind of implicit knowledge structures employed by Type 1 processes. Here, then, is a plausible explanation of what goes on in Herzog's example where Bert reveals proprietary information to Anne (section 2.2.4): Anne's collegial behavior matches examples of collegial behavior that Bert has experienced. This causes Bert's Type 1 processes to match his current situation to previous examples of collegial experiences and activate the script that applies to such situations. The Type 1 processes apply this script to recommend a default action of disclosing his company's budget when Anne notes that a certain solution's feasibility depends on the budget. He could—and should—override this recommendation, but instead he ratifies it (or simply acts on it automatically). Notice that the kind of procedural knowledge here resembles the experiential information that is applied to new situations in Gary Klein's model of recognition-primed decision-making. Anne exploits what is often a source of fast but good decisions to get Bert to make a bad decision. Other forms of manipulation that exploit tendencies to react automatically are likely to follow this same pattern. The "tailgating" tactic (section 2.2.4) where someone gains entry into a secured area simply by walking closely behind someone authorized to enter, so that the authorized person holds the door open out of habit, would be an example.[8]

As we have seen, agents can override default actions recommended by Type 1 processes. But this typically requires the agent to engage their Type 2 processes. An agent who *fails* to engage them will often simply ratify the course of action suggested by the Type 1 processes. This fact creates another vulnerability to manipulation. Suppose that T's Type 1 processes have recommended some course of action, **A**, that **M** wants T to choose. Suppose that **A** is something that T has reason *not* to choose, but T will only notice this reason if T consciously attends to some fact about the situation. In such a case, **M** might try to get T not to pay conscious attention to that fact. The most straightforward way for **M** to do this is to induce T to make an attention mistake. This might be done by drawing T's attention away from anything that might help T notice the reasons not to do what T's Type 1 processes have suggested. This, in turn, might involve drawing T's attention *to* some other (irrelevant) thing. It might also involve imposing time pressure on the decision to prevent T's Type 2 critical thinking processes from evaluating the advice T's Type 1 processes offered. Thus, mistakes of attention can be used not only to induce a mistake, but also to prevent the discovery of a mistake that has already been made. The original mistake might be one that the manipulator has deliberately gotten the Type 1 processes to make, as Anne does with Bert. But it might also be a mistake that the Type 1 processes made without any intervention by the manipulator.

[8] For a brief overview of some empirical work relevant to the effects of social norms on behavior, see Fennis and Stroebe (2021, 278–79).

Thus, **M** might notice that T has embarked on a course of action that **M** wants T to complete, but that T will likely abort if T notices some fact. In such a case, **M** might need only to distract T's attention from that fact.

These examples involve manipulators exploiting the fact that our behavior is often driven by a perfunctory ratification of recommendations from Type 1 processes, and that Type 2 deliberative processes are typically triggered only when we *notice* a reason for rejecting the recommendation. Indeed, the cybersecurity expert Christopher Hadnagy writes that "the goal of the social engineer is to get you to make a decision without thinking. The more you think, the more likely you are to realize that you are being manipulated" (Hadnagy 2018, 4).

If the agent engages the Type 2 deliberative processes, then a manipulator may induce mistakes by exploiting vulnerabilities in the *Type 1* processes that provide inputs for them. This may involve exploiting the vulnerabilities to error that are the price Type 1 processes pay for their astonishing speed. Some of these specific vulnerabilities will be discussed in more detail in the next section. But Type 2 processes are themselves hardly invulnerable to errors. So when an agent employs them, their vulnerabilities can also be targeted by manipulators. Manipulators frequently induce mistakes in conscious deliberation and reasoning processes. For example, part of Iago's manipulation of Othello involves getting Othello to draw mistaken conclusions from evidence that Iago arranges (such as the famous misplaced handkerchief). The processes by which Othello draws these mistaken conclusions are clearly Type 2 processes. Indeed, inducing mistakes into conscious Type 2 processes is probably a common way to induce mistaken beliefs. Since mistaken beliefs often drive emotional manipulation and gaslighting, Type 2 processes will often contribute to those forms of manipulation as well. As we know from Gigerenzer's work, heuristics can be employed consciously as well as nonconsciously. Thus, forms of manipulation that rely on heuristic mistakes, such as social proof, will often involve mistakes made by Type 2 processes. Finally, since akratic mistakes are often made during conscious deliberation, pressure-based forms of manipulation will often involve mistakes that are made by Type 2 processes.

A final way to induce mistakes in Type 2 processes involves degrading those processes themselves. There are many ways to do this: The manipulator might induce the target to deliberate while under the influence of alcohol or drugs. Strong emotions, fatigue, anxiety, agitation, or negative moods like depression can also degrade the quality of deliberation. Some ways of degrading the deliberative processes push a person in certain directions. Agitation seems more likely to push a person toward impulsive and aggressive behavior, while depression seems more likely to push a person toward defeatism. By choosing which mood to induce, the manipulator can nudge the target in whatever direction the manipulator wants.

8.6. Biases and Manipulation

As we noted earlier, many of the decision-making shortcuts that cut off the deliberative regress are vulnerable to errors. Some of these vulnerabilities constitute systematic cognitive, motivational, and decision-making biases. The literature on these biases is vast, as is the number of such biases that have been described and catalogued. It is neither possible nor necessary to cover them all here. Instead, we will examine those that are especially useful to manipulators.

8.6.1. The Availability Heuristic

This well-known heuristic has been extensively studied since it was first discussed in a groundbreaking article by Kahneman and Tversky, who define it as a "judgmental heuristic in which a person evaluates the frequency of classes or the probability of events by availability, i.e., by the ease with which relevant instances come to mind" (Tversky and Kahneman 1973, 207). Amanda Safford and Mark Pingle put it more succinctly: "People make judgments about the probability or likelihood of an event based on the ease with which examples come to mind" (Safford and Pingle 2015, 201).

For example, consider the question: Which is more common, fatalities from automobile accidents or fatalities from lightning strikes? Most people can answer this question easily without consulting mortality statistics, simply by noticing that they can recall instances of automobile fatalities much more readily than lightning fatalities. However, like most heuristics, the availability heuristic can lead one astray—a fact that Tversky and Kahneman noted early on:

> Availability is an ecologically valid clue for the judgment of frequency because, in general, frequent events are easier to recall or imagine than infrequent ones. However, availability is also affected by various factors which are unrelated to actual frequency. If the availability heuristic is applied, then such factors will affect the perceived frequency of classes and the subjective probability of events. Consequently, the use of the availability heuristic leads to systematic biases. (Tversky and Kahneman 1973, 209)

Here is a commonly-offered example where the availability *heuristic* becomes the availability *bias*:

> Are you more likely to die from a shark attack or from being hit by falling airplane parts? Most people would answer that the shark attack is more likely, but this is incorrect. This inaccurate judgment is due to the ability to more easily recall

news stories about shark attacks (at a small cost) than about falling airplane parts. (Safford and Pingle 2015, 201)[9]

Availability is related to salience, as Anine Riege and Rolf Reber note, "vividness and imaginability of an instance increase availability of the respective category that in turn increases judged frequency (or . . . judged probability) of occurrence of instances of the category" (Riege and Reber 2022, 181). Thus, things that make something salient also make it easier to remember. And things that are easier to remember are often judged more likely. This, in turn, can lead an agent to give them greater weight in decision-making. For example, sensationalistic media coverage of violent crime makes it more salient and thus more available to memory. The increased availability of such incidents then leads to their probability being overestimated. This can lead to excessive fear of improbable events, and the diversion of effort and resources away from protecting against objectively more likely threats toward protecting against less likely ones.

In effect, then, we may think of availability as a sort of salience within memory. But availability also seems to be partly an artefact of salience: the more vivid or salient something is, the more available it will be to memory. Thus, for the purposes of a manipulator, the availability heuristic might function as a way to "store" a deliberate salience distortion. Thus, Mandy from the case of ***University I*** in section 4.2 might use the availability heuristic to get Tara to overestimate the city's crime rate by recounting recent high-profile (and easy-to-remember) crimes there. Consequently, when Tara thinks about crime in the city, instances of crime will be easy to remember, which will make them seem more common than they are.

8.6.2. Framing Effects

Eric Kirchler and Christoph Kogler describe framing as "the various ways decision situations can be presented, resulting in markedly different representations of the same situation, and as a consequence leading to different choices" (Kirchler and Kogler 2015, 164). According to Anton Kühberger, the "framing effect" consists of a set of "well-established empirical findings showing that the wording of an utterance has predictable effects on peoples' responses even in equivalent situations" (Kühberger 2022, 61).

An influential taxonomy put forward by Irwin Levin, Sandra Schneider, and Gary Gaeth (Levin, Schneider, and Gaeth 1998) divides framing effects into three types: Attribute framing, goal framing, and risky choice framing. Attribute and

[9] Although this example is frequently used to illustrate the availability bias, there is some reason for skepticism about its accuracy; see Helman (2009) for a discussion.

goal framing seem especially likely as potential vectors for manipulation.[10] In attribute framing, a single attribute is framed in either a positive or a negative way. One common example is labelling ground beef as "90% lean" rather than "10% fat." Another example comes from a study discussed by Kahneman in *Thinking, Fast and Slow*:

> Physician participants were given statistics about the outcomes of two treatments for lung cancer: surgery and radiation. The five-year survival rates clearly favor surgery, but in the short term surgery is riskier than radiation. Half the participants read statistics about survival rates, the others received the same information in terms of mortality rates. The two descriptions of the short-term outcomes of surgery were:
>
> The one-month survival rate is 90%.
>
> There is 10% mortality in the first month.
>
> You already know the results: surgery was much more popular in the former frame (84% of physicians chose it) than in the latter (where 50% favored radiation). (Kahneman 2013, 367)[11]

Of course, a 90 percent survival rate and a 10 percent fatality rate are simply two ways of saying the same thing. How the information was framed, however, made a significant difference in the physicians' judgments. Attribute framing involves what is sometimes called a "'valence-consistent shift,' wherein the positive framing of attributes leads to more favorable evaluations than negative framing" (Levin, Schneider, and Gaeth 1998, 160). In other words, expressing an attribute (e.g., a treatment outcome) in a positive frame makes the possessor of that attribute more appealing than expressing the attribute in a negative frame.

In goal framing, a single option can be described either as achieving a gain or as avoiding a loss. Goal framing effects occur when an option is more appealing when it is framed as avoiding a loss than as achieving a gain. Thus, an energy conservation message might be more effective if it is framed in terms of how much money consumers will lose if they do not conserve than if it is framed in terms of how much they will save if they do conserve (Thaler and Sunstein 2009, 37). Because people are often more motivated to avoid a loss than to achieve a gain, framing an

[10] Risky choice framing, which appears in the famous "Asian Disease Problem," involves differences in risk tolerance depending on whether the outcome is framed in negative or positive terms (Kühberger 2022, 63–64; Levin, Schneider, and Gaeth 1998, 152–58). These effects appear to involve loss aversion, in that people are more willing to tolerate a risk to avoid losses than to achieve gains, so that "we end up with risk aversion in the domain of gains, and risk seeking in the domain of losses" (Kühberger 2022, 64)

[11] Kahneman cites a 1982 study by Amos Tversky and colleagues (McNeil et al. 1982) as the source of this data (Kahneman 2013, 478). However, it seems possible that he meant to cite (McNeil, Pauker, and Tversky 1988) instead, as the latter study (and the data from it—see esp. pages 563–64) seem like a better match for what he says in the passage quoted here.

option as avoiding a loss may be more motivating than framing it as achieving a gain.[12]

Framing effects are thought to involve automatic, Type 1 processing, and to engage emotional reactions. Kahneman and Carey Morewedge write:

> Framing is an automatic System 1 response, which is not eliminated by expertise. For example, "10% mortality" is a more frightening description of surgery outcomes than "90% survival" and the two formulations elicit different preferences for surgery versus radiation therapy even among experienced physicians. (Morewedge and Kahneman 2010, 436)

The fact that framing effects can alter choices without seeming to provide reasons suggests that they are a potential vector for manipulation. While neither of the competing frames may be clearly mistaken, it seems like a mistake to change one's preference depending on which frame is used. We will discuss the potential for framing effects to be used in manipulation in more detail in Chapter 11.

8.6.3. Metaphor

Metaphors resemble framing in many ways, and there is considerable overlap between the two concepts (Bermúdez 2020, 11–14). Perhaps somewhat artificially, I will distinguish them as follows: Whereas framing simply organizes the information relevant to the decision, metaphor goes beyond merely organizing *what is* and suggests *what is to be done* (see, e.g., Boeynaems et al. 2017, 119; Lakoff and Johnson 2003, 158). Thus, we can think of a metaphor as an implicit analogy which not only compares two things, but suggests conclusions based on that comparison. For example, the metaphor of crime as a beast might suggest different strategies for addressing it than the metaphor of crime as a virus (Thibodeau and Boroditsky 2011).

Often, solving an unfamiliar problem involves seeing how it resembles a problem for which a solution has already been found. Thus, metaphor can be a powerful problem-solving tool and a useful cognitive shortcut (Keefer and Landau 2016). But metaphor can also lead us astray. Faulty metaphors, like faulty analogies, can induce errors. Explicitly offering an analogy to support one's claim alerts the audience that an attempt to persuade is under way. Such "fair warning" can serve as a cue to engage one's Type 2 reasoning processes to subject the analogy to critical scrutiny. But when metaphors are slipped into conversation, they may

[12] However, according to Anton Kühberger, "the evidence for goal-framing effects is still weak, even after a considerable amount of empirical work" (Kühberger 2022, 68).

retain their persuasive force without alerting the audience to be on guard. Indeed, metaphors can be suggested through subtle word choice, so that the analogy is implied rather than stated, and thus less likely to be noticed. Thus, the audience may simply accept a metaphor—and the conclusions that it suggests—without critically evaluating it. Consequently, it seems likely that metaphors can shape people's thinking in ways that may pass unnoticed and thus unchallenged.

It is not surprising, then, that the potential for metaphor to influence attitudes and behavior has interested scholars. In their helpful review of the scholarly literature on this topic, Amber Boeynaems and colleagues note that work on metaphor falls into two main categories (Boeynaems et al. 2017). Some scholars (e.g., Lederer 2013; Charteris-Black 2006; Musolff 2014) take a "critical discourse approach" to metaphor. They study real-life uses of metaphor, often in political messaging, to understand their semantic and cognitive properties. Although work taking this approach sometimes tries to assess the effectiveness of the metaphors being studied, such effects are difficult to detect and measure due to confounding variables. For example, one such study seems to suggest that the Bush Administration's "war on terror" metaphor caused an increase in violence against people with perceived Middle Eastern ethnicities (Bartolucci 2012, 573–74). While such an effect is plausible, it is difficult to isolate and measure the causal impact (if any) of a particular metaphor on the increase of such violence.

The other group of scholars study the effectiveness of metaphor in changing attitudes under tightly controlled conditions. Scholars taking this approach seek to understand the psychological effects of metaphors on attitudes and behavior in the laboratory. While some defend this approach as more empirically rigorous, others question its ecological validity, since it typically studies invented messages under tightly controlled—and thus very artificial—conditions.

One of the most famous laboratory studies of metaphor was conducted by Paul Thibodeau and Lera Boroditsky. They gave participants written texts about a fictional crime wave. For half of the participants, the text invoked the metaphor of crime as a virus. For the other half, it invoked the metaphor of crime as a beast. They found that those exposed to the beast metaphor were more likely to suggest enforcement rather than prevention strategies than those exposed to the virus metaphor (Thibodeau and Boroditsky 2011). However, follow-up studies by other researchers raise questions about this finding.[13]

Nevertheless, there is good reason to think that metaphors have some effect on attitudes and behavior, though this effect might be complicated and difficult to measure. In an especially interesting study, Mark Landau, Jamie Arndt, and Linda

[13] For a failed replication, see Steen, Reijnierse, and Burgers (2014); for a follow-up suggesting that the effects of the metaphors depended on political affiliation, see Reijnierse et al. (2015). For a response to such challenges, see Thibodeau (2017).

Cameron tested whether metaphors of the sun as an enemy ready to attack affected how people reacted to warnings about skin cancer (Landau, Arndt, and Cameron 2018). They found that such metaphors increased concerns about skin cancer and intentions to use sunscreen *but only in participants with a pre-existing fear of confrontation with an enemy*. In another study, Mark Landau, Daniel Sullivan, and Jeff Greenberg exposed participants in the experimental condition to material meant to raise concerns about contamination before exposing them to a metaphor comparing the US to a body (Landau, Sullivan, and Greenberg 2009). Participants exposed to *both* materials expressed significantly stronger anti-immigration attitudes than other participants.

The power of metaphor to influence remains somewhat under-studied. Nevertheless, there is some empirical support for the claim that metaphors can, under certain circumstances, exert *some* influence on attitudes. Indeed, it would be rather surprising if this were not the case. After all, the conscious use of analogies can be persuasive; it would be surprising if the implicit analogies suggested by metaphors lacked any power to influence attitudes and behavior.

8.6.4. Status Quo Bias and Loss Aversion

Sometimes "if it ain't broke, don't fix it" is a good policy. When departures from a satisfactory status quo could be disastrous, or when transition costs are likely to outweigh expected gains from switching, letting well enough alone is often wise. Such a policy can, in fact, be seen as an embodiment of the policy of satisficing rather than optimizing.

But this policy—or heuristic—is not always rational, and there is some evidence that people follow it even when it is not rational, that is, when it constitutes a status quo *bias*.[14] In a classic study (Samuelson and Zeckhauser 1988), William Samuelson and Richard Zeckhauser analyzed choices by Harvard university faculty among retirement investment plans. They found that a new plan was far more likely to be chosen by new hires than by those who had been on an older plan for many years. The effect persisted even when age differences—and thus target retirement dates—were controlled for. Thus, it appears that many faculty preferred their current plan simply because it was the plan they were already on. Laboratory and field studies suggest that our bias in favor of the status quo is stronger than is rational, and persists in contexts where it is clearly irrational.

[14] For a discussion of some early studies and their relevance to economic theory, see Kahneman, Knetsch, and Thaler (1991); for an analytical review of recent literature on decision avoidance, see Christopher J. Anderson (2003); for an especially thorough recent review of the literature on both the bias and how to counter it, see Godefroid, Plattfaut, and Niehaves (2022).

The status quo bias seems to be related to the loss aversion bias, in which a loss of **X** is regarded as being worse than a failure to gain **X**. Ilana Ritov and Jonathan Baron explain the connection to loss aversion this way:

> Since the current state serves as a reference point, a change usually entails expected loss on some dimensions and expected gains on other dimensions. Since people are loss averse, the losses are weighed more heavily than the gains. Hence, people are unlikely to prefer an alternative in which the expected gains are only slightly higher than the expected losses. (Ritov and Baron 1992, 49)

Ritov and Baron also suggest that the status quo bias might reflect a more basic bias in favor of doing nothing over doing something (Ritov and Baron 1992, 60). This, in turn, suggests a connection with some features of akrasia that were noted in section 4.5. Taking action usually imposes some cost, whether it be decision costs, transition costs, or just the effort of performing the action that changes the status quo. Since those costs will often be more immediate than the benefits of taking action, a bias that overvalues immediate costs relative to later benefits would often favor akratic inaction in situations where taking action would be beneficial in the long run. Thus, the status quo bias may sometimes reflect the more general human tendency to temporal myopia (a tendency discussed in more detail below).

8.6.5. Conformity

The influence tactic of social proof harnesses a heuristic that Gigerenzer describes as "do what the majority of your peers do" (Gigerenzer 2007, 217). Obviously, this heuristic helps to promote social cohesion. It can be invaluable in helping to solve coordination problems, especially in contexts where it matters less *what* we all do than it does that we all do *the same thing*.

As Gigerenzer notes, this heuristic works particularly well in relatively stable environments, and when mistakes are likely to be dangerous: "Relying only on individual experience to learn which berries found in the forest are poisonous is obviously a bad strategy" (Gigerenzer 2007, 219). This example suggests two conditions for the heuristic to work well: first, that choices are likely to affect different people in the same way, and second, that other people's actions are obtaining satisfactory results. Both conditions are met in Gigerenzer's example: Something non-poisonous to one person is likely to be non-poisonous to another, and we are assuming that other people are not falling over dead from eating the berries they selected. The less well these conditions are met, the more the rule becomes a bias rather than a useful heuristic.

The double-sided nature of conformity is strikingly illustrated by Amanda Ripley's analysis of disasters (Ripley 2009). Her case studies suggest that survival rates during mass casualty disasters often depend on whether the crowd knows what it's doing—and, sadly, it often does not. Thus, when some people freeze or respond unwisely to a disaster, conformity may make others follow suit. On the other hand, a competent and calm leader who takes charge can often count on conformity to convert a chaotic mob into an organized body capable of unified, intelligent action.

Social conformity can lead to groupthink, which can lead to poor decisions. As Kahneman, Sibony, and Sunstein observe:

> Under favorable circumstances, in which people share what they know, deliberating groups can indeed do well. But independence is a prerequisite for the wisdom of crowds. If people are not making their own judgments and are relying instead on what other people think, crowds might not be so wise after all. (Kahneman, Sibony, and Sunstein 2021, 99)

Moreover, the tendency to defer to others can lead to what Kahneman, Sibony, and Sunstein call an "informational cascade" where irrelevant factors such as who speaks first produce a "herding effect that undermines the wisdom of crowds" (Kahneman, Sibony, and Sunstein 2021, 99). They ask us to imagine a ten-person hiring committee considering three candidates. If the first committee member to take the floor speaks strongly in favor of one candidate, others who are on the fence may be persuaded and chime in. This might persuade other fence-sitters. As the consensus grows, others who supported a different candidate may reconsider, or may decide not to speak up for fear of seeming contrary. The longer this process continues, the more difficult it becomes to sway the group from its emerging consensus, and the more psychological pressure there is to avoid rocking the boat. In this way, a group could come to very different decisions depending only on which member spoke first. Assuming that some candidates are indeed better than others, this dynamic could lead to the group making a worse decision simply because the first person to speak favored it.

It is easy to see how a clever manipulator could employ these facts about group dynamics to drive a group decision the way the manipulator prefers. Herodotus tells us in Book V (ch 97) of his *Histories*, that Aristagoras failed to get the Spartan king to agree to help the Ionians against Persia. But he succeeded in getting Athens to do so. According to Herodotus, this was because a group is more easily deceived than a single person. He does not say exactly how Aristagoras got the Athenians to agree to help the Ionians, but one can easily imagine this sort of "informational cascade" playing a role.

8.6.6. Temporal Myopia and the Immediacy Bias

Is it better to have something pretty good sooner, or to wait for something even better? It depends on how much better the second thing is, how long the wait is, and how likely it is that something could change during that time that would change its value. The longer the wait, the better the second thing must be for it to be worth waiting for. None of this is surprising or puzzling. Nor is it irrational to discount the value of a good according to how long one must wait for it to become available.

However, not all ways of discounting future goods are rational. Consider this example from George Ainslie:

> If I ask a room full of people to imagine that they've won a contest and can choose between a certified check for $100 that they can cash immediately and a postdated certified check for $200 that they can't cash for three years, more than half of the people usually say they would rather have the $100 now. If I then ask what about $100 in six years versus $200 in nine years, virtually everyone picks the $200. But this is the same choice seen at six years' greater distance (Ainslie 2001, 33).

Ainslie and others have demonstrated that humans often display preference patterns like these. Notice that this phenomenon is more than just valuing a smaller good available sooner over a larger good available later. That, after all, is often quite rational. For example, there is nothing inherently irrational about preferring, say, $100 now over $120 next week. But if that same person prefers $120 in 53 weeks over $100 in 52 weeks, then something about "right now" makes that person's preferences reverse. In other words, the person prefers waiting an extra week for a 20% larger payoff, unless that extra week starts *now*. This seems irrational, not because it is irrational to discount future goods, but because it seems irrational to *change* how one discounts future goods when one good is available *immediately*.

Someone's willingness to wait a week for a 20% gain if that wait happens in the future can be seen as that person's all things considered judgment that it is better to wait a week for a 20% gain. Thus, that same person's choice of $100 *now* rather than $120 one week from now can be seen as an akratic choice. Such choices are not uncommon. As time passes, and the availability of the smaller good becomes imminent, we may change our mind and choose it over a larger good—even though from a greater temporal distance, we would have chosen the larger good. In short, immediacy seems to distort our preferences relative to what they would be if viewed from the perspective of greater temporal distance.

These preference patterns can be modelled mathematically. The mathematical functions that describe a stable pattern of discounting future goods—one that does not change as the availability of the smaller good draws near—are exponential. When plotted on graphs, they form gentle curves that describe a steady increase in our preference for a later good as the time when it is available draws near. Exponential preference functions treat a given delay in a good's availability the same no matter when that delay happens. If it's worth waiting an extra week for an extra 20 percent payoff that will happen in fifty-three weeks rather than fifty-two weeks, then it's worth waiting that same week even if it starts today.

However, as we have seen, people commonly reverse their preferences when the availability of the smaller good becomes imminent. The mathematical functions that describe preference patterns that reverse in this way are hyperbolic rather than exponential. The curves created by such functions have an interesting property: When the good's availability is far in the future, they grow slowly, almost as though they are in a dormant phase. But when the good's availability draws near, they shoot up sharply. This feature can create preference reversals: Suppose that a person prefers the larger good L over the smaller good S when neither S nor L is available for a while. Suppose, however, that S will become available sooner than L will, so that when S becomes available, L still won't be available for a while. As the time when S becomes available draws near, the preference for S enters its "explosive" phase. If the availability of L is not also imminent, it will remain in its "dormant" phase. Consequently, the rapidly strengthening preference for S may become larger than the still sharply discounted preference for L, simply because the availability of S has become imminent. So, it is not just that we prefer smaller goods available sooner over larger goods available later. It is that *how much* we prefer the smaller good sometimes increases drastically as the time when it is available draws near.

We can call this the *immediacy bias*: The immediate availability of some good changes how we evaluate it relative to other goods not yet available. This bias amounts to what Ainslie calls a "warp in how we evaluate the future" (Ainslie 2001, 27). This warp or bias is not just the often rational preference for sooner goods; rather, it is an extreme and explosive preference for goods that are available *immediately*.

There is some debate about whether hyperbolic discounting curves are the best mathematical models for observed preference shifts in favor of immediately available goods (McKerchar et al. 2009; Luhmann 2013; Read, Frederick, and Airoldi 2012). Be that as it may, a great deal of empirical work demonstrates that human (and animal) choices often display the kind of immediacy bias that the hyperbolic discounting model seeks to describe (Frederick, Loewenstein, and O'Donoghue 2002, 360–62; Vanderveldt, Oliveira, and Green 2016, 147–48). For our purposes, the precise mathematical description is less important than the phenomenon itself, namely that preferences for a good often increase sharply when that good is immediately available.[15]

[15] Matters are more complicated when we consider bad things (like pain), where temporal discounting has received much less attention. Sometimes people prefer getting a pain over with, even if doing so increases the amount of pain somewhat, apparently because anticipating a future pain contributes to its badness (Story et al. 2013). However, sometimes people prefer to delay a pain even if the delayed pain is worse (Tompkins et al. 2016; Story et al. 2013). It is possible that these studies simply confirm that it is usually better to get something unpleasant over with, but that we sometimes give in to the temptation to put off unpleasant or painful things anyway—even knowing that this will make things worse later.

Like many phenomena commonly called biases, the immediacy bias can be adaptive in certain environments and conditions (Vanderveldt, Oliveira, and Green 2016, 154–57; Dasgupta and Maskin 2005). The more likely it is that the birds in the bush will evade capture, or that you might not be around long enough to capture them, the more sense it makes to prefer the bird in the hand. In uncertain environments, it might be adaptive to prefer immediate and thus certain access to vital goods over later and thus less certain access to greater amounts of them. The less certain the future is, the more sense it makes to put a premium on immediate consumption. Indeed, in certain situations, delaying gratification can amount to a gamble on the future—one which it might not always be rational to engage in.[16] But in the stable environments most of us face most of the time, a strong bias in favor of immediacy is often unreasonable. Yet the immediacy effect often still operates. Even when we know that it is unreasonable, the immediacy of a good makes it tempting to choose it over a larger good that will only become available later.

Moreover, the longer such a temptation persists, the more difficult resisting it often becomes.[17] This phenomenon may play a role in the effectiveness of one of the simplest manipulative tactics: nagging. Resisting nagging is somewhat like holding one's hand in cold water. Initially, it is unpleasant but tolerable. But over time, it becomes ever more difficult to resist the urge to remove one's hand. So too with nagging: It may be unpleasant but tolerable in the short term, but if it persists long enough, it can be difficult for even a strong-willed person to resist the urge to give in. This may be true even when the person knows that giving in is, overall, a worse option than enduring the unpleasantness of the nagging. A similar dynamic may apply in other kinds of manipulative pressure. For example, some forms of emotional blackmail involve imposing mildly aversive—but persistent—consequences that, over time, may wear down a person's ability to resist, even when that person knows that giving in is sub-optimal.

Certain goods are especially tempting, and thus especially apt to induce akratic choices. This is obviously true of objects of powerful psychological drives like food, sex, addictive substances, and relief from pain. It should come as no surprise, then, that such goods are notoriously effective levers for the manipulator. While the "honey trap" is probably more prevalent in spy fiction, it is not unheard-of in real life espionage (Knightley 2010). Charm offensives often have at least an implicit sexual or romantic component. When they do not, they often involve another important drive, the need for affiliation.

However, more subtle motivations can also lead to akratic choices. For example, Robert Cialdini offers the following observations about the motivational force of the social norm of reciprocity:

[16] This point echoes a common critique of studies that treat the propensity to delay gratification as an unquestioned virtue; e.g., that of Calarco (2018).

[17] On this point, see Cholbi (2014) and Noggle (2016a).

> Most of us find it highly disagreeable to be in a state of obligation. It weighs heavily on us and demands to be removed. It is not difficult to trace the source of this feeling. Because reciprocal arrangements are so vital in human social systems, we have been conditioned to feel uncomfortable when beholden . . . For this reason alone, then, we may be willing to agree to perform a larger favor than the one we received, merely to relieve ourselves of the psychological burden of debt. (Cialdini 2008, 33–34)

In a classic study, Dennis Regan found that participants who were given a Coke before being asked to buy raffle tickets bought about twice as many as participants not given a Coke (Regan 1971). This effect appears to operate even when the favor is merely *offered* (Guéguen et al. 2016), and even in the absence of social approval or disapproval (Burger et al. 2009). Interestingly, this effect often motivates people to give back more than what was given. As Joop van der Pligt and Michael Vliek note about the Regan study, conducted in 1971, "a bottle of cola cost 10 cents at the time. In the reciprocity condition, however, the test subjects spent an average of 50 cents on raffle tickets. Meanwhile, the participants in the control group spent an average of just 25 cents" (Pligt and Vliek 2016, 89). Cialdini relates this anecdote from one of his students as an illustration of lopsided reciprocity:

> About one year ago, I couldn't start my car. As I was sitting there, a guy in the parking lot came over and eventually jump-started the car . . . [A]s he was leaving, I said that if he ever needed a favor to stop by. About a month later, the guy knocked on my door and asked to borrow my car for two hours as his was in the shop. I felt somewhat obligated but uncertain, since the car was pretty new and he looked very young. Later, I found out that he was underage and had no insurance. Anyway, I lent him the car. He totalled it. (Cialdini 2008, 33)

There are two ways that this "psychological burden of debt" can figure in manipulation. First, it may induce an akratic choice simply because the discomfort from being in debt, while small, is more immediate than the objectively larger costs of the favor being requested in return. Second, the feeling of being obligated may be unfitting, either because it is too strong given the magnitude of the original favor, or because the original favor was unwanted and thus not a genuine source of reciprocal obligation.

Finally, we often care more about our self-esteem than we might expect—or like to admit. Moreover, our self-esteem is often more fragile than we realize—or like to admit. Consequently, we are liable to act akratically to improve it, to protect it from harm, or to restore it after it has been injured. This can affect behavior in ways that we might not expect. For example, blows to their self-esteem appear to make people more likely to purchase items on credit, perhaps to compensate somehow for the injury (Pettit and Sivanathan 2011). Interventions designed to improve self-esteem may decrease the hyperbolic discounting that typifies temporal myopia and the immediacy bias (Moeini-Jazani, Albalooshi, and Seljeseth 2019). Thus, reductions in self-esteem may encourage the sorts of akratic behavior the induction of which is the goal of manipulative pressure.

But our attachment to our self-esteem can be used more directly by manipulators. A manipulator might offer a glowing picture of the target and suggest a course of action that will confirm that picture.[18] Or a manipulator might knock a person's self-esteem down a few notches and then offer a course of action that will restore it. Such tactics might well induce an otherwise rational person to choose a sub-optimal course of action that improves or restores their self-esteem, especially when the improvement or restoration is more immediate than the costs of the action. In this way, the manipulative tactics of conditional flattery and negging likely draw on both the immediacy bias and our strong motivations to maintain our self-esteem.

8.7. Conclusion

This chapter drew heavily on current psychological findings and theories. As a working science, psychology is a work in progress. Consequently, some of what has been said here is almost certainly incorrect and subject to revision as psychology progresses. However, it seems likely that the general outlines are largely correct, even if some of the details must be revised as our understanding of the psychology of influence improves. Any such revisions, however, would not affect the substance of the Mistake Account. For that account is a *conceptual* claim that manipulation involves inducing mistakes; it is not tied to any particular empirical claims about how mistakes are induced. But given our current—no doubt imperfect—understanding of psychology, we can begin to understand some of the mechanisms by which manipulators induce the mistakes that are the core of manipulation. And, thus, we can begin to understand how manipulation works.

It is tempting to regard the mechanisms exploited by manipulators as design flaws. But this would be misleading. As we have seen, mechanisms like heuristics, Type 1 processes, satisficing, and recognition-primed decision-making, are all ways of reconciling the limits of human deliberative capacities with the open-ended nature of deliberation. Such mechanisms enable us to settle the question of

[18] The empirical literature on flattery as a tool for gaining compliance is not vast, and much of it assumes that flattery works by increasing the flatterer's likability (Grant, Fabrigar, and Lim 2010; Grant, Krieger et al. 2022), which seems likely to be how flattery operates in charm offensives. The efficacy of conditional flattery to produce compliance has apparently been the subject of a single, unpublished study (Goodall et al. 1996), which found that participants told that they looked like helpful people were more likely to agree to complete a five page questionnaire than those subjected to no flattery or a compliment unrelated to the request.

what to do in a timely manner. Usually, the actions they help us choose are effective, adaptive, and conducive to achieving our goals. But because they employ the kinds of short-cuts necessary to make them fast, they can be derailed by manipulators. Other mechanisms are adaptive in conditions that were more common when our ancestors walked the earth than they are now. These mechanisms can bias decision-making in favor of immediate consumption, false positives in detecting danger, and so on. These mechanisms can likewise be exploited by manipulators.

It is inevitable that the mechanisms that enable finite creatures like ourselves to settle questions of what to do in a timely way are imperfect. This is partly because it is inevitable that they must pay for their astonishing speed with some loss of accuracy. Thus, rather than design flaws, we should see these mechanisms as embodying inevitable speed-accuracy trade-offs that are optimal most of the time, and mechanisms that were optimal under the conditions prevailing for our ancestors.

Thus, many of the mechanisms that leave us vulnerable to manipulation are inevitable features of minds instantiated in brains made of the kinds of materials that compose our brains, and which allowed our ancestors to win the evolutionary struggle for survival. They embody the inevitable trade-off between accuracy and speed that must underlie the kind of rationality available to creatures like us. These facts should make us a little more understanding of the vulnerability to manipulation that is part and parcel of the human condition. And they should make us a little more forgiving of *ourselves* when we fall prey to manipulation. By and large, the mechanisms exploited by manipulators are not *flaws* but *features* that allow us to be as rational as we are, given the limitations of human biology and our evolutionary past.

9
Manipulation and Morality

9.1. Introduction

In ordinary conversation, calling someone "manipulative" is a criticism of that person's character in a way that calling someone "influential" is not. In ordinary conversation, saying, "Smith manipulated me" is a moral complaint about Smith's conduct in a way that saying, "Smith influenced me," is not. If we ignore or stipulate away these negative moral connotations, then we cease to give an account of the concept of manipulation as we normally think of it and talk about it.[1]

An analysis of the ordinary concept of manipulation which recognizes its negative moral connotations should answer three important questions:

1. Is manipulation always morally wrong?
2. What makes manipulation morally wrong (when it is morally wrong)?
3. If manipulation is not always morally wrong, what determines when it is not?

This chapter will attempt to answer these questions. As is typical in moral philosophy, I shall use the terms 'immoral,' 'wrong,' and 'morally wrong' interchangeably.

9.2. Is Manipulation Always Wrong?

Consider this case[2]:

Terrorist Terry hid an atomic bomb somewhere in Chicago. FBI agent Mindy has apprehended Terry and must now locate the bomb. Rational persuasion and offers of lenient punishment have not induced Terry to reveal the bomb's

[1] There has been some discussion of whether we should seek a "moralized" definition of manipulation (Wood 2014; Baron 2014). In my view, the answer depends on what 'moralized' means. If it means defining manipulation in explicitly moral terms—as when murder is defined as a *wrongful* killing—then I do not favor such a definition. If it means defining the concept in a way that takes seriously and helps to explain the negative moral connotations that the term 'manipulation' has in ordinary conversation, then not only do I favor such a definition, but I shall argue in this chapter that the Mistake Account provides such a definition.

[2] The argument and conclusions in this and the next two sections draw on arguments made by Marcia Baron (2014).

Manipulation. Robert Noggle, Oxford University Press. © Robert Noggle 2025.
DOI: 10.1093/9780198924920.003.0009

location. Mindy knows that Terry was recruited into this plot by his beloved spouse Stella. Mindy also knows that Stella is a loving, devoted, and faithful spouse to Terry. Mindy employs the same tactics that Iago used on Othello to drive Terry into a jealous rage at Stella, and this makes him abandon the plot and reveal the bomb's location.

It seems clear that Mindy's manipulation of Terry is not wrong, all things considered. So, while manipulation may be *usually* wrong, it is clearly not *always* wrong.

When we say that manipulation is usually but not always wrong, we might mean that it is *prima facie* wrong, or we might mean that it is *pro tanto* wrong, or both. To call an action *pro tanto* wrong is to say that there is always *some* moral reason *against* performing it; but that this reason can sometimes be outweighed by "countervailing" reasons in favor of performing it.[3] These countervailing reasons are typically situation specific. For example, it is *pro tanto* wrong to shove someone without that person's consent. But suppose that the only way to save someone from being squashed by a falling piano is to shove that person immediately, without waiting to acquire consent. In this situation, the fact that the non-consensual shove is the only way to save that person's life constitutes a countervailing reason that outweighs the wrongness of the non-consensual shove. It is as though the *pro tanto* moral reasons against the action lose a tug-of-war against the countervailing reasons favoring the action. But they do not vanish. Their effects linger in two ways. First, if there is a less wrong alternative to shoving, such as shouting a warning, then there is a moral reason to do that instead. Second, if there is no less wrong alternative, then that fact is a reason for regret. A morally conscientious agent might say: "If I could have prevented the accident without shoving you, I would have, and I regret that there was no other way to save you."

By contrast, to say that something is *prima facie* wrong is to say that it is usually wrong, but that some kinds of countervailing reasons can *nullify* the action's usual wrongness. In such cases, the moral reason to refrain from the action does not merely lose a moral tug-of-war with another reason; instead, it disappears entirely. For example, it is *prima facie* wrong for Smith to punch Jones in the face. However, if Smith has validly consented to a properly-supervised boxing match against Jones, then it is no longer wrong—at all—for Jones to punch Smith. Moreover, there is no residual moral reason for Jones to choose some other course of action besides punching Smith. Nor is there any reason for Jones to regret his lack of alternatives.

[3] My discussion and use of terminology here follows that of Shelly Kagan (1991).

9.3. Manipulation as *Prima Facie* Wrong

It seems reasonable to think that countervailing moral reasons can sometimes completely nullify the reason to refrain from manipulation. In the case of Terrorist Terry, we might deny that Mindy had any obligation to try rational persuasion before resorting to manipulation, or to regret the inability of rational persuasion to get the job done. It also seems reasonable to think that it is not wrong *at all* for law enforcement to use certain kinds of tricks to catch a serial killer or even a car thief. And it seems reasonable to deny that there is any residual reason to seek alternative, non-manipulative means before, say, having a police officer pose as a potential victim or parking a well-monitored sports car as bait for car thieves, or to regret the lack of feasible alternatives if none are available. Of course, there are limits: Some forms of manipulation might amount to entrapment if they are likely or intended to induce someone not already inclined to criminality to attempt a crime.[4] But that is just to say that the wrongness of manipulation might be nullified when it is used to *thwart* an active evil-doer, and *not* when it is used to *recruit* a new one.[5]

Similar remarks seem applicable to certain competitive activities—from chess to combat sports—where certain forms of manipulation are accepted as part of the activity or contest. In such cases it seems reasonable to think that voluntary participation in the activity completely nullifies the moral reasons that ordinarily oppose those forms of manipulation. Some forms of entertainment—from literature and theater to magic shows—also involve practices like misdirection, evoking misplaced emotions, etc., that fit the definition of manipulation. But if people choose to be in the audience, there seems to be no reason to regret that a magician employed misdirection to create an entertaining illusion, or that a playwright played on the emotions to elicit sympathy for a fictitious character.[6]

Apparently, then, manipulation's moral wrongness might sometimes be completely nullified—and not merely outweighed—in situations where it is used to thwart evil-doers, or where it is allowed by the rules of an activity in which people participate voluntarily. Consequently, manipulation seems to be *prima facie* wrong.

[4] For an argument that it is morally wrong for the state to punish people who have been entrapped by the use of certain forms of manipulation, see Haeg (2022).

[5] As an anonymous reviewer notes, some might claim that in such cases it is still *pro tanto* wrong to manipulate the evil-doer, but that the countervailing reasons for doing so vastly outweigh this *pro tanto* wrongness. I am unsure how to adjudicate between these two views. Fortunately, very little turns on the matter. Readers who think that there is always some *pro tanto* reason to refrain from manipulation are free to treat cases where I suggest that the reason against manipulation has been nullified as ones where it has been vastly outweighed.

[6] Such examples might tell us less about the moral status of manipulation than they do about "the moral magic of consent" (Hurd 1996). What is wrong absent consent is very often morally legitimate if consented to. In this, manipulation resembles many other actions that are wrong without consent but not wrong if consented to. Similar remarks might apply to using ordinarily immoral means to thwart an evil-doer.

9.4. Manipulation as Pro Tanto Wrong

Recall this case from Chapter 3:

> ***Bad Boyfriend***: Theresa has left a toxic relationship with Al, who is abusive, but also scrupulously monogamous. Theresa values Al's faithfulness so highly that she is considering going back to Al. Her friends know that if Theresa does this, Al's abuse will resume and escalate, and that this poses a grave threat to Theresa's mental and physical well-being. Unfortunately, their attempts to use rational persuasion to get Theresa to abandon her plan to reconcile with Al have failed. So, Theresa's friends employ Iago's manipulative tactics to drive Theresa into a jealous rage that quashes any thoughts of reconciling with Al.

It seems reasonable to think that the grave risk to Theresa justifies her friends' use of manipulation. If so, then part of the reason why it is justified is the fact that rational persuasion has failed. Had it been possible to use rational persuasion to convince Theresa not to reunite with Al, then her friends should have chosen that method rather than manipulation. Moreover, the fact that rational persuasion was not a viable option is a cause for regret. These facts indicate that, while the reasons favoring protecting Theresa might *outweigh* the reasons to avoid manipulation, they do not *nullify* them. Cases like this support the claim that manipulation is *pro tanto* wrong.

Thus, it seems correct to say that manipulation is *both pro tanto* and *prima facie* wrong. Consent or the need to thwart an evil-doer can completely nullify the wrongness of manipulation. But other moral considerations, such as those generated by the desirability of protecting someone from harm, can sometimes outweigh (without nullifying) the wrongness of manipulation. In such cases, the wrongness of manipulation continues to exert a residual moral force, in the form of an obligation to use any available less wrong alternative to manipulation, and a reason for regret if no such alternative is available.

Let us understand the claim that manipulation is *presumptively* wrong to include both the claim that it is *prima facie* wrong and that it is *pro tanto* wrong. That is, manipulation is wrong except when its wrongness is outweighed or nullified by countervailing reasons. So, what makes manipulation presumptively wrong?

9.5. Manipulation and Harm

An obvious answer would be that manipulation harms the person being manipulated. The harms done by manipulation are many and various. Con artists use manipulation to inflict financial harms—sometimes grave ones—on their victims. Manipulation can induce people to remain in relationships that are unequal, oppressive, and even abusive. Systematic political manipulation may weaken democratic institutions and perhaps even lead to tyranny. Undoubtedly, manipulation often harms the target. Such harm is often *one* moral reason—and often the most important one—against a given instance of manipulation.

But manipulation does not always harm its target. Moreover, even when it does not, it remains presumptively wrong. In the ***Bad Boyfriend*** example, Theresa's friends employ the same tactics that Iago uses on Othello—tactics that any credible account of manipulation must count as manipulative. Their use of those tactics remains *presumptively* wrong even though it benefits Theresa, and even if that fact makes it justified *on balance*. This is why it would have been morally preferable for Theresa's friends to use a less wrongful method to protect Theresa from the harm of going back to Al, and why the lack of any such alternative would be a cause for regret.

Thus, harmfulness cannot be the ultimate source of manipulation's presumptive wrongness, even though manipulation *often* causes significant, even devastating, harm.

9.6. Manipulation and Treating Persons as Things

The term 'manipulate' carries a negative moral connotation when it applies to something done to a person, but not when it applies to something done to a mere thing, such as a steering wheel or a remote-controlled drone. Consequently, it seems natural to link manipulation with Kant's claim that it is wrong to treat a person as a mere thing: While there is nothing wrong with manipulating the controls on a drone, there is something wrong with manipulating a person.[7]

Kant's claim that morally wrong actions involve treating a person as a mere thing, or a mere means to an end,[8] is extremely compelling. Unfortunately, it is notoriously difficult to spell out precisely, and there is a great deal of philosophical debate about how this should be done (Kerstein 2019, Audi 2015). We cannot define *treating someone as a thing* to mean *treating someone in a way that it is wrong to treat a person*, for that just takes us in a circle: It is wrong to treat a person in a way that it is wrong to treat a person. Nor will it help to define "treating someone as a mere means" as profiting at that person's expense. As the case of ***Bad Boyfriend*** demonstrates, it is possible to manipulate someone for that person's own benefit, rather than that of the manipulator. Manipulation remains presumptively wrong even when it benefits the target.

[7] For a recent attempt to work out how some of Kant's views might apply to manipulation, see M. H. Werner (2022).

[8] I will treat "treating as a mere thing" and "treating as a mere means" as synonyms here. If there is a difference between them, it is too subtle to make any significant difference here.

Since the Mistake Account draws a parallel between manipulation and deception, perhaps we might apply Kant's analysis of lies and deception to manipulation. Roughly, his account goes like this: To treat you as a person, I must give you the opportunity to consent to how I plan to treat you. But if I lie about this, you cannot consent, since you do not know what you are consenting to (Kant 1785, 429–30). Unfortunately, it is difficult to see how this idea applies to forms of manipulation that do not involve trickery or deception. If I use nagging or peer pressure—tactics that any credible theory must recognize as manipulation—to get you to do something, I do not typically hide what I want you to do, or how I am trying to get you to do it.

It is also tempting to say that, since persons are rational beings, influences that do not engage with our rationality fail to treat us as persons. But this idea faces obstacles like those facing the Bypassing Reason Account of manipulation (section 3.5): If we say that only rational persuasion engages our rationality and treats us as persons, then we condemn as manipulative the sincere appeal to emotions like empathy in moral persuasion. And if we allow that emotions can sometimes engage with our rationality, we need to know when emotions do engage with our rationality and when they do not.

Still, something seems right about the idea that manipulation treats a person like a thing, just as something seems right about the idea that manipulation is somehow opposed to reason. Later in this chapter, I shall suggest that the Mistake Account offers a way to understand and endorse both ideas.

9.7. Manipulation and Autonomy

Closely related to the idea that manipulation is wrong because it treats a person as a thing is the idea that manipulation is wrong because it undermines the target's autonomy. This idea is both common[9] and appealing. Spelling out the precise connection between autonomy and manipulation is difficult, however, because there is no philosophical consensus about what autonomy is (Buss and Westlund 2018).

However, we need not settle the debate over autonomy to see problems with the suggestion that manipulation's presumptive wrongness derives from undermining the target's autonomy. Consider this example from Jonathan Pugh, which I will call "***Becky and the Beast***." It begins as follows:

[9] Scholars who either assert that manipulation often or typically undermines autonomy, or who report the commonness of this claim, include Raz (1988, 373, 375–76), Hill (1984, 257), Dworkin (1976, 25–27), Berofsky (2003, 204, 214–15), Phillips (1997, 85, 190), Sunstein (2016, 84, 96), Wilkinson (2013, 345), Coons and Weber (2014, 8), Blumenthal-Barby (2014, 128), and Taylor (2009, 41).

> Jim and Becky are being pursued by a beast deep in the jungle and running for their lives. Jim is some way ahead of Becky and comes to a ravine; he realises that they must somehow get across it to escape. (Pugh 2015, 90)

Pugh gives several versions of the rest of the story. The one most relevant for our purposes picks up with Jim considering the width of the ravine:

> Jim ... calculates it as being 5 metres wide. He knows that in their state of high adrenalin, both he and Becky can jump this distance. However, he also knows that Becky will fail to make the jump if she knows that the ravine is 5 metres wide; her fear will hold her back. So he calls Becky and tells her that the only way to escape is to jump a ravine that is 4 metres wide. Since he knows that this is at the limit of the distances that Becky believes she can jump, Jim has good grounds for believing that she will put all her effort into it, and leap at least 5 metres ... Becky successfully clears the ravine. (Pugh 2015, 92)

Pugh offers this story as a counterexample to the claim that *lies* always undermine the autonomy of the person to whom they are told. Indeed, on any credible theory of autonomy, Jim's lie *enhances* Becky's autonomy, since it enables her to act on her preference to escape the beast—an action and preference that any credible theory of autonomy must surely recognize as autonomous.[10] Jim's lie has this unusual effect because it *counteracts* the effects of Becky's *false* belief that she can only leap four meters. This false belief undermines Becky's autonomy, either by preventing her from making the autonomous decision to jump the ravine, or by thwarting her autonomously chosen plan to escape the beast. Thus, Jim's lie prevents this false belief from undermining Becky's autonomy.

Pugh's example involves lying, but it is relevant to the question of the relationship between *manipulation* and autonomy, for two reasons. First, the Mistake Account identifies Jim's lie as an instance of manipulation, so it treats Pugh's case as a counterexample to the claim that *manipulation* always undermines the target's autonomy. Second, it provides a template for constructing cases where autonomy is enhanced by forms of manipulation that do not involve lies. Consider this case (Noggle 2018, 169):

Smokin' Joe: Joe desires to quit smoking, and acting on this desire would fulfil whatever criteria for autonomy you prefer. However, Joe cannot act on this desire because his willpower is insufficient to counter his nicotine

[10] Alan Strudler (2016) gives a similar argument. An example similar to Pugh's appears in an incisive paper by Suzy Killmister (2013, 528), which argues that, while false beliefs *often* undermine autonomy, in special cases they do not.

addiction. His physician, Phoebe, knows that Joe has contamination-related phobias, of which Joe himself is unaware. Phoebe decides to trigger these phobias by telling a humorous story about seeing large birds dropping their droppings over a tobacco field on a recent vacation to South Carolina. She successfully disguises this as idle conversation rather than an attempt to influence Joe's behavior. She recognizes that the cigarette manufacturing process removes any trace of bird droppings, so that the fact that tobacco leaves once had bird droppings on them is not a good reason to find them disgusting. Nevertheless, Phoebe's story triggers Joe's phobia, making him disgusted at the thought of putting cigarettes in his mouth. This disgust counters his addiction, allowing him to act on his desire to quit smoking—just as Phoebe intended.

On *any* credible theory of *manipulation*, Phoebe manipulated Joe: Her influence is covert, it employs an irrational mechanism, it bypasses Joe's reason, and it induces mistaken disgust at bird droppings that are no longer present in his cigarettes. And yet, on *any* credible theory of *autonomy*, Joe is more autonomous when he becomes able to act on his desire to quit smoking. Moreover, this is not a case of decreasing short-term autonomy to increase long-term autonomy. The influence increases Joe's autonomy directly and immediately. So manipulation does not always undermine autonomy.

A defender of the claim that manipulation's presumptive wrongness derives from its negative effects on autonomy might concede that manipulation does not always undermine autonomy, while maintaining that manipulation is presumptively wrong *only in those cases when it does undermine autonomy*. But this claim does not pan out either. Phoebe's manipulation of Joe does not undermine his autonomy, but it is nevertheless *pro tanto* wrong. This is true even if we judge it to be justified on balance. This is clear from the following observation: If rational persuasion could have gotten Joe to quit smoking (e.g., by convincing him to undertake a smoking-cessation program), Phoebe should have done that instead of resorting to manipulation. And if rational persuasion would not have worked, then this fact would be a cause for regret. These observations indicate that Phoebe's manipulation of Joe was *pro tanto* wrong, even though it enhanced Joe's autonomy, and even *if* we think that it was justified on balance. So, the example of ***Smokin' Joe*** demonstrates that manipulation does not always undermine autonomy, and in such cases, it remains presumptively wrong.

None of this is to deny that manipulation *usually* undermines the target's autonomy, and that when it does, that fact contributes to its wrongness. But it does show that manipulation is presumptively wrong for some reason other than its effect on the target's autonomy.

9.8. Mistakes and Manipulation's Presumptive Wrongness

So what *does* account for the fact that manipulation remains presumptively wrong even in cases—like that of ***Smokin' Joe*** and ***Becky and the Beast***—where it neither harms nor undermines the autonomy of the target?

9.8.1 The Parallel with Deception

In section 5.6, I suggested that the Mistake Account ties the moral status of manipulation to two distinct concerns: The misfortune of making a mistake, and the manipulator's intention to inflict that misfortune upon someone. Thus, the Mistake Account rests the fundamental normative status of manipulation on the normative status of mistakes. Or, to put it more simply, manipulation is bad because mistakes are bad.

The badness of mistakes is easiest to see with beliefs. Beliefs are states whose function is to reflect accurate information; they are often said to have a "mind to world direction of fit," or to "aim" at truth.[11] These are just different ways to make the same point: Beliefs are governed by a norm of truth, so that a false belief is defective, and believing falsely is a kind of *failure*. Such a failure is a *misfortune*.[12]

To say that believing falsely is a misfortune is *not* to say that having a false belief is always a *harm*.[13] Quite the contrary; sometimes it is the truth that hurts, and some false beliefs protect the believer from harm. In Joseph Conrad's novel, *Heart of Darkness* (Conrad 1973), Marlow tells Kurtz's fiancée that Kurtz's final word was her name, when in reality he had abandoned his love for her in his descent into madness. The resulting false belief probably makes Kurtz's fiancée better off, all things considered, than she would have been if she knew the truth. Yet it seems clear that something unfortunate has occurred in her believing falsely, even if it is less unfortunate than knowing the truth.

A misfortune, as I understand it, is simply *one* respect in which things could have gone better. It is a misfortune to believe falsely because a false belief is defective, and to have one is to have something that, in one respect, it would have been better not to have. It is clearly a misfortune to be "living a lie," even if doing so makes us happier than the truth would. Aristotle wrote that "it would perhaps be thought to be better, indeed to be our duty, for the sake of maintaining the truth

[11] For important accounts of this idea, see Searle (1983, 7–8), Smith (1987), and Humberstone (1992). For philosophers who question the claim that direction of fit can distinguish belief from desire, see Frost (2014), Gregory (2012), and Sobel and Copp (2001). However, nothing I say here turns on the question of whether direction of fit suffices to distinguish belief from desire.

[12] For similar ideas about the badness of false belief, see Fried (1978, 62–64), B. Williams (2004, esp. ch. 6), and Gorin (2018, 242–43).

[13] For an interesting argument that everyone desires to believe what is true, so that if we adopt a desire-based theory of welfare, believing falsely *is* always a harm, see Fehige and Wessels (2019).

even to destroy what touches us closely" (Aristotle, n.d. Book 1, section 6). We need not go *that* far to recognize that believing falsely is a misfortune. We might disagree with Aristotle's ranking of the relative badness of living a lie versus facing a harsh truth, without denying that living a lie is a misfortune.

Thus, something can be a misfortune even if it is the lesser of two evils. Seeing this is key to answering a question one might have about the case of ***Becky and the Beast***: How can Becky's false belief be a misfortune when it saves her from the beast? The answer is that it is unfortunate in one respect, but fortunate in another. It is unfortunate in the way that false beliefs are always misfortunes. But it is fortunate in that it allowed her to jump the ravine. Becky's false belief about how far she could jump made it the case that, lacking time to correct *that* false belief, the only way for Jim to save Becky from disaster was to get her to acquire *another* false belief. This does not change the fact that the false belief Jim got Becky to acquire was a misfortune. It simply means that this misfortune saved her from the larger misfortune of becoming supper for the beast.

Becky's situation is something like that of a patient whose gangrenous limb must be amputated to save his life. The loss of the limb is a misfortune, even though it is necessary to prevent an even larger misfortune. Indeed, part of that larger misfortune is the very fact that the patient's life depends on imposing something upon him that is, taken by itself, a misfortune. To see that removing the limb remains a misfortune even if it is the only way to avoid a larger misfortune, we need only notice that if it were possible, it would be preferable to save the patient without inflicting the misfortune of the amputation. Likewise, Becky's false belief about how far she can leap is a misfortune. But, like a gangrenous limb, it threatens a harm that can only be prevented by imposing on her another, lesser misfortune (the false belief about the width of the ravine). Had it been possible to get Becky to leap the ravine without imposing on her the misfortune of another false belief, this would have been preferable. The fact that imposing this misfortune is the only way to prevent an even larger misfortune explains why Jim is morally justified in lying to Becky: Jim's *pro tanto* reason to refrain from inflicting the misfortune of a false belief on Becky is outweighed by the stronger reason to help her save herself from the beast.

The Mistake Account extends the idea that a mistaken belief is a misfortune to other kinds of mistakes. It is a mistake to ignore something important, to feel an unfitting emotion or one that is too strong or too weak, to react too strongly to an incentive or disincentive, and so on. These various mistakes are also misfortunes, since they are ways in which something has *gone wrong*. Something has *gone wrong* when an emotion is unfitting, or when it is too strong or too weak for the circumstances. Something has *gone wrong* when someone fails to pay attention to something important. Something has *gone wrong* when someone acts against their judgment about what it is best to do. Having something go wrong is a misfortune, for it would have been better in at least one respect if what went wrong had gone right instead. Mistakes of any sort are misfortunes in the same way that mistaken beliefs are misfortunes. This is so even though there are worse misfortunes, and even when such a misfortune is the only way to prevent an even larger misfortune.

9.8.2. Getting Things Right: Kantian Intuitions Revisited

To err is human, of course. But that doesn't mean that we must like it, and generally we don't. We are chagrined if we discover that we overreacted to something that is not as important as we had imagined. We metaphorically kick ourselves if we realize we were so focused on a red herring that we failed to notice something important. We regret acting akratically and resolve to make what we *will* do better reflect what we believe we *should* do. By and large, we do care about getting things right, and regard it as a misfortune when we do not.

Seldom is anyone truly indifferent to a suggestion that they might be mistaken in how they feel, what they pay attention to, how they react to some incentive, and the like. The suggestion that one has gotten things wrong is disturbing, whether it prompts humble soul-searching or indignant denial. Those who put little effort into getting things right do not thereby display an indifference to whether they have made a mistake. Instead, they display an irrational confidence in their ability to get things right consistently and with little effort. But even that dysfunctional attitude embodies a recognition that making a mistake is a kind of failure, and thus a misfortune.

Evolution has probably favored a general preference for getting things right. It is usually advantageous to have accurate rather than faulty information. Having too much or too little fear can be either hazardous or needlessly debilitating. Having too much or too little anger can mark you out as either a threat or as prey, either of which can cause trouble with others. Paying attention to the wrong things can spell disaster. Akrasia can produce impulsive behavior which sacrifices long-term interests for short-term gain.

Of course, there are exceptions. Evolution often settles speed-accuracy tradeoffs in favor of the least dangerous bias, such as a tendency to err on the side of false positives when detecting danger, or to favor immediate consumption when the future is uncertain. And it seems likely that certain false beliefs and feelings, such as an unjustified optimism in our own abilities, might be more advantageous than the more dismal but less empowering truth (Zimmerman and Walker 2022). But evolution often deals in general dispositions, and it seems likely that our evolutionary heritage gives us a general disposition—with lots of exceptions, to be sure—to favor getting things right.

Although an evolutionary story may help explain why we generally *do* care about getting things right, to see why we *should* care about it, we must turn from a Darwinian perspective to a more Kantian one. From that perspective, it is plausible to regard a preference for getting things right as partly constitutive of rational agency. It is difficult to see how one could *be* a rational agent if one is indifferent to whether one has gotten things right. To be a rational agent is to accept norms of rationality, including norms that apply to our mental states. These include the norm of truth for belief, the norm of relevance for attention, norms of fittingness for emotion, and the norm that one's decisions should conform to one's judgment about what is best to do. These norms entail that our beliefs, patterns of attention, emotions, decision-making, and so on can be mistaken, and that such mistakes are failures and thus misfortunes.

Of course, we are not *perfectly* rational agents. Evolution is still true, after all, and it puts limits on how well we can approximate the ideal of rational agency. Given the finite nature of our brains, and the evolutionary processes from which they arose, imperfections in our rational agency are inevitable. Many of these arise from the fact that evolution often trades accuracy for speed. Others arise because mechanisms that were adaptive in conditions that our ancestors faced may produce mistakes in contemporary environments. Still others arise because mechanisms that take advantage of regularities that normally exist in nature can be made to misfire by other agents. Even our beloved conscious reasoning and deliberative faculties are imperfect evolutionary outgrowths of more primitive processes and structures, and this too leaves them imperfect and vulnerable to mistakes.

But while the imperfect nature of our rational agency compromises our *ability* to get things right, it does not eliminate our reason for *caring about* doing so. Perfect and imperfect rational agency both have the same goal—getting things right. What makes imperfect rational agency imperfect is simply that it is not always able to achieve this goal. To be an imperfectly rational agent is still to be embarked on the same project that defines rational agency—the project of getting things right. To value rational agency at all, even the imperfect version of which we are capable, is to value getting things right. Thus, the imperfect nature of our rational agency does not eliminate the reason we have to care about getting things right, and to regard our failures to do so as misfortunes. It simply means that such failures are inevitable.

Of course, the fact that we have a reason to care about getting things right does not preclude us from caring about other things as well, or from sometimes ranking other cares above getting things right. But to place no value at all on getting things right is, ultimately, to renounce the rational agency to which we aspire, and which we largely but imperfectly manage to achieve.

These remarks suggest how the Mistake Account fills in the otherwise vague idea that the manipulator fails to treat the target as a person. Rational agents seek to avoid mistakes in what they believe, how they feel, what they pay attention to, how they react to incentives and disincentives, and so on. If we accept the Kantian idea that rational agency (or even our imperfect version of it) is part of what makes us persons, then manipulation thwarts a goal that is essential to our status as persons.[14]

9.8.3. Adding Insult to Injury

We all make mistakes, and often we have no one to blame but ourselves. But when someone deliberately induces us to make mistakes, it is not only worse but qualitatively different. When you make a mistake, a misfortune *happens* to you. When someone deliberately gets you to make a mistake, that person *inflicts* a misfortune upon you. Its being deliberately inflicted adds a new element to the badness of the misfortune.[15]

This is why, all other things being equal, believing a lie is not only qualitatively different from, but in an important way worse than, acquiring a false belief on one's own. We do not merely show ourselves to have been foolish, but we have been actively made a fool of—and thus victimized—by another person. This applies not only to mistaken beliefs, but to other mistakes as well. If someone gets you to pay attention to the wrong thing, or gets your emotions out of kilter, or makes you doubt your own sound judgment, or gets you to make what you judge to be a sub-optimal choice, then that person inflicts a misfortune upon you.

Consider the difference between getting hit by a loose stone that falls accidentally from a ledge above, versus getting hit by a stone deliberately thrown at you. While both are misfortunes, the difference between them is not trivial. There is a relational component in the second case that is lacking in the first. In the second case, you have not merely suffered an accidental misfortune. Instead, someone has deliberately inflicted one upon you. When this is done out of malice, it will be natural and fitting to have what P. F. Strawson (1962) famously called "reactive attitudes" like resentment toward the person who deliberately inflicted the misfortune. While you may *lament* being hit by a stone that fell by accident, it is fitting to *resent* someone who deliberately threw a stone at you. Similarly, while you may *lament* making a mistake accidentally, it is fitting to *resent* someone who deliberately induced you to make a mistake. In both cases, the fact that the action deliberately inflicts a misfortune upon someone else gives it what we might call an

[14] An anonymous reviewer suggested that this account of the misfortune of mistakes might not apply to very young children. I am inclined to agree that, for children too young even to approximate rational agency, what counts as a mistake for a rational agent might not count as a mistake, and might not be a misfortune even if it does. Obviously, such a view aligns with the common intuition that some forms of influence that would be manipulative when directed at adults might not be manipulative when directed at very young children, and that even when they are, they might be less wrong, if wrong at all. A fuller response along these lines would likely draw on Schapiro (1999) and Noggle (2002).

[15] I am grateful to Thomas Douglas for help in developing the ideas in the next few paragraphs.

"assaultive character." With manipulation, the assault is not on one's body but on one's mind.

The claim that manipulation has this assaultive character is not a claim about the *overall attitude* of the manipulator. It is simply an observation that it is the nature of manipulation to inflict a misfortune. In this sense, an action can have an assaultive character even if it is done from a benevolent motive: If the only way to get Jones to see the landslide headed his way is to chuck a stone at him so that its hitting him makes him look up from his phone, then the action retains its assaultive character even though it was done precisely because the misfortune it inflicts is smaller than the one it prevents. Similarly, benevolent manipulation that saves the target from something terrible retains its assaultive character even if it was done precisely because the misfortune it inflicts is smaller than the one it prevents. Of course, someone inflicts a misfortune on you *benevolently* only if it is true that *if* there *had* been a better way to prevent the larger misfortune, the person would have chosen it, and if the person regrets the fact that no such alternative was available. Part of what is being regretted here is the fact that the lesser of the two evils was still an action with an assaultive character. In such cases, it is no longer fitting to *resent* the benevolent infliction of the misfortune. But deliberately inflicted misfortunes are *candidates* for resentment in a way that accidental misfortunes are not.

9.9. Complicity and Manipulation

Although the analogy between manipulation and hitting someone with a stone is informative in one way, it is misleading in another. The stone-thrower's victim is passive in a way that the manipulator's victim is not.[16] When I am manipulated, I am the one who makes the mistake. The manipulator may *invite* or *induce* me to make a mistake, but the manipulator cannot make the mistake *for* me. Only *I* can do that. Consequently, if manipulation is to succeed, I *must* participate in the bad thing that is done to me in a way that I do not participate when I am passively hit by a stone. In an insightful psychological study of con artists—who are, after all, professional manipulators—Maria Konnikova puts the point this way:

> The true con artist doesn't force us to do anything; he makes us complicit in our own undoing. He doesn't steal. We give. He doesn't have to threaten us . . . We believe because we want to, not because anyone made us. (Konnikova 2016, 6)

This is why, despite its popularity, the metaphor of the manipulator as puppet-master is profoundly misleading. The puppet-master acts on the body of the

[16] Abramson makes a similar point about the more elaborate form of gaslighting that she discusses (Abramson 2024, 63–64).

puppet, directly controlling its limbs with strings. Even if the puppet *had* a mind, it would play no role in the puppet-master's control over the puppet. The puppet performs no actions of its own. It is merely a tool through which the puppet-master acts. By contrast, the manipulator's influence operates *through* the target's *mind*. Unlike the puppet, the target of manipulation is, and remains, an *agent* who performs genuine actions. As we have seen, manipulation does not bypass the target's decision-making capacities. Instead, it employs them, by causing them to make mistakes.

At first glance, this observation may seem to make manipulation less blameworthy than forms of wrongdoing in which the victim plays no causal role: If I contribute causally to what the manipulator does to me, doesn't that mean that part of the blame for what the manipulator does transfers from him to me? A similar idea is sometimes thought to justify the common belief that it is less bad to deceive someone without lying than it is to lie outright. The idea is that if you deceive me into thinking you are planning a trip by arranging for me to see your packed suitcases, then I must make the effort to infer from the suitcases that you are planning a trip. But if you simply lie to me, I do not put forth this mental effort. According to the argument, the fact that I contribute to being deceived shifts some of the blame for being deceived from the deceiver to me, and thus makes (non-lying) deception less bad than lying.[17]

This argument may seem plausible at first glance, but it does not survive scrutiny. For it rests on a principle that has unacceptable, indeed morally odious, implications. As Jennifer Saul observes, we do not say that it is less bad to mug someone walking through a less safe neighborhood because this contributed causally to the mugging (Saul 2012b, 82–84). Similarly, it is not less bad to steal a car from someone who left the keys in it than from someone who did not (Hurd 2005, 510). It is not less bad to assault someone too drunk to put up an effective defense than to assault a sober person. As Saul puts it, "We cannot move from a claim that responsibility is shared to a claim that the act is less bad or that the actor is less culpable" (Saul 2012a, 5). This is surely correct. There is no reason to think that the fact that the victim of manipulation must be the one to make the mistake makes manipulation any less bad.

This is not to say that victims of manipulation are *never* blameworthy. Some of the traits on which manipulators prey *are* blameworthy. These include vices like greed, lust, arrogance, hate, and, perhaps under certain conditions, gullibility. When a manipulator exploits a target's blameworthy trait, it seems reasonable to blame the target, at least indirectly, for having the bad quality exploited by the

[17] This argument is often attributed to Kant; see, e.g., MacIntyre (1994, 337). Jennifer Saul has developed a decisive critique of this argument (Saul 2012a; 2012b). While I agree with Saul's critique of this *argument* for the claim that lying is worse than mere deception, I remain agnostic about whether lying is, in fact, worse than deception. If it is, then I suspect that the reason is that asserting a claim involves something like a promise or warrant or invitation to trust that one only asserts what one believes true. For examples of this view, see Chisholm and Feehan (1977, 153), and Fallis (2010, 17–18). Saul rejects this view (Saul 2012a, 5–6).

manipulator. We might even experience *schadenfreude* when bad people get their comeuppance because a manipulator has exploited the very qualities that make them bad. Moreover, it is no doubt better, *ceteris paribus*, if manipulators target bad people rather than good people. But all this is consistent with the claim that the mere fact that the target must make a mistake if manipulation is to occur does not, in and of itself, make manipulation less bad or the manipulator less blameworthy.

In fact, there are good reasons to think that the target's contribution to being manipulated makes manipulation *worse* than it would otherwise be. Someone who manipulates me does not only do something bad to me, but that person gets me to do something bad to myself. Thus, the manipulator does two things at once: He makes a fool of me, but he also gets me to make a fool of myself. The fact that the manipulator induces me to become complicit in my own victimization makes that victimization worse, not less bad.[18]

Massimo Renzo makes a similar point, writing that

> What makes manipulation distinctively objectionable is the fact that it co-opts the capacity of the manipulee to respond to their reasons for action and uses it to induce them to fail to do so. In this way, the manipulee becomes an accomplice in the very wrong they suffer. (Renzo 2023, 254)[19]

As we have seen, manipulation does not *bypass* the target's capacity for rational agency; instead, it makes it misfire in a way that the manipulator wants. On the Mistake Account, manipulation does this by feeding a mistake into the reasoning and decision-making processes that make us rational agents. But manipulation harnesses the capacities that make us rational agents to thwart a goal that is constitutive of rational agency, namely the goal of getting things right. Thus, Renzo's remarks reveal a cruel irony at the heart of manipulation: It harnesses a person's rational agency to thwart a goal that is an essential component *of* rational agency.

Renzo's insight is both correct and profound. But there is another way that the target's complicity makes manipulation not just an especially bad way to treat someone's rational agency, but a bad *experience* to inflict upon someone. In describing what happens to the victim of deception, Jonathan Adler writes:

> Not only has he been misled, but the embarrassment or horror of it is that he has been duped into collaborating on his own harm. Afterward, he cannot secure the relief of wholly locating blame externally. (Adler 1997, 442)

[18] Clea Rees (2014) defends a similar claim about non-lying deception, though her argument does not appear to generalize to manipulation. Christian Coons and Michael Weber make a similar suggestion about manipulation (Coons and Weber 2014, 16).

[19] My thinking about the ideas in this and the next couple of paragraphs has benefitted from the work of, and discussions with, Massimo Renzo.

The victim that Adler describes is not distressed so much by the cruel irony of his rational agency being used against him. Rather, he is distressed by the realization of his own personal failure in allowing that to happen.

Adler's remarks apply more generally to all victims of manipulation. Manipulation is always at least partly a self-inflicted misfortune, and the *experience* of inflicting it upon oneself contributes to its insidious cruelty. R. Paul Wilson, an expert on con artists (and a former con artist himself) writes that

> Con games can have a powerful, damaging effect on a mark. Loss of money or property is amplified by a loss of faith or self-respect. Because of this, few victims are motivated to admit what's happened to them. Their primary fear is that they will be regarded as foolish, naïve, greedy, or gullible. These are normal human frailties that are preyed upon by con men, and when the ride is over, the victim is suddenly faced with a naked truth that can cut deeper than any knife. (Wilson 2014, 340)

Con artists rely on this shame to shield themselves from the consequences of their actions. As Wilson writes, "Shame is a powerful emotion, and the smarter the mark is, or the higher their standing in society, the greater the chances that he won't tell a soul about being conned" (Wilson 2014, 131–32; see also Konnikova 2016, 291–96).

The fact that manipulation enlists the victim in his own victimization makes it especially devious. When we fall for it, the value we place on getting things right, and our sense of ourselves as rational beings who normally *do* get things right, contributes to a deep sense of failure and shame. And yet, somewhat ironically, that sense of failure and shame is itself largely mistaken. The imperfections of human reason and the human character are inevitable given our evolutionary history and the limits of biological intelligence. As we saw throughout Chapter 8, many of the features of our minds that manipulators exploit are not flaws so much as inevitable trade-offs between accuracy and speed, or between annoying false positives and deadly false negatives. While it is natural to feel shame at having been manipulated, and while manipulators sometimes exploit genuine character flaws, our susceptibility to being manipulated is part and parcel of the human condition. Certainly, we should be on guard against manipulation. But when we inevitably do fall for it anyway, we should also be a little more forgiving of ourselves. For the most part, our vulnerabilities to manipulation reflect our status as finite beings made of mushy stuff honed through the vicissitudes of evolution, whose instantiation of rational agency is inevitably imperfect.

9.10. The Moral Evaluation of Manipulation

The forgoing discussion suggests some practical advice about assessing the moral status of individual instances of manipulation.

9.10.1. Manipulation, Harm, and Autonomy

Although the *intrinsic* presumptive wrongness of manipulation derives from the misfortune of being mistaken, it remains true that manipulation *usually* has negative effects on the target's well-being or autonomy, or both. When they are present, these negative effects are usually larger misfortunes than the misfortune of being induced to make a mistake. Thus, while the misfortune of making a mistake explains the intrinsic presumptive wrongness of *all* cases of manipulation, the most morally egregious cases of manipulation are egregious when and because they harm the target or undermine the target's autonomy.

Indeed, the Mistake Account explains *why* manipulation so often harms the target or undermines the target's autonomy. People normally try to promote their own well-being. Consequently, getting them to do something that reduces it will often require getting them to make a mistake. Similarly, people normally try to protect their autonomy and to pursue their autonomously chosen goals. Consequently, getting them to do something that undermines their autonomy or thwarts their autonomously chosen goals will often require getting them to make a mistake. The flipside of this also holds: Because people normally promote their own interests, choices based on mistakes will often thwart their interests. Because people normally protect their autonomy and advance their autonomously chosen goals, choices based on mistakes will often compromise their autonomy or thwart their autonomously chosen goals. Consequently, in analyzing a given instance of manipulation, we should begin by examining its effects on the target's well-being and autonomy.

Even when manipulation harms the target or undermines the target's autonomy, it might be justified in the same ways that other harmful or autonomy-undermining actions are sometimes justified. All but the most fanatical deontologists concede that an action that is harmful or autonomy-reducing to one person might be justified if its positive effects on others outweigh—by a sufficiently great amount—the negative effects on the one. *When* this happens, and *how much* a "sufficiently great amount" is, are among the central questions of moral philosophy. The simplest and least plausible versions of utilitarianism allow any action with bad consequences to be justified if its *net* consequences are even slightly better than the alternatives. More plausible theories require the good effects on others to be significantly larger than the bad effects on the one for the action to be justified.

These matters lie at the heart of the perennial debate between proponents of consequentialist and deontological theories of morality, as well as debates over the most plausible deontological theories.[20] Settling them is far beyond the scope of this book. But however we do settle them, we must keep in mind that one of

[20] For a concise overview of deontological approaches to trade-offs of this sort, see Alexander and Moore (2021, esp. sections 4 and 5). See also Kagan (1997 ch. 3).

the harms of manipulation is the psychological harm of complicity in one's own victimization.

Unless we take an unreasonably absolutist approach to manipulation, there will be at least three kinds of cases where even harmful or autonomy-undermining manipulation will be morally justified. First, there are situations like ***Terrorist Terry***, where manipulation prevents the target from deliberately harming others. As we noted earlier, in such cases manipulation may not even be *pro tanto* immoral. Instead, the need to thwart an evil-doer might completely nullify the moral reasons against manipulation. If so, then justifying manipulation in such cases will be a matter of determining what sorts, and perhaps what magnitudes, of evil the target must be embarked on for the presumption against manipulation to be nullified.

Second, there are cases where manipulation is the only (or least bad) way to prevent some great harm to one or more innocent persons. There are two variations of this kind of case. In one, neither the manipulation itself, nor the action that the manipulation gets the target to perform, harms the target or anyone else. Suppose that FBI Agent Mindy from the case of ***Terrorist Terry*** has gotten Terry to tell her that the bomb is in a nearby high-security building. With the clock ticking, Mindy rushes to the secured entrance of that building so quickly that she forgets her FBI credentials. Thus, Mindy cannot gain entrance by using her badge, and if she tries to explain why she needs access to the building, she will either sound unhinged or start a panic. So, Mindy employs the manipulative tactic of "tailgating" (see section 2.2.4) to gain access: She follows closely behind an employee with a key card, who enters and then absent-mindedly holds the door open for Mindy. Mindy's manipulation does not harm or undermine the autonomy of the employee, or anyone else. And it saves many others from harm. Such cases are probably uncommon: Innocent people who can easily help prevent some great harm without harming themselves or anyone else, or undermining their own or anyone else's autonomy, will normally do so voluntarily. So, there will usually be no reason to manipulate them; asking them will usually suffice to enlist their assistance. Hence such cases are most likely to arise when something prevents the innocent person from doing the harmless thing that would prevent the great harm, and manipulation is the only feasible way to overcome the obstacle. When cases like this do occur, it will often be possible to justify manipulation to the target *afterwards*, for the same reason that such cases are rather uncommon: The manipulation helps the person do what they would have been inclined to do were it not for the impediment. Such a person is likely, after the fact, to waive any objection to being manipulated into doing what the impediment prevented them from doing.

Matters become more difficult if either the harm-preventing action or the manipulation required to get the target to perform it, would harm the target or some other innocent person(s). But most of what makes cases like this complicated is the question of when it is permissible to harm one person to protect others from harm. The fact that the harms to some will be brought about through manipulation simply adds another layer of complexity to the problem: The intrinsic wrongness of manipulation will add to the moral reasons not to impose harms on some to prevent larger harms to others.

A third kind of case is when manipulating one person will protect *that same person* from harm, or bestow some benefit on *that same person*. Such cases still involve trade-offs, but the trade-offs are *intra*-personal rather than *inter*-personal. Presumably, it is easier for considerations of harm and benefit to justify manipulating someone if that same person will suffer the harm or enjoy the benefit.[21] Hence, it seems reasonable to think that, in at least some version of the ***Bad Boyfriend*** case (section 3.4), Theresa's friends are justified in manipulating her because this is the least bad thing they can do to protect her from the harms with which she is threatened. Moreover, it seems plausible that less potential harm to Theresa is needed to justify manipulating Theresa than would be needed to justify manipulating some innocent bystander if doing so would somehow protect Theresa from harm.

9.10.2. The Rough Parity Principle

As we have just seen, determining whether a harmful or autonomy-reducing instance of manipulation is justified begins with the same moral calculus that we use to determine whether any other harmful or autonomy-reducing action is justified. But since the Mistake Account denies that the entire moral status of manipulation derives from its effects on well-being and autonomy, reasoning about the effects of manipulation on well-being and autonomy is only *part* of the moral analysis of a given instance of manipulation. The misfortune of making a mistake must also play a role in our analysis of the moral status of manipulation, even if that role is often less than the role played by considerations of autonomy and well-being. How, then, should we think about the magnitude of the badness of mistakes, and how should we factor it into our analysis of the moral status of a given instance of manipulation?

Here the parallel that the Mistake Account draws between manipulation and deception can play an important role. In fact, there is good reason to endorse what I shall call the

> ***Rough Parity Principle***: The moral status of any given instance of non-deceptive manipulation is similar to that of a relevantly similar instance of deception.

[21] See Hanna (2018, 127–28) for an argument for this claim.

The strongest argument for the Rough Parity Principle derives from the fact that cases of non-deceptive manipulation can often be redescribed as cases of deception. As we saw in section 4.7, cases of successful manipulative pressure can be described as involving either "classical" akrasia or a temporary change in beliefs about what is optimal. For example, in ***University I*** from section 4.2, if Mandy's manipulative use of emotional blackmail gets Tara to withdraw her application to university, either of two things might have happened:

Scenario A: Tara chose akratically against her considered and stable judgment that forgoing university would be worse than losing Mandy's friendship.
Scenario B: Tara temporarily and irrationally adopted, and acted on, the false belief that losing Mandy's friendship would be worse than forgoing university.

Similarly, as we saw in section 6.9, we can often redescribe cases of emotional manipulation in terms of changes in beliefs. Thus, if Maddie from ***Snow Flurries I*** (section 5.3) manipulates Tim into staying home from a party by inducing in him an excessive fear of snow flurries, either of two things might have happened:

Scenario A: Maddie's vivid descriptions of gruesome car accidents on slippery roads increased Tim's fear of a crash without changing any of his beliefs.
Scenario B: Maddie's vivid descriptions of gruesome car accidents on slippery roads caused Tim to acquire one or more false beliefs about the probability of the flurries turning worse, the effects on road conditions of mere flurries, or his ability to cope with a minor deterioration in road conditions.

For pairs of cases like these, there may be no empirical facts that make one description more apt than the other. And if there *are* empirical facts that make one description more apt, those facts are likely to be so subtle that it would be difficult to believe that they make a significant moral difference. Since Scenario B in both pairs involves the adoption of a false belief, the manipulator's behavior in each B scenario would count as deception. Since it is difficult to believe that there is a significant moral difference between the members of each pair of scenarios, it seems reasonable to think that the moral status of a given instance of non-deceptive manipulation is on a par with a relevantly similar instance of deception. Such cases, which could easily be multiplied, support the Rough Parity Principle.

Moreover, the Rough Parity Principle reflects the conceptual and moral parallels that the Mistake Account draws between manipulation and deception. For both manipulation and deception, the most morally egregious instances will be morally egregious because of bad effects on the target's autonomy or well-being.

The core moral status of both manipulation and deception (the part that does not stem from their effects on autonomy and well-being) is the misfortune of making a mistake and the wrongness of inflicting that misfortune on someone else. These parallels lend additional support to the Rough Parity Principle.

To apply the principle to a particular case of non-deceptive manipulation, we would redescribe it as a case of deception. In doing so, we must be careful to ensure that the "deceptive redescription" is as similar as possible to the actual case. Most obviously, we must ensure that the effects on the target's well-being and autonomy are the same in both cases. Moreover, we must ensure that, in both cases, the influencer has a relevantly similar state of mind, e.g., the intent to do what, from the influencer's perspective, amounts to inducing the target to make a mistake. Finally, we must ensure that the magnitude or size of the mistakes are as similar as possible in the two cases.

Once we have a "deceptive redescription" that is similar in all relevant respects to the case of manipulation we are evaluating, then we need only consult our intuitions about whether the case of deception would be morally justified. Of course, in some cases our intuitions about the deceptive case will be weak or varied. But the reason why the Rough Parity Principle is promising is that we have fairly well-behaved intuitions about when deception is morally justified. Consequently, while the Rough Parity Principle will not yield a clear and unanimous verdict on every case of manipulation, it will help us achieve principled answers to at least some moral questions involving manipulation where we lack clear and uniform intuitions.

9.10.3. Manipulation and Mistake Size

The discussion of the Rough Parity Principle just now referred to the "size" of the mistake as something that must be kept similar when we re-describe a case of non-deceptive manipulation as a case of deception. But how do we determine the size of a mistake?

To answer this question, it will be helpful to begin with what we might call *morally trivial* deception. These are instances of deception that are morally innocuous because (1) they have no serious negative effects on the target's autonomy or well-being, and (2) because the false beliefs induced constitute relatively trivial mistakes.[22] Here are some examples of morally trivial deception:

1. Daphne misleads Tim into thinking that they are embarking on a shopping excursion, but she is really taking him to his surprise birthday party.

[22] For views sympathetic to the idea that some forms of deception are morally innocuous, see S. Buss (2005), Baier (2010), Nyberg (1995), Adler (1997), and Strudler (2016).

2. On the way home from a terrible day at work, Don stops at a coffee shop. When the barista asks how his day is going, he smiles and answers (unironically), "Great."
3. Tate is usually a competent baker. But the cake he just baked for Delilah's birthday is dry and flavorless. Delilah pretends to enjoy it, and thanks Tate profusely for making it.

If these acts of deception are wrong at all, they would seem to be only trivial wrongs. Some may even be morally justified. For example, it is possible that the institution of surprise parties is sufficiently valuable to justify some instances of trivial deception like the one that Daphne engages in (Strudler 2016).

The most obvious reason why these cases of deception are morally innocuous is that none of them have, or are intended to have, any significant negative effect on the target's well-being or autonomy. But they are also innocuous because the falsehoods themselves seem fairly trivial. They are small mistakes rather than large ones. At least three factors seem to make them so.

The first is how far the false belief deviates from the truth. Tate's false belief that this particular cake was good is a fairly small deviation given that the bad cake is itself a minor deviation from Tate's normal run of good cakes. The difference between believing that his cakes *always* turn out well and believing that they *almost always* turn out well is small. A second factor is the duration of the false belief. Tim's false belief that he is going shopping with Daphne lasts only until they reach the location of the surprise party. A third factor is the level of psychological investment the target has in the matter that the false belief concerns. Even if the barista has a general concern for the well-being of all her customers, she is presumably far less invested in Don's well-being than she is in the well-being of her loved ones.

By contrast, a false belief which deviates significantly from the truth, which persists for a long time, and which concerns matters important to the deceived person, is a much larger mistake. The false belief that Marlow induces in Kurtz's fiancée, namely that Kurtz's last word was her name, constitutes a far more significant mistake: It is a large deviation from the truth, it likely persists for the rest of her life, and it concerns a matter of great importance to her. Thus, Marlow's deception creates a much larger mistake than does that of Daphne, the barista, or Delilah. Even though its badness is at least partly outweighed by the fact that it protects her from a painful truth, it remains, in and of itself, a significant misfortune precisely because it is such a large mistake. By contrast, the mistakes that Daphne, the barista, and Delilah induce are trivial, so much so that their badness can be outweighed by fairly minor countervailing considerations.

All other things being equal, then, a larger mistake is a worse misfortune, in and of itself, than a smaller one.[23] But larger mistakes are also more likely to spread or

[23] Charles Fried makes this same point (Fried 1978, 64–66).

propagate than smaller ones. If Tate is a terrible baker, then the false belief that almost all his baked goods are delicious could reverberate through his psychology in all sorts of ways. And some of these ways might lead him to make bad choices—like quitting a good job to open a bakery. If Daphne tells Tim that his fiancée was in a car accident and they need to go to the hospital, this mistake will certainly cause all sorts of other mistaken beliefs and emotions before it is dispelled when the party guests yell, "Surprise!" If Don misleads *his best friend* that his day was great when it was terrible, that friend might forgo offering support and advice that he would otherwise offer, and he might mistake Don's sour mood for a response to something that he said or did.

Thus, there are two reasons why a larger mistake is worse than a smaller one: First, a larger mistake is a larger misfortune, in and of itself, than a smaller one. Second, a larger mistake is more likely than a smaller one to propagate and give rise to additional mistakes and bad decisions. Consequently, when we apply the Rough Parity Principle, we must make sure that the size of the mistake in the hypothetical case of deception resembles that of the mistake involved in the case of non-deceptive manipulation that we are evaluating.

Looking at the various kinds of mistakes induced in (non-deceptive) manipulation, we can see that they, too, vary in terms of their size, and that this variation reflects factors like their duration, the importance to the target of their subject-matter, and how far they deviate from what is correct. Generally, the larger the influence that the manipulator wants to produce, the larger the mistake must be. Thus, Iago must induce a very large mistake—turning trust into suspicion and love into hate—to get Othello to murder his beloved Desdemona. In such cases, where the mistaken emotion differs significantly in "shape" from what is correct, the mistake is quite large. When the emotional mistake consists of the right emotion being felt too strongly or too weakly, the size of the mistake will depend on how excessive or deficient the emotion is. Moreover, lasting emotions often propagate, since they often affect what we are inclined to believe. In particular, feeling an emotion tends to make one more likely to believe things that would make the emotion fitting. Thus, it is easier to believe the worst of someone whom one dislikes than of someone whom one likes. And, as Shakespeare so deftly illustrates in *Othello*, once suspicion and jealousy are kindled, they can incline a person to believe the very things that would make such emotions fitting.

Mistakes of attention or weighting can likewise vary in how far they deviate from what is correct. The more important the thing one is gotten not to notice, or the greater the difference between something's true importance and the importance one places on it during deliberation, the larger the mistake.

Similarly, an akratic overreaction to an incentive can be larger or smaller. A trivially small overreaction might be strong enough only to induce a sub-optimal choice when that choice is only very slightly less than optimal. For example, if a parent's reaction to a teen's nagging for a new cell phone is only slight, then it might only induce an akratic choice if the parent sees the reasons against buying the new phone as being only a bit stronger than the reasons for doing so. But a slight overreaction would be insufficient to induce an akratic choice if the parent regards the reasons against buying the phone as being much stronger than those in favor of doing so.

Script and heuristic mistakes can, likewise, be smaller or larger. Mistakenly using the "fast food restaurant" script while in a fancy restaurant is not as big a mistake as using the "politely holding the door" script when entering a secured area. Generally, the size of the heuristic mistake depends on how much the employed heuristic differs from the appropriate one. But it can also be a mistake to rely on any heuristic in high-stakes situations where time permits the use of more elaborate reasoning, and the size of this mistake depends on how much more appropriate elaborate reasoning is relative to the heuristic employed.

The size of the mistakes induced in (non-deceptive) manipulation can also be affected by their duration. While many forms of manipulation are isolated instances that require only fleeting, one-off mistakes, manipulation can also take the form of an ongoing process. In such cases, the mistakes often persist much longer.

As we noted earlier, as a practical matter, it will often be possible to estimate the size of the mistake induced by the manipulator from the magnitude of the influence. A manipulative influence that is so weak that it can only produce a slight deflection in the target's behavior will typically involve a relatively small mistake. By contrast, a large effect on the target's behavior—such as the one Iago induces in Othello—typically requires inducing a much larger mistake.

9.10.4. Trivial Manipulation

The Rough Parity Principle, together with the existence of trivial deception, suggests that some forms of manipulation are likewise trivial and thus morally innocuous. More precisely, some instances of manipulation are trivial and thus morally innocuous because they are neither harmful nor autonomy-undermining, and because they induce only small mistakes.

The existence of a category of trivial manipulation helps us deal with borderline cases of manipulation, where it is difficult for anyone—including the target—to say whether a mistake has been induced, or where it is difficult for anyone—including the influencer—to say whether the influencer regards what is induced as a mistake.

Suppose that Tammy is attending a karaoke party, but she prefers not to sing. Her friends all call for her to take a turn, shouting encouragement and sincerely complimenting her singing voice, until she gives in and belts out a tune. Whether this counts as manipulation may be difficult to determine. Did Tammy weigh her friends' encouragement properly? How strong was her preference not to sing? Was her choice to sing akratic, or was it a measured response to the joy it would bring her friends? Were her friends trying to make it difficult for Tammy to decline even if she regarded that as her optimal choice? Or were they simply making a request and combining it with sincere compliments on her singing?

Or suppose that Tom has never lived where snow is common until moving to Chicago. Suppose that, while warning him of the dangers of driving in snow and ice, I decide to "lay it on a little thick," to make sure he gets the point. Have I induced Tom to feel the proper amount of fear, or too much fear, of winter driving? What is the proper amount of fear? Did my attempt to counteract what I took to be his nonchalance cross the line between trying to induce the right amount of fear, and trying to induce a little too much fear because it is more dangerous to fear winter driving too little than to fear it too much?

In practice, such questions can be difficult, if not impossible, to answer. The existence of a category of morally trivial manipulation allows us to soften the moral line between manipulation and non-manipulative influence. Being able to say that a given influence is, at most, morally trivial manipulation, or that if it is manipulation, it is a morally trivial instance of it, prevents us from having to say that large moral distinctions turn on extremely fine distinctions that may be impossible for the influencer, the target, or anyone else to make.

9.11. Conclusion

Its ability to give a convincing account of the moral status of manipulation, and advice about how to assess the moral status of individual instances of manipulation, are important advantages of the Mistake Account. In the final two chapters, we will see that the Mistake Account has another important advantage, namely, that it can be applied to a wide range of examples of influence, and that it offers plausible verdicts about whether they are manipulative.

10
Exotic Influences and Problem Cases

10.1. Introduction

We have seen that the Mistake Account aligns with and explains our intuitive judgments about a wide variety of *ordinary* forms of influence, such as those discussed in Chapter 2. Indeed, its ability to do this is the strongest argument in favor of the Mistake Account. This chapter will consider influences that are more exotic than those we have discussed so far. It will also consider some ordinary forms of influence that may seem to pose difficulties for the Mistake Account.

10.2. Priming

Let's begin with one of the most interesting and controversial examples of a purported influence, which, if real, would certainly count as exotic: *social priming*. The term 'priming' refers to the "facilitative effects of some event or action on subsequent associated responses" (Molden 2014, 3). Thus, a prime "greases the wheels" for a response that is somehow related to the prime, making the response more likely to occur, or making it occur more quickly or efficiently.

Both cognitive and social psychologists study priming, but they study different sorts of priming in different ways. As Stéphane Doyen and colleagues note, cognitive psychologists usually study priming effects

> to infer the structure of semantic representations. For example, they might present the prime word "nurse" and then measure the speed with which people can determine that another word (e.g., "doctor," "uniform," or "house") is a word or non-word... The closer the semantic association..., the faster the response on such a lexical decision task. (Doyen et al. 2014, 17)

Priming effects of this sort—sometimes called "semantic priming"—influence cognitive tasks like word recognition and recall, and they tend to be subtle and fleeting. The existence of semantic priming is relatively uncontroversial. The main debates about it concern its underlying mechanisms and whether it requires conscious awareness of the prime (Doyen et al. 2014).

By contrast, social psychologists study priming effects on overt behavior or its immediate psychological precursors, such as affective states and evaluative judgments. As Daniel Molden writes:

Manipulation. Robert Noggle, Oxford University Press. © Robert Noggle 2025.
DOI: 10.1093/9780198924920.003.0010

> priming effects in social psychology all involve some stimulation of people's mental representations of social targets, events, or situations that then influences subsequent evaluations, judgments, or actions. (Molden 2014, 4)

This "social" priming (as it is often called[1]) is thought to influence behavior more directly than semantic priming, since it affects either behavior or mental states that often influence behavior. Moreover, the *way* that social priming is thought to influence action is significant. As Molden writes,

> the influence of this priming is assumed to occur outside of *either* (a) awareness of this potential influence *or* (b) intention to utilize the activated representations during judgment or action . . . That is, the effects of the prime are presumed to arise because people either do not recognize its potential effects on their subsequent responses or, even if they do, still do not intend to utilize the primed representations when making these responses. Thus, in general, priming research in social psychology is largely concerned with how cues that call to mind particular social situations or relationships can subtly influence people's responses even when they do not deliberately connect these cues to their current thoughts and actions. (Molden 2014, 4–5)

A much-discussed example of social priming was reported in a pair of studies conducted by John Bargh, Mark Chen, and Lara Burrows (Bargh, Chen, and Burrows 1996). Participants were asked to unscramble words to form sentences. In one study, the scrambled sentences assigned to the experimental group included words related to rudeness; in the other, they included words related to ageing or the elderly. After the unscrambling task, the participants' behavior was observed surreptitiously. In the first study, Bargh, Chen and Burrows reported that participants who were primed with words relating to rudeness were quicker to interrupt a staged conversation than participants in the control group. In the second study, they reported that participants who were primed with words related to the elderly walked more slowly down a hallway than participants in the control group.

In another interesting study, Kathleen Vohs, Nicole Mead, and Miranda Goode examined the effects of primes related to money (Vohs, Mead, and Goode 2006). In some experiments, participants in the experimental group were exposed to money-related words during a sentence-descrambling task. In others, they were asked to read an essay about growing up in an affluent household. In still others, they could see large amounts of Monopoly money during the experiment. The researchers then compared the behavior of participants subjected to money-related

[1] Some psychologists find the term 'social priming' unhelpful: see, e.g., Payne, Brown-Iannuzzi, and Loersch (2016, 1270) and Sherman and Rivers (2021, 2).

primes to that of participants who were either not subjected to money-related primes at all, or who were subjected to primes associated with less money (e.g., a smaller amount of Monopoly money, or an essay about growing up in a non-affluent family). Vohs, Meade, and Goode reported that participants subjected to money or high money primes were slower to ask for help on a difficult task, picked up fewer pencils dropped by a researcher in a staged accident, spent less time helping a confederate posing as a confused fellow participant, and donated less money to a charity.

These studies examined the effects of a prime on behavior—what is sometimes called "behavioral priming." Other social priming studies examine the effect of priming on attitudes and evaluative judgments—what is sometimes called "affective" or "evaluative" priming. Although such primes might still affect behavior, this effect would be indirect, with the prime changing how we feel, and how we feel affecting how we behave (Ferguson and Mann 2014).

A classic study of affective or evaluative priming was done by E. Tory Higgins, William Rholes, and Carl Jones (Higgins, Rholes, and Jones 1977). Participants were given a written description of a fictional person named "Donald." Given this description, Donald could be described equally well as "adventurous" or "reckless," as "self-confident" or "conceited," as "independent" or "aloof," and as "persistent" or "stubborn." Participants in the experimental groups were first primed with either the positive or negative words that could describe Donald. They then read the description of Donald and rated their attitudes toward him. Participants primed with the positive words evaluated Donald more favorably than those primed with the negative words.

A particularly striking example of affective priming was reported by Bargh and Lawrence Williams (Williams and Bargh 2008). This study drew on earlier work suggesting that when we form first impressions of people, we tend to categorize them as either "warm" or "cold." The study investigated whether exposure to different physical temperatures could influence these impressions of a fictitious person. At the start of the experiment, a researcher pretended to need both hands free to complete some paperwork and asked each participant to hold the researcher's drink. For some participants, the drink was hot coffee; for others it was iced coffee. All participants were then asked to rate a fictitious person based on a written description. Bargh and Williams reported that participants who held the hot coffee rated the person as "warmer"—having more personality traits connected with being a socially warm person—than the participants who held the iced coffee. In a second experiment, participants were asked to handle either a hot pack or cold pack as part of a feigned product evaluation study. Later, participants were given the opportunity to choose a small gift for themselves or one to be donated to a friend. Bargh and Williams reported that significantly more participants primed with the warm pack chose to donate the gift than did those primed with the cold pack.

10.3. Questions about the Efficacy of Priming

It is easy to see how effects like these—if they are genuine and robust—could influence someone's behavior in significant ways. This possibility is not lost on influence expert Robert Cialdini. In his best-selling book, *Pre-suasion* (Cialdini 2018), which is a follow-up to his best-selling book, *Influence* (Cialdini 2008), he draws on various priming studies to advise readers to offer potential customers a warm rather than cold drink to prime feelings of social warmth (Cialdini 2018, 108–9), to ask people whether they are adventurous before asking them to try a new product to prime the idea of openness to new experiences (Cialdini 2018, 26–27), and to post pictures of a person winning a race to prime workers with ideas of achievement (Cialdini 2018, 103–4).

Unfortunately for those seeking to deploy priming effects to influence others, many of the findings in social priming research have been called into question (Bartlett 2013; Chivers 2019; Yong 2012) and proven difficult to replicate (Doyen et al. 2012; Lynott et al. 2014; Vadillo, Hardwicke, and Shanks 2016, Schimmack, Heene, and Kesavan 2017). This situation is often characterized as a replication *crisis*; Kahneman has called it a "train wreck" (Goldstein 2012). Reactions to this situation vary. Some seem to regard it as seriously undermining the credibility of prominent findings in social priming research. Others seem to regard declarations of a crisis as overblown or at least premature. Still others tread a middle ground, suggesting that some social priming effects may be real, but are probably more subtle, less powerful, or more dependent on moderating variables than has been claimed.[2] A consensus about the existence and strength of social priming effects is unlikely to emerge anytime soon.

In the meantime, there are three reasons why we should ask whether the Mistake Account properly identifies manipulation in cases of social priming. First, these effects *might* be real and strong enough to constitute a significant effect on behavior, in which case a credible theory of manipulation should account for our intuitions in cases where they are used. Second, even if social priming effects are weak or non-existent, a plausible theory of manipulation should yield intuitively correct judgments about counterfactual cases where they are real and powerful. Third, thinking about how the Mistake Account applies to social priming may guide its application to other exotic forms of influence that might exist.

[2] For a sample of the various reactions to the replication crisis, see Chivers 2019, Stroebe and Strack 2014, Ferguson and Mann 2014, Payne, Brown-Iannuzzi, and Loersch 2016, Bargh 2012, Krpan 2017, Di Nucci 2012, Weingarten et al. 2016, and Sherman and Rivers 2021. One challenge in (so-called) social priming research is that the studies in which the most interesting priming effects have been reported tend to be ones that employ between-subject designs that are less powerful than within-subject designs, especially given the low numbers of participants tested (Sherman and Rivers 2021).

10.4. The Mistake Account and Priming

So let us suppose that these priming effects are real and powerful enough to influence behavior. Suppose, for example, that you could get someone to walk more slowly by peppering your speech with words that evoke stereotypes of the elderly. Or suppose that a businessperson could increase the chances of making a sale by offering the potential customer a hot coffee instead of a cold soft drink. How would the Mistake Account handle such cases? Our analysis will depend on a crucial question: Are these influences strong enough to overcome a contrary behavioral inclination? Assume, first, that they are. Consider these two cases:

Risky Investments: Byron is about to meet with a financial consultant selling risky investments. Byron has no interest in these risky investments, but he agreed to meet the consultant as a favor to a mutual friend. The consultant's partner, Mike, has read Cialdini's advice, and hands Byron a hot cup of coffee just before the meeting. This makes Byron develop "socially warm feelings," which make him want to do business with the consultant. As a result, he buys into one of the consultant's risky investments, just as Mike had planned. If Mike had handed Byron a cold drink, he would not have invested.

Missed Train: Walker is rushing to catch a train so that he will be on time for a job interview. Michelle, a rival candidate for that same job, wants Walker to *miss* the train. So she regales Walker with jokes about the residents of the Del Boca Vista retirement community from the American sitcom, *Seinfeld*. Although Walker knows that he should hurry, Michelle's priming of elderly-related stereotypes causes him to walk slowly enough to miss the train. Had Michelle not exposed Walker to elderly-related primes, he would have walked quickly enough to catch the train.

In both cases, the prime overcomes a disposition to do something else. This might make the cases less realistic. But it also makes them clear examples of manipulation—so clear, in fact, that it would be bad for a theory not to identify them as such, whether or not they are psychologically possible.

As we have seen, the Mistake Account can label an influence as manipulation *only* if it works by getting the target to make a mistake. So, what mistakes do Byron and Walker make? Let's begin with Byron.

There are two mistakes that Mike's priming might induce Byron to make. First it might activate an inappropriate script—that is, an inappropriate package of procedural knowledge and behavioral norms and expectations (see section 7.4). It seems likely that scripts can be activated automatically in response to cues typical in situations for which the script is appropriate. It is conceivable that primes might sometimes function as cues of this sort. Thus, we might imagine that the warm coffee activates a script that would be appropriate for interactions between close friends—a script that is *not* appropriate to Byron's *actual* situation. This inappropriate script might, in turn, suggest a default behavior that Byron might ratify without realizing that the script suggesting it is inappropriate. In Byron's case, that default behavior might consist of agreeing to help out a close friend, and ratifying that default behavior might amount to buying into the investment. If this is how Mike's influence operates, then it induced a mistake, since the "close friend" script is inappropriate for Byron's actual situation. And so the Mistake Account would properly identify Mike's influence as manipulation.

Alternatively, the feelings of "social warmth" might cause Byron to *trust* the consultant, since social warmth and trust often go together. We can think of trust either as an epistemic attitude, or an emotion. Either way, it seems clearly mistaken here: Trust is clearly an inappropriate epistemic attitude when a stranger is trying to sell you something risky. And it is an unfitting emotion to feel *toward* a stranger who is trying to sell you something risky. Again, the Mistake Account would properly identify this as manipulation.

Byron is subjected to affective priming, which affects behavior *indirectly*: The hot coffee prime induces warm feelings, and those feelings influence his behavior. By contrast, Walker's case is based on the Bargh, Chen, and Burrows experiments in which priming appears to influence behavior *directly*. Bargh and colleagues claim that their experiment demonstrates a *direct* link between priming and behavior, via some sort of "ideomotor effect" (Bargh, Chen, and Burrows 1996, 231–33). Of course, it is possible that Bargh and colleagues are mistaken, and that the priming actually changed some attitude, and this change in attitude affected behavior. In that case, the analysis of ***Missed Train*** would be similar to that of ***Risky Investments***. But let us imagine that the primes reported by Bargh and colleagues affect behavior directly, without creating an intermediate mental state.

This assumption makes ***Missed Train*** more challenging, since we cannot claim that the priming creates a mistaken mental state that then shapes Walker's behavior. So where is Walker's mistake?

It is tempting to locate Walker's mistake in his *behavior*, i.e., to say that his *walking too slowly* was a mistake, and that Michelle's priming was manipulative because it induced this mistake. In section 4.2 we saw that the Trickery Account cannot treat a bad decision as a faulty mental state without losing the ability to properly identify cases of *paternalistic* manipulation. A similar problem arises for the suggestion that Walker's behavior of walking slowly is a mistake, and that Michelle manipulates Walker because she gets him to make this mistake. To see this problem, suppose that Walker plans to take the train to meet an old friend for lunch, something he naively judges to be his best course of action. Michelle knows that this will become a five-martini lunch that will render Walker inebriated for an important meeting with his boss this afternoon. So she employs the elderly prime to make him miss the train. Here, Michelle's intervention seems like a clear case of paternalistic manipulation. But we cannot say that Michelle's manipulation consists of inducing in Walker the mistake of walking slowly enough to miss the train. Since walking slowly saves Walker from inopportune inebriation, it is difficult to see it as a mistake. Thus, if we say in the original case that Michelle's prime is manipulative because it induces in Walker the mistake of walking slowly, we will be unable to point to the same mistake in the paternalistic version, since in that version walking slowly is not a mistake.

But there *is* a mistake that Walker makes in *both* versions of the case: He fails to act according to his judgment about what he has most reason to do. He behaves akratically. It's just that in the paternalistic version of the case, his behavior displays *inverse* akrasia, since he fails to conform his behavior to an *incorrect* assessment of what he has most reason to do. As we saw in section 4.8, the Mistake Account should treat inverse akrasia as the same sort of mistake as "regular" akrasia. Thus, the Mistake account will treat Walker's akrasia as mistaken in both cases, and thus it will properly classify both cases as manipulation.

One might object that Walker does not *make a decision* to walk slowly, so that a charge of akrasia is misplaced. However, there is no reason to insist that akratic behavior must always result from a conscious decision. If I resolve to go running in the morning but simply lie in bed all day without making any specific decision to skip my run, I surely acted akratically, even though I never made an akratic decision. But even if Walker's mistake does not fit some particular definition of akratic action, it is clearly a mistake. Anyone who insists on defining akrasia so that it only applies to conscious decisions is welcome to label Walker's mistake as "akrasia-like."

The point about Walker not making a deliberate decision, though, illuminates another mistake that Walker probably makes. Suppose that if Walker had realized that he was walking slowly, he would have sped up. If he nevertheless failed to do so, then he mistakenly failed to attend to the time and his walking speed and thus failed to notice that he was walking too slowly to catch the train. Thus, his akratic mistake may have been compounded by an attention mistake, that is, his failure to notice his inadequate walking speed.

Of course, if the priming effect is so strong that Walker would have continued walking slowly even if he *had* noticed this and tried to speed up, then the priming effect would be very strong indeed. There are two ways that we might imagine this happening. First, we might imagine Walker realizing that he is walking too slowly to catch the train, and the prime somehow inducing him not to decide to speed up. This would be a fairly common kind of akratic mistake. It would resemble my realizing that I should put down my phone and go to sleep, but failing to decide to do so. Second, we might imagine that Walker decides to speed up, but that the prime somehow makes him continue walking slowly anyway. This is the most bizarre version of the case, for it would involve something like Walker's legs refusing to obey his commands, not because of fatigue or paralysis (which *would* be easy enough to imagine), but simply because of Michelle's earlier allusion to retirees playing shuffleboard at Del Boca Vista. On this version of the case, the prime would operate something like an artificially induced compulsion. It is not clear that even the most ardent believers in priming effects would claim that they are *that* strong. But even if they had that power, it would be the power to force Walker to make the mistake of acting against what he takes to be the balance of his reasons. And to do that is to induce the mistake of akrasia, which, according to the Mistake Account, suffices to make the prime manipulative.

10.5. Non-Manipulative Priming?

A strength of the Mistake Account is its ability to recognize that many forms of influence can be used either manipulatively or non-manipulatively (section 6.8). This raises the question: Can priming be used non-manipulatively?

Suppose that Walker has a strong habit of walking very quickly, but he has volunteered to take his child's preschool class on a walking tour. He knows that he needs to walk slowly, but also that he is very bad at doing so. Michelle knows all this, too, so she regales him with tales of retirees playing shuffleboard at Del Boca Vista. This primes him to slow down to a pleasant amble appropriate for the task at hand. Here the priming *helps* Walker do what he takes himself to have most reason to do—walk slowly so the kids can keep up. Provided that the prime does *not* achieve this effect by introducing some *mistaken* intermediate mental state that produces this behavior, the Mistake Account would *not* classify this case as manipulation.

Let's turn now to Byron. Imagine that he suffers from a sort of psychological tunnel vision. At the office he focuses so intensely on the job that he becomes unresponsive to the needs of his children or his deep love for them. He is about to cancel a long-promised family outing to attend a trivial business meeting. His assistant, Mike, knows that Byron would not make this decision were it not for his tunnel vision, and that Byron will regret it as soon as he gets home. So, Mike hands Byron a cup of hot coffee, which gives Byron feelings of social warmth. This makes his love for his children salient enough to break through his tunnel vision. Alternatively (and perhaps a bit more realistically), we might imagine Mike deliberately humming one of Byron's children's favorite tunes, or slipping into his office to move his family photos to a more conspicuous location. Either way, the influence *enhances* Byron's ability to pay appropriate attention to, and give proper weight to, the values that he places on meeting his children's needs—values that his tunnel vision threatens to obscure. It helps him do what, on reflection, he takes himself to have most reason to do. The Mistake Account would not classify this case as manipulation. The influence here prevents a mistake rather than inducing one.

As these examples suggest, how the Mistake Account handles a given case of priming will depend on the causal path by which the priming affects the target's behavior. To see this, consider the "honest eyes" effect. Melissa Bateson, Daniel

Nettle, and Gilbert Roberts report (Bateson, Nettle, and Roberts 2006) that pictures of human eyes led to significantly better compliance with the honor system governing contributions to an office's coffee fund than did a control picture. Supposing this effect to be real,[3] how does it happen? Bateson and colleagues theorize that "images of eyes . . . motivate cooperative behaviour because they induce a perception in participants of being watched" (Bateson, Nettle, and Roberts 2006, 413). Now, if this is the mechanism by which the effect operates, then the Mistake Account will identify it as manipulation, for the simple reason that no one *is* actually watching, so any "perception" of being watched is mistaken.

However, the "honest eyes" effect is interesting because it seems clear that the employees have good reasons—apart from being watched—to honor the collective obligation to maintain a resource from which they benefit, and thus to pay for whatever coffee supplies they use. Of course, the fact that employees have good reasons to contribute to the coffee fund does not preclude the honest eyes effect from being manipulative, since a person can be manipulated into doing the right thing. However, let us now suppose that the honest eyes effect is real, but that Bateson and colleagues are incorrect about the mechanism behind it. Suppose that instead of inducing a feeling of being watched, the eyes remind people of the *other* parties to this social contract, who are all counting on each other to do their part in this cooperative endeavor for mutual benefit. Reminding someone of other people might help that person frame the choice as a "we" problem rather than an "I" problem, so that it becomes easier to see the reason for participating in the solution to the collective action problem of funding the office coffee. If this is the mechanism behind the honest eyes effect, then it is a mechanism that *helps* people recognize genuine reasons to do their fair share. The Mistake Account would *not* classify *that* mechanism as manipulative.

One might worry that this makes the verdict of whether a priming effect is manipulative depend on fine details about how it operates. Certainly, this fact poses a practical challenge for assessing whether an influence is manipulative when we know very little about how it works. But a moment's reflection shows that it should neither surprise us nor pose a *theoretical* problem for the Mistake Account. For judgments about whether an influence is manipulative often depend on how it gets the target to behave in the way that the influencer wants.

Take nagging for example. Whether a given instance of nagging is manipulation will depend in part on whether it operates merely by reminding the target of a request the target might have forgotten, or whether it induces the target to comply akratically, knowing that it would be better not to. Or consider this variation of ***Missed Train***:

[3] For a literature review that is optimistic about the existence of this effect, see Dear, Dutton, and Fox (2019); for one that is more skeptical, see Northover et al. (2017). For an interesting response to the debate by one of the study's authors, see Nettle (2022).

Convoluted Missed Train: Walker sees through Michelle's attempt to manipulate him, but he realizes that she would only stoop to such subterfuge if she really needed the job. Walker already has a decent job, and he knows that he is Michelle's only serious competition for this job. Out of concern for Michelle, he decides to take himself out of contention. But he knows that doing this openly will hurt Michelle's pride. So, he deliberately walks slowly enough to miss the train, and thus the interview.

Clearly, we would not want to say that Michelle's priming manipulated Walker in this version of the case, even though it played a decisive causal role in his missing the train. (We should, of course, still say that Michelle acted manipulatively.) Granted, this is a somewhat contrived example. But it should suffice to demonstrate that any credible analysis of whether a given use of priming manipulates must be sensitive to the nature of the causal pathway by which it affects the target's behavior.[4]

10.6. Influences in Buridan Situations

For all we know right now, social priming effects might be real but too weak to cause the kinds of behavior changes imagined in cases like ***Risky Investments*** or ***Missed Train***. This possibility would make priming less potent as a tool for manipulators. Somewhat ironically, though, this possibility might pose a bigger problem for the Mistake Account than would more robust priming effects.

When we imagine a prime deflecting someone from a course of action toward which the person had a prior inclination, the Mistake Account has straightforward ways to detect manipulation. We ask whether the prime induced a mistaken mental state that explained this change, or whether it induced the person to act akratically against their judgment about what they had most reason to do. But what if an agent has no prior inclination—and no reason—to do one thing rather than another?

This is the situation in which Buridan's famous ass finds himself: hungry and equidistant between two equally appealing piles of hay. Although the ass has a strong reason—and a strong inclination—to approach *one* of the piles of hay, it has no reason to choose one over the other. To avoid starvation, it must simply choose one pile without having any reason to choose that pile over the other. The

[4] The differences that matter in determining whether an influence is manipulation in cases like those discussed here are far more substantive than those that I argued (Chapters 4, 6, and 9) should *not* make a difference to whether an influence is manipulation. Psychological distinctions that *are* too subtle to be plausible determinants of whether an influence is manipulation include the difference between thinking of akrasia as momentarily changing one's judgment about what is best versus acting against one's judgment about what is best, and the difference between attributing versus not attributing a change in belief to explain a change in emotion.

moral of the story is that *sometimes* it can be rational to make an arbitrary decision, to choose an option without a reason to choose that option rather than another. People can find themselves in what we might call "Buridan situations" with similar structures. If a piano is falling on me and I have no good reason to prefer dodging to the left versus dodging to the right, it would be a mistake to stand still while I wait to discover a reason to choose one direction over the other.

Situations in which the reasons for and against each of a person's options are *exactly* equal might be as rare as a tossed coin landing on its edge. But this is not the only way that a Buridan situation can arise. Even if there is *some* difference in choice-worthiness between options, it might be too small for the decision-maker to notice, or too small to be worth the time and effort to discover. Or the options might involve incommensurable values that lack a determinate ranking. Perhaps the most common way for a Buridan situation to arise, though, is when the agent has adopted a satisficing rather than a maximizing approach to the choice. If I seek only a good *enough* option, encountering two good-enough options will be more common than encountering two options that are precisely as good as one another. Indeed, for satisficers, Buridan situations are likely to be quite common.

Even if priming effects are too weak to overcome significant pre-existing behavioral inclinations, they might nevertheless be strong enough to break ties in Buridan situations, where the agent lacks any reason or any inclination to choose one option over another.[5] Indeed, even *semantic* priming—the existence of which is not in serious dispute—might do that. One might break a Buridan tie by choosing the "first thing that comes to mind," and the first thing that comes to mind might depend on a semantic priming effect. For example, a well-known study found that priming participants with the words 'ocean' and 'moon' made them more likely to mention the brand "Tide" when asked to name a laundry detergent (Nisbett and Wilson 1977, 243). One could easily imagine a semantic priming effect of this sort being enough to tip the scales for customers in a Buridan situation with regard to which laundry detergent to buy.

Other subtle influences besides priming effects might also be too weak to affect behavior *unless* the target is in a Buridan situation. Consider, for example, the "shelf position effect." There is evidence that product purchasing choices can be influenced by the location on a shelf where products are placed (Chandon et al. 2009; Christenfeld 1995; Porcheddu and Venturi 2011).[6] This effect is often studied in laboratory experiments where the attempt to control for confounding variables puts participants into Buridan situations. And it is often used to influence purchasing decisions in situations where shoppers face an array of very similar choices. So it is

[5] For similar observations, see Krpan (2017) and Di Nucci (2012).

[6] Since this effect is commonly demonstrated in laboratory situations designed to approximate Buridan situations, it is not clear how strong the effect is, but we can put that question aside precisely because we are considering the operation of this effect in Buridan situations.

altogether possible that this effect is just strong enough to break ties for choosers in Buridan situations. Let us assume, for now, that this is the case.

How, then, should the Mistake Account handle influences that are only strong enough to break ties in Buridan situations? Consider this case:

> ***Dish Soap***: I am in a supermarket choosing between two packages of dish soap: Squeaky Clean, and Pro Clean. I have no brand loyalty, and the products are virtually indistinguishable in terms of price, effectiveness, environmental impact, and any other quality that I do or should care about. Moreover, I am satisficing—looking for a dish soap that is good enough rather than the absolute best—and both soaps are good enough. Pro Clean paid the store extra to ensure that it would be displayed in the most advantageous shelf position (in the middle of the shelf, and at eye level), while Squeaky Clean is displayed at the least advantageous position (the bottom and off to one side). If you think that the relative ease of grabbing something at eye level is a reason to choose Pro Clean, then assume that Squeaky Clean's price is lower by just enough to offset that advantage. Suppose that the better shelf position for Pro Clean breaks the tie that puts me in the Buridan situation.

Was I manipulated by Pro Clean's superior shelf position? The answer depends on how the shelf position effect operates. If it creates a false belief, or even a false impression, that Pro Clean is *better* than Squeaky Clean,[7] then the effect would be manipulative. Suppose, however, that the effect does *not* create any false belief or any false impression that Pro Clean is the superior choice. In that case, it is difficult to see how it has induced me to make a mistake. True, my choice was arbitrary. And it *would* be a mistake to choose arbitrarily *against* what I have most reason to do. But here the reasons are equally balanced, and so it cannot be a mistake to break the tie in some arbitrary way. Indeed, *refusing* to choose arbitrarily *would* be a mistake, for it would mean leaving the store without any dish soap. If it is rational to choose arbitrarily between the equally reasonable options in a Buridan situation, then it is difficult to see how an influence that induces me to make an arbitrary choice induces me to make a mistake. Thus, it appears that the Mistake Account does not classify Pro Clean's use of the shelf position effect as manipulation.

Whether this is a *problem* depends on whether we are convinced that ***Dish Soap*** *is* a case of manipulation. If so, then it will be a counterexample to the Mistake Account. But I suspect that intuitive reactions to this case will be a mixed bag. Some may be pretty sure that it is a case of manipulation, some may be pretty sure that it is not, and the rest will be somewhere in between. However, I suspect that many

[7] Some researchers suggest that the effect might be mediated by the belief that items placed in the most favorable positions are more popular (Valenzuela and Raghubir 2009), and it is plausible to think that customers might treat popularity as a proxy for quality.

people will find something at least a bit *unsettling* about what Pro Clean does, even if they are uncertain whether to call it *manipulation*. If we can explain what is unsettling about the case in a way that does not label it as *manipulation*, then perhaps those who see it as manipulation will decide that it is not manipulation after all, but something else unsettling.

10.7. Manipulation versus Meddling

So what, exactly, is unsettling about the ***Dish Soap*** case? It cannot be that someone gets me to make a mistake, since it is not a mistake to use something arbitrary to break a tie. But even if I must break the tie *somehow*, I might regard it as *my* tie to break, and I might resent interference with how I do this. If I were to decide to break the tie by flipping a coin, I might nevertheless object to Pro Clean rigging my coin in a way that favors Pro Clean. Even if I break the tie by acting on a whim, I might care that the whim is authentically *mine*, and not one engineered by Pro Clean's marketing team.

Some people might not care whether someone rigs a coin they will use to break a tie that they have no reason to break one way rather than another. I suspect that such people would *also* not object to Pro Clean's interference with my arbitrary decision, and that they will not find the ***Dish Soap*** case unsettling. By contrast, I suspect that people who *are* uneasy with how Pro Clean gains its advantage *would* also be uneasy with someone rigging the coin they use to break a tie in a Buridan situation.

Notice that *this* source of unease about Pro Clean's use of the shelf position effect is quite different from the source of unease with Iago's manipulation of Othello. Iago induces Othello to make a mistake—and a terrible one at that. Pro Clean gets me to make a decision that I *must* make arbitrarily, in a way that benefits Pro Clean. It intrudes on my choice, but it does not get me to make any mistakes in how I make that choice. My suggestion, then, is that the ***Dish Soap*** case does not demonstrate a problem with the Mistake Account. Instead, it demonstrates the existence of a distinct way that we might find an influence objectionable. Pro Clean does not manipulate. Instead, it *meddles*.

This might sound like an *ad hoc* invention of a new category of influence into which to sweep the difficulties that Buridan cases pose for the Mistake Account. The charge might have some merit if there were no independent reason to distinguish between manipulating and meddling. But there is. Consider these cases:

New Job 1: Dan is deliberating about whether to take a new job. Dan decides that another perspective would be helpful. So, he asks Anne for advice, which Anne provides. This advice is wise, sincere, and unbiased.

New Job 2: Dan is deliberating about whether to take a new job. Dan has politely declined Mel's offer of advice, but Mel continually pesters Dan with his advice anyway. This advice is wise, sincere, and unbiased. But Dan does not want it, and prefers to deliberate in private.

Assume that nothing about Anne's advice or how she presents it would normally count as manipulation, and that everything about Mel's advice is identical, except for its being unwelcome. Clearly, Anne does not act manipulatively. What about Mel? I suspect that intuitions might differ, but it is certainly not a *paradigm* case of manipulation. Mel merely foists his otherwise non-manipulative advice on Dan, and I doubt that most people would *insist* on calling Mel's behavior a *clear* case of manipulation. It is pushy, meddlesome, and rude, and it seems clear that Dan has a legitimate complaint about it. But Dan's complaint seems more naturally framed in terms of meddling rather than manipulation. Of course, nothing prevents an influence from being *both* manipulative *and* meddlesome. Indeed, such cases are likely quite common, and this may be one reason why the two concepts are easily run together.

Notice that these two ***New Job*** cases do not involve Buridan situations. Rather, they illustrate a distinct kind of complaint one might make about someone's influence. It might be objectionable not because it is mistake-inducing, but simply because it is unwelcome meddling. The difference is a bit like the difference between assault and trespassing. As we saw in section 9.8.3, manipulation has an assaultive character in that it inflicts a misfortune upon someone. Trespassing, though, wrongs someone by violating a boundary that the victim has a right to enforce. While the two often go together, they can come apart. Non-manipulative meddling is thus a bit like someone trespassing on your property but doing no damage to it (or to you). Taken together, these considerations suggest that it is not *ad hoc* to claim that what seems unsettling about the ***Dish Soap*** case is that it involves meddling rather than manipulation.

Working out a complete theory of meddling would probably require a book of its own, so a few quick observations must suffice here. As a first approximation, an influence is meddlesome if it interferes in an illegitimate way with someone's decision-making or other aspects of someone's mental life. Presumably, various considerations interact to determine whether something interferes in an *illegitimate* way, and thus constitutes meddling. The most obvious is whether the influence is unwelcome. But it seems plausible that other factors also play a role. One of these is whether the influence targets a self- or other-regarding decision. Other things being equal, an unwelcome influence on someone's purely self-regarding decision seems more meddlesome than an unwelcome influence on a decision that could affect others. Another factor is how avoidable the influence is. Part of what makes Mel's influence meddlesome is that Dan is unable to escape it simply by telling Mel he does not want it. Finally, it seems plausible that facts about the kind of influence or the situation in which it occurs play a role in determining whether it is an illegitimate interference. For example, unwanted influences that assail us in our homes seem especially meddlesome, as do unwanted influences that operate by impinging on our bodies.[8] By contrast, it seems less intrusive for such influences to operate within a clearly designated commercial space, like the supermarket selling Pro Clean.

Let's return, then, to the ***Dish Soap*** case. I suggest that any intuitive unease about it is better framed in terms of meddling than manipulation. What seems unsettling about the case is that Pro Clean is meddling in a choice that should be mine to decide how to make. If I am correct that the more someone cares about breaking one's *own* ties in Buridan situations, the more unsettling they will find this case, then the unwelcomeness of the influence seems to be the source of the unease. To the extent that the shelf position effect tends to go unnoticed, it is difficult to avoid, and this fact may contribute to this unease. If this is correct, then the fact that the Mistake Account does not label it as manipulation is not a problem.

None of this is to insist that the ***Dish Soap*** case is a *paradigm* example of meddling. Indeed, reasonable people can disagree about whether Pro Clean's use of the shelf position effect is meddling, and, if so, whether and to what extent this meddling is immoral. My point is simply that the factors that best explain why some people find a case like ***Dish Soap*** unsettling have more to do with it being a possible instance of meddling rather than a possible instance of manipulation. It appears, then, that the ***Dish Soap*** case does not pose a problem for the Mistake Account.

Let's turn to a different case, the outlines of which were suggested[9] by Massimo Renzo as a potential problem for the Mistake Account.

> ***Gardener:*** Ian wants to help his friend George find a gardening job. So, he approaches another friend, Tarek, who currently employs a gardener, and—without being asked—points out various flaws in that gardener's work. They are genuine flaws, and Ian thinks that they give Tarek sufficient reason to fire his current gardener. Nothing about Ian's remarks induces Tarek to make a mistake. However, Ian's reason for pointing out these flaws is to get Tarek to fire the gardener so he can then recommend hiring George.

I think that many people would find Ian's behavior unsettling, or at least a bit unsavory. However, Ian does not induce Tarek to make any mistakes, so the Mistake Account is unable to label this case as manipulation. But I contend that any unease we might feel about Ian's behavior is better framed as unease about whether Ian is meddling than whether he is manipulating.

[8] It seems likely that meddling as I am thinking of it might violate what Thomas Douglas and Lisa Forsberg (2021) call a right to mental integrity.

[9] Personal communication, 2021.

Some readers might insist that what I am calling meddling *really is* manipulation, and that if the Mistake Account cannot identify it as such, then so much the worse for the Mistake Account. Indeed, they might wonder: Why not simply define manipulation as unwelcome influence?

One reason not to do this is that many clear examples of manipulation do not involve *unwelcome* influences. Othello *seeks out* Iago's counsel, saying to Iago at one point, "I prithee speak to me as to thy thinkings . . . and give thy worst of thoughts."[10] But the counsel Iago gives is clearly manipulative despite its being invited. Indeed, manipulation is often either welcome or at least not clearly unwelcome. Manipulation is often most effective—and definitely still manipulative—when it is perpetrated by a trusted person whose influence the target welcomes.

But perhaps it will be objected that someone who welcomes another person's influence does *not* welcome *mistake-inducing* influences. So perhaps we should regard Othello's welcome of Iago's influence as containing the implicit condition that it only applies to non-mistake-inducing influences. More generally, we might construe any welcoming of an influence as containing the implicit proviso that the welcome only applies to influences that are not intended to induce mistakes. If we say that mistake-inducing influences are unwelcome, then any influence that the Mistake Account identifies as manipulative would be unwelcome, so the revised proposal would also count them as manipulative.

But this revised proposal faces problems. First, it seems to get the order of explanation backwards. On this proposal, what makes Iago's advice unwelcome is that it is mistake-inducing. But it seems more sensible to say that the advice is unwelcome because it is manipulative than to say that it is manipulative because it is unwelcome. Second, this proposal makes it conceptually impossible to consent to manipulation. Yet it does seem possible to do this. I might authorize my physician, or a psychologist studying priming effects, to engage in conduct that would normally count as manipulation. While my consent may render such conduct morally justified, it would seem odd to say that it is no longer manipulation. Here, as elsewhere, I think that the concept of deception is a good guide for how to think about manipulation: If I consent to being deceived, say, on an informed consent form for a psychology experiment, the deception may no longer be immoral, but it is still deception. I think that we should say a similar thing about manipulation: Consent may render it morally unobjectionable, but it is still manipulation. But defining manipulation as unwelcome influence would make it conceptually impossible to consent to being manipulated.

Finally, this proposal faces an objection like the one that dooms the Subjective Endorsement Account of manipulation discussed in section 3.7: It makes whether an influence is manipulative depend too much on whether the target wants to be subjected to it. It seems correct to say that my decision whether to welcome an

[10] *Othello*, Act III, Scene iii.

influence plays a role in determining whether it is meddling. It seems less correct to say that it plays a role in determining whether it is manipulation.

But even if these problems can be addressed, defining manipulation as unwelcome influence would still leave us with a major subtype of influences that are unwelcome *because they are mistake-inducing*. By contrast, if we retain the Mistake Account's characterization of manipulation, we get a picture where manipulation and meddling are both subtypes of a larger category of objectionable influences. A moment's reflection reveals that both proposals divide things up the same way; they just move the labels around. I'm less interested in the labels than I am in the fact that there seem to be two distinct reasons for objecting to an influence: One based on whether the influence transgresses a boundary that I have a moral right to impose on other people's attempts to influence me, and one based on what an influence does to my psychological processes. Anyone who insists on using the term 'manipulation' to apply to *all* unwelcome influences should treat my use of that term to apply only to that subset of unwelcome influences that are unwelcome because they are, or are intended to be, mistake-inducing.

10.8. Expanding the Analysis

The analysis developed here of priming effects provides a template for analyzing other exotic influences. For any such influence, we must ask a series of questions.

First, does the influence produce behavior directly, or does it create some *intermediate* mental state that helps produce the behavior? If the influence produces behavior directly, then the analysis will proceed in a way similar to the analysis of behavioral primes like the one in ***Missed Train***. For influences like this, the next question will be: Does the influence impede the target from doing what the target judges there to be most reason to do? If so, it is akrasia-inducing and thus manipulative.

If the influence causes behavior *indirectly*, by inducing in the target a mental state that helps produce the behavior, then the next question is: Is the mental state caused by this influence mistaken? If so, then the influence is manipulative.

By contrast, if an influence does not directly cause behavior that is contrary to what the target regards there being most reason to do, and does not induce any mistakes in the target's mental states or processes, then it is not manipulation. However, an influence that is not manipulation might nevertheless be meddling, and this might make it immoral—perhaps just as immoral as it would have been if it *had* been manipulation. This might be true, for example, of the cases of non-manipulative priming discussed earlier—i.e., the ones where Michelle gets Walker to walk slowly so that the children on the walking tour can keep up, and where

Mike uses affective priming to help Byron pay what he regards as the right amount of attention to his children's needs.[11]

Let's apply this template to one last example of an exotic influence: the urban legend of the "trained professor" (Brunvand 2001, 326–27):

> ***Trained Professor:*** A group of students conspire to appear more attentive to their professor when she stands closer to the door, and vice versa. Over time, their plan leads to the professor becoming conditioned to teach from the doorway.

This urban legend is probably fiction; it might even be psychologically impossible. But that doesn't prevent us from applying the template to it. Suppose that the professor doesn't care where she stands when she teaches, so that she is in a Buridan situation with regard to her location in the classroom. Here, the influence would not be manipulative, though it is probably meddling. Now suppose that the professor thinks that there *is* some reason—even just her own preference or convenience—for standing in some particular spot, such as behind the podium where she can see her notes and reach her coffee. On this assumption, the conditioning would induce akratic behavior against what she takes herself to have most reason to do. Thus, the Mistake Account would identify the influence as manipulation. Finally, suppose that the conditioning creates in the professor a false belief, or even a false impression, that she teaches more effectively from the doorway, or that it induces her to acquire a defective "how to" belief about how best to lecture. On this assumption, the influence would also be manipulation, since the belief, impression, or item of procedural knowledge would be mistaken.

10.9. Moods, Drugs, and Other Systemic Influences

In comments on material that became part of Chapter 5, David Schwan noted that

> mental states like puzzlement, confusion, or affective states like moods or even displeasure . . . seem like interesting targets for a potential manipulator. For example, they might slow a target down, or incline them to other attitudes. But, it's also less clear how such states are capable of being mistaken. (Schwan 2019)

Along similar lines, Thomas Douglas raised the question of whether it would be manipulative to paint prison cells a certain color on the theory that some colors

[11] I thank Jennifer Blumenthal-Barby for suggesting this possibility.

were more calming than others.[12] Both remarks highlight a potential worry for the Mistake Account: Changes to someone's mood seem like they can be manipulative, but it is difficult to see how a mood can be mistaken.

Perhaps, though, the difficulty is only apparent, and moods really *can* be mistaken. Being light-hearted at a loved one's funeral, or being irritable and agitated while on vacation, may resemble unfitting—and thus mistaken—emotions. In addition, we might ascribe a derivative kind of mistakenness to a mood if it is caused by some other mistaken mental state. Thus, if I am wildly afraid of a harmless spider, then the agitation that accompanies my fear would seem to be just as unfitting, and just as mistaken, as the fear that caused it. If I am irritated at a colleague because I falsely believe that he shirked his part of our joint task, then my irritation seems misplaced and thus mistaken.

I am unsure what to say about this suggestion. Obviously, if moods can be assessed for their mistakenness, then the question of whether mood alterations can be manipulative needn't trouble the Mistake Account. But I hesitate to rest a response to worries about mood alterations on such a claim, for two reasons. First, it may involve an illicit slide between moods and emotions. That is, it may treat moods as having intentional objects in the way that emotions do when, properly speaking, they do not have such objects. Sorting this out would require sorting out the nature of both moods and emotions in more detail and more definitively than is practical here. Second, even if *some* moods can be appropriate or inappropriate, it seems doubtful that this is true of *all* moods. Consequently, I will assume for the sake of argument that moods at least sometimes lack clear criteria according to which they can be judged to be mistaken. If this assumption turns out to be false, then the problem moods pose for the Mistake Account disappears, which would make me (appropriately) delighted.

There are several ways that the Mistake Account can recognize the role that influencing someone's mood can be manipulative, even if that mood lacks clear criteria for being mistaken. First, and perhaps most importantly, changes to moods play a role in manipulation by making it easier for the manipulator to get the target to make mistakes. Often, they do this by impairing or impeding the decision-making process, tying up attention, or otherwise hampering the processes that must operate efficiently to avoid mistakes. Negative moods can make a person mentally sluggish. Anxiety and agitation can make a person impulsive, akratic, and likely to make snap decisions. Moods might also induce mistaken optimism

[12] Thomas Douglas, personal communication. For reviews of work on the effect of color on mood, see Elliot and Maier (2014) and Elliot (2015); for the classic study of using color in a prison context, see Pellegrini (1981); for a later, unsuccessful, attempt to replicate those findings, see Genschow et al. (2015).

or pessimism and otherwise warp the judgments that go into deliberation.[13] In all these ways, changing a person's moods might be part of a larger manipulative *process* of the kind discussed in section 6.6.

Similar remarks apply to the use of intoxicants, fatigue, sleep deprivation, extreme distraction, and other interventions that impair the functioning of the reasoning and deliberative faculties.[14] Deliberately using such tactics will often be morally wrong independent of their use in manipulation. When they are used to increase the likelihood that the target will make mistakes or fail to notice existing mistakes, their use facilitates manipulation in the same way that mood alterations do. Either way, the influence is manipulative insofar as it is meant to increase the chances that the target will make a mistake.

Second, alterations to mood can play a role in manipulative pressure. There are "good moods" and "bad moods," and people generally prefer being in the former and avoiding the latter. This fact allows mood alteration to play a role in manipulative pressure. Recall that manipulative pressure involves creating incentives for performing the solicited action and disincentives for refraining from the solicited action. A moment's reflection reveals that pleasant moods are often part of these incentives, and unpleasant moods part of the disincentives. A charm offensive, for example, works in part by making the target feel good. Emotional blackmail works in part by threatening to make the target feel bad.

Third, changes to mood can facilitate emotional manipulation. Emotions and moods are closely related, and altering a person's mood can facilitate inducing that person to enter an emotional state related to that mood. For example, agitation and anxiety are not emotions *per se*, but they are closely related to the emotion of fear. This relationship makes it easier to get someone who is already anxious and agitated to acquire the emotion of fear than someone who is not. Similarly, it is probably easier to get someone in an irritable mood to feel angry, to get someone in a depressed mood to feel disappointment, and so on.

10.10. Conclusion

We have not, of course, discussed every possible form of influence that is either exotic or a potential counterexample to the Mistake Account. Indeed, the mysteries

[13] For a brief discussion of the effect of mood on decision-making, see Fennis and Stroebe (2021, 168–69; 199).

[14] Joel Dimsdale (2021), Jay Lifton (1989), and John Marks (1991) have documented the use of such tactics in what is often called "brainwashing" or "mind control." This phenomenon, which Dimsdale calls "coercive persuasion," is clearly related to manipulation, but working out the exact relationship is beyond the scope of this book.

of the human mind, and the imagination of philosophers, will yield many more—be they real or hypothetical. However, I am optimistic that the analysis done in this chapter provides tools that will allow the Mistake Account to handle such influences in convincing ways. In the next and final chapter, we will apply the Mistake Account to more ordinary forms of influence that raise pressing moral and public policy questions.

11

Ordinary Influences

Applying the Mistake Account

11.1. Introduction

A good philosophical account of manipulation should help us think about real-world cases of influence. This chapter will argue that the Mistake Account does that. After a few general remarks about applying the Mistake Account, the chapter will discuss manipulation in nudges, advertising, sales, and online. The goal is not to cover *every* form of influence. Nor is it to have the last word on those forms of influence that we will discuss. Many conclusions drawn here will be tentative and subject to revision. This is because they will often be based on our current understandings of the psychological mechanisms involved in various forms of influence—understandings which are tentative and subject to revision. This chapter's goal is to demonstrate that the Mistake Account offers helpful guidance in a variety of real-world cases. However, sometimes that guidance involves determining what more we must learn before we can decide whether an influence is manipulation.

11.2. Preliminary Remarks

As we saw in Chapter 6, the Mistake Account takes the central case of manipulation to be one where ***M manipulates T***. It characterizes this as a direct, one-on-one interaction where *M* gets *T* to make a mistake, which causes *T* to do what *M* wanted. In such cases, the Mistake Account places equal emphasis on what the influencer does and what happens to the target. But sometimes we are less interested in what happens to *T* than in what *M* does. Thus, we might ask instead whether *M* ***acts manipulatively toward T***. To answer this question, we focus only on what *M* tries to do.

But not all cases of manipulation involve a *person* acting directly on another person. Some involve inanimate objects, and the Mistake Account recognizes several senses in which some*thing* rather than some*one* can be manipulative. Something *designed* to influence behavior in a way that induces targets to make (what the designer regards as) a mistake is manipulative in the *derivative* sense. Something that merely *tends* to influence behavior by inducing a mistake (even if no one intended for it to do so) is manipulative in the *metaphorical* sense.

Manipulation. Robert Noggle, Oxford University Press. © Robert Noggle 2025.
DOI: 10.1093/9780198924920.003.0011

Something is manipulative in the broadest, *disjunctive* sense, if it *either* tends *or* is intended to influence behavior by inducing a mistake.

Defining the metaphorical—and, by extension, the broad, disjunctive—sense of 'manipulative' in terms of a tendency to induce a mistake raises obvious questions: How strong must this tendency be for something to count as manipulative? How likely must it be that the influence causes the target to make a mistake? What portion of those exposed to the influence must make the mistake? How much effort must it take for someone to counter the influence's tendency to induce a mistake? These questions are vital because virtually *anything* might induce *someone* to make a mistake. A sign warning of poisonous snakes in the water will inspire healthy caution in most people, but an irrational panic in a few. Presumably, we do not want to count such a sign as manipulative simply because it causes a few rare souls to overreact. Determining how strong something's mistake-inducing tendency must be for it to count as manipulative is vital if we wish to prohibit or regulate certain forms of manipulation.

Fortunately, we need not start from scratch. The Mistake Account recommends defining 'manipulation' and related terms in ways parallel to how we define 'deception' and related terms. Consequently, we should approach questions about when to call something manipulative by thinking about when we call something deceptive. For example, when we call black ice deceptive, we mean that it could cause a mistaken belief in a typical person, especially if that person is not on guard. It seems reasonable to adopt a similar standard for calling something manipulative.

Sometimes, however, it makes better sense to think of deceptiveness as a matter of degree. We might say that black ice is *more* deceptive at night than in daylight. Or we might say that a highway mirage is only *somewhat* deceptive because relatively few people experiencing it come to believe that it is water. Similarly, it makes sense to think of manipulativeness as a matter of degree. The degree of manipulativeness depends on the strength of the tendency to induce a mistake, the amount of effort required to resist that tendency, and the likelihood that it will induce a given person to make a mistake.

But seeing manipulativeness as a matter of degree simply restates our original question: How manipulative must something be for it to be an appropriate target for regulation or prohibition? Sometimes we may want to set a relatively strict standard for prohibited manipulation. Presumably we should not give scam artists a free pass on manipulative schemes that succeed only on people who are especially susceptible simply because *most* people see through them. Indeed, those who are especially susceptible to manipulation may deserve more rather than less legal and regulatory protection against it. This seems especially appropriate when the manipulation is targeted at those who are especially vulnerable, and when it enriches the manipulators at their expense.

This assumes, of course, that manipulation is an appropriate target for laws and regulation. It is true that, in US law, there is no *general* prohibition against manipulation. That is also true of deception. However, while there is no *overarching* law against deception, in many contexts, deception is legally prohibited, tortious, or grounds to invalidate a contract. Legal scholar Gregory Klass argues that the laws that address deception "collectively constitute a coherent body," which he calls "the law of deception" (Klass 2018, 708). It would be an exaggeration to make a similar claim about a "law of manipulation." Nevertheless, legal scholar Eric Posner observes that "one finds many examples of lawsuits in which plaintiffs complain that they were manipulated by defendants and courts lend a sympathetic ear" (Posner 2016, 270). Such cases often arise in contract and probate law, where the doctrines of "undue influence" and "unconscionability" allow contracts to be invalidated due to behavior aptly described as manipulation (Turkat 2003; Quinn 2014; 2012; 2000). Moreover, Cass Sunstein observes that "in some contexts, regulators do aim at manipulation, at least implicitly" (Sunstein 2016, 86). This is especially true in commercial law, where there has been some attempt to regulate tactics aptly described as manipulation. The US Bureau of Consumer Protection focuses on protecting consumers against "unfair, deceptive and fraudulent business practices." While the Bureau's activities have traditionally focused mainly on *deceptive* practices, it has become increasingly concerned with "unfair" practices, some of which fit the definition of (non-deceptive) manipulation. Several legal scholars have called for increasing regulation of non-deceptive manipulation in commerce.[1]

Since manipulation is commonly thought to undermine the voluntariness of consent, one might wonder whether it has a similar effect on legal and moral responsibility. Answering this question is far from straightforward. On the one hand, it seems reasonable to think manipulation can sometimes undermine the conditions for responsibility. But it also seems implausible to think that manipulation completely absolves the manipulated person from responsibility. Othello seems to be responsible for Desdemona's murder despite having been manipulated by Iago. Moreover, as Massimo Renzo argues, how manipulation affects responsibility probably depends on which of several notions of responsibility one has in mind (Renzo 2023). These complications put the question of how manipulation affects responsibility, despite its importance, beyond the scope of this book.[2]

[1] Scholars noting increasing calls for such regulation include Edwards (2008). Scholars calling for such regulation include Calo (2014), Becher and Feldman (2016), Berman (2015), and Norton (2021).

[2] Philosophical discussions of the connection between ordinary manipulation and responsibility are uncommon. They include Renzo (2023) and Haeg (2022).

11.3. Nudges and Manipulation

Richard Thaler and Cass Sunstein define a nudge as a change to the choice situation that "alters people's behavior in a predictable way without forbidding any options or significantly changing their economic incentives" (Thaler and Sunstein 2009, 6).[3] The term 'nudge' is often limited to interventions that benefit the target, though it is sometimes used more broadly to include those that encourage altruistic behavior (Thaler and Sunstein 2009, 231–32).[4] Some nudges, such as more readable food nutrition labels and credit card agreements, merely improve the quality and quantity of information available to decision-makers. These nudges do not seem manipulative, provided that the information is neither false nor misleading, and does not create mismatches between the salience of information and its relevance. Let us focus, then, on nudges that operate by means other than improving the quality and quantity of information. Here are a few:

Retirement Choices: Encouraging employees to save for retirement by making saving the default (Thaler and Sunstein 2009, 110–11, 131–32).

Cafeteria: Encouraging healthier eating by arranging a school cafeteria so that more nutritious foods are first in line and at eye level (Thaler and Sunstein 2009, 1–3).

Success Framing: Framing a medical treatment in terms of its survival or success rate rather than its fatality or failure rate to make people more likely to choose it.[5]

Road Lines: Painting regularly-spaced lines across a roadway, but placing them closer together before a curve, to create the illusion of increased speed in order to get drivers to slow down (Thaler and Sunstein 2009, 37–39).

Save More Tomorrow: Enabling employees to pre-commit to having future raises directed to retirement savings (Thaler and Sunstein 2009, 114–17).

[3] For an interesting review of the efficacy of nudges in real-world contexts, see DellaVigna and Linos (2022).

[4] For an important discussion of the conceptual puzzles in attempting to precisely define nudges, see Saghai (2013). Occasionally, the term is used to apply to influences that otherwise would count as nudges regardless of whom they benefit, though this seems to be a non-standard use of the term.

[5] Ethical questions about nudges in the clinical context are especially complicated due to the nature of the physician-patient relationship and the high standards for informed consent. The use of such nudges has been defended by Director (2024), Cohen (2013), and, under certain conditions and with some important caveats, Blumenthal-Barby (2012).

11.4. Are Nudges Manipulative?

Many scholars have argued that *at least some* non-informational nudges are manipulative.[6] Most of these arguments employ one of two strategies. The first characterizes manipulation as hidden influence and observes that we are often unaware of the influences harnessed by non-informational nudges. The second characterizes manipulation as irrational influence and claims that non-informational nudges are irrational influences. The first strategy need not concern us here, since it rests on the Covert Influence Account of manipulation, which we have already rejected (section 3.6).

The second strategy cannot be dismissed so easily, however. If nudges employ irrational influences, then they might also induce mistakes. Some defenders of nudges argue that the claim that nudges employ irrational influences rests on the wrong notion of rationality. They claim that we should understand rationality in terms of reliably advancing one's interests. This would make *paternalistic* nudges rational, since they help people make decisions that better serve their own interests.[7] Andreas Schmidt (2019) and Bart Engelen (2019) offer this defense of nudges. Other defenders of nudges argue that, even on the more standard instrumentalist and procedural view of rationality, non-informational nudges are not necessarily irrational influences. Neil Levy (2019; 2022, ch. 6) offers an especially persuasive version of this argument.[8] He claims that "nudges work by targeting mechanisms that satisfy the conditions for being reasoning mechanisms" (Levy 2019, 289–90).

Levy claims that many nudges function as implicit recommendations (Levy 2019, 289–90; 2022, 140). Consider default nudges. Levy cites empirical work by Craig McKenzie and colleagues (McKenzie, Liersch, and Finkelstein 2006) showing that participants often infer that a default option is being *recommended* by the default setter. For example, if enrollment in a retirement plan is the default, people are likely to infer that whoever set the default recommends enrolling. Evidence also suggests that people react to defaults in ways that resemble how people react to recommendations. For example, it seems likely that defaults are less

[6] See, for example, Grüne-yanoff (2012, 636), Wilkinson (2013, 347), Pugh (2020, 68), Kumar (2016, 862), Blumenthal-Barby and Burroughs (2012, 5), and Nys and Engelen (2017, 210). The aforementioned scholars take a wide range of views about *which* nudges are manipulative and *when*. Sunstein concedes that some nudges can be manipulative (Sunstein 2015, 444–46), but when he describes several of the sorts of nudges that he advocates (including those similar to ***Cafeteria*** and ***Success Framing***) that might be manipulative, he claims that "any manipulation seems modest, and in all of them, I believe that the relevant choice architecture can be justified" (Sunstein 2015, 446). For similar claims, see Blumenthal-Barby and Burroughs (2012, 5), and Nys and Engelen (2017, 12). For overviews of additional criticisms of nudges and libertarian paternalism, see Medina (2021) and Schmidt and Engelen (2020).

[7] This idea is sometimes combined with the claim that nudges are influences that are too weak to get people to make choices *contrary* to their own interests. See, e.g., Houk (2019, 410).

[8] Andrés Moles (2015, 657), Jason Hanna (2015, 625–27), and Timothy Houk (2019, 415–16) also offer versions of this approach.

influential when people have stronger preferences and more information about the choice prior to encountering the default (McKenzie, Liersch, and Finkelstein 2006, 419).

Framing effects are more complicated. Craig McKenzie and Jonathan Nelson (McKenzie and Nelson 2003) provide evidence that many framing effects are caused by "information leakage," whereby additional information is suggested by the choice of frame, and inferred by those encountering the frame. For example, people are more likely to describe a glass as "half full" when it was previously empty, and to describe it as "half empty" when it was previously full. And people are more likely to infer that a glass described as "half full" was previously empty, and that one described as "half empty" was previously full. As Sarah Fisher writes, both speakers and listeners tend to treat "half empty" as "emptier than before" and "half full" as "fuller than before" (Fisher 2022, 972).

McKenzie and Nelson (2003) report similar findings for the framing of medical treatments in terms of their survival and fatality rates. Speakers were more likely to describe a treatment *in terms of its survival rate* when its *survival* rate was *better than* that of the alternative. And speakers were more likely to describe it in terms of its *fatality* rate when its fatality rate was *worse than* that of the alternative. In other words, speakers were more likely to frame a treatment in positive terms (survival) if it was better than the alternative, and in negative terms (fatality) if it was worse than the alternative. When a treatment was described in terms of its survival rate, listeners were more likely to infer that its survival rate was better than that of the alternative, and vice versa.[9]

It seldom matters very much whether a glass was previously full or empty. It matters quite a lot whether a medical treatment has a higher or lower survival rate than the alternative. Thus, choosing a frame that signals an answer to the latter question signals something quite important. As Gigerenzer writes, "by choosing a survival frame, the doctor can communicate that surgery has a substantial benefit compared to no surgery, and make an implicit recommendation" (Gigerenzer 2015, 368). In this way, "a doctor's choice between logically equivalent frames can communicate unspoken information, *including recommendations*" (Gigerenzer 2014, 24, emphasis added).[10] Thus, the implicit information "leaked" by the frame choice can be regarded as an implicit recommendation. Or, as Levy puts it, "people frame options in ways that highlight particular choices because they take them to be good ones, and their communicative intent is recognized by those who respond to the framing" (Levy 2019, 290).

[9] For studies corroborating and extending these findings, see Sher and McKenzie (2006), Leong et al. (2017), Honda et al. (2018), Honda and Yamagishi (2017), Teigen and Karevold (2005), and Juanchich, Teigen, and Villejoubert (2010).

[10] See Leong et al. (2017, 1155) and Sher and McKenzie (2006, 481, 486) for similar observations.

Levy observes that framing and default effects are stronger when the decision-maker is under cognitive load (Levy 2019, 290–91). This is what we should expect if framing and defaults operate as implicit recommendations. When one lacks the cognitive resources to make one's own decision, it makes sense to rely on recommendations. The same is true of the finding that domain-relevant expertise can weaken framing effects (Leong et al. 2017, 1152–54). The more one already knows about the facts relevant to the choice at hand, the less it makes sense to rely on recommendations. Levy concludes that "canonical nudges and supposedly irrational heuristics and biases very often work by functioning as implicit recommendations" (Levy 2019, 290). He further concludes that "it's rational to be guided by a nudge because it's rational to give due weight to a recommendation, implicit or not" (Levy 2022, 141; see also 2019, 290).

Levy's analysis of framing as implicit recommendations seems most plausible when one frame describes something positively and the other negatively. It seems less plausible for less evaluatively loaded frames, such as whether a glass is described as half full or half empty. Perhaps the information leakage account explains framing effects generally, and the implicit recommendation account shows how those effects can sometimes be harnessed to form implicit recommendations (which is how they are most likely to be used in nudges).[11] But Levy's overall point could be amended easily to account for this. He could simply claim that it is rational to consider *any* additional information encoded in frames, including *but not limited to* implicit recommendations.

11.5. Nudges, Manipulation, and the Mistake Account

Levy claims that the recommendations implicit in frame selection and defaults constitute a form of evidence. But he notes that it is not always *reliable* evidence:

> We can nudge people by designing the choice architecture so that they are presented with bad reasons: bad defaults, or inappropriate frames, for example. Such nudges don't *bypass* reasoning, any more than overt lies bypass reasoning. Rather, they subvert autonomy by giving *bad* reasons. (Levy 2019, 298, emphasis original)

These remarks are relevant for the Mistake Account, since Levy's claim that nudges can offer "bad reasons," suggests that they can induce mistakes. Thus, Levy's view seems to allow that nudges can *sometimes* be manipulative.

[11] For a discussion of the relationship between the two accounts, see Sher and McKenzie (2006, 482–83)

Consider the default in ***Retirement Choices***. Levy's view treats it as an implicit recommendation to contribute to a retirement account. But that does not settle the question of whether it is manipulative. To recommend an option to someone is simply to claim that the option is a good choice for the recipient of the recommendation. According to the Mistake Account, a recommendation is manipulative under the same conditions that any other claim would be manipulative. If the recommender does not regard the recommended option as a good choice for the recipient, then the recommender seeks to induce the recipient to make (what the recommender regards as) a mistake. Such a recommendation would be manipulative.

Thus, the test for whether a recommender *acts manipulatively* is whether the recommender sincerely regards the recommended option as a good choice for the recipient of the recommendation. If, in ***Irene's New Coworkers*** (section 5.2), Irene recommends that Todd distance himself from Billy, she still acts manipulatively because, *as far as Irene knows*, Billy is a good friend to Todd and distancing himself from Billy would be a *bad* option for Todd. The fact that, unbeknownst to Irene, Billy is really a bully, so that what Irene recommends is, *in fact*, a *good* option for Todd does not change the fact that Irene acts manipulatively in recommending it. Similarly, ***Aunt Vicky*** (section 5.2) does not act manipulatively in recommending vaccine refusal, since she sincerely believes that vaccine refusal is a good choice. However, her recommendation is manipulative in the metaphorical sense, since vaccine-refusal is, in fact, a bad choice.

It is important to distinguish bad recommendations from good recommendations that nevertheless turn out badly. This is especially important for what we might call probabilistic recommendations. A recommendation of a treatment with a 90 percent success rate over one with a 50 percent success rate is non-mistaken (and thus non-manipulative), *even if* we find out after the fact that the recipient was one of the unlucky 10 percent for whom the recommended treatment fails. Moreover, we should not even say that this recommendation was manipulative in the metaphorical sense. It is no mistake to claim that an action with the highest chance of success is the best option to choose. This remains true even if that option nevertheless fails. Because it was still the decision-maker's best bet given the probabilities, it was not a mistake to recommend it or to accept that recommendation. Of course, from an omniscient perspective, such a choice might seem like a mistake (especially if the chooser was also part of the "lucky" 50% for whom the less effective treatment *would* have succeeded). But this is not the perspective from which the Mistake Account should define mistaken recommendations. For doing so would entail that recommending a procedure with a 90 percent success rate is manipulative 10 percent of the time. This seems like an incorrect thing to say.

There is another, more subtle, way that a recommendation can be manipulative. Typically, one only offers a recommendation if one has information relevant to the decision, especially information that the decision-maker lacks. Consequently, it is natural for recipients of recommendations to assume that recommenders have some basis for their recommendations. A recommendation can be misleading—mistake-inducing—if it is made in a way that encourages the recipient to assume that the recommender has some expertise or competence that the recommender does not, in fact, have.

Thus, a recommendation is manipulative if it does not reflect the recommender's sincere belief about the recipient's best option, or if it is made in a way that suggests a level of competence about the relevant topic that the recommender lacks. By contrast, let us say that a recommendation is *reliable*, and thus non-manipulative, when it is based on sufficient expertise—or at least competence—about the options, and when it reflects the recommender's sincere judgment about which option is best for the recipient of the recommendation.

Consequently, the default in ***Retirement Choices*** is not manipulative if it embodies a reliable recommendation, i.e., a sincere and well-informed judgment about what is best for the employees' financial interests. But we could easily imagine an unscrupulous employer defaulting employees into investments that serve the employer's rather than the employees' interests. *That* default *would* be manipulative, since it would embody an *unreliable* recommendation.

The analysis of ***Success Framing*** is slightly more complicated since we have uncovered two distinct ways to assess when framing is manipulative. According to Levy's framing-as-recommendation theory, we should treat the positive framing of a procedure as a recommendation for that procedure. We can then ask whether the recommendation meets the conditions for reliability. If it does, then the framing is not manipulative. Presumably, in most medical contexts, these conditions will be met, since physicians generally have superior knowledge and benevolent motives. Thus, on the framing-as-recommendations view, most cases of medical framing would not seem to be manipulative. According to the "information leakage" analysis of McKenzie and colleagues, positive framing implicitly suggests that the positively framed option surpasses the best alternative in terms of the attribute in question. On this analysis, a frame would be manipulative if what it suggests is false. For example, if surgery's success rate is 80 percent and medication's is 90 percent, then framing medication as 90 percent effective implicitly suggests—accurately—that medication has a higher success rate than surgery. Thus, such framing would not be manipulative because it suggests something true. By contrast, framing the medication as having a 10 percent failure rate would be manipulative, since it suggests—falsely—that medication has a worse failure rate than surgery.

This analysis is tentative because it rests on claims about framing effects that could turn out to be incorrect. But even if it is correct, it does not settle the question of whether such nudges are permissible in clinical contexts, where standards of informed consent are especially high. Indeed, there is a strong case that physicians should make their implicit recommendations explicit, and disclose that their framing of an option in a certain way reflects a recommendation about it.

Indeed, one could hardly defend the claim that framing is unproblematic because it constitutes *implicit* recommendations, while rejecting the suggestion that physicians should make their recommendations *explicit*. Moreover, for many medical decisions there is no uniquely rational option. In such cases, it seems appropriate for physicians not only to avoid making *any* recommendation, explicit or implicit, but also to employ "debiasing" tactics (e.g., framing the options in multiple ways), to avoid influencing the patient's decision.[12]

The ***Cafeteria*** nudge is more challenging. Levy argues that it, too, involves an implicit recommendation: "changing the visual accessibility of food in the cafeteria . . . can be understood as providing implicit recommendations" (Levy 2022, 140). But while Levy cites empirical evidence to support his claim that people treat defaults and frames as recommendations, he offers no evidence that people treat the ***Cafeteria*** nudge as a recommendation. As Thomas Douglas observes about a version of the ***Cafeteria*** case, "It is plausible to suppose that, when we respond to salience-based nudges, we are responding to the salience, not the intentions for which it was created" (Douglas 2022, 380). The mere fact that this nudge has the same behavioral effect as a recommendation does not show that the effect is caused by people *treating* salience *as a recommendation*.

People probably do treat *some* salience nudges as recommendations, especially when it is clear that someone deliberately made the option salient. It seems reasonable to expect customers to infer a recommendation when a particular dish is displayed prominently on a menu, or when a particular car is displayed in the dealer's showroom. It is less clear that customers will infer a recommendation from a food's placement on a buffet line.

So how do salience nudges influence behavior if they are not treated as recommendations? Sometimes they make salient something about an option that makes it choice-worthy. For example, putting patient photographs on their files may induce radiologists to be more careful when interpreting their scans (Turner and Hadas-Halpern 2008).[13] It seems likely that the pictures make salient the fact that the scans are of *people* whose lives may depend on careful rather than cursory reading of the scans. A nudge like this would not be manipulative since it raises the salience of something genuinely important, thereby encouraging decision-makers to give it proper weight (Noggle 2018, 168). But a nudge that drives some fact's salience out of alignment with its actual importance is manipulative, since it is intended or likely to induce a mistake of attention or weighting.

However, the ***Cafeteria*** nudge raises the salience of *an option itself*, and not any fact that makes it choice-worthy. I once argued (Noggle 2018) that nudges like this are manipulative, since they induce people to choose an option without

[12] Discussions of the permissibility of nudges-as-recommendations in such contexts include Douglas and Proudfoot (2013) and Sagoff (2013).

[13] Cited and discussed in Blumenthal-Barby and Burroughs (2012, 4).

making salient any reason for choosing it. But I now believe that this was a mistake. There are ways that a salience nudge that highlights an option itself rather than some choice-worthy feature of it can be non-manipulative. For one, *some* salience nudges probably *are* treated as recommendations, and when those recommendations are reliable, they are not manipulative.

But, as we noted earlier, it is not clear that this is what happens in ***Cafeteria***. So let us consider some other possibilities.[14] Perhaps increasing the salience of healthy food options simply causes people to consider those options before considering other options. Even an effect this weak might influence some customers. Consider those customers who are *satisficers* for whom the healthy option is good enough. A nudge that gets them to consider the healthy option first will result in their choosing the healthy option by making it the first satisfactory choice they consider. If the healthy option really does meet their conditions for being good enough, such a nudge would induce no mistake and thus not be manipulative. Similarly, a weak influence might serve as a tie-breaker for customers in Buridan situations with regard to the healthy option and some other option. For reasons discussed in the previous chapter, such an influence would not manipulate these customers because arbitrarily breaking a Buridan tie is not a mistake.

However, there are also plausible mechanisms by which the ***Cafeteria*** nudge might operate that *would* be manipulative. One would be for it to produce a mistaken intermediate mental state that influences behavior. Perhaps there are circumstances in which salience creates an impression that the salient option is better than the alternatives. If this is how the ***Cafeteria*** nudge operates, then it would be manipulative to use it to create a *faulty* impression of superior quality. For example, it would be manipulative to harness such an effect to get customers to purchase sub-standard but higher-profit items by creating a false impression of their quality or value. Perhaps some salience nudges produce direct behavioral inclinations to choose the salient option. If the ***Cafeteria*** nudge operates this way, we would need to know whether it creates an inclination powerful enough to induce customers to choose an item against their better judgment. If so, then it would be manipulative to deploy such a mechanism in a way that is intended or likely to induce an akratic choice.

There is empirical support for the claim that nudges like the one in ***Cafeteria*** have some—perhaps modest—effects on behavior.[15] But without a better understanding of the mechanism behind this effect, the question of whether such nudges are manipulative remains unsettled. In the meantime, all we can say is that there are some plausible mechanisms by which the ***Cafeteria*** nudge might operate that *would* entail that it is manipulative, and some that would not.

[14] My thinking in this and the next few paragraphs has benefitted from Engelen (2019) and Nys and Engelen (2017).

[15] On the efficacy such nudges, see A. L. Wilson et al. (2016) and Arno and Thomas (2016).

The nudge in ***Road Lines*** is more straightforward. Of course, it is not a mistake to slow down when approaching a curve. But the nudge encourages that behavior by creating a false impression of one's speed. In effect, the evenly spaced lines invite drivers to treat them as a speed indicator. The more closely placed lines cause this indicator to "misfire," and produce a false impression of increasing speed. Thus, the Mistake Account regards this nudge as manipulative. However, this nudge also seems like a prime example of morally justified manipulation. The mistake induced is small, temporary, and unlikely to cause additional mistakes. And the benefits that it produces—not just for the target, but for third parties as well—are very large.

Finally, consider ***Save More Tomorrow***. It is a pre-commitment device that assists the decision-maker in implementing a plan that it would be tempting to akratically abandon. Used in this way, a pre-commitment device is, in a sense, the opposite of manipulative. Rather than inducing a mistake, it helps the target make a decision while free of the immediacy bias, and it makes the decision less susceptible to akrasia because a definite action needs to be taken to *undo* it.[16]

No doubt some readers will be disappointed with the tentative nature of some of the conclusions drawn here. But this is an inevitable result of two facts. First, according to the Mistake Account (and I would argue, *any* credible account of manipulation) whether an influence is manipulative depends on the mechanisms by which it operates. Second, there is no consensus about the exact mechanisms by which many prominent nudges operate. Nevertheless, the Mistake Account *does* provide us with a sense of what we would need to know to determine whether these nudges are manipulative.

11.6. Manipulation in Advertising

Because advertising results in the transfer of money from the target to the influencer, it is sometimes denounced, either implicitly or explicitly, as manipulation. An especially influential version of this critique is John Kenneth Galbraith's portrayal of advertising as "the competitive manipulation of consumer desire," by which producers create desires for their products instead of producing products to satisfy customers' existing desires.[17]

Philosophical work on advertising has been surprisingly sparse, especially in comparison to nudges.[18] But those philosophers who have critiqued advertising

[16] For a defense of commitment devices in medical contexts, see Hodson (2023).

[17] A related criticism of advertising alleges that it implicitly promises that products will provide intangible goods that they cannot deliver, such as love and happiness. For versions of this criticism, see Graaf, Wann, and Naylor (2005), Kilbourne and Pipher (2000), and Piety (2001).

[18] By contrast, the *psychological* literature on advertising is vast, so much so that it is difficult to navigate without guidance. I have found Bob Fennis and Wolfgang Stroebe's *The Psychology of Advertising* (Fennis and Stroebe 2021) especially helpful in this regard.

have often invoked the concept of manipulation. Thus, Thomas Beauchamp (1984) argues that advertising often manipulates by non-persuasively changing the person's perceptions of their options. Roger Crisp (1987) argues that non-informational advertising is manipulative because it creates desires in people against their will and without their knowledge. Shlomo Sher (2011) develops a version of Joel Rudinow's classic account of manipulation (Rudinow 1978) to argue that advertising tactics that deceive or play on customer weaknesses are manipulative.[19]

Sophisticated discussions of manipulation in advertising are more common among legal theorists. Many of these draw on philosophical accounts of manipulation.[20] One that does not is the influential view put forward by Jon Hanson and Douglas Kysar (Hanson and Kysar 1999; 1998).[21] They draw on behavioral economics to define manipulation as the "utilization of cognitive biases to influence peoples' perceptions and, in turn, behavior" (Hanson and Kysar 1999, 637).[22] But even though it far surpasses its philosophical counterpart, the legal literature on manipulation in advertising is far from complete. Let us see, then, what the Mistake Account might contribute.

One function of advertising is to provide information about products. As with purely informational nudges, it seems difficult to label purely informational advertising as manipulation, unless it is intended or likely to induce false beliefs, false impressions, or mistakes of attention or weighting. Purely informational advertising is manipulative if it suggests that the product has attractive properties that it lacks, or if it hides or diverts attention away from significant drawbacks. For example, advertisements for evaporative cooling devices are manipulative when they deliberately obscure the fact that they operate efficiently only in dry environments.

However, advertising often does more than simply impart information. The non-informational forms or components of advertising raise the most serious concerns about manipulation, since they seem to operate by mechanisms other than rational persuasion. Of course, a major theme of this book is that we cannot simply conclude that an influence that does not operate by rational persuasion is

[19] For related criticisms that advertising subverts autonomy, see Villarán (2017), Santilli (1983), and Sneddon (2001). For a philosophical argument that advertising seldom manipulates consumers, see Arrington (1982). Philosophically sophisticated work by non-philosophers on whether advertising is manipulative incudes Drumwright (2018), Saucier (2008), and Phillips (1997).

[20] For example, Norton (2021) and Kilovaty (2019) draw on the Covert Influence Account of Susser, Roessler, and Nissenbaum (2019). Goodman (2013) draws on the Trickery Account in Noggle (1996). For an eclectic account that includes elements of the Covert Influence Account, see Becher and Feldman (2016, 475–76).

[21] Discussions that have been influenced by Hanson and Kysar include Piety (2001), Berman (2015), and Calo (2014).

[22] Given its emphasis on behavioral economics, one could interpret their view as a version of the approach that characterizes manipulation in terms of Type 1 processes. But given its focus on "biases," which, after all, are tendencies to make mistakes, one could also interpret their view as a cousin of the Mistake Account. Their inclusion of temporal myopia among the biases (Hanson and Kysar 1999, 678–80) brings their view even closer to the Mistake Account.

automatically manipulative. We must instead determine whether the influence works by inducing a mistake. To do that, we must understand how the influence operates.

One non-informational function of advertising is simply to propose a sales transaction and draw attention to that proposal. This often involves increasing the salience of the product on offer. There does not seem to be anything inherently mistake-inducing—and thus manipulative—about a transparent and salient sales proposal. Matters are different when the sales proposal is not transparent. For example, it is manipulative to disguise a sales proposal as something else, like a reliable recommendation meant purely for the customer's benefit. The fact that transparent sales proposals (and efforts to make them salient to potential customers) often lead to purchasing decisions does not make them manipulative. There is nothing inherently mistaken about agreeing to a sales proposal, or purchasing something one wants or needs when given and made aware of the opportunity. Thus, proposing a sales transaction, and drawing attention to that proposal, can increase sales without being inherently manipulative.

However, non-informational advertising often does more than proposing a sales transaction and drawing attention to that proposal. In most cases, it also seeks to steer customer choice toward the advertised product and away from competing products. Often this involves highlighting some advantage—such as price, quality, or convenience—that the advertised product has over competitors. However, differences in price, quality, or convenience of competing products are often negligible. In such situations, advertising seeks to induce customers to choose one product over another, despite there being very little difference between them.

A common way to do this is to employ a tactic that is sometimes called "associative advertising" (Waide 1987). This form of advertising associates a product with some other thing that customers find appealing. Frequent choices include sex, success, health, vigor, popularity, etc. Often, the association is made by showing the product with, or being used by, a person who possesses some desirable quality. Linking a product with something independently appealing suggests, without asserting, that there is a connection between them. For some targets of advertising, these associations may induce beliefs that the product will produce the thing with which it is associated. For others, the association may induce only an *impression* to this effect. Either way, though, this form of advertising can be manipulative if the belief or impression is mistaken.

Sometimes, the product bears a strong enough relationship to the thing to which it is associated that the association is unlikely to induce mistaken beliefs or impressions. Thus, the beliefs or impressions most likely to be created by associating excitement with a sports car, health and vigor with athletic equipment, or attractiveness with clothes or cosmetics, are not necessarily mistaken. Of course, such associations might induce mistaken levels of *optimism* about the efficacy of the product to produce the thing with which it is associated. In such cases, the advertisement would be at least somewhat manipulative (depending on how excessive the optimism produced). But it is not necessarily manipulative to suggest a connection between a product and something else to which it is plausibly related, even if this is done through associations rather than explicit assertions.

But sometimes it clearly is a mistake to associate two things. Consider the Marlboro Man. This advertising campaign associated Marlboro cigarettes with an actor who was the very image of rugged vigor. In reality, of course, smoking Marlboros—or any other cigarettes—*undermines* rugged vigor. Indeed, several actors who portrayed the Marlboro Man died of smoking-induced lung cancer (Pearce 2014). Thus, the impression of a connection between Marlboro and rugged vigor is clearly a mistake.[23] The Mistake Account correctly classifies this advertising campaign as manipulative.

Associative advertising might also operate via psychological mechanisms like the halo effect (Laham and Forgas 2022) or evaluative conditioning (Fennis and Stroebe 2021, 133, 162–68). That is, the positive feelings about the person or thing with which the product is associated may transfer to the product. This transference might even take place implicitly rather than consciously (Fennis and Stroebe 2021, 135–37). The analysis above needs only minor modification to address this possibility. It is a mistake to regard something in a positive light simply because it is linked to something else positive to which it is not genuinely related. For example, it is a mistake to form a positive attitude toward Marlboros based on its association with qualities of health and vigor that the product actually undermines.

Informational advertising *asserts* that something is the case. Associative advertising *suggests* that something is the case. A third form of advertising—puffery—is often claimed to do neither of these things. Puffery consists of positive statements about a product. However, these statements are often said to make no actual claims because they are unfalsifiable, vague, subjective, or so exaggerated that no reasonable person would take them seriously. "World's Best Coffee" is a paradigm example. A prominent theory sees puffery as expressing optimism or excitement about a product rather than asserting or even suggesting factual claims about it. As legal theorist David Hoffman notes, this theory provides much of the rationale for not prohibiting puffery as deceptive advertising (Hoffman 2006, 137). The optimism expressed by puffery is often sincere. As Hoffman notes, sellers, like everyone else, are prone to the optimism bias (Hoffman 2006, 136). Moreover, those who are not initially optimistic about the products they sell may face psychological pressure to *become* optimistic to avoid a negative self-image of being an insincere seller of inferior products.

[23] In a detailed discussion of tobacco advertising more generally, Hanson and Kysar (1998) argue that it is manipulative because it employs biases that lead consumers to underestimate their personal risk from smoking. The Mistake Account would agree with their conclusion, but its emphasis is on the outcomes—i.e., mistaken estimates of personal risk—rather than the biases that produce them.

Despite the common idea that no one believes puffery, it seems likely that some people *do* take it literally and believe it.[24] This could happen because some people mistakenly take literally a message not meant to be taken literally. In other cases, puffery might be *intended* to induce false beliefs in a subset of potential customers. An unscrupulous seller might calibrate its puffery to deceive enough customers to be profitable, but not so many for the messages to be judged as deceptive by regulators (Hoffman 2006, 144–45). (This is one reason for favoring regulations protecting those who are especially vulnerable to manipulation—see section 11.2) For those who do not believe its claims, puffery may work primarily by drawing attention to the availability of the goods being sold. In such cases, it need not be manipulative for the reasons discussed earlier. It is not inherently manipulative to propose a business transaction, to draw attention to that proposal, or to express sincere optimism about the product one proposes to sell.

Finally, some of puffery's influence—and that of advertising more generally—may involve simply making a product or its brand more familiar. This is widely assumed to occur because of the "mere exposure effect" (Fennis and Stroebe 2021, 160–62). This effect involves "increased liking for a stimulus that follows repeated, unreinforced exposure to that stimulus" (Bornstein and Craver-Lemley 2022, 255). This effect has been studied extensively since Robert Zajonc's seminal work on the topic (Zajonc 1968), and its existence does not appear to be in serious dispute. While the exact psychological mechanisms that underlie it are subject to debate, most proposed explanations involve basic neural processes that occur without or below the level of conscious processing.[25]

Suppose that the mere exposure effect causes Ted to choose a familiar brand of laundry soap over an unfamiliar one, even though the two products are identical in every way that matters to Ted. Was Ted manipulated? The answer depends on the details of *how* this effect influenced Ted's choice. One possibility is that it created a *false* belief or impression that the familiar brand is superior to the unfamiliar brand. In this case, of course, the effect of the advertising would be manipulative, since it would create a *false* belief or impression. But suppose that the mere exposure effect merely created a *preference* for the familiar brand, without any faulty belief or impression of its superiority. Perhaps people simply like what is familiar, without having any impression or belief that what is familiar is better. Inducing such a preference can be manipulative if it leads to akratic choices. For example, if Ted had judged the unfamiliar brand to be a better choice, a familiarity-based preference might lead him to act against his judgment about what is best to choose. However, a familiarity-based preference that is only strong enough to break a tie in

[24] Empirical literature on puffery includes Xu and Wyer (2010), Cowley (2006), Amyx and Lumpkin (2016), Lee (2014), Gao and Scorpio (2011), and Yang et al. (2019); see Hoffman (2006) for an overview. The overall empirical picture seems mixed, with some studies demonstrating the effectiveness of puffery at least under certain conditions, and others failing to find significant effects.

[25] For reviews of the theoretical debates, see Bornstein and Craver-Lemley (2022).

a Buridan situation is not manipulative, since it is not a mistake to arbitrarily break such a tie.

This analysis assumes that brand recognition advertising works through the mere exposure effect. But there is another line of thought about how brand recognition advertising works. According to this line of thought, advertising, even when it lacks any informational content, provides signals about product quality. There are several versions of this idea.[26] One is that only successful companies can afford ambitious advertising campaigns, and they would not be successful if they produced low quality products. Similarly, customers may reason that if a well-known brand produced low-quality products, it would have a poor reputation. Consequently, well-known brands *without* poor reputations probably make acceptable quality products. Another is that producers who have invested in brand advertising have an incentive to ensure that branded products are of good quality. Otherwise, branding would backfire, by making it easy for customers to avoid purchasing from that brand again. Each version of this idea suggests that it is reasonable to assume that products of a heavily advertised brand are of acceptable quality, unless that brand has acquired a reputation for poor quality.

The idea that advertising can signal quality appears in some legal defenses of puffery (Hoffman 2006) and trademark protection regulations (Sheff 2010). If some version of this idea is correct, then one reason for advertising's influence is that customers sometimes treat familiarity as a signal for product quality. Thus, even advertising that does not look like it is communicating information might still work at least partly because customers treat it as a signal for product quality.

If brand recognition advertising functions as a signal for quality, it is easy to see how unscrupulous marketers might exploit its signalling function to send *faulty* signals. Jeremy Sheff calls this process "psychological arbitrage" (Sheff 2010, 1296). A producer of low-quality products might mount an aggressive advertising campaign to create a sense of familiarity that customers mistakenly treat as an indicator of quality.[27] Sheff recounts how the makers of a bogus headache remedy avoided US FDA rules against deceptive claims by using advertisements that did little more than repeat the product's name. In this way, the "mere repetition of a brand name in advertising generated multimillion-dollar sales of a placebo to treat a condition for which numerous inexpensive and more efficacious treatments were readily available" (Sheff 2010, 1297).

What Sheff calls "psychological arbitrage" the Mistake Account calls manipulation. Since brand familiarity can create an impression of quality, companies producing low-quality products act manipulatively when they mount vast advertising campaigns to create *false* impressions of quality. A similar form of manipulation

[26] For examples, see Ambler and Hollier (2004), Nelson (1974), and Gigerenzer (2007, 126–29). For a useful discussion, see Sheff (2010).

[27] For a similar observation, see Gigerenzer (2007, 128).

occurs when a producer of lower quality products imitates the trademarks and other markers of a higher-quality brand. This may get customers to mistakenly believe that the low-quality products are those of the higher-quality brand. Or, more subtly, it may get customers to mistakenly transfer the impression of high quality from the reputable brand to that of the imitator.

Of course, it is an empirical matter whether brand-recognition advertising works through the mere exposure effect, or because people treat it as evidence of quality. But either way, we can see how the Mistake Account allows us to distinguish manipulative from non-manipulative uses of this form of advertising.

11.7. Manipulation in Sales

As with advertising, the topic of manipulation in sales has been relatively neglected by philosophers. Not surprisingly, there is consensus that deception in sales is unethical. And there has been some debate about how much information sellers are morally obligated to provide to buyers.[28] But philosophical discussions of non-deceptive manipulation in sales are rare.[29]

We have already discussed several sales tactics that the Mistake Account characterizes as manipulation. These include misemphasis to increase the salience of a product's advantages while decreasing the salience of its disadvantages (section 7.6), and insincere friendliness that triggers the buyer's "friendly interaction" script instead of the "evaluating a sales pitch" script (section 7.4).

Many high-pressure sales tactics are manipulative precisely because the pressure they employ is manipulative, that is, intended or likely to induce akratic purchasing decisions. A common example is the creation of false urgency, through limited time offers that are arbitrary or artificial, or through scarcity that is either engineered or feigned (Fennis and Stroebe 2021, 333–36). Urgency can put pressure on decision-making by increasing the "fear of missing out," and by compressing the time available to decide. These factors can lead to impulsive decision-making that is often akratic. Since consumers may sometimes infer quality from scarcity (Fennis and Stroebe 2021, 335), false scarcity might also create a false impression of quality, which may strengthen the manipulative pressure created by false urgency.

Another use of manipulative pressure occurs when a salesperson asserts that the customer has agreed to a purchase and begins discussing payment options, etc., when the customer has not, in fact, agreed to buy. This tactic exploits conflict

[28] See, for example, Ebejer and Morden (1988), Holley (1986; 1998), Mooradian (2004), Brockway (1993), and Carson (1998, 2001, 2012).

[29] See Holley (1986) for a brief discussion of manipulative sales tactics. Sophisticated accounts of manipulative sales tactics by non-philosophers include Saucier (2008) and Alessandra, Wexler, and Barrera (1992).

aversion to raise the emotional cost of declining to purchase. The psychological cost of interrupting and then contradicting the salesperson is, for many people, significantly greater than that of simply not saying yes to the transaction. Some customers in this situation might have purchased anyway, and others might endure the psychological costs of refusing to purchase. But some customers will akratically avoid the conflict involved in extricating themselves from the unwanted transaction, and thus be manipulated. As with many forms of manipulative commerce, this tactic may be profitable even if it only manipulates a fraction of those subjected to it.

Similar remarks apply to the "impulse purchase area" tactic (Almy and Wootan 2015; Fennis and Stroebe 2021, 277, 292–94). This involves placing tempting snacks in the check-out aisle—a place that shoppers cannot avoid—so that they are easily accessed and impossible not to notice. The combination of unavoidable temptation and hungry, tired customers virtually guarantees that some customers will make akratic purchases. Consequently, the practice is manipulative in effect and probably intent as well. By contrast, placing batteries or other items frequently forgotten by shoppers at the checkout aisle would be unlikely to induce akratic purchases. Nor would placing less tempting and more healthful snacks at the checkout aisle for the benefit of those who have grown hungry while shopping. In these latter two cases, the product placement would not be manipulative because it would not be intended or likely to induce customers to make akratic choices.

In their discussion of commercial manipulation, legal theorists Shmuel Becher and Yuval Feldman discuss various ways in which "a store's atmosphere can influence consumers' emotions, as well as level of comfort, mood, and time spent shopping—all of which may impact purchase decisions" (Becher and Feldman 2016, 477). Likely candidates for such "atmospherics" include certain colors and other pleasing visual elements, appealing music, and pleasant scents. Indeed, the use of pleasant scents to induce sales appears in a common puzzle in philosophical discussions of manipulation, namely whether it is manipulative to use the scent of fresh baked goods to sell a house (Cohen 2017, 486, Barnhill 2014, 58).

Empirical research suggests that pleasant atmospherics can influence sales. A literature review by L. W. Turley and Ronald Milliman concludes that "there is enough evidence to be able to clearly state that the atmosphere has an effect on consumer spending and that variations of atmospheric variables affect the amount of money people spend and the number of items they purchase" (Turley and Milliman 2000, 209; see also Fennis and Stroebe 2021, 168–69, Becher and Feldman 2016, 476–81). Becher and Feldman offer an eclectic definition of 'manipulation' as influence that exploits customer vulnerabilities to covertly change their perceptions of the product. On the basis of this definition, they argue that atmospherics are manipulative (Becher and Feldman 2016, 475–76). The Mistake Account's analysis is more nuanced. It ties questions about whether an influence is manipulative to the question of whether it operates in a way that induces the audience to make a mistake. To answer this question, we need to know more about how these influences work.

It seems unlikely that atmospherics drive behavior directly, without affecting any intermediate mental state. If they did, then the Mistake Account's analysis of them would parallel the analysis given in section 10.4 of direct behavioral primes. In particular, if the atmospheric influence gets a customer to choose what the customer judges to be an inferior product, or to pay more than the customer judges it to be worth, then it is akrasia-inducing and thus manipulative. On the other hand, if the direct behavioral influence is only strong enough to break a tie between comparable products, then the influence would not be manipulative.

It seems more likely that atmospherics operate more indirectly, by inducing intermediate mental states that then affect behavior. One plausible candidate for an intermediate mental state is mood. In section 10.9, we noted that moods like agitation, anxiety, etc., can be indirectly manipulative by making mistakes more likely. Of course, these *bad* moods are the opposite of what atmospherics are designed to induce. But especially *good* moods might make people less likely to consider purchases carefully, and thus contribute to akratic or otherwise mistaken purchasing decisions (Fennis and Stroebe 2021, 198–99).

Atmospherics might also work through mechanisms like the halo effect or evaluative conditioning, which may transfer positive feelings from the environment to the products being sold. Here the intention or effect would not simply be to create a pleasant shopping environment, but to enhance the perception of the value of products being sold. As before, it matters *how* this effect operates on the buyer's decision-making process. If it creates a false impression that *this* store's products are superior to those of competing stores, then the effect would be manipulative.

It is also possible that atmospherics often do little more than make a shopping experience more pleasant. Presumably, customers tend to spend more time in pleasant places than unpleasant ones, and thus have more opportunities to encounter products that they might wish to purchase. This mechanism for the influence exerted by atmospherics would simply be a version of the legitimate, non-manipulative attempt to draw attention to a proposed sales transaction. Since people can respond to such proposals without making any mistakes, the mere fact that they increase sales does not prove that they are manipulative.

For establishments like coffee shops, bookstores, etc., the atmospherics may be a large part of what the customer seeks when entering the establishment. Patrons may regard purchases partly as a quid pro quo for providing a pleasant environment. There is little basis, either in intuition or in the Mistake Account, for thinking that it is manipulative to increase sales this way.[30]

[30] For a somewhat different assessment of atmospherics in coffee shops, see Ariely (2010, 40–41).

As with the discussion of nudges, the discussion of advertising and sales tactics must remain tentative and open to revision, for two reasons. First, our understanding of the psychology of sales and advertising is far from complete. Second, according to the Mistake Account (or *any* credible account of manipulation) whether a tactic is manipulative depends on the psychological mechanisms by which it influences behavior. It is no doubt disappointing that the Mistake Account sometimes offers as many questions as answers. However, those questions offer guidance about how future research on the psychological mechanisms underlying various sales and advertising tactics can help determine whether they are manipulative.

One final caveat: Determining that an advertising or sales tactic is manipulative is not the final word in determining its moral status or whether it ought to be legally regulated. Some forms of commercial manipulation might resemble the sort of trivial manipulation discussed in section 9.10.4—minor attempts at manipulation that we expect to encounter in commercial contexts. One could argue that voluntarily entering a commercial space might constitute consent to at least some trivial forms of manipulation.

11.8. Online Manipulation

As more of our commercial, social, and professional lives move into online environments, it is natural to worry about the distinctive ways that manipulation can occur there. Online manipulation has attracted significant attention from both philosophers[31] and legal scholars.[32] In these discussions, the work of Susser, Roessler, and Nissenbaum (2019; 2020) and that of Hanson and Kysar (1999) have been especially influential.

Discussions of online manipulation often focus on what Harry Brignull famously labelled as "dark patterns," which he defined as "tricks used in websites and apps that make you do things that you didn't mean to" (Brignull et al. 2023).[33] These tactics are frequently described as "tricks used to manipulate . . . a user" (Khindri 2021), or as "manipulative design practices" (Federal Trade Commission 2022). Examples include:[34]

Tricky buttons designed to confuse users into clicking a button that they would not otherwise click, often through misleading instructions or giving

[31] See Klenk (2022a, 2022b); Susser, Roessler, and Nissenbaum (2019; 2020), and the papers collected in Jongepier and Klenk (2022).

[32] Notable examples include Calo (2014), Spencer (2020), Willis (2020), Luguri and Strahilevitz (2021), and Day and Stemler (2020).

[33] Brignull (2023, 5) now calls them "deceptive patterns," but the original term is still in wide use; moreover, many of them do not involve deception.

[34] The examples are from Brignull et al. (2023), Khindri (2021), and Morrison (2021).

the button design features associated with a button that people often want to click.

Disguised advertisements that mimic news items, impartial reviews, or other neutral sources.

Pre-selected options that are generally disadvantageous to the user, but which users may mistakenly fail to deselect.

"***Roach motels***," in which deliberately placed obstacles make it more difficult to cancel an account or service, especially one that was easy to initiate.

Electronic nagging, such as periodic pop-ups asking users to do something they may not want to do, but which they cannot deactivate without doing.

Some of these—like ***Tricky Buttons*** and ***Disguised Advertisements***—are straightforwardly deceptive. The first induces a false belief that, say, the button granting access to your personal data is actually the button to refuse access. The second induces the faulty belief that a given body of information is unbiased when it is really a sales pitch. The Mistake Account clearly identifies these tactics as manipulation.

Pre-selected Options are a form of default, and their analysis simply applies what was said earlier. If defaults constitute recommendations, then they are manipulative when they are designed to appear reliable when they are not. Typically, manipulative defaults are unreliable because the default option is not a good choice for the target. This tactic becomes even more manipulative when surrounding text or other context creates the impression that the pre-selection reflects expert advice about what will benefit the target.

Many dark patterns involve pressure rather than trickery. Take the ***Roach Motel***, for example. In 2023, the US Federal Trade Commission sued Amazon over obstacles it used to make it difficult to cancel an Amazon Prime account, alleging that "the primary purpose of the Prime cancellation process was not to enable subscribers to cancel, but rather to thwart them" (Federal Trade Commission 2023, 3).[35] The entry point for the process to cancel a Prime account was difficult to find. The process itself then "required consumers intending to cancel to navigate a four-page, six-click, fifteen-option cancellation process. In contrast, customers could enroll in Prime with one or two clicks" (Federal Trade Commission 2023, 43). Customers ensnared by this labyrinthine cancellation process are, no doubt, frustrated. But they are not tricked or deceived. And nothing about this situation, or the influence that it exerts, is covert. Hence, the Covert Influence Account commonly used in discussions of online manipulation (e.g., Susser, Roessler, and Nissenbaum 2019) seems inadequate to account for the widespread intuition that Roach Motels are manipulative.

[35] See also McCabe (2023) for an overview.

But the Mistake Account easily identifies this tactic as manipulation. This is not to say that it successfully manipulates everyone who encounters it. Some will persist in cancelling despite the obstacles. Others will not cancel, but only because their preference to cancel was weaker than their preference to avoid the hassle of navigating the roach motel. Members of a third group judge it better overall to cancel, but they give up before doing so. Thus, the Roach Motel induces members of this third group to behave akratically. According to the Mistake Account, members of this group are manipulated.[36] The FTC observes that customers succumb to roach motels "likely out of frustration" (Federal Trade Commission 2022, 16), and that they "become fatigued and give up" (Federal Trade Commission 2022, 14). Frustration and fatigue are both explanations for the akratic behavior of those users who are successfully manipulated by the Roach Motel.[37]

Another common dark pattern that operates by manipulative pressure is ***Electronic Nagging***. As with Roach Motels, electronic nagging manipulates only a subset of those who encounter it. Others will successfully resist, or their preference for not doing what they are being nagged to do is too weak for their giving in to be akratic. But some will give in despite judging that doing so is not their best option. According to the Mistake Account, they have been manipulated.

Not all concerns about online manipulation focus on specific elements of website design. Many focus on the entire phenomenon of social media (Orlowski 2020; Alter 2018). Tristan Harris, a web designer turned technology ethicist, suggests that, with the rise of social media, we have "moved away from having a tools-based technology environment to an addiction- and manipulation-based technology environment."[38] In Jeff Orlowski's documentary, *The Social Dilemma*, the former president of Pinterest, Tim Kendal, describes social media's hold on him: "I couldn't get off my phone once I got home, despite having two young kids who needed my love and attention . . . I couldn't help myself."[39] Psychiatrist Anna Lembke adds that: "social media is a drug . . . [W]e have a basic biological imperative to connect with other people . . . A vehicle like social media, which optimizes this connection between people, is going to have the potential for addiction."[40]

[36] That is not to deny that the other two groups have been mistreated. They have. Both have been subjected to an unjustified cost. This cost is, essentially, a tax on exercising what ought to be their unfettered right to choose whether to engage in a certain economic transaction based on whether it will benefit them. Of the two groups who are not manipulated, one group chooses to pay this tax and one does not.

[37] For a similar analysis of mail-in rebates, which consumers treat as price reductions but do not always redeem, see Edwards (2008, 353–59).

[38] Tristan Harris, quoted in Orlowski (2020).

[39] Tim Kendal, quoted in Orlowski (2020). For similar claims, see Day and Stemler (2020, part 1) and Alter (2018).

[40] Anna Lembke, quoted in Orlowski (2020).

Lembke, Kendall, and Harris are not alone in calling social media addictive, and several scholars have proposed theories about the nature of social media addiction (Sun and Zhang 2021). The concept of addiction is tricky, as is the question of whether excessive social media use is a "genuine" addiction. Fortunately, we need not settle these questions here. We need only observe that social media tends to induce akrasia. This tendency probably reflects a combination of the general features of social media that Lembke identifies, and design features like notifications, "like" buttons, "gamification," and other elements that provide intermittent reinforcement.[41] This combination enables social media to induce us to engage akratically, that is, more than we know is good for us. Because their revenues come from advertising, social media platforms profit from maximizing engagement. Thus, it is not surprising that their imperative would be, as Kendal puts it, "Let's figure out how to get as much of this person's attention as we possibly can."[42]

Moreover, several new technologies provide efficient ways to do this. One is rapid A/B testing. This allows web designers to quickly compare design features, layouts, color schemes, word choices, etc. for their effectiveness in getting users to do what the designer wants (Kohavi and Longbotham 2023; Kohavi and Thomke 2017). Rapid A/B testing is likely to discover design features that exploit *general* human vulnerabilities to manipulation. Microtargeting is likely to discover vulnerabilities *specific* to individuals.[43] The more information that the microtargeting algorithms collect, the more likely they will be to find not only our interests but our weaknesses and vulnerabilities. If the system's only goal is maximizing engagement, it will not care whether it achieves this by providing users with valuable content or by appealing to their weaknesses to entice them to engage more than they judge valuable. Such technologies make it inevitable that web designers will discover manipulative forms of influence along with non-manipulative ones—perhaps without bothering to raise questions about the distinction.[44]

Thus, we should not be surprised to find in social media a mix of (1) valuable content that gives us good reasons to engage, and (2) design elements that manipulate us into engaging *more* than those good reasons warrant. That is, we should expect social media and other profit-driven platforms to contain a combination of manipulative and non-manipulative content.

The most immediate harms from online manipulation are time wasted on the internet and money wasted on purchases we would not have made had we not been manipulated. But there is reason to worry about larger, more systemic harms

[41] On features of social media that make it addictive, see Alter (2018); on gamification see Parmer (2022) and Gorin (2022).

[42] Kendal, quoted in Orlowski (2020); on the market forces incentivizing manipulation, see Hanson and Kysar (1998).

[43] On the manipulative potential of microtargeting see Gorton (2016), Jongepier and Wieland (2022), Gehl and Lawson (2022, chap. 7), Susser, Roessler, and Nissenbaum (2019), Calo (2014), Turow (2013).

[44] Harry Brignull (2023, 22) makes a similar point.

from online manipulation. Harris and others note that people find outrage more engaging than analysis, and information that confirms their pre-existing ideas more engaging than information that encourages critical thinking. Consequently, social media's engagement-maximizing algorithms will tend to increase social and political polarization (Harris 2019). Assessing this allegation is beyond the scope of this book. But in the wake of the disinformation campaigns around the 2020 and 2024 US elections and the COVID-19 pandemic, it seems unwise to dismiss it as hyperbole.

11.9. A Few Comments on Political Manipulation

These last observations bring us to the topic of manipulation in politics. Concerns about political manipulation are continuous with older worries about propaganda, ideology, demagoguery, and the like. The ancients were aware of the power of deception, misdirection, and appeals to vanity, greed, and fear as tools for political influence. Although the term 'manipulation' as applied to interpersonal influence has only been around since the mid-1800s, it clearly applies to many of these age-old tactics.[45]

While political theorists have written extensively about political influence, they have written far less about the distinction between manipulative and non-manipulative influence.[46] The Mistake Account offers a way to draw this distinction, for it applies just as readily to political influence as it does to any other form of influence. Indeed, political manipulation involves many of the same devices and tactics that we have already discussed. For example, traditional advertising tactics and newer forms of online influence can be harnessed to sell candidates and policies as easily as products.

There are, no doubt, some differences in content and emphasis. Political manipulators are more likely than advertisers to appeal to *negative* emotions. Baseless fear, unwarranted anger, and irrational hatred are particularly potent emotions for political manipulators to incite and play upon. Political influence often involves metaphors (Lakoff, Dean, and Hazen 2004), some of which are manipulative. Political manipulation often involves the confirmation bias, where current events are portrayed as confirming a certain narrative. Misemphasis and misdirection are also common, so that facts at odds with a particular message or narrative are

[45] For the relative newness of term 'manipulation,' see Oxford English Dictionary (2023); I am grateful to Michael Klenk for pointing this out to me. For a discussion of forms of influence known in antiquity that we would likely describe as manipulation, see Ball (2011).

[46] Notable exceptions include Dowding (2016; 2018), Ware (1981), Gorton (2016), Whitfield (2022), as well as the papers collected in Le Cheminant and Parrish (2011); work by philosophers includes Goodin (1980), Claudia Mills (1995), and Saul (2024). For a survey, see Noggle (2021). For a theory of situational manipulation in politics, see Riker (1986).

downplayed or hidden. The fragmentation of the media assists in these processes. Similarly, microtargeting allows political manipulators to determine just which facts to emphasize to, and which to hide from, a given voter.[47]

Recent history abounds with examples of political manipulation, such as disinformation about the 2020 and 2024 US presidential elections, COVID denialism, and the rise of xenophobic populism. A list of specific examples of recent political manipulation would be all too easy to construct. I have resisted the temptation to use such examples in this book, however, for two reasons. First, a sophisticated discussion of manipulation in contemporary politics is best undertaken with a well worked-out and defended theory about what manipulation is, how it works, and why it is bad. Second, for me, at least, it is much easier to develop and test such a theory outside of the heated context of contemporary politics.[48]

Thus, my decision to steer clear of recent examples of political manipulation does not reflect any doubt about its existence or importance. Quite the contrary. The manipulation of a single person can be tragic. Although *Othello* is fiction, real-life abusers, psychopaths, and common criminals use manipulation to perpetrate real tragedies every bit as bad as Othello's murder of Desdemona. But when someone manipulates a *multitude*, the stakes can be even higher. When Elizabeth Powel asked Benjamin Franklin whether the Framers of the US Constitution had created a monarchy or a republic, he was said to have answered, "a Republic, if you can keep it."[49] If the US does not manage to keep its republic, it seems likely that political manipulation will be a large part of the reason. The ancients were right to worry about democracies being drawn into disastrous wars or devolving into tyrannies due to what we would now call political manipulation. This book was written during a time in US history when the first danger is a recent memory and the second is a looming threat.

As a philosopher, I have tried to clarify the concept of manipulation, to understand what it is, how it works, and why it is bad. As a citizen, I hope that this project might be of some small help in addressing real-world manipulation and the challenges it poses for contemporary democracies. I have no illusions about the size of this contribution. The practical challenge of combatting manipulation in our social and political lives is vastly greater than the theoretical challenge of defining manipulation. The threat posed by political manipulation, and the potential of emerging technologies to facilitate it, make this practical challenge especially pressing.[50] Policymakers do not need a philosophical theory of manipulation to

[47] As Jennifer Saul (2024) demonstrates, racist dogwhistles achieve a similar effect of enabling politicians to play to racial resentments of some voters, while hiding such appeals from others.

[48] By contrast, Jennifer Saul (2024) has achieved remarkable analytical clarity about forms of influence related to manipulation while delving into contemporary politics.

[49] For discussions of the context and historicity of this story, see Miller (2022) and Anishanslin (2019).

[50] For a sobering examination of the current technologies that can facilitate political manipulation, see A. Wilson (2023).

identify its most egregious instances. Yet such a theory may be helpful in providing a principled way to distinguish manipulation from sincere advocacy of views one does not share, and in providing a clear rationale for treating it as a unified—and uniformly pernicious—phenomenon. So, while the heavy lifting needed to combat political manipulation is not a philosophical task, a viable philosophical theory might lighten the load just a bit.

11.10. Conclusion

This book has offered and defended answers to the three questions about manipulation posed in Chapter 1: What is it? How does it work? Why is it bad?

Stated simply, manipulation is a form of influence that operates by getting us to make mistakes in our psychological states or processes. It works by exploiting the imperfections in our rational agency that are part and parcel of the human condition. It is bad because it involves inducing mistakes, and mistakes are bad.

However, as we have just seen, while the core moral status of manipulation derives from the fact that it gets people to make mistakes, the worst cases of manipulation are especially bad because of their consequences. For the individual, the consequences can be as dire as death and murder, as in the case of Othello. For groups, they can be as tragic as the mass suicide of the People's Temple. For society at large, they can be tyranny, war, and genocide.

Given the imperfect state of human nature, manipulation will always be a tempting way for unscrupulous people to get what they want, and even wise and good people will sometimes fall for it. My hope is that having a better understanding of manipulation—what it is, how it works, and why it's bad—will help us avoid the worst effects of the manipulation that will probably always be part of the human landscape.

Bibliography

Abramson, Kate. 2024. *On Gaslighting*. Princeton: Princeton University Press.
Ackerman, Felicia. 1995. "The Concept of Manipulativeness." *Philosophical Perspectives* 9: 335–40.
Adler, Jonathan E. 1997. "Lying, Deceiving, or Falsely Implicating." *The Journal of Philosophy* 94 (9): 435–52.
Ainslie, George. 2001. *Breakdown of Will*. Cambridge: Cambridge University Press.
Alessandra, Tony, Phil Wexler, and Rick Barrera. 1992. *Non-Manipulative Selling*. 2nd edition. New York: Simon & Shuster.
Alexander, Larry, and Michael Moore. 2021. "Deontological Ethics." In *The Stanford Encyclopedia of Philosophy*, edited by Edward N. Zalta, Winter 2021. https://plato.stanford.edu/archives/win2021/entries/ethics-deontological/.
Almy, Jessica, and Margo Wootan. 2015. "Temptation at Checkout." Center for Science in the Public Interest. www.cspinet.org/temptation-checkout.
Alter, Adam. 2018. *Irresistible: The Rise of Addictive Technology and the Business of Keeping Us Hooked*. New York: Penguin Books.
Ambler, Tim, and E. Ann Hollier. 2004. "The Waste in Advertising Is the Part That Works." *Journal of Advertising Research* 44 (4): 375–89.
Amyx, Douglas Alan, and James R. Lumpkin. 2016. "Interaction Effect of Ad Puffery and Ad Skepticism on Consumer Persuasion." *Journal of Promotion Management* 22 (3): 403–24.
Anderson, Christopher J. 2003. "The Psychology of Doing Nothing: Forms of Decision Avoidance Result from Reason and Emotion." *Psychological Bulletin* 129 (1): 139–67.
Anderson, Scott. 2011. "Coercion." In *The Stanford Encyclopedia of Philosophy*, edited by Edward N. Zalta, Summer 2021. https://plato.stanford.edu/archives/sum2021/entries/coercion/.
Anishanslin, Zara. 2019. "Perspective | What We Get Wrong about Ben Franklin's 'a Republic, If You Can Keep It.'" *Washington Post*, October 29, 2019.
Ariely, Dan. 2010. *Predictably Irrational: The Hidden Forces That Shape Our Decisions*. New York: Harper Perennial.
Aristotle. n.d. *Nicomachean Ethics*. Translated by W. D. Ross. http://classics.mit.edu/Aristotle/nicomachaen.1.i.html. Accessed October 19, 2022.
Arno, Anneliese, and Steve Thomas. 2016. "The Efficacy of Nudge Theory Strategies in Influencing Adult Dietary Behaviour: A Systematic Review and Meta-Analysis." *BMC Public Health* 16 (1): 676.
Arpaly, Nomy, and Timothy Schroeder. 1999. "Praise, Blame and the Whole Self." *Philosophical Studies* 93 (2): 161–88.
Arpaly, Nomy, and Timothy Schroeder. 2012. "Deliberation and Acting for Reasons." *The Philosophical Review* 121 (2): 209–39.
Arrington, Robert L. 1982. "Advertising and Behavior Control." *Journal of Business Ethics* 1 (1): 3–12.
Audi, Robert. 1994. "Dispositional Beliefs and Dispositions to Believe." *Noûs* 28 (4): 419–34.
Audi, Robert. 2015. *Means, Ends, and Persons: The Meaning and Psychological Dimensions of Kant's Humanity Formula*. New York: Oxford University Press.
Austin, Elizabeth J., Daniel Farrelly, Carolyn Black, and Helen Moore. 2007. "Emotional Intelligence, Machiavellianism and Emotional Manipulation: Does EI Have a Dark Side?" *Personality and Individual Differences* 43 (1): 179–89.
Austin, Elizabeth J., and Michael M. O'Donnell. 2013. "Development and Preliminary Validation of a Scale to Assess Managing the Emotions of Others." *Personality and Individual Differences* 55 (7): 834–39.

Baier, Annette. 2010. "Why Honesty Is a Hard Virtue." In *Reflections On How We Live.* Oxford: Oxford University Press.

Ball, Terence. 2011. "Manipulation: As Old as Democracy Itself (and Sometimes Dangerous)." In *Manipulating Democracy: Democratic Theory, Political Psychology, and Mass Media*, edited by Wayne Le Cheminant and John M. Parrish. New York: Routledge.

Bargh, John A. 2012. "Priming Effects Replicate Just Fine, Thanks | Psychology Today." May 11, 2012. www.psychologytoday.com/us/blog/the-natural-unconscious/201205/priming-effects-replicate-just-fine-thanks.

Bargh, John A., Mark Chen, and Lara Burrows. 1996. "Automaticity of Social Behavior: Direct Effects of Trait Construct and Stereotype Activation on Action." *Journal of Personality and Social Psychology* 71 (2): 230–44.

Barnhill, Anne. 2014. "What Is Manipulation?" In *Manipulation: Theory and Practice*, edited by Christian Coons and Michael Weber. New York: Oxford University Press.

Baron, Marcia. 2003. "Manipulativeness." *Proceedings and Addresses of the American Philosophical Association* 77 (2): 37–54.

Baron, Marcia. 2014. "The Mens Rea and Moral Status of Manipulation." In *Manipulation: Theory and Practice*, edited by Christian Coons and Michael Weber. New York: Oxford University Press.

Bartlett, Tom. 2013. "Power of Suggestion." *The Chronicle of Higher Education.* 59 (22): B5–B10.

Bartolucci, Valentina. 2012. "Terrorism Rhetoric under the Bush Administration: Discourses and Effects." *Journal of Language and Politics* 11 (4): 562–82.

Bateson, Melissa, Daniel Nettle, and Gilbert Roberts. 2006. "Cues of Being Watched Enhance Cooperation in a Real-World Setting." *Biology Letters* 2 (3): 412–14.

Beauchamp, Tom L. 1984. "Manipulative Advertising." *Business and Professional Ethics Journal* 3 (3/4): 1–22.

Becher, Shmuel I, and Yuval Feldman. 2016. "Manipulating, Fast and Slow: The Law of Non-Verbal Market Manipulations." *Cardozo Law Review* 38 (2): 459–507.

Bělohrad, Radim. 2019. "The Nature and Moral Status of Manipulation." *Acta Analytica* 34: 447–62.

Berman, Micah L. 2015. "Manipulative Marketing and the First Amendment." *Georgetown Law Journal* 103: 497–546.

Bermúdez, José Luis. 2020. *Frame It Again: New Tools for Rational Decision-Making.* Cambridge: Cambridge University Press.

Berofsky, Bernard. 2003. "Identification, the Self, and Autonomy." *Social Philosophy and Policy* 20 (2): 199–220.

Blumenthal-Barby, Jennifer S. 2012. "Between Reason and Coercion: Ethically Permissible Influence in Health Care and Health Policy Contexts." *Kennedy Institute of Ethics Journal* 22 (4): 345–66.

Blumenthal-Barby, Jennifer S. 2014. "A Framework for Assessing the Moral Status of Manipulation." In *Manipulation: Theory and Practice*, edited by Christian Coons and Michael Weber. New York: Oxford University Press.

Blumenthal-Barby, Jennifer S., and Hadley Burroughs. 2012. "Seeking Better Health Outcomes: The Ethics of Using the 'Nudge.'" *American Journal of Bioethics* 12: 1–10.

Boeynaems, Amber, Christian Burgers, Elly A. Konijn, and Gerard J. Steen. 2017. "The Effects of Metaphorical Framing on Political Persuasion: A Systematic Literature Review." *Metaphor and Symbol* 32 (2): 118–34.

Bornstein, Robert F., and Catherine Craver-Lemley. 2022. "Mere Exposure Effect." In *Cognitive Illusions*, edited by Rüdiger F. Pohl. New York: Routledge.

Bortolotti, Lisa. 2010. *Delusions and Other Irrational Beliefs.* Oxford: Oxford University Press.

Bowers, Len. 2003. "Manipulation: Description, Identification and Ambiguity." *Journal of Psychiatric and Mental Health Nursing* 10 (3): 323–28.

Braiker, Harriet. 2004. *Who's Pulling Your Strings?: How to Break the Cycle of Manipulation and Regain Control of Your Life.* New York: McGraw-Hill.

Brignull, Harry. 2023. *Deceptive Patterns: Exposing the Tricks Tech Companies Use to Control You.* Orlando, FL: Testimonium Ltd.

Brignull, Harry, Mark Leiser, Cristina Santos, and Kosha Doshi. 2023. "Deceptive Patterns—User Interfaces Designed to Trick You." April 25, 2023. www.deceptive.design/.

Brockway, George. 1993. "Limited Paternalism and the Salesperson: A Reconsideration." *Journal of Business Ethics* 12 (4): 275–79.

Brunvand, Jan Harold. 2001. *Too Good to Be True: The Colossal Book of Urban Legends*. New York: W. W. Norton & Co.

Burger, Jerry M., Jackeline Sanchez, Jenny E. Imberi, and Lucia R. Grande. 2009. "The Norm of Reciprocity as an Internalized Social Norm: Returning Favors Even When No One Finds Out." *Social Influence* 4 (1): 11–17.

Buss, David M. 1992. "Manipulation in Close Relationships: Five Personality Factors in Interactional Context." *Journal of Personality* 60 (2): 477–99.

Buss, Sarah. 2005. "Valuing Autonomy and Respecting Persons: Manipulation, Seduction, and the Basis of Moral Constraints." *Ethics* 115 (2): 195–235.

Buss, Sarah, and Andrea Westlund. 2018. "Personal Autonomy." In *The Stanford Encyclopedia of Philosophy*, edited by Edward N. Zalta, Spring 2018. https://plato.stanford.edu/archives/spr2018/entries/personal-autonomy/.

Byron, Michael, ed. 2004. *Satisficing and Maximizing: Moral Theorists on Practical Reason*. New York: Cambridge University Press.

Calarco, Jessica McCrory. 2018. "Why Rich Kids Are So Good at the Marshmallow Test." The *Atlantic*. June 1, 2018.

Calo, Ryan. 2014. "Digital Market Manipulation." *George Washington Law Review* 82 (January): 995–1051.

Carson, Thomas L. 1998. "Ethical Issues in Sales: Two Case Studies." *Journal of Business Ethics* 17 (7): 725–28.

Carson, Thomas L. 2001. "Deception and Withholding Information in Sales." *Business Ethics Quarterly* 11 (2): 275–306.

Carson, Thomas L. 2012. *Lying and Deception: Theory and Practice*. Oxford: Oxford University Press.

Chandon, Pierre, J. Wesley Hutchinson, Eric T. Bradlow, and Scott H. Young. 2009. "Does In-Store Marketing Work? Effects of the Number and Position of Shelf Facings on Brand Attention and Evaluation at the Point of Purchase." *Journal of Marketing* 73 (6): 1–17.

Charteris-Black, Jonathan. 2006. "Britain as a Container: Immigration Metaphors in the 2005 Election Campaign." *Discourse & Society* 17 (5): 563–81.

Chisholm, Roderick M., and Thomas D. Feehan. 1977. "The Intent to Deceive." *The Journal of Philosophy* 74 (3): 143–59.

Chivers, Tom. 2019. "What's next for Psychology's Embattled Field of Social Priming." *Nature* 576 (7786): 200–202.

Cholbi, Michael. 2014. "The Implications of Ego Depletion for the Ethics and Politics of Manipulation." In *Manipulation: Theory and Practice*, edited by Christian Coons and Michael Weber. New York: Oxford University Press.

Christenfeld, Nicholas. 1995. "Choices from Identical Options." *Psychological Science* 6 (1): 50–55.

Christie, Richard, and Florence L. Geis. 1970. *Studies in Machiavellianism*. New York: Academic Press.

Cialdini, Robert. 2008. *Influence: Science and Practice*. 5th edition. Boston: Allyn and Bacon.

Cialdini, Robert. 2018. *Pre-Suasion: A Revolutionary Way to Influence and Persuade*. New York: Simon & Schuster.

Cicero, M. Tullius. BCE 49. "Letter to L. Cornelius Lentulus Crus." Translated by Evelyn Shuckburgh. Perseus Collection—Tufts University. BCE 49. www.perseus.tufts.edu/hopper/text?doc=Perseus%3Atext%3A1999.02.0022%3Ayear%3D49&force=y.

Clark, Bob, dir. 1983. *A Christmas Story*. Comedy, Family. Metro-Goldwyn-Mayer (MGM), Christmas Tree Films.

Cohen, Shlomo. 2013. "Nudging and Informed Consent." *American Journal of Bioethics* 13 (6): 3–11.

Cohen, Shlomo. 2017. "Manipulation and Deception." *Australasian Journal of Philosophy* 96(3): 483–497.
Conrad, Joseph. 1973. *Heart of Darkness*. Baltimore: Penguin.
Coons, Christian, and Michael Weber, eds. 2014. *Manipulation: Theory and Practice*. New York: Oxford University Press.
Coppola, Francis Ford, dir. 1972. *The Godfather*. Crime, Drama. Paramount Pictures, Albert S. Ruddy Productions, Alfran Productions.
Cowley, Elizabeth. 2006. "Processing Exaggerated Advertising Claims." *Journal of Business Research* 59 (6): 728–34.
Crisp, Roger. 1987. "Persuasive Advertising, Autonomy, and the Creation of Desire." *Journal of Business Ethics* 6 (5): 413–18.
Cukor, George, dir. 1944. *Gaslight*. Crime, Drama, Mystery. Metro-Goldwyn-Mayer (MGM).
Cukor, George, dir. 1949. *Adam's Rib*. Comedy, Romance. Metro-Goldwyn-Mayer (MGM).
Damasio, Antonio R. 2005. *Descartes' Error: Emotion, Reason, and the Human Brain*. London: Penguin.
Daniels, Norman. 2020. "Reflective Equilibrium." In *The Stanford Encyclopedia of Philosophy*, edited by Edward N. Zalta, Summer 2020. https://plato.stanford.edu/archives/sum2020/entries/reflective-equilibrium/.
D'Arms, Justin, and Daniel Jacobson. 2000. "The Moralistic Fallacy: On the 'Appropriateness' of Emotions." *Philosophy and Phenomenological Research* 61 (1): 65–90.
Dasgupta, Partha, and Eric Maskin. 2005. "Uncertainty and Hyperbolic Discounting." *The American Economic Review* 95 (4): 1290–99.
Day, Gregory, and Abbey Stemler. 2020. "Are Dark Patterns Anticompetitive?" *Alabama Law Review* 72 (1): 1–46.
Dear, Keith, Kevin Dutton, and Elaine Fox. 2019. "Do 'Watching Eyes' Influence Antisocial Behavior? A Systematic Review & Meta-Analysis." *Evolution and Human Behavior* 40 (3): 269–80.
DellaVigna, Stefano, and Elizabeth Linos. 2022. "RCTs to Scale: Comprehensive Evidence From Two Nudge Units." *Econometrica* 90 (1): 81–116.
Di Nucci, Ezio. 2012. "Priming Effects and Free Will." *International Journal of Philosophical Studies* 20 (5): 725–34.
Dimsdale, Joel E. 2021. *Dark Persuasion: A History of Brainwashing from Pavlov to Social Media*. New Haven: Yale University Press.
Director, Samuel. 2024. "Framing Effects Do Not Undermine Consent." *Ethical Theory and Moral Practice* 27 (2): 221–235.
Douglas, Charles, and Emily Proudfoot. 2013. "Nudging and the Complicated Real Life of 'Informed Consent.'" *American Journal of Bioethics* 13 (6): 16–17.
Douglas, Thomas. 2022. "If Nudges Treat Their Targets as Rational Agents, Nonconsensual Neurointerventions Can Too." *Ethical Theory and Moral Practice* 25 (2): 369–84.
Douglas, Thomas, and Lisa Forsberg. 2021. "Three Rationales for a Legal Right to Mental Integrity." In *Neurolaw: Advances in Neuroscience, Justice and Security*, edited by S. Ligthart, D. van Toor, T. Kooijmans, T. Douglas, and G. Meynen. Cham: Palgrave Macmillan.
Dowding, Keith. 2016. "Power and Persuasion." *Political Studies* 64 (1 suppl): 4–18.
Dowding, Keith. 2018. "Emotional Appeals in Politics and Deliberation." *Critical Review of International Social and Political Philosophy* 21 (2): 242–60.
Doyen, Stéphane, Olivier Klein, Cora-Lise Pichon, and Axel Cleeremans. 2012. "Behavioral Priming: It's All in the Mind, but Whose Mind?" *PLoS ONE* 7 (1): e29081.
Doyen, Stéphane, Olivier Klein, Daniel J. Simons, and Axel Cleeremans. 2014. "On the Other Side of the Mirror: Priming in Cognitive and Social Psychology." *Social Cognition* 32 (Supplement): 12–32.
Drumwright, Minette. 2018. "Ethical Issues in Marketing, Advertising, and Sales." In *The Routledge Companion to Business Ethics*, edited by Eugene Heath, Byron Kaldis, and Alexei M. Marcoux. New York: Routledge.

Dworkin, Gerald. 1976. "Autonomy and Behavior Control." *The Hastings Center Report* 6 (1): 23–28.
Ebejer, James M., and Michael J. Morden. 1988. "Paternalism in the Marketplace: Should a Salesman Be His Buyer's Keeper?" *Journal of Business Ethics* 7 (5): 337–39.
Edwards, Matthew A. 2008. "The FTC and New Paternalism." *Administrative Law Review* 60 (2): 323–70.
Egan, Andy. 2008. "Imagination, Delusion, and Self-Deception." In *Delusion and Self-Deception: Affective and Motivational Influences on Belief Formation*, edited by Tim Bayne and Jordi Fernandez. New York: Psychology Press.
Elliot, Andrew J. 2015. "Color and Psychological Functioning: A Review of Theoretical and Empirical Work." *Frontiers in Psychology* 6 (April 2): 368.
Elliot, Andrew J., and Markus A. Maier. 2014. "Color Psychology: Effects of Perceiving Color on Psychological Functioning in Humans." *Annual Review of Psychology* 65 (1): 95–120.
Engelen, Bart. 2019. "Nudging and Rationality: What Is There to Worry?" *Rationality and Society* 31 (2): 204–32.
Evans, Dylan. 2002. "The Search Hypothesis of Emotion." *The British Journal for the Philosophy of Science* 53 (4): 497–509.
Evans, Jonathan St B. T. 2010. *Thinking Twice: Two Minds in One Brain.* New York: Oxford University Press.
Evans, Jonathan St B. T., and Keith E. Stanovich. 2013. "Dual-Process Theories of Higher Cognition: Advancing the Debate." *Perspectives on Psychological Science* 8 (3): 223–41.
Faden, Ruth R., Tom L. Beauchamp, and Nancy M. P. King. 1986. *A History and Theory of Informed Consent.* New York: Oxford University Press.
Fallis, Don. 2010. "Lying and Deception." *Philosopher's Imprint* 10 (11): 1–22
Federal Trade Commission. 2023. Complaint in *Federal Trade Commission v Amazon.com, Inc.*. United States District Court. Western District of Washington. Case 2:23-cv-01495.
Federal Trade Commission, Bureau of Consumer Protection. 2022. "Bringing Dark Patterns to Light." Staff report. Available at www.ftc.gov/system/files/ftc_gov/pdf/P214800%20Dark%20Patterns%20Report%209.14.2022%20-%20FINAL.pdf.
Fehige, Christoph, and Ulla Wessels. 2019. "II—Deception and the Desires That Speak against It." *Aristotelian Society Supplementary Volume* 93 (1): 91–110.
Feinberg, Joel. 1989. *Harm to Self.* New York: Oxford University Press.
Fennis, Bob M., and Wolfgang Stroebe. 2021. *The Psychology of Advertising.* 3rd edition. New York: Routledge.
Ferguson, Melissa J., and Thomas C. Mann. 2014. "Effects of Evaluation: An Example of Robust 'Social' Priming.'" *Social Cognition* 32 (Supplement): 33–46.
Fisher, Sarah A. 2022. "Meaning and Framing: The Semantic Implications of Psychological Framing Effects." *Inquiry* 65 (8): 967–90.
Fishkin, James S. 2011. "Manipulation and Democratic Theory." In *Manipulating Democracy : Democratic Theory, Political Psychology, and Mass Media*, edited by Wayne Le Cheminant and John M. Parrish. New York: Routledge.
Forward, Susan. 2001. *Emotional Blackmail: When the People in Your Life Use Fear, Obligation and Guilt to Manipulate You.* New York: Quill.
Frederick, Shane, George Loewenstein, and Ted O'Donoghue. 2002. "Time Discounting and Time Preference: A Critical Review." *Journal of Economic Literature* 40 (2): 351–401.
Fried, Charles. 1978. *Right and Wrong.* Cambridge, MA: Harvard University Press.
Frost, Kim. 2014. "On the Very Idea of Direction of Fit." *The Philosophical Review* 123 (4): 429–84.
Galbraith, John Kenneth. 1958. *The Affluent Society.* Cambridge, MA: Houghton Mifflin.
Gao, Zhihong, and Elaine A. Scorpio. 2011. "Does Puffery Deceive? An Empirical Investigation." *Journal of Consumer Policy* 34 (2): 249–64.
Garandeau, Claire F., and Antonius H. N. Cillessen. 2006. "From Indirect Aggression to Invisible Aggression: A Conceptual View on Bullying and Peer Group Manipulation." *Aggression and Violent Behavior* 11 (6): 612–25.

Gass, Robert H., and John S. Seiter. 2013. *Persuasion: Social Influence and Compliance Gaining*, 5th edition. Boston: Routledge.

Gehl, Robert W., and Sean T. Lawson. 2022. *Social Engineering: How Crowdmasters, Phreaks, Hackers, and Trolls Created a New Form of Manipulative Communication*. Cambridge, MA: The MIT Press.

Gendler, Tamar Szabó. 2008. "Alief and Belief." *The Journal of Philosophy* 105 (10): 634–63.

Genschow, Oliver, Thomas Noll, Michaela Wänke, and Robert Gersbach. 2015. "Does Baker-Miller Pink Reduce Aggression in Prison Detention Cells? A Critical Empirical Examination." *Psychology, Crime & Law* 21 (5): 482–89.

Gibert, Sophie. 2023. "The Wrong of Wrongful Manipulation." *Philosophy & Public Affairs* 51 (4): 333–72.

Gigerenzer, Gerd. 2007. *Gut Feelings: The Intelligence of the Unconscious*. East Rutherford: Penguin.

Gigerenzer, Gerd. 2014. "Should Patients Listen to How Doctors Frame Messages?" *BMJ* 349 (Nov 27): g7091–g7091.

Gigerenzer, Gerd. 2015. "On the Supposed Evidence for Libertarian Paternalism." *Review of Philosophy and Psychology* 6 (3): 361–83.

Gigerenzer, Gerd, and Peter M. Todd. 1999. "Fast and Frugal Heuristics: The Adaptive Toolbox." In *Simple Heuristics That Make Us Smart*. New York: Oxford University Press.

Godefroid, Marie-E., Ralf Plattfaut, and Björn Niehaves. 2022. "How to Measure the Status Quo Bias? A Review of Current Literature." *Management Review Quarterly* 73 (4): 1667–1711.

Goldstein, Dan. 2012. "Kahneman on the 'Storm of Doubts' Surrounding Social Priming Research." *Decision Science News* (blog). October 5, 2012. www.decisionsciencenews.com/2012/10/05/kahneman-on-the-storm-of-doubts-surrounding-social-priming-research/.

Goodall, Jill, Irma Ilustre, Catherine Marquis, Nicholas Nicolella, and Joline Sikaitis. 1996. "Effects of Flattery in Obtaining Compliance." *The Sloping Halls Review, Vol. 3* (College of Humanities and Social Science, Carnegie Mellon University). https://kilthub.cmu.edu/articles/journal_contribution/Effects_of_Flattery_in_Obtaining_Compliance/6712625/1. Accessed June 1, 2024.

Goodin, Robert E. 1980. *Manipulatory Politics*. New Haven: Yale University Press.

Goodman, Ellen P. 2013. "Visual Gut Punch: Persuasion, Emotion, and the Constitutional Meaning of Graphic Disclosure." *Cornell Law Review* 99 (3): 513–70.

Gorin, Moti. 2014a. "Do Manipulators Always Threaten Rationality?" *American Philosophical Quarterly* 51 (1): 51–61.

Gorin, Moti. 2014b. "Towards a Theory of Interpersonal Manipulation." In *Manipulation: Theory and Practice*, edited by Christian Coons and Michael Weber. New York: Oxford University Press.

Gorin, Moti. 2018. "Paternalistic Manipulation." In *The Routledge Handbook of the Philosophy of Paternalism*. New York: Routledge.

Gorin, Moti. 2022. "Gamification, Manipulation, and Domination." In *The Philosophy of Online Manipulation*, edited by Fleur Jongepier and Michael Klenk. New York: Routledge.

Gorton, William A. 2016. "Manipulating Citizens: How Political Campaigns' Use of Behavioral Social Science Harms Democracy." *New Political Science* 38 (1): 61–80.

Graaf, John de, David Wann, and Thomas H. Naylor. 2005. *Affluenza: The All-Consuming Epidemic*. 2nd edition. San Francisco: Berrett-Koehler.

Grant, Naomi, Leandre Fabrigar, and Heidi Lim. 2010. "Exploring the Efficacy of Compliments as a Tactic for Securing Compliance." *Basic and Applied Social Psychology* 32 (3): 226–33.

Grant, Naomi K., Laura R. Krieger, Harrison Nemirov, Leandre R. Fabrigar, and Meghan E. Norris. 2022. "I'll Scratch Your Back If You Give Me a Compliment: Exploring Psychological Mechanisms Underlying Compliments' Effects on Compliance." *British Journal of Social Psychology* 61 (1): 37–54.

Green, Kathleen, Zoe Kukan, and Ruth J. Tully. 2017. "Public Perceptions of 'Negging': Lowering Women's Self-Esteem to Increase the Male's Attractiveness and Achieve Sexual Conquest." *Journal of Aggression, Conflict and Peace Research* 9 (2): 95–105.

Greenspan, Patricia. 2004. "Practical Reasoning and Emotion." In *The Oxford Handbook of Rationality*, edited by Alfred R. Mele and Piers Rawling. Oxford: Oxford University Press.

Gregory, Alex. 2012. "Changing Direction on Direction of Fit." *Ethical Theory and Moral Practice* 15 (5): 603–14.

Grüne-yanoff, Till. 2012. "Old Wine in New Casks: Libertarian Paternalism Still Violates Liberal Principles." *Social Choice and Welfare* 38 (4): 635–45.

Guéguen, Nicolas, Sébastien Meineri, Clément Ruiz, and Alexandre Pascual. 2016. "Promising Reciprocity: When Proposing a Favor for a Request Increases Compliance Even If the Favor Is Not Accepted." *The Journal of Social Psychology* 156 (5): 498–512.

Hadnagy, Christopher. 2018. *Social Engineering: The Science of Human Hacking*. 2nd edition. Indianapolis: Wiley.

Haeg, Jonas. 2022. "Entrapment and Manipulation." *Res Publica* 28 (4): 557–83.

Hamilton, Patrick. 1939. *Gas Light: A Victorian Thriller in Three Acts*. London: Constable.

Hanna, Jason. 2015. "Libertarian Paternalism, Manipulation, and the Shaping of Preferences." *Social Theory and Practice* 41 (4): 618–43.

Hanna, Jason. 2018. *In Our Best Interest: A Defense of Paternalism*. New York: Oxford University Press.

Hanson, Jon D., and Douglas A. Kysar. 1998. "Taking Behavioralism Seriously: Some Evidence of Market Manipulation." *Harvard Law Review* 112 (7): 1420–1573.

Hanson, Jon D., and Douglas A. Kysar. 1999. "Taking Behavioralism Seriously: The Problem of Market Manipulation." *NYU Law Review* 74 (3): 630–749.

Hare, Robert D. 2011. *Without Conscience: The Disturbing World of the Psychopaths Among Us*. New York: The Guilford Press.

Harris, Tristan. 2019. "Our Brains Are No Match for Our Technology." *The New York Times*. Opinion. December 5, 2019.

Hart, Shelley R., Karlie M. Garcia, Stormie Pyle, and Pamela Goldberg. 2022. "Trashy Tricks Rating Scale: Initial Evidence for a Youth Self-Report Scale of Manipulative Behaviors." *SN Social Sciences* 2 (5): 68.

Hausman, Daniel M., and Brynn Welch. 2010. "Debate: To Nudge or Not to Nudge*." *Journal of Political Philosophy* 18 (1): 123–36.

Helman, Danny. 2009. "Careful Phrasing: A Matter of Life and Death." *Skeptical Inquirer* 33 (4): 51–52.

Herodotus. 2008. *Oxford World's Classics: Herodotus: The Histories*. Translated by Robin Waterfield and Carolyn Dewald. Oxford: Oxford University Press.

Herzog, Lisa. 2017. "The Game You Are in: Misleading through Social Norms and What's Wrong with It." *Filozofija I Društvo* 28 (2): 250–69.

Higgins, Tory E., William S. Rholes, and Carl R. Jones. 1977. "Category Accessibility and Impression Formation." *Journal of Experimental Social Psychology* 13 (2): 141–54.

Hill, Thomas E. 1984. "Autonomy and Benevolent Lies." *The Journal of Value Inquiry* 18 (4): 251–67.

Hodson, Nathan. 2023. "Commitment Devices: Beyond the Medical Ethics of Nudges." *Journal of Medical Ethics* 49 (2): 125–30.

Hoffman, David. 2006. "The Best Puffery Article Ever." *Iowa Law Review* 91 (January): 101–51.

Holley, David M. 1986. "A Moral Evaluation of Sales Practices." *Business and Professional Ethics Journal* 5 (1): 3–21.

Holley, David M. 1998. "Information Disclosure in Sales." *Journal of Business Ethics* 17 (6): 631–41.

Holton, Richard. 2009. *Willing, Wanting, Waiting*. Oxford: Oxford University Press.

Honda, Hidehito, Masaru Shirasuna, Toshihiko Matsuka, and Kazuhiro Ueda. 2018. "Do People Explicitly Make a Frame Choice Based on the Reference Point?" *Frontiers in Psychology* 9: 2552.

Honda, Hidehito, and Kimihiko Yamagishi. 2017. "Communicative Functions of Directional Verbal Probabilities: Speaker's Choice, Listener's Inference, and Reference Points." *The Quarterly Journal of Experimental Psychology* 70 (10): 2141–58.

Houk, Timothy. 2019. "On Nudging's Supposed Threat to Rational Decision-Making." *The Journal of Medicine and Philosophy* 44 (4): 403–22.

Humberstone, Lloyd. 1992. "Direction of Fit." *Mind* 101 (401): 59–83.
Hurd, Heidi M. 1996. "The Moral Magic of Consent." *Legal Theory* 2 (2): 121–46.
Hurd, Heidi M. 2005. "Blaming the Victim: A Response to the Proposal That Criminal Law Recognize a General Defense of Contributory Responsibility." *Buffalo Criminal Law Review* 8 (2): 503–22.
Ioannidis, Pavlos. 2021. "The Development of the MATRRESS; A Multidimensional Scale of Manipulation Tactics in Romantic Relationships." *International Journal of Science and Research* 10 (10): 1510–15.
Jongepier, Fleur, and Michael Klenk, eds. 2022. *The Philosophy of Online Manipulation*. New York: Routledge.
Jongepier, Fleur, and Jan Willem Wieland. 2022. "Microtargeting People as a Mere Means." In *The Philosophy of Online Manipulation*, edited by Fleur Jongepier and Michael Klenk. New York: Routledge.
Juanchich, Marie, Karl Halvor Teigen, and Gaëlle Villejoubert. 2010. "Is Guilt 'Likely' or 'Not Certain'?: Contrast with Previous Probabilities Determines Choice of Verbal Terms." *Acta Psychologica* 135 (3): 267–77.
Kagan, Shelly. 1991. *The Limits of Morality*. Oxford: Oxford University Press.
Kagan, Shelly. 1997. *Normative Ethics*. Boulder, Colo: Routledge.
Kahneman, Daniel. 2013. *Thinking, Fast and Slow*. New York: Farrar, Straus and Giroux.
Kahneman, Daniel, and Gary Klein. 2009. "Conditions for Intuitive Expertise: A Failure to Disagree." *American Psychologist* 64 (6): 515–26.
Kahneman, Daniel, Jack L. Knetsch, and Richard H. Thaler. 1991. "Anomalies: The Endowment Effect, Loss Aversion, and Status Quo Bias." *Journal of Economic Perspectives* 5 (1): 193–206.
Kahneman, Daniel, Olivier Sibony, and Cass R. Sunstein. 2021. *Noise: A Flaw in Human Judgment*. New York: Little, Brown Spark.
Kant, Immanuel. 1785. *Immanuel Kant: Groundwork of the Metaphysics of Morals*. Edited and translated by Mary Gregor and Jens Timmermann. Cambridge: Cambridge University Press.
Kasten, Vance. 1980. "Manipulation and Teaching." *Philosophy of Education* 14 (1): 53–62.
Keefer, Lucas A., and Mark J. Landau. 2016. "Metaphor and Analogy in Everyday Problem Solving." *WIREs Cognitive Science* 7 (6): 394–405.
Kerstein, Samuel. 2019. "Treating Persons as Means." In *The Stanford Encyclopedia of Philosophy*, edited by Edward N. Zalta, Summer 2019. https://plato.stanford.edu/archives/sum2019/entries/persons-means/.
Khindri, Dheeraj. 2021. "10 Common Dark Patterns in UX and How to Avoid Them." *Insights—Web and Mobile Development Services and Solutions* (blog). July 9, 2021. www.netsolutions.com/insights/dark-patterns-in-ux-disadvantages/.
Kiener, Maximilian. 2020. "Coercion." In *Routledge Encyclopedia of Philosophy*, edited by Edward Craig. London: Routledge.
Kilbourne, Jean, and Mary Pipher. 2000. *Can't Buy My Love: How Advertising Changes the Way We Think and Feel*. New York: Free Press.
Killmister, Suzy. 2013. "Autonomy and False Beliefs." *Philosophical Studies* 164 (2): 513–31.
Kilovaty, Ido. 2019. "Legally Cognizable Manipulation." *Berkeley Technology Law Journal* 34 (2): 449–502.
Kirchler, Erich, and Christoph Kogler. 2015. "Framing." In *Real-World Decision Making: An Encyclopedia of Behavioral Economics*, edited by Morris Altman. Santa Barbara, CA: Greenwood.
Klass, Gregory. 2018. "The Law of Deception: A Research Agenda." *University of Colorado Law Review* 89 (707): 711–40.
Klein, Gary. 2017. *Sources of Power: How People Make Decisions*. 20th anniversary edition. Cambridge, MA: MIT Press.
Klenk, Michael. 2022a. "Manipulation, Injustice, and Technology." In *The Philosophy of Online Manipulation*, edited by Fleur Jongepier and Michael Klenk. New York: Routledge.
Klenk, Michael. 2022b. "(Online) Manipulation: Sometimes Hidden, Always Careless." *Review of Social Economy* 80 (1): 85–105.

Knightley, Phillip. 2010. "The History of the Honey Trap." *Foreign Policy*, March 12, 2010 . https://foreignpolicy.com/2010/03/12/the-history-of-the-honey-trap/
Kohavi, Ron, and Roger Longbotham. 2023. "Online Controlled Experiments and A/B Tests." In *Encyclopedia of Machine Learning and Data Science*, edited by Dinh Phung, Geoffrey I. Webb, and Claude Sammut. New York: Springer.
Kohavi, Ron, and Stefan Thomke. 2017. "The Surprising Power of Online Experiments: Getting the Most Out of A/B and Other Controlled Tests." *Harvard Business Review* 95 (5): 74–82.
Konnikova, Maria. 2016. *The Confidence Game: Why We Fall for It ... Every Time*. New York: Viking.
Krpan, Dario. 2017. "Behavioral Priming 2.0: Enter a Dynamical Systems Perspective." *Frontiers in Psychology* 8 (July): 1204.
Kruglanski, Arie W., and Gerd Gigerenzer. 2011. "Intuitive and Deliberate Judgments Are Based on Common Principles." *Psychological Review* 118 (1): 97–109.
Kühberger, Anton. 2022. "Framing." In *Cognitive Illusions*, edited by Rüdiger F. Pohl. New York: Routledge.
Kumar, Victor. 2016. "Nudges and Bumps." *Georgetown Journal of Law & Public Policy* 14 (special): 861–76.
Laham, Simon M., and Joseph P. Forgas. 2022. "Halo Effects." In *Cognitive Illusions*, edited by Rüdiger F. Pohl. New York: Routledge.
Lakoff, George, Howard Dean, and Don Hazen. 2004. *Don't Think of an Elephant!: Know Your Values and Frame the Debate—The Essential Guide for Progressives*. White River Junction, VT: Chelsea Green.
Lakoff, George, and Mark Johnson. 2003. *Metaphors We Live By*. Chicago: University of Chicago Press.
Landau, Mark J., Jamie Arndt, and Linda D. Cameron. 2018. "Do Metaphors in Health Messages Work? Exploring Emotional and Cognitive Factors." *Journal of Experimental Social Psychology* 74 (January): 135–49.
Landau, Mark J., Daniel Sullivan, and Jeff Greenberg. 2009. "Evidence That Self-Relevant Motives and Metaphoric Framing Interact to Influence Political and Social Attitudes." *Psychological Science* 20 (11): 1421–27.
Le Cheminant, Wayne, and John M. Parrish, eds. 2011. *Manipulating Democracy: Democratic Theory, Political Psychology, and Mass Media*. New York: Routledge.
Lederer, Jenny. 2013. "'Anchor Baby': A Conceptual Explanation for Pejoration." *Journal of Pragmatics* 57 (October): 248–66.
Lee, Sang Yeal. 2014. "When Do Consumers Believe Puffery Claims? The Moderating Role of Brand Familiarity and Repetition." *Journal of Promotion Management* 20 (2): 219–39.
Leong, Lim M., Craig R. M. McKenzie, Shlomi Sher, and Johannes Müller-Trede. 2017. "The Role of Inference in Attribute Framing Effects." *Journal of Behavioral Decision Making* 30 (5): 1147–56.
Levin, Irwin P., Sandra L. Schneider, and Gary J. Gaeth. 1998. "All Frames Are Not Created Equal: A Typology and Critical Analysis of Framing Effects." *Organizational Behavior and Human Decision Processes* 76 (2): 149–88.
Levy, Neil. 2019. "Nudge, Nudge, Wink, Wink: Nudging Is Giving Reasons." *Ergo: An Open Access Journal of Philosophy* 6 (10): 281–302.
Levy, Neil. 2022. *Bad Beliefs: Why They Happen to Good People*. New York: Oxford University Press.
Lifton, Robert Jay. 1989. *Thought Reform and the Psychology of Totalism: A Study of "Brainwashing" in China*. Chapel Hill: University of North Carolina Press.
Lippke, Richard L. 1999. "The 'Necessary Evil' Defense of Manipulative Advertising." *Business & Professional Ethics Journal* 18 (1): 3–20.
Luguri, Jamie, and Lior Jacob Strahilevitz. 2021. "Shining a Light on Dark Patterns." *Journal of Legal Analysis* 13 (1): 43–109.
Luhmann, Christian C. 2013. "Discounting of Delayed Rewards Is Not Hyperbolic." *Journal of Experimental Psychology: Learning, Memory, and Cognition* 39 (4): 1274–79.

Lycan, William G. 1986. "Tacit Belief." In *Belief: Form, Content, and Function*, edited by R. Bogdan. Oxford: Oxford University Press.

Lynott, Dermot, Katherine S. Corker, Jessica Wortman, Louise Connell, M. Brent Donnellan, Richard E. Lucas, and Kerry O'Brien. 2014. "Replication of 'Experiencing Physical Warmth Promotes Interpersonal Warmth' by Williams and Bargh (2008)." *Social Psychology* 45 (3): 216–22.

MacIntyre, Alasdair. 1994. "Truthfulness, Lies, and Moral Philosophers : What Can We Learn From Mill and Kant?" In *Tanner Lectures on Human Values* 16 (1994–95): 307–361.

Mahon, James Edwin. 2016. "The Definition of Lying and Deception." In *The Stanford Encyclopedia of Philosophy*, edited by Edward N. Zalta, Winter 2016. https://plato.stanford.edu/archives/win2016/entries/lying-definition/.

Marks, John. 1991. *The Search for the "Manchurian Candidate."* New York: W.W. Norton & Co.

McAllister, Blake. 2018. "Seemings as Sui Generis." *Synthese* 195 (7): 3079–96.

McCabe, David. 2023. "F.T.C. Accuses Amazon of Tricking Users Into Subscribing to Prime." *The New York Times*, June 21, 2023, sec. Technology. www.nytimes.com/2023/06/21/technology/ftc-amazon-prime-lawsuit.html.

McIntyre, Alison. 2006. "What Is Wrong with Weakness of Will?" *The Journal of Philosophy* 103 (6): 284–311.

McKenzie, Craig R. M., Michael J. Liersch, and Stacey R. Finkelstein. 2006. "Recommendations Implicit in Policy Defaults." *Psychological Science* 17 (5): 414–20.

McKenzie, Craig R. M., and Jonathan D. Nelson. 2003. "What a Speaker's Choice of Frame Reveals: Reference Points, Frame Selection, and Framing Effects." *Psychonomic Bulletin & Review* 10 (3): 596–602.

McKerchar, Todd L., Leonard Green, Joel Myerson, T. Stephen Pickford, Jade C. Hill, and Steven C. Stout. 2009. "A Comparison of Four Models of Delay Discounting in Humans." *Behavioural Processes* 81 (2): 256–59.

McNeil, Barbara J., Stephen G. Pauker, Harold C. Sox, and Amos Tversky. 1982. "On the Elicitation of Preferences for Alternative Therapies." *The New England Journal of Medicine* 306 (21): 1259–62.

McNeil, Barbara J., Stephen G. Pauker, and Amos Tversky. 1988. "On the Framing of Medical Decisions." In *Decision Making: Descriptive, Normative, and Prescriptive Interactions*, edited by Amos Tversky, David E. Bell, and Howard Raiffa. Cambridge: Cambridge University Press.

Medina, Júlia de Quintana. 2021. "What Is Wrong with Nudges? Addressing Normative Objections to the Aims and the Means of Nudges." *Gestión y Análisis de Políticas Públicas* 25 (March): 23–37.

Mele, Alfred. 2010. "Weakness of Will and Akrasia." *Philosophical Studies* 150 (3): 391–404.

Melendez, Bill, and Phil Roman, dirs. 1973. *A Charlie Brown Thanksgiving*. Animation, Short, Comedy. Lee Mendelson Film Productions, Bill Melendez Productions, United Feature Syndicate (UFS).

Miller, Julie. 2022. "'A Republic If You Can Keep It': Elizabeth Willing Powel, Benjamin Franklin, and the James McHenry Journal | Unfolding History." Webpage. The Library of Congress. January 6, 2022. //blogs.loc.gov/manuscripts/2022/01/a-republic-if-you-can-keep-it-elizabeth-willing-powel-benjamin-franklin-and-the-james-mchenry-journal.

Mills, Chris. 2018. "The Choice Architect's Trilemma." *Res Publica* 24 (3): 395–414.

Mills, Claudia. 1995. "Politics and Manipulation." *Social Theory and Practice* 21 (1): 97–112.

Moeini-Jazani, Mehrad, Sumaya Albalooshi, and Ingvild Müller Seljeseth. 2019. "Self-Affirmation Reduces Delay Discounting of the Financially Deprived." *Frontiers in Psychology* 10 (July): 1729.

Molden, Daniel C. 2014. "Understanding Priming Effects in Social Psychology: What Is 'Social Priming' and How Does It Occur?" *Social Cognition* 32 (Supplement): 1–11.

Moles, Andrés. 2015. "Nudging for Liberals." *Social Theory and Practice* 41 (4): 644–67.

Mooradian, Norman. 2004. "Information Requirements and the Characteristics of Sales Situations." *Business Ethics Quarterly* 14 (1): 123–39.

Morewedge, Carey K., and Daniel Kahneman. 2010. "Associative Processes in Intuitive Judgment." *Trends in Cognitive Sciences* 14 (10): 435–40.

Morrison, Sara. 2021. "Dark Patterns, the Tricks Websites Use to Make You Say Yes, Explained." Vox. April 1, 2021. www.vox.com/recode/22351108/dark-patterns-ui-web-design-privacy.

Moseley, Ralph. 2021. *Advanced Cybersecurity Technologies*. Milton Park, UK: Taylor & Francis.

Musolff, Andreas. 2014. "Metaphorical Parasites and 'Parasitic' Metaphors: Semantic Exchanges between Political and Scientific Vocabularies." *Journal of Language & Politics* 13 (2): 218–33.

Nelson, Phillip. 1974. "Advertising as Information." *The Journal of Political Economy* 82 (4): 729–54.

Nettle, Daniel. 2022. "Breaking Cover on the Watching Eyes Effect." *Daniel Nettle* (blog). March 28, 2022. www.danielnettle.org.uk/2022/03/28/breaking-cover-on-the-watching-eyes-effect/ Accessed June 2, 2024.

Nicholson, Jeremy. 2013. "Can an Insult Make You Fall in Love?" *Psychology Today*. August 31, 2013. https://www.psychologytoday.com/us/blog/the-attraction-doctor/201308/can-insult-make-you-fall-in-love

Nisbett, Richard E., and Timothy D. Wilson. 1977. "Telling More than We Can Know: Verbal Reports on Mental Processes." *Psychological Review* 84 (3): 231–59.

Noggle, Robert. 1996. "Manipulative Actions: A Conceptual and Moral Analysis." *American Philosophical Quarterly* 33 (1): 43–55.

Noggle, Robert. 2002. "Special Agents: Children's Autonomy and Parental Authority." In *The Moral and Political Status of Children*, edited by David Archard and Colin M. Macleod, Oxford: Oxford University Press.

Noggle, Robert. 2016a. "Addiction, Compulsion, and Persistent Temptation." *Neuroethics* 9 (3): 213–23.

Noggle, Robert. 2016b. "Belief, Quasi-Belief, and Obsessive-Compulsive Disorder." *Philosophical Psychology* 29 (5): 654–68.

Noggle, Robert. 2018. "Manipulation, Salience, and Nudges." *Bioethics* 32 (3): 164–70.

Noggle, Robert. 2020. "Pressure, Trickery, and a Unified Account of Manipulation." *American Philosophical Quarterly* 57 (4): 241–52.

Noggle, Robert. 2021. "Manipulation in Politics." In *Oxford Research Encyclopedia of Politics*, edited by William R. Thompson.

Noggle, Robert. 2022. "The Ethics of Manipulation." In *The Stanford Encyclopedia of Philosophy*, edited by Edward N. Zalta, Summer 2022. https://plato.stanford.edu/archives/sum2022/entries/ethics-manipulation/.

Northover, Stefanie B., William C. Pedersen, Adam B. Cohen, and Paul W. Andrews. 2017. "Artificial Surveillance Cues Do Not Increase Generosity: Two Meta-Analyses." *Evolution and Human Behavior* 38 (1): 144–53.

Norton, Helen. 2021. "Manipulation and the First Amendment Symposium: Algorithms and the Bill of Rights." *William & Mary Bill of Rights Journal* 30 (2): 221–44.

Nozick, Robert. 1969. "Coercion." In *Philosophy, Science, and Method: Essays in Honor of Ernest Nagel*, edited by Sidney Morgenbesser, Patrick Suppes, and Morton White. New York: St Martin's Press.

Nyberg, David. 1995. *The Varnished Truth: Truth Telling and Deceiving in Ordinary Life*. Chicago: University of Chicago Press.

Nyholm, Sven. 2022. "Technological Manipulation and Threats to Meaning in Life." In *The Philosophy of Online Manipulation*, edited by Fleur Jongepier and Michael Klenk. New York: Routledge.

Nys, Thomas R.V., and Bart Engelen. 2017. "Judging Nudging: Answering the Manipulation Objection." *Political Studies* 65 (1): 199–214.

Öhman, Arne, Anders Flykt, and Francisco Esteves. 2001. "Emotion Drives Attention: Detecting the Snake in the Grass." *Journal of Experimental Psychology: General* 130 (3): 466–78.

Orlowski, Jeff, dir. 2020. *The Social Dilemma*. Documentary. Exposure Labs. netflix.com/title/81254224.

Osman, Magda, and Christos Bechlivanidis. 2024a. "Public Perceptions of Manipulations on Behavior Outside of Awareness." *Psychology of Consciousness: Theory, Research, and Practice* 11 (2): 154–176.

Osman, Magda, and Christos Bechlivanidis. 2024b. "Impact of Personalizing Experiences of Manipulation Outside of Awareness on Autonomy." *Psychology of Consciousness: Theory, Research, and Practice* 11 (3): 324–347.

Oxford English Dictionary. 2023. "Manipulate, v. Meanings, Etymology and More | Oxford English Dictionary." July 2023. www.oed.com/dictionary/manipulate_v?tab=meaning_and_use#38434998.

Parmer, W. Jared. 2022. "Manipulative Design Through Gamification." In *The Philosophy of Online Manipulation*, edited by Fleur Jongepier and Michael Klenk. New York: Routledge.

Payne, B. Keith, Jazmin L. Brown-Iannuzzi, and Chris Loersch. 2016. "Replicable Effects of Primes on Human Behavior." *Journal of Experimental Psychology: General* 145 (10): 1269–79.

Pearce, Matt. 2014. "At Least Four Marlboro Men Have Died of Smoking-Related Diseases." *Los Angeles Times*. January 28, 2014.

Pellegrini, Robert J. 1981. "Room Color and Aggression in A Criminal Detention Holding Cell: A Test of the 'Tranquilizing Pink' Hypothesis." *Orthomolecular Psychiatry* 10 (3): 174–81.

Pepp, Jessica, Rachel Sterken, Matthew McKeever, and Eliot Michaelson. 2022. "Manipulative Machines." In *The Philosophy of Online Manipulation*, edited by Fleur Jongepier and Michael Klenk. New York: Routledge.

Pettit, Nathan C., and Niro Sivanathan. 2011. "The Plastic Trap: Self-Threat Drives Credit Usage and Status Consumption." *Social Psychological and Personality Science* 2 (2): 146–53.

Philips, Lee, dir. 1975. "Love and Marriage." *M*A*S*H*.

Phillips, Michael J. 1997. *Ethics and Manipulation in Advertising*. Westport, CT: Quorum.

Piety, Tamara R. 2001. "Merchants of Discontent: An Exploration of the Psychology of Advertising, Addiction, and the Implications for Commercial Speech." *Seattle University Law Review* 25 (2): 377–450.

Plessner, Henning, and Sabine Czenna. 2008. "The Benefits of Intuition." In *Intuition in Judgment and Decision Making*, edited by Henning Plessner, Cornelia Betsch, Tilmann Betsch. Mahwah, New Jersey: Lawrence Erlbaum.

Pligt, Joop van der, and Michael Vliek. 2016. *The Psychology of Influence: Theory, Research and Practice*. New York: Routledge.

Porcheddu, Daniele, and Alberto Venturi. 2011. "Choices from Identical Options in a Virtual Shopping Aisle." *The Open Business Journal* 4 (1): 36–45.

Posner, Eric. 2016. "The Law, Economics, and Psychology of Manipulation." *Journal of Marketing Behavior* 1 (3-4): 267–82.

Potter, Nancy Nyquist. 2006. "What Is Manipulative Behavior, Anyway?" *Journal of Personality Disorders* 20 (2): 139–56.

Pugh, Jonathan. 2015. "Ravines and Sugar Pills: Defending Deceptive Placebo Use." *Journal of Medicine & Philosophy* 40 (1): 83–101.

Pugh, Jonathan. 2020. *Autonomy, Rationality, and Contemporary Bioethics*. Oxford: Oxford University Press.

Quinn, Mary Joy. 2000. "Undoing Undue Influence." *Generations: Journal of the American Society on Aging* 24 (2): 65–69.

Quinn, Mary Joy. 2012. "Friendly Persuasion, Good Salesmanship, or Undue Influence." *Marquette Elder's Advisor* 2 (4): 49.

Quinn, Mary Joy. 2014. "Defining Undue Influence." *BIFOCAL: A Journal of the Commission on Law and Aging* 35 (3): 72–75.

Rawls, John. 1971. *A Theory of Justice*. Cambridge, MA: Harvard University Press.

Raz, Joseph. 1988. *The Morality of Freedom*. Oxford: Oxford University Press.

Read, Daniel, Shane Frederick, and Mara Airoldi. 2012. "Four Days Later in Cincinnati: Longitudinal Tests of Hyperbolic Discounting." *Acta Psychologica* 140 (2): 177–85.

Recker, Narcy. 1993. "The Conditional Compliment—Verbal Manipulation." *Nursing Management* 24 (6): 72–73.

Rees, Clea F. 2014. "Better Lie!" *Analysis* 74 (1): 59–64.
Regan, Dennis T. 1971. "Effects of a Favor and Liking on Compliance." *Journal of Experimental Social Psychology* 7 (6): 627–39.
Reijnierse, Gudrun, Christian Burgers, Tina Krennmayr, and Gerard Steen. 2015. "How Viruses and Beasts Affect Our Opinions (or Not): The Role of Extendedness in Metaphorical Framing." *Metaphor and the Social World* 5 (2): 245–63.
Renzo, Massimo. 2023. "Responsibility and Manipulation." In *The Routledge Handbook of Philosophy of Responsibility*. Abingdon, Oxon: Routledge.
Riege, Anine, and Rolf Reber. 2022. "Availability." In *Cognitive Illusions*, edited by Rüdiger F. Pohl. New York: Routledge.
Riker, William H. 1986. *The Art of Political Manipulation*. New Haven: Yale University Press.
Ripley, Amanda. 2009. *The Unthinkable: Who Survives When Disaster Strikes and Why*. New York: Three Rivers Press.
Ritov, Ilana, and Jonathan Baron. 1992. "Status-Quo and Omission Biases." *Journal of Risk and Uncertainty* 5 (1): 49–61.
Rizzo, Mario J. 2016. "Behavioral Economics and Deficient Willpower: Searching for Akrasia." *Georgetown Journal of Law & Public Policy* 14 (Special): 789–806.
Rudinow, Joel. 1978. "Manipulation." *Ethics* 88 (4): 338–47.
Safford, Amanda, and Mark Pingle. 2015. "Heuristics." In *Real-World Decision Making: An Encyclopedia of Behavioral Economics*, edited by Morris Altman. Santa Barbara, CA: Greenwood.
Saghai, Yashar. 2013. "Salvaging the Concept of Nudge." *Journal of Medical Ethics* 39 (8): 487–93.
Sagoff, Mark. 2013. "Trust versus Paternalism Open Peer Commentaries." *American Journal of Bioethics* 13 (6): 20–21.
Samuelson, William, and Richard Zeckhauser. 1988. "Status Quo Bias in Decision Making." *Journal of Risk & Uncertainty* 1 (1): 7–59.
Santilli, Paul C. 1983. "The Informative and Persuasive Functions of Advertising: A Moral Appraisal." *Journal of Business Ethics* 2 (1): 27–33.
Sarkis, Stephanie Moulton. 2018. *Gaslighting: Recognize Manipulative and Emotionally Abusive People—and Break Free*. New York: Da Capo.
Saucier, Rick D. 2008. *Marketing Ethics*. Lewiston, NY: The Edwin Mellen Press.
Saul, Jennifer Mather. 2012a. "Just Go Ahead and Lie." *Analysis* 72 (1): 3–9.
Saul, Jennifer Mather. 2012b. *Lying, Misleading, and What Is Said: An Exploration in Philosophy of Language and in Ethics*. Oxford: Oxford University Press.
Saul, Jennifer Mather. 2024. *Dogwhistles and Figleaves: How Manipulative Language Spreads Racism and Falsehood*. Oxford: Oxford University Press.
Scanlon, T. M. 1998. *What We Owe to Each Other*. Cambridge, MA: Harvard University/Belknap Press.
Scarantino, Andrea. 2006. "Review of *Thinking about Feeling: Contemporary Philosophers on Emotions* and *Emotion, Evolution, and Rationality*." *Mind* 115 (459): 812–20.
Scarantino, Andrea, and Ronald de Sousa. 2018. "Emotion." In *The Stanford Encyclopedia of Philosophy*, edited by Edward N. Zalta, Winter 2018. https://plato.stanford.edu/archives/win2018/entries/emotion/.
Schank, Roger C., and Robert P. Abelson. 1977. *Scripts, Plans, Goals, and Understanding: An Inquiry into Human Knowledge Structures*. Hillsdale, N.J: L. Erlbaum Associates.
Schapiro, Tamar. 1999. "What Is a Child?" *Ethics* 109 (4): 715–38.
Schimmack, Ulrich, Moritz Heene, and Kamini Kesavan. 2017. "Reconstruction of a Train Wreck: How Priming Research Went off the Rails." *Replicability-Index* (blog). February 2, 2017. https://replicationindex.com/2017/02/02/reconstruction-of-a-train-wreck-how-priming-research-went-of-the-rails/.
Schmidt, Andreas T. 2019. "Getting Real on Rationality—Behavioral Science, Nudging, and Public Policy." *Ethics* 129 (4): 511–43.
Schmidt, Andreas T., and Bart Engelen. 2020. "The Ethics of Nudging: An Overview." *Philosophy Compass* 15 (4): 12658.

Schwan, David. 2019. "Comments on Robert Noggle, 'Manipulation, Mistakes, and Perspective.'" Unpublished comments presented at the Northwest Philosophy Conference, October 26.
Schwartz, Barry. 2005. *The Paradox of Choice: Why More Is Less*. New York: Harper Perennial.
Schwitzgebel, Eric. 2001. "In-Between Believing." *The Philosophical Quarterly* 51 (202): 76–82.
Schwitzgebel, Eric. 2021. "Belief." In *The Stanford Encyclopedia of Philosophy*, edited by Edward N. Zalta, Winter 2021. https://plato.stanford.edu/archives/win2021/entries/belief/.
Searle, John R. 1983. *Intentionality: An Essay in the Philosophy of Mind*. Cambridge: Cambridge University Press.
Sheff, Jeremy N. 2010. "Biasing Brands." *Cardozo Law Review* 32 (4): 1245–1314.
Sher, Shlomi, and Craig R. M. McKenzie. 2006. "Information Leakage from Logically Equivalent Frames." *Cognition* 101 (3): 467–94.
Sher, Shlomo. 2011. "A Framework for Assessing Immorally Manipulative Marketing Tactics." *Journal of Business Ethics* 102 (1): 97–118.
Sherman, Jeffrey W., and Andrew M. Rivers. 2021. "There's Nothing Social about Social Priming: Derailing the 'Train Wreck.'" *Psychological Inquiry* 32 (1): 1–11.
Shiffrin, Seana Valentine. 2019. "Learning about Deception from Lawyers." *Aristotelian Society Supplementary Volume* 93 (1): 69–90.
Simon, George K. 2010. *In Sheep's Clothing: Understanding and Dealing with Manipulative People*. Little Rock, AR: Parkhurst Brothers Publishers.
Simon, Herbert. A. 1956. "Rational Choice and the Structure of the Environment." *Psychological Review* 63 (2): 129–38.
Smith, Michael. 1987. "The Humean Theory of Motivation." *Mind* 96 (381): 36–61
Sneddon, Andrew. 2001. "Advertising and Deep Autonomy." *Journal of Business Ethics* 33 (1): 15–28.
Sobel, David, and David Copp. 2001. "Against Direction of Fit Accounts of Belief and Desire." *Analysis* 61 (1): 44–53.
Spencer, Shaun. 2020. "The Problem of Online Manipulation." *University of Illinois Law Review* 2020 (3): 959–1005.
Stanovich, Keith E. 2011. *Rationality and the Reflective Mind*. Oxford: Oxford University Press.
Stark, Cynthia A. 2019. "Gaslighting, Misogyny, and Psychological Oppression." *The Monist* 102 (2): 221–35.
Steen, Gerard J., W. Gudrun Reijnierse, and Christian Burgers. 2014. "When Do Natural Language Metaphors Influence Reasoning? A Follow-Up Study to Thibodeau and Boroditsky (2013)." *PLoS ONE* 9 (12): e113536.
Stern, Robin. 2018. *The Gaslight Effect: How to Spot and Survive the Hidden Manipulation Others Use to Control Your Life*. New York: Harmony.
Story, Giles W., Ivaylo Vlaev, Ben Seymour, Joel S. Winston, Ara Darzi, and Raymond J. Dolan. 2013. "Dread and the Disvalue of Future Pain." *PLOS Computational Biology* 9 (11): e1003335.
Strawson, Peter. 1962. "Freedom and Resentment." *Proceedings of the British Academy* 48: 187–211.
Stroebe, Wolfgang, and Fritz Strack. 2014. "The Alleged Crisis and the Illusion of Exact Replication." *Perspectives on Psychological Science* 9 (1): 59–71.
Stroud, Sarah, and Larisa Svirsky. 2019. "Weakness of Will." In *The Stanford Encyclopedia of Philosophy*, edited by Edward N. Zalta, Fall 2019. https://plato.stanford.edu/archives/fall2019/entries/weakness-will/.
Strudler, Alan. 2005. "Deception Unraveled." *Journal of Philosophy* 102 (9): 458–73.
Strudler, Alan. 2016. "Respectful Lying." *Ethical Theory & Moral Practice* 19 (4): 961–72.
Sun, Yalin, and Yan Zhang. 2021. "A Review of Theories and Models Applied in Studies of Social Media Addiction and Implications for Future Research." *Addictive Behaviors* 114 (March): 106699.
Sunstein, Cass R. 2014. *Why Nudge?: The Politics of Libertarian Paternalism*. New Haven: Yale University Press.
Sunstein, Cass R. 2015. "The Ethics of Nudging." *Yale Journal on Regulation* 32 (2): 413–50.

Sunstein, Cass R. 2016. *The Ethics of Influence: Government in the Age of Behavioral Science.* New York: Cambridge University Press.

Susser, Daniel, Beate Roessler, and Helen Nissenbaum. 2019. "Technology, Autonomy, and Manipulation." *Internet Policy Review* 8 (2): 1–22.

Susser, Daniel, Beate Roessler, and Helen Nissenbaum. 2020. "Online Manipulation: Hidden Influences in a Digital World." *Georgetown Law and Technology Review* 4 (1): 1–45.

Tappolet, Christine. 2016. *Emotions, Value, and Agency.* Oxford: Oxford University Press.

Taylor, James Stacey. 2009. *Practical Autonomy and Bioethics.* London: Routledge.

Teigen, Karl, and Knut Karevold. 2005. "Looking Back versus Looking Ahead: Framing of Time and Work at Different Stages of a Project." *Journal of Behavioral Decision Making* 18 (4): 229–46.

Thaler, Richard H., and Cass R. Sunstein. 2009. *Nudge: Improving Decisions About Health, Wealth, and Happiness.* New York: Penguin.

Thibodeau, Paul. 2017. "The Function of Metaphor Framing, Deliberate or Otherwise, in a Social World." *Metaphor and the Social World* 7 (2): 270–90.

Thibodeau, Paul, and Lera Boroditsky. 2011. "Metaphors We Think With: The Role of Metaphor in Reasoning." *PLOS ONE* 6 (2): e16782.

Tolhurst, William. 1998. "Seemings." *American Philosophical Quarterly* 35 (3): 293–302.

Tompkins, D. Andrew, Patrick S. Johnson, Michael T. Smith, Eric C. Strain, Robert R. Edwards, and Matthew W. Johnson. 2016. "Temporal Preference in Individuals Reporting Chronic Pain: Discounting of Delayed Pain-Related and Monetary Outcomes." *Pain* 157 (8): 1724–32.

Turkat, Ira Daniel. 2003. "Psychological Aspects of Undue Influence." *Probate and Property* 17 (1): 36–40.

Turley, L. W, and Ronald E Milliman. 2000. "Atmospheric Effects on Shopping Behavior: A Review of the Experimental Evidence." *Journal of Business Research* 49 (2): 193–211.

Turner, Yehonatan Nizan, and Irith Hadas-Halpern. 2008. "The Effects of Including a Patient's Photograph to the Radiographic Examination." Radiological Society of North America Scientific Assembly and Annual meeting. Oak Brook, Ill: Radiological Society of North America, 2008; 576. Available at https://archive.rsna.org/2008/6008880.html.

Turow, Joseph. 2013. *The Daily You: How the New Advertising Industry Is Defining Your Identity and Your Worth.* New Haven: Yale University Press.

Tversky, Amos, and Daniel Kahneman. 1973. "Availability: A Heuristic for Judging Frequency and Probability." *Cognitive Psychology* 5 (2): 207–32.

Vadillo, Miguel A., Tom E. Hardwicke, and David R. Shanks. 2016. "Selection Bias, Vote Counting, and Money-Priming Effects: A Comment on Rohrer, Pashler, and Harris (2015) and Vohs (2015)." *Journal of Experimental Psychology: General* 145 (5): 655–63.

Valenzuela, Ana, and Priya Raghubir. 2009. "Position-Based Beliefs: The Center-Stage Effect." *Journal of Consumer Psychology* 19 (2): 185–96.

Vanderveldt, Ariana, Luís Oliveira, and Leonard Green. 2016. "Delay Discounting: Pigeon, Rat, Human—Does It Matter?" *Journal of Experimental Psychology. Animal Learning and Cognition* 42 (2): 141–62.

Villarán, Alonso. 2017. "Irrational Advertising and Moral Autonomy." *Journal of Business Ethics* 144 (3): 479–90.

Vohs, Kathleen D., Nicole L. Mead, and Miranda R. Goode. 2006. "The Psychological Consequences of Money." *Science* 314 (5802): 1154–56.

Waide, John. 1987. "The Making of Self and World in Advertising." *Journal of Business Ethics* 6 (2): 73–79.

Ware, Alan. 1981. "The Concept of Manipulation: Its Relation to Democracy and Power." *British Journal of Political Science* 11 (2): 163–81.

Weingarten, Evan, Qijia Chen, Maxwell McAdams, Jessica Yi, Justin Hepler, and Dolores Albarracín. 2016. "From Primed Concepts to Action: A Meta-Analysis of the Behavioral Effects of Incidentally Presented Words." *Psychological Bulletin* 142 (5): 472–97.

Werner, Micha H. 2022. "Manipulation and the Value of Rational Agency." In *Kant's Theory of Value*, edited by Christoph Horn and Robinson dos Santos. Berlin: De Gruyter.

Werner, Preston J. 2014. "Seemings: Still Dispositions to Believe." *Synthese* 191 (8): 1761–74.

Wertheimer, Alan. 1990. *Coercion*. Princeton: Princeton University Press.

Whitfield, Gregory. 2022. "On the Concept of Political Manipulation." *European Journal of Political Theory* 21 (4): 783–807.

Wilkinson, T. M. 2013. "Nudging and Manipulation." *Political Studies* 61 (2): 341–55.

Williams, Bernard. 2004. *Truth and Truthfulness: An Essay in Genealogy*. Princeton: Princeton University Press.

Williams, Lawrence E., and John A. Bargh. 2008. "Experiencing Physical Warmth Promotes Interpersonal Warmth." *Science* 322 (5901): 606–7.

Willis, Lauren E. 2020. "Deception by Design." *Harvard Journal of Law & Technology* 34 (1): 115–90.

Wilson, Amy L., Elizabeth Buckley, Jonathan D. Buckley, and Svetlana Bogomolova. 2016. "Nudging Healthier Food and Beverage Choices through Salience and Priming. Evidence from a Systematic Review." *Food Quality and Preference* 51: 47–64.

Wilson, Andrew. 2023. *Political Technology: The Globalisation of Political Manipulation*. Cambridge: Cambridge University Press.

Wilson, R. Paul. 2014. *The Art of the Con: How to Think Like a Real Hustler and Avoid Being Scammed*. Guilford, CT: Lyons Press.

Wood, Allen W. 2014. "Coercion, Manipulation, Exploitation." In *Manipulation: Theory and Practice*, edited by Christian Coons and Michael Weber. New York: Oxford University Press.

Woolf, Nicky. 2012. "'Negging': The Anatomy of a Dating Trend." *New Statesman*, May 25, 2012. www.newstatesman.com/blogs/voices/2012/05/negging-latest-dating-trend.

Xu, Alison Jing, and Robert S. Wyer Jr. 2010. "Puffery in Advertisements: The Effects of Media Context, Communication Norms, and Consumer Knowledge." *Journal of Consumer Research* 37 (2): 329–43.

Yang, Defeng, Ninghui Xie, and Sarena J. Su. 2019. "Claiming Best or Better? The Effect of Target Brand's and Competitor's Puffery on Holistic and Analytic Thinkers." *Journal of Consumer Behaviour* 18 (2): 151–65.

Yong, Ed. 2012. "Replication Studies: Bad Copy." *Nature* 485 (7398): 298–300.

Zajonc, Robert B. 1968. "Attitudinal Effects of Mere Exposure." *Journal of Personality and Social Psychology* 9 (2): 1–27.

Zimmerman, Carla A., and Richard Walker. 2022. "Positivity Biases." In *Cognitive Illusions*, edited by Rüdiger F. Pohl. New York: Routledge.

Index

For the benefit of digital users, indexed terms that span two pages (e.g., 52–53) may, on occasion, appear on only one of those pages.